THE SECURITY RISK
ASSESSMENT HANDBOOK

OTHER INFORMATION SECURITY BOOKS FROM AUERBACH

AUERBACH PUBLICATIONS

www.auerbach-publications.com
To Order Call: 1-800-272-7737 • Fax: 1-800-374-3401
E-mail: orders@crcpress.com

THE SECURITY RISK ASSESSMENT HANDBOOK

A Complete Guide for Performing Security Risk Assessments

DOUGLAS J. LANDOLL

Auerbach Publications
Taylor & Francis Group
Boca Raton   New York

Published in 2006 by
Auerbach Publications
Taylor & Francis Group
6000 Broken Sound Parkway NW, Suite 300
Boca Raton, FL 33487-2742

International Standard Book Number-10: 0-8493-2998-1 (Hardcover)
International Standard Book Number-13: 978-0-8493-2998-2 (Hardcover)
Library of Congress Card Number 2005050717

Library of Congress Cataloging-in-Publication Data

Landoll, Douglas J.
   The security risk assessment handbook : a complete guide for performing security risk assessments / Douglas J. Landoll.
          p. cm.
   Includes bibliographical references and index.
   ISBN 0-8493-2998-1
   1. Business--Data processing--Security measures. 2. Computer security. 3. Data protection. 4. Risk assessment. I. Title.

HF5548.37.L358 2005
658.4'7--dc22   2005050717

Taylor & Francis Group
is the Academic Division of Informa plc.

Visit the Taylor & Francis Web site at
http://www.taylorandfrancis.com

and the Auerbach Publications Web site at
http://www.auerbach-publications.com

Dedication

To my family: without their support, this and many other accomplishments would not be possible and would mean little.

The Author

Douglas Landoll has 17 years of information security experience. He has led security risk assessments establishing security programs within top corporations and government agencies. He is an expert in security risk assessment, security risk management, security criteria, and building corporate security programs.

His background includes evaluating security at the National Security Agency (NSA), North Atlantic Treaty Organization (NATO), Central Intelligence Agency (CIA), and other government agencies; co-founding the Area Common Criteria Testing Laboratory, co-authoring the systems security engineering capability maturity model (SSE-CMM); teaching at NSA's National Cryptologic School; and running the southwest security services division for Exodus Communications. Presently he is the president of Veridyn, a provider of network security solutions. He is a certified information systems security professional (CISSP) and certified information systems auditor (CISA) He holds a BS degree from James Madison University and an MBA from the University of Texas at Austin. He has published numerous information security articles, speaks regularly at conferences, and serves as an advisor for several high-tech companies.

Contents

List of Figures

List of Tables

List of Sidebars

Chapter 1

Introduction

Heavy financial losses, breaches of privacy, and even the downfall of corporations have recently been attributed to the inability of corporations to protect themselves from cyber-risks. Cyber-risks are generated from hackers, malicious software, disgruntled employees, competitors, and many other sources both internal and external. These external and internal cyber-attacks on corporate assets and an increasingly technology-savvy corporate management have led to a more appropriate awareness of the information security risks to corporate information than ever previously experienced in corporations and government agencies.

Understandably, information security is now a major concern for most corporations. A recent survey reported that computer security is the critical attribute of corporate networks for 78 percent of corporate executives. Another survey reported that security outweighed other concerns by a factor of three as the driving concern for IT improvements.

Many corporations are putting their money where their mouth is by increasing security spending. In a survey of chief security officers, corporations have increased their information security budget fivefold to 10 percent of their IT budget from 2002 to 2003. Another survey reported that information security spending has increased by 28 percent globally from 2001 to 2003. But even with all this spending, many corporate executives are unsure about the effectiveness of their information security programs or the security controls that have been put in place. A 2003 survey found that 34 percent of organizations see their own security controls as inadequate to detect a security breach.

It should be rather clear from the discussion above that organizations need a reliable method for measuring the effectiveness of their information security program. An information security risk assessment is designed specifically for that task. An information security risk assessment, when performed correctly, can give corporate managers the information they need to understand and control the risks to their assets. The subject of this book is how to perform a security risk assessment correctly, efficiently, and effectively.

1.1 The Need for an Information Security Program

Recent attention to information security breaches has led to an increased awareness of information security issues. The development of legislation addressing these risks has forced corporations in many sectors to measure and address the information security risk to corporate assets.

Although the recent flurry of attention in this area seems to be new, regulations that require information security practices have been introduced and revised since the 1980s. Figure 1.1 shows the increasing frequency of these regulations. Regardless of the differences in these regulations, they all ultimately call for the

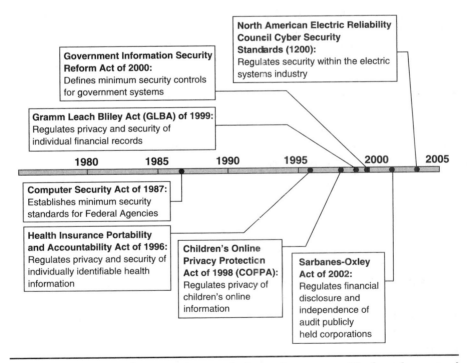

Figure 1.1 Information security regulations. As more critical and personal information is stored, transmitted, and processed on information systems, more information security regulations are being developed and applied. Notice the surge of information security regulations since 1995.

implementation of an adequate set of information security practices. There has been considerable attention and discussion on the proliferation of information security regulations. Many corporate managers wonder why these regulations are being imposed on them and why now. The answer is that, in the eyes of the federal government, corporations have failed to "police themselves."

In the movies, cyber-security breaches are enacted by highly skilled and motivated evildoers, who go to great lengths to break corporate security measures. In the real world, most cyber-security breaches are performed by mischievous adolescents, disgruntled employees, or even novice computer users. None of these "villains" require expertise, timing, motivation, or even much time to breach corporate security. Security breaches happen through the simple act of opening an e-mail, running a hacker program, or placing a phone call. As easy as these threats are to counter, many corporations do not bother to enact even rudimentary security measures. The lack of adequate protection is demonstrated by the increase in security breaches and the escalating costs incurred in dealing with these incidents.

Unwilling to wait for government agencies and corporations in certain industries to police themselves, the U.S. Federal Government (and other foreign governments as well) has determined that it needs to step into the process and force these agencies and corporations to implement a minimum set of information security practices. As seen in Figure 1.1, industries already affected include state and federal government, financial, healthcare, energy, "critical infrastructure," and all publicly traded companies.

These affected agencies and corporations have now found the motivation (avoidance of fines and jail) to at least implement minimum security practices. After decades of underspending other industries in information technology improvements, the healthcare industry more recently began outspending these industries to make up for lost time and to comply with the Health Insurance Portability and Accountability Act (HIPAA). Similar increases can be found in other industry verticals that have been affected by information security regulations applicable to them.

Each of the information security regulations applying to these industries has a unique set of information security requirements. However, there are significant similarities between these information security regulations. One striking similarity is that each of these information security regulations requires the affected organization to perform an information security risk assessment.[1] Those remaining corporations (apparently) unaffected by such legislation still find it necessary to understand and mitigate the risks to their treasured assets. As such, establishing an information security program is not simply a reaction to regulations and the avoidance of jail time, but is instead a reaction to the impending threat to corporate assets and an avoidance of loss of capital and corporate value. In this way, information security practices are a necessary element of good corporate governance. Even if information security practices are not required by law, they are still a good idea.

1.2 Elements of an Information Security Program

Organizations that are determined to develop or improve their information security program are still left with the challenge of identifying the important elements that make up their program. There is no doubt that for almost every conceivable threat there is a multitude of safeguards that can counter that threat to some extent. The answer is not to enact every countermeasure available. Instead an organization should take a risk-based approach to determining the security controls that reduce their threat to a reasonable level.

Such subjective measurements as "reasonable" typically lead to the development of guidelines and regulations. The information security field is no exception. Below is a discussion of various guidelines and regulations that seek to identify a "reasonable" set of safeguards for a given industry or organization.

Safeguards are generally identified as administrative, physical, and technical security controls. The collection of these safeguards is commonly referred to as an information security program. The objective of an organization's information security program is to protect organizational assets from security threats. It is assumed here that an organization seeks to establish and maintain adequate information security programs.

The establishment of an information security practice for an organization is not a task to be taken lightly. Care must be taken to establish adequate reporting structures, create appropriate budgets, understand information security requirements, adequately staff the information security department, develop policies and procedures, define and perform information security activities, and ensure the success of the organization. Such an important task should be performed by a professional or with the assistance of a professional organization.

Although this book will discuss many of the elements of a successful information security program and how to spot gaps, the establishment of an information security program is not the topic of this book. The topic of this book is how to perform and review an information security program. This is commonly referred to as an information security risk assessment. In this book, we assume that no matter how the information security department is established and run within your organization (or your client's organization), an information security risk assessment is part of your (or your client's) process of ensuring the information security program runs efficiently.

Clearly, not all information security practices are appropriate for all organizations. The selection of information security practices for an organization should be based on the business objectives of the organization. Without a proper understanding of the organization's business you cannot hope to understand their needs and to select the appropriate information security requirements for the organization. Understanding the organization's business mission will be discussed in more detail later in the book, but for now it is important to understand that it is not possible to prescribe, prima facie, the information security activities that are appropriate for any specific organization.

Despite the understanding that all organizations are different and therefore have different information security requirements, there have been a number of efforts to prescribe "minimum" information security standards or industry "best practices" for information security practice. For as simple as the concept of "minimum" information security requirements and industry "best practices" sounds, it can be rather complex to determine precisely what "best practices" comprise. In fact there are at least a dozen definitions covering various aspects of "information security best practices." Among the standards and regulations that provide a list of required security controls are the following:

1.2.1 Security Control Standards and Regulations

- Generally Accepted Information Security Practices (GAISP).
- Common Objectives for IT (COBIT).
- Information Technology — Code of Practice for Information Security Management (ISO 17799).
- National Institute of Standards and Technology (NIST) Special Publication 800-12 (*NIST Computer Security Handbook*).
- Health Insurance Portability and Accountability Act (HIPAA), Final Security Rule (HIPAA Security).
- Financial Modernization Act of 1999, also known as Gramm-Leach-Bliley Act (GLB Act).
- DCID 6/3 Manual — Protecting Sensitive Compartmented Information within Information Systems.
- NIST Special Publication 800-53 (Recommended Controls For Federal Information Systems.

1.3 Common Core Information Security Practices

A high-level analysis of the core information security practices described above (i.e., GAISP, COBIT, ISO 17799, NIST Handbook, HIPAA, GLB Act) shows a considerable amount of overlap. Such an overlap reinforces the definition of "information security core practices" as the activities found in multiple approaches can surely be regarded as essential or core best practices.

However, there is no single definition of the "best practices" for an information security program. Each of these sources (e.g., NIST, ISO 17799, HIPAA) are reliable sources for information security practices yet none of them seem to agree. This should not be as disturbing as it sounds. After all, most information security professionals agree that information security controls should be selected on a risk-based approach. Therefore, industries or organizations with different risk environments would be expected to select a different set of security controls. In fact, the term "best practices" for information security is really a misnomer or even could be considered a myth.

There exists no definition for minimum security practices either. Various regulations, books, and standards define what is required for specific industries or environments. To the extent that these environments have common elements and common threats, the corresponding regulations seem to have common elements. A review of these common elements gives us a good basis for a discussion in baseline security practices.

1.3.1 Unanimous Core Security Practices

Most security control standards and regulations seem to agree that the following elements would comprise an information security program consistent with core security practices. In fact, all of the information security guidelines and regulations mentioned here included all of the following elements as a required practice:

- Security Responsibility — Security responsibility should be assigned to an individual or entity with the proper authority, visibility, and expertise to perform the job adequately.
- Risk Management — The organization's management needs to have an understanding of the risk to its assets and have an approach for addressing those risks. This typically consists of periodic security risk assessments and risk mitigation.
- Risk Assessment — In support of risk management, an organization needs a periodic and objective analysis of the effectiveness of the current security controls that protect an organization's assets.
- Network Security — An organization must ensure the confidentiality, integrity, and availability of information assets and resources while in transit, processing, or storage. This includes considerations for the entire information system, its networked components, interfaces to other networks, authorized users, and procedures dictating their behavior.
- Security Awareness Training — An effective security awareness training program should be developed and administered to all those who will be given access to the organization's facilities or information systems. This training should take place annually with periodic security reminders.
- Incident Management — The organization should have a process in place that identifies security incidents in progress or evidence of such incidents in the past. Incident management includes the identification, investigation, and reporting of these incidents to the appropriate individuals within the organization.

1.3.2 Majority Core Security Practices

The information security regulations and guidelines discussed in this book do not require the same security practices. However, the overwhelming majority (e.g., all but one in each case) agree that the following elements would comprise an information security program consistent with core security practices:

- Information Security Policies — The basis of any information security program is the definition of security. Information security policies define the security policies to be enforced within the organization and the organization's information systems. Additional policies dictate the expected behaviors of individuals within the corporation.
- Access Control — Mechanisms must be in place to ensure that only authorized individuals will have access to sensitive information and resources.
- Physical Security — Mechanisms must be in place to physically protect organizational equipment, locations, and employees.
- BCP and DRP — Business continuity planning and disaster recovery planning ensures that the organization has identified its critical processes and assets, developed a plan for minimizing the loss in the event of a disaster, and periodically tests the plan.
- Secure Development Life Cycle — The best way to ensure that an information system or information system component enforces its security policy is to design it securely from the start. Secure development life-cycle activities include the involvement of security professionals in the requirements analysis, design, test, deployment, acceptance and disposal phases of the development life cycle.
- Accountability — The security-relevant actions of users must be recorded and reviewed by security personnel. This is typically accomplished through identification/authentication and auditing, but other techniques such as intrusion detection systems can hold authorized and unauthorized users accountable.
- Secure Media Handling — Sensitive information stored on media (e.g., disks, hard drives, or CDs) must be handled appropriately to ensure that unauthorized users do not gain access to the data stored on the media. Controls include procedures for labeling, transportation, storage, and destruction of media.
- Oversight of Third Parties — Many organizations allow other service organizations to access or process their sensitive information. When such arrangements are made, the owner of the sensitive information must ensure that their sensitive information continues to be protected. Controls include contractual language and audits.

1.3.3 Core Security Practice Conclusions

The preceding analysis of relevant information security guidelines and regulations was an attempt at unifying the various claims of information security best practices. As stated before, the term "best practices" should not be applied as a requirement for all systems or even for any specific system because each system operates within a unique threat environment. Instead, it is recognized that information security controls are determined based on the risk to the system in its given environment.

However, the commonality of many aspects of the environmental threat provides a basis for claiming some usefulness in analyzing the common program elements mentioned in these regulations and guidelines. For example, since there is a real threat to most all organizations of disgruntled employees exposing critical assets, security practices such as policies, security awareness, termination procedures, and accountability apply to most organizations.

Conclusion 1: Core security practices are applicable to most organizations.

- Unanimous Core Practices — security responsibility, risk management, security risk assessment, network security, security awareness training, incident management.
- Majority Core Practices — information security policies, access control, physical security, BCP/DRP, developmental life cycle, accountability, secure media handling, oversight of third parties.

Rather than go into a more involved discussion of all unanimous core security practices, the subject of this book is limited security risk assessments. Based on the analysis above, it is unanimous that security risk assessments are central to an organization's information security program.

Conclusion 2: Security risk assessment is a unanimous core security practice.

1.4 Security Risk Assessment

Within the core of best practices is the security risk assessment. It is this activity that measures the strength of the overall security program and provides the information necessary to make planned improvements based on information security risks. The security risk assessment is the tool of senior management that gives them an effectiveness measurement of their security controls and an indication of how well their assets are protected.

1.4.1 The Role of the Security Risk Assessment

A security risk assessment is an important element in the overall security risk management process. Security risk management involves the process of ensuring that the risk posture of an organization is within acceptable bounds as defined by senior management. There are four stages of the security risk management process: security risk assessment; test and review; security risk mitigation; and operational security (see Figure 1.2).

- Security Risk Assessment — This is an objective analysis of the effectiveness of the current security controls that protect an organization's assets and a determination of the probability of losses to those assets. A security risk assessment reviews the threat environment of the organization, the value of assets, the criticality of systems, the vulnerabilities of the security controls, the impact of expected losses, and recommendations for additional controls to reduce risk to an acceptable level. Based on this information the senior management of the organization can determine if additional security controls are required.
- Test and Review — Security testing is the examination of the security controls against the security requirements. Security controls are determined during the security risk assessment and tested during security testing efforts. Security testing is performed more frequently than security risk assessments.
- Risk Mitigation — Risks to an organization's assets are reduced through the implementation of new security controls or the improvement of existing controls. Security risk assessments provide information to allow the senior management to make risk-based decisions for the development of new controls or expenditure of resources on security improvements on

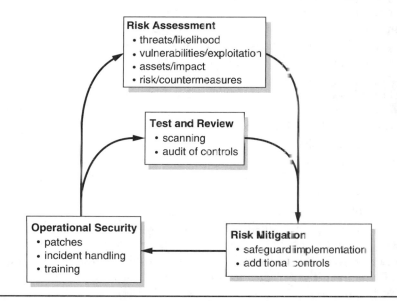

Figure 1.2   The role of the security risk assessment. Security risk assessments play a critical role in the security management process, providing information on the threats, assets, and risks to an organization.

existing controls. Security test and review efforts provide information on how to keep existing controls up to date. Risk can be mitigated through corrections and additional controls or accepted or transferred.

- Operational Security — The implementation and operation of most security controls are performed by operational personnel. Daily and weekly activities such as applying patches, performing account maintenance, and providing security awareness training are essential for maintaining an adequate security posture.

1.4.2 Definition of a Security Risk Assessment

The security risk assessment takes on many names and can vary greatly in terms of method, rigor, and scope, but the core goal remains the same: assess the risks to the organization's information assets. This information is used to determine how best to mitigate those risks and effectively preserve the organization's mission.

There exists no shortage of definitions for a security risk assessment (and many other closely associated names). Many of these definitions are overly complex or may be specifically geared to an industry segment such as the federal government. For example, the National Institute of Standards and Technology provides two alternative definitions for the term "risk assessment." One definition, found in the NIST *Risk Management Guide*, states that risk assessment is "the process of identifying the risks to system security and determining the probability of occurrence, the resulting impact, and additional safeguards that would mitigate this impact." Yet another definition found in the NIST *Guide for Security Certification and Accreditation* expands the definition to describe the process required for the certification and accreditation of federal systems. It reads as follows:

> The periodic assessment of risk to agency operations or assets resulting from the operation of an information system is an important activity required by [Federal Information Security Management Act of 2002] FISMA. The risk assessment brings together important information for agency officials with regard to the protection of the information system and generates essential information required for the security plan. The risk assessment includes: (i) the identification of threats to and vulnerabilities in the information system; (ii) the potential impact or magnitude of harm that a loss of confidentiality, integrity, or availability would have on agency operations (including mission, functions, image, or reputation) or agency assets should there be a threat exploitation of identified vulnerabilities; and (iii) the identification and analysis of security controls for the information system.

Other uses of the term "risk assessment" are geared toward a specific use such as complying with the Sarbanes-Oxley Bill. The IT Governance Institute defines risk assessment as the identification and analysis by management of relevant risks to achieve predetermined objectives, which form the basis for determining control activities.[3] Furthermore, the IT Governance Institute recognizes that risk assessments may be performed at the company level or at the level of an individual activity. A risk assessment performed at the company level is concerned with the overall risks to the company. Such a risk assessment would require senior-level management oversight, the integration of a strategic plan for measuring and controlling risk throughout the company, and, of course, the assessment of information technology risks. A risk assessment performed at the activity level would encompass formalized or built-in risk assessments in individual control activities. Examples of activities include change management control, application testing, and account creation, maintenance, and termination.

The ISO 17799 takes an integrated approach to security management and recognizes the value of security risk assessments in that process. The basic structure of security management involves selecting security requirements, assessing the risks, and selecting controls. The security risk assessment is central to this approach as it assesses the risks that the security requirements may not be met and provides the basis for a risk-based decision for selecting security controls.

The ISO 17799 defines risk assessment as the "systematic consideration of the business harm likely to result from a security failure ... and the realistic likelihood of such a failure occurring in the light of prevailing threats and vulnerabilities, and the controls currently implemented."

In all the regulations, guidelines, and standards, "security risk assessment" has been defined in numerous ways. Some definitions are more detailed than others in terms of how an assessment is performed. Some definitions focus on the result of the assessment, while other focus on the approach. For our purposes, a simpler security risk assessment definition is needed to cover any such approach or detail. Since this book will discuss the various methods of performing a security risk assessment, the definition used here is designed to fit all such methods. For the purposes of this book, security risk assessment if defined as follows:

> Security Risk Assessment — An objective analysis of the effectiveness of the current security controls that protect an organization's assets and a determination of the probability of losses to those assets.

1.4.3 The Need for a Security Risk Assessment

Aside from being required, a security risk assessment is an essential element of any corporation seeking to protect its information assets. A security risk assessment has the following benefits to an organization.

1.4.3.1 Checks and Balances

A security risk assessment provides a review of the organization's current implementation of information asset protection. The work of the information security officer and the security operations staff should be assessed by an objective party to determine the adequacy of the program and to note areas for improvement. Those who have architected the security program and those who are administering security controls are too close to the decisions that have been made and are not likely to be able to provide an objective analysis. (More on this under project staffing.)

1.4.3.2 Periodic Review

Even the most carefully constructed information security program requires a periodic review. A periodic review of an information security program can provide a measure of the effectiveness of the program and information necessary to properly adjust the program for the changing threat environment and business mission.

Many elements of an information security program require periodic review to measure their effectiveness. For example, the security awareness training program should be reviewed to measure and improve its effectiveness. Such measurements should not be limited to student evaluations of courses delivered, but the actual security awareness that has been instilled into the culture of employees and others who have access to an organization's information assets. Additional measurements could be obtained through physical inspections, policy quizzes, and social engineering experiments, to name a few.

Moreover, the landscape in which an information security program is developed is constantly changing. Threats to the origination's information assets change as technology advances, information is promulgated, skills (or tools) are acquired by would-be intruders, and interfaces to your organization's assets increase. Prior to widespread knowledge, tools, and tutorials, a SQL injection attack on a database required the skills of a determined intruder. Nowadays, less skilled and more abundant script-kiddies possess the ability to launch the same attack through tools circulated freely on the Internet.

Similarly, several years ago many organizations could state, with reasonable confidence, that they were aware of and controlled all interfaces to their network. However, if an organization lacks the proper controls, the introduction of cheap wireless routers that can be added to connected laptops rendered such a statement wishful thinking.

Lastly, your organization's mission may have changed since information security controls were first devised. Changes in mission can change everything from the reclassification of sensitive data, the addition of partners and extended networks, to the development of new systems, connections, and risks. Without a

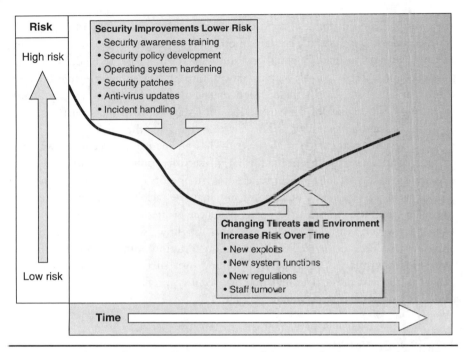

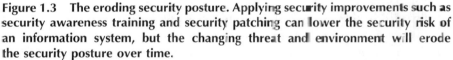

Figure 1.3   The eroding security posture. Applying security improvements such as security awareness training and security patching can lower the security risk of an information system, but the changing threat and environment will erode the security posture over time.

periodic security risk assessment, an organization's information security program would remain stagnant while threats, attacker skills and business missions change. The result would be a steady decline of the effectiveness of the information security program and an increased risk, as illustrated in Figure 1.3.

1.4.3.3 Risk-Based Spending

Resource allocation can be based on risk to assets. Organizations have limited resources to address their information security issues. If a security risk assessment is not performed, the organization does not have an understanding of the risks to its information assets. In the absence of risk information, resources are allocated on a variety of other factors including convenience, existing familiarity or skill, or simply interest.

When deciding how to spend the information security budget, the decision maker may choose the latest gadgets offered by vendors who have an existing relationship to the organization. Similarly, the decision maker may chose to expand the capabilities of the organization within an area with which they are familiar.

For example, the information security manager may be an expert in configuring perimeter devices to filter the content of outgoing messages. There may be exciting advances within this field. It would be natural for this manager to be drawn toward pursuing the integration of such advances into the existing information asset control architecture. Lastly, the decision maker may simply be swayed by "cool" technology. While each of these controls will likely improve the security posture of the organization, they may not be the best "bang for the buck."

Consider an organization that currently has an inadequate security awareness program and lacks the proper information security policies. Recognizing that security programs break at the weakest link, it is not a stretch to imagine that a security risk assessment would point out that the lack of an adequate security awareness program and security policies poses the greatest risk to an organization's assets. However, without a consideration of how security controls would ultimately reduce the overall risk to an organization, other more familiar or interesting controls will likely receive funding over such administrative controls. When is the last time you remember a security professional being interested in developing a security awareness program?

1.4.3.4 Requirement

As discussed in the introduction, a security risk assessment is a required element of a security program according to multiple information security regulations. These regulations include HIPAA, GLBA, FERC Cyber Security Standards, ISO 17799, OMB A-130, and many others. If for no other reason, many organizations obtain a security risk assessment simply because it is required.

1.4.4 Security Risk Assessment Secondary Benefits

Aside from the obvious benefits mentioned in section 1.4.3, a security risk assessment may provide some secondary benefits to an organization as well. Among those benefits are the transfer of knowledge from the security assessment team to the organization's staff, increased communications regarding security among business units, increased security awareness within the organization, and the results of the security risk assessment may be used as a measure of the security posture and compared to previous and future results.

There is an expectation that the members of the security assessment team will be experts in the field of information security. As we shall discuss in this book, the ability to observe, estimate, assess, and recommend is largely based on having experience with security mechanisms, how they work, and how they fail. An experienced security risk assessment team will be able to apply that knowledge to specific implementations of security mechanisms within the unique environment of the organization. Throughout the data-gathering process and the draft and final security risk assessment report, the experience of the team will be shared with the organization. Many of the insights shared may prove valuable to the organization and would not otherwise have been gained.

The fact that a security risk assessment team is focused solely on the security risks to the organization requires that the interaction of security mechanisms between business units need to be addressed—perhaps for the first time. The security risk assessment may allow for or even force a security discussion among the business units. For example, when assessing the effectiveness of termination procedures, the legal, human resources, physical security, and information technology departments will all need to work together to ensure an effective approach and execution of these procedures.

A security risk assessment includes many activities that may test the security awareness of the employees within the organization. A security risk assessment will include physical security walk-throughs, checks on perimeter controls, interviews with employees and key personnel, and may include social engineering. All of these activities will result in an indication of how effective security awareness training is within the organization. Making specific results known to the employees of the organization will increase the overall security awareness. For example, if the security risk assessment team was able to "piggyback" through physical access controls (e.g., badge swipe to open a door), consider letting the organization's employees know. This will increase their awareness that such breaches can actually occur and that it is their responsibility to help enforce current policies.

The security risk assessment should conclude with a list of risks to the organization's assets and an indication of the organization's overall security posture. These results can be compared to the previous and future results to assist in tracking the progress of the information security program. Organizations who consistently find that their security posture indicates that they are taking a larger risk than they are comfortable with should consider increasing the resources allocated to information security. The organization should also ask the security risk assessment team for a comparison of the organization's security program with similar organizations. As mentioned above, the members of the security risk assessment team will have experience with other organizations and should be able to provide a rough comparison of how this organization measures up to its peers in the industry.

1.5 Related Activities

There is much confusion surrounding the terms used to describe an assessment of the security mechanisms within an organization. Although there are clearly different approaches, objectives, levels, or rigor within various assessments, there does not seem to be a well-understood and accepted method for describing each of these assessments. For the purposes of this book and for clearly describing our topic, the following descriptions are offered.

A security risk assessment (see Tables 1.1 and 1.2) is related to these services but should not be confused with the services. A security risk assessment and the services described may be performed by professionals with similar credentials and use similar tools and checklists. However, a security risk assessment is differentiated from the other services in that only a security risk assessment takes a risk-based approach at identifying vulnerabilities within the organization's security controls. Only a security risk assessment provides recommendations for improvement based on the actual and perceived risks to your organization.

1.5.1 Gap Assessment

A gap assessment is the comparison between what exists within a corporation and what is required. Typically gap assessments are associated with specific criteria, e.g., HIPAA Gap Assessment, or ISO 17799 Gap Assessment. These assessments compare the existence of security policies, procedures, and mechanisms, along with activities (which may include a security risk assessment), against the required security policies, procedures, mechanisms, and activities dictated in the HIPAA regulation or in the ISO 17799 guidelines. There is no measure of risk associated with this assessment; it is merely a review of what exists against an interpretation of what the regulation or guideline requires.

A gap assessment is performed at the beginning of the organization's compliance pursuit with a standard or regulation. Since the gap assessment will result in a list of "gaps" or things that need to be done prior to declaring compliance, these assessments do not require verification of findings. If an interview with key personnel and a review of the materials reveals that the security awareness program is adequate, then the assessment team need go no further with this line of review. The point is to efficiently reach the point where the organization knows what the compliance project entails. An efficient gap assessment helps them get a quicker start. The customer should realize that deceiving the gap assessment team will only result in an inaccurate compliance plan.

1.5.2 Compliance Audit

When the time comes to attest to the organization's compliance with a regulation or a standard, a more in-depth review is required. This review requires that all findings are verified. The same interview and review of the security awareness training program would be followed up with review of a sample of employee training records and interviews with some employees. A compliance audit still does not result in a measure of the risk to the organization's assets. A compliance audit is an objective review of the organization's compliance with a security

Table 1.1   Addressing Security Risks. Vulnerability scans and penetration testing provide a review of some of the elements of a security program. However, many key elements of the security program are left unchecked. The security risk assessment provides a complete review of an organization's security program.

Security Program Elements	Vulnerability Scan	Penetration Test	Security Risk Assessment
Organization			Organizational effectiveness analysis
Policy and Procedure			Security policy and procedure review
Architecture			Security architecture review
Applications		Common mistakes, perform ad-hoc testing, side effects	Common mistakes, perform ad-hoc testing, side effects
External I/F	Scan for known vulnerabilities	Scan for known vulnerabilities	Scan for known vulnerabilities
Internal I/F	Scan for known vulnerabilities	Scan for known vulnerabilities	Scan for known vulnerabilities
Security awareness		Social engineering	Assess security awareness social engineering
External modems		Wardialing	Wardialing configuration review

Table 1.2 Security Assessment Definitions. There are a great many different ways to review the security controls of an organization. Terms such as "assessment," "audit," and "test" are commonly used as synonyms, yet it is important to understand the distinctive use and limitations of these industry terms.

Term	Definition	Purpose
Gap assessment	A review of security controls against a standard	To provide a list of controls required to become compliant
Compliance audit	Verification that all required security controls are in place	To attest to an organization's compliance with a standard
Security audit	A verification that specified security controls are in place	To attest to an organization's adherence to industry standards
Penetration testing	A methodical and planned attack on a system's security controls	To test the adequacy of security controls in place
Vulnerability scanning	An element of penetration testing that searches for obvious vulnerabilities	To test for the existence of obvious vulnerabilities in the system's security controls

standard, such as HIPAA Privacy and Security Rule, Gramm-Leach-Bliley Act, ISO 17799, or other regulations and standards that specify security controls that need to be in place.

1.5.3 Security Audit

A security audit, also called a security controls review, is a verification that the security controls that have been specified are properly implemented. Proper implementation may be further defined in existing organizational security policy and procedures or within industry standards, such as COBIT, ISO 17799, and others. Depending on how detailed the standards are, these security audits can be quite detailed and even involve statistically relevant sampling techniques and verification of all findings.

One thing that is common to all security audits is the overhead implicit in the assessment to ensure consistency with the standard. Many information security standards have associated assessment standards that specify the degree to which the assessor must analyze the data, sample the controls, and other such requirements. Many information security standards also require the assessors to obtain the proper credentials or require the assessor's company to be an auditing firm. While these requirements ensure consistency, they also add significantly to the cost of the audit. In most cases a "security audit" would cost far more than a security risk assessment.

The major differences here are level of rigor and formality of the statement. For example, a security audit performed under SAS No. 70[4] is said to be an "attestation." This means that a certified public accountant (CPA) has expressed a conclusion about the reliability of a written statement that is the responsibility of someone else. There are two key elements of this definition. First, a CPA provides a conclusion as to the reliability of a written statement. Security audits incur significant overhead since they must be overseen by a licensed CPA, the reports are issued by a licensed CPA firm, and the report is a formal input into the accounting process. Second, the written statement is a statement regarding the presence of reasonable assurance that control objectives are met. Control objectives are statements of the intended result or purpose achieved by implementing security controls. These statements are tailored to the organization and the security it is intended to provide.

It is important to understand that, because of the way the SAS 70 audit is structured, the SAS 70 audit (and most standard-driven audits) does not perform a security risk assessment. These security audit methodologies review an organization against a standard and do not provide an analysis of the effectiveness of the current security controls. Instead these security audits review the current security controls against a standard or a statement produced by the organization being assessed.[5]

1.5.4 Vulnerability Scanning

Vulnerability scanning is the testing of the external or internal interfaces of a system in order to identify obvious vulnerabilities. At a bare minimum, this service involves running a vulnerability scanning tool to test the known interfaces to the system and providing the tool-generated report. These tools are constantly updated with the knowledge of common system vulnerabilities. A more in-depth vulnerability scanning service would perform additional analyses and checks to remove false positives generated by the tool. A false positive is an indication by a security engineer, using his knowledge of the system, that identifies a vulnerability identified by the tool that does not really exist. These false positives are typically quite numerous.

1.5.5 Penetration Testing

Also called ethical hacking, whitehat hacking, security testing, and attack and penetration studies, this service is provided by an objective team who attempt to penetrate the defenses of an organization in order to demonstrate the effectiveness of the current controls. A vulnerability scan is typically performed as the first stage of a penetration test. The vulnerability scan would provide one source of information to the security testers for their use in attempting to penetrate the system. Penetration testing actually comprises several elements, including vulnerability scanning, ad-hoc testing, wardialing, social engineering, and other techniques. These elements can also be performed as a stand-alone test or as part of the security risk assessment data-gathering phase.

1.5.6 Ad Hoc Testing

Whereas vulnerability scans test for obvious vulnerabilities, *ad hoc* testing is a search for less obvious vulnerabilities. This type of testing must be performed by experts who use various techniques and knowledge gained from years of experience. This is more of an art than a science, but methods and some tools are available or developed in-house to assist in the process.

1.5.7 Social Engineering

This type of testing involves an assessment of the security training, policies, and procedures of the organization by attempting to gain unauthorized access through the human element. Social engineering by its nature is ad hoc and varies each time. Examples of this testing include gaining unauthorized physical access through "piggybacking," obtaining user identification and passwords through the help desk, and gaining unauthorized information through temporary or new employees.

Basically, social engineering involves gaining the confidence of authorized users in order to obtain sensitive information or gain access.

1.5.8 Wardialing

Another way of threatening an organization's assets is to gain access to its information systems or control systems through unprotected modems. This method is referred to as wardialing. A wardialing effort consists of identifying all organizational phone numbers that have modems attached (footprinting), determining the vulnerabilities of these various modems (preparation), and finally gaining access to the organization's systems through vulnerable modems. Systems targeted include not only information systems but also environmental systems such as the HVAC, security systems, and telephone systems (or private branch exchanges — PBXs).

1.6 The Need for This Book

The proliferation of information security and privacy laws, not to mention lawsuits, has mandated that businesses perform information security risk assessments. Five to ten years ago an analysis of the effectiveness of security controls was rarely performed outside of government agencies and organizations with the highest security concerns. Now most organizations are incorporating a security risk assessment into their information security programs as a way to continually improve their controls and remain compliant with information security regulations. At the same time, the demand for security risk assessments has exploded, but the supply of experienced information security engineers to perform them has not kept up with the demand.

In order to provide relief to this situation, there have been several promising advances in the area of security risk assessments. There are many sources of information that describe various information security risk assessment processes. These resources include (a) general security program guidance, which includes discussions on security risk assessments; (b) descriptions of security risk assessment methodologies; and (c) information on security risk assessment tools. These resources are useful to most information security professionals involved with commissioning or performing a security risk assessment.

- General Security Program Guidance — Groups such as ASIS and federal agencies such as NIST have provided general guidance that covers some aspects of performing security risk assessments. Below are a few examples.
- NIST Special Publication 800–12: An Introduction to Computer Security: The NIST Handbook — This publication provides an excellent overview of the security risk management process, which includes security risk assessment and security risk mitigation, and uncertainty analysis. Chapter

7 of the handbook provides a general description of the objectives and the processes involved in security risk management. This handbook is useful to anyone wanting to understand the various processes in computer security, their objectives, and how they interrelate. The coverage of security risk assessment is at a high level, but it provides the reader with a strong explanation of the phases of the process in terms of how the phases work together to provide management with the information required to make an informed decision regarding the risk decisions for the organization.

- NIST Special Publication 800–30: Risk Management Guide for Information Technology Systems — This publication provides a detailed discussion of a nine-step process for security risk assessments. The nine-step process includes system, threat, and vulnerability identification, control and impact analysis, likelihood and risk determination, control recommendation, and results documentation. For each of these steps, the NIST publication provides a discussion of the relevant point, offers some advice, and references several other useful sources of information. This publication also offers a simplistic approach to calculating the risk level for each system procedure/vulnerability pair. The publication also offers a list of general categories of risk prevention, detection, and recovery controls and advice on cost/benefit analysis.

- ASIS International: General Security Risk Assessment Guideline — This guideline was published to obtain a consensus regarding general practices for performing security risk assessments. The document outlines a seven-step process which comprises system and assess identification, specification of vulnerabilities, determining risk probabilities and event impact, developing risk mitigation options, studying the feasibility of options, and performing a cost/benefit analysis. The bulk of the ASIS security risk assessment guideline is the practice advisories contained in Appendix I: Qualitative Approach. These practice advisories include several examples to help illustrate the seven-step process. The ASIS guideline also provides many useful references.

- Security Risk Assessment Methods — Other groups and individuals such as Carnegie Mellon University have produced general security risk assessment models and methods that are designed to be used in the performance of a security risk assessment. For a more complete discussion of security risk assessment methods see Chapter 13.

- Security Risk Assessment Tools — There is even a good set of security risk assessment tools available to those looking at providing a security risk assessment service or with performing a security risk assessment within their own organization. Security risk assessment tools include everything from the simple checklists to the complex software packages. For a more complete discussion of security risk assessment methods see Chapter 13.

However, none of these resources is able to provide an explanation of the complete and detailed security risk assessment process sufficient to assist an information security professional in actually performing the work.

Although many information security risk assessment products, services, and approaches exist, little guidance is available to those who need to perform them. For all the literature that exists on the topic, there still is nothing that tells the security practitioner how to get started, how to behave, how to present the results, or any one of several dozen skills required to actually perform a security risk assessment. There is a frustration commonly experienced by information security professionals when attempting to perform a security risk assessment. That frustration is that, although existing material describes in detail the components of a security risk assessment, little information is available on how to execute those components. The "why" and the "what" are well explained, but there seems to be no information on the "how."

For example, most guidance currently available outlines the step in which the security risk assessment team must determine the impact of an event. The available guidance provides the structure for a risk assessment team to work within by describing that losses may be direct and indirect, the team must understand the business mission and consider the various security policies that could be threatened, and even gives sample qualitative categories and descriptions such as "low," "medium," and "high." However, none of the guidance documents tells the team exactly how to come up with the impact classification for each of the risk statements. No examples are given. No guidelines on ideal team size or decision techniques. No specific guidance on how to actually get this job done exists. Until now that specific guidance has only been developed by experienced information security professionals and absorbed by less experienced team members during an actual engagement.

This book will attempt to document just that experience and advice. By providing real examples, step-by-step descriptions, checklists, decision techniques, and other tricks of the trade, this book will provide a detailed insight into precisely how to conduct an information security risk assessment from a practical point of view.

1.7 Who Is This Book For?

This book is designed and intended for anyone who wants a more detailed understanding of how to perform an information security risk assessment. The audience for this book includes security professionals who want a more in-depth understanding of the process of performing a security risk assessment and for security consumers who want a better understanding of what goes into completing a security risk assessment project.

Security professionals will benefit from this book by becoming a more valuable member of or even leading a security risk assessment team. The information contained in this book contains practical real-world advice that will help develop the experience of the security professional reader.

Security consumers will benefit from this book by having greater insight into the security risk assessment process. The process descriptions and examples in this book will give the security consumer a more in-depth understanding of the entire process. Enlightened security consumers are then better educated to negotiate the scope and rigor of a security assessment, interface with the security assessment team more effectively, provide insightful comments on the draft report, and have a greater understanding of the final report recommendations.

As a result of reading and using this book, it is envisioned that the reader will save both time and money. Students of this text can expect to save time since they will spend less time figuring out what activities to do next and precisely how to perform them. In addition, the charts, checklists, examples, and templates included in this text can speed up the process of data gathering, analysis, and document development for the security risk assessment effort.

It is also expected that students of this text can save money as well. In the world of information security consulting, time is money. This text is designed to increase the quality of a consultant's product and reduce the amount of effort it takes to create that product. Such advances can lead to consultants providing a better, less expensive service for their customers and perhaps even making a larger profit in the process.

The security service consumer will benefit from reading this book as well. In addition to being the recipient of better, cheaper, faster security risk assessments, security consumers who have a more in-depth understanding of the security risk assessment process will be able to more confidently scope their risk assessments to meet their objectives in the most effective manner. Security assessment services can range from a low of about $35,000 to a high of well over $350,000, depending on various factors (see section 2.2 for a discussion of these factors).

A more educated consumer will be better suited to solicit and review proposals presented by various security service consultancies. Security service consumers who understand the process, components, skills, and experience required and other factors of a security risk assessment will be well positioned to commission a security risk assessment that meets their needs from a quality security service provider at a competitive price.

Notes

1. A more complete comparison of these information security regulations is presented in Chapter 13.
2. The reader should be careful not to draw too many conclusions from such a high-level analysis of these regulations and guidelines. For example, some

regulations or guidelines may not explicitly call for information security policies (as in GLBA) or configuration management (as in GAISP, HIPAA, and GLB Act). However, this does not mean that those security practices should not or do not need to be part of an information security program under those regulations or guidelines. Every guideline and regulation includes security risk assessment and therefore the inclusion of many security practices is a matter of analysis and judgment.

3.   IT Governance Institute, *IT Control Objectives for Sarbanes-Oxley: The Importance of IT in the Design, Implementation, and Sustainability of Internal Control over Disclosure and Financial Reporting,* 2004.

4.   Statement on Auditing Standards (SAS) No. 70, Service Organizations, was developed by the American Institute of Certified Public Accountants (AICPA) and provides a methodology for the service organization to claim internal control objectives and for the auditors to check the validity of such claims.

5.   There is considerable debate as to the usefulness of SAS No. 70 and other control objective-based audits. In these types of audits the organization being assessed is responsible for creating its own statements of security. For example, if the organization believes that it provides effective controls over stored data, then it makes a statement regarding those controls. The debate centers around the practice of assessed organizations simply deleting or rewording any control objectives for which they cannot show reasonable assurance that those objectives are met. This practice leads security professionals to question the value of a SAS 70 audit report when it may contain few relevant control objectives. On the other side of the debate, security audit professionals are responsible for ensuring that a reasonable set of control objectives is applied to their customers. Any suggested wording or deletion of control objectives should be approved by the auditing firm. In either case, a consumer of a SAS 70 or other control objective-based audit would be well advised to study the control objectives contained in the report and base their assurance in the report on the relevance of the control objectives for which the organization was audited.

References

[1]   AT&T Corp. PR Newswire, "Security Is Top Concern for Corporate Networks, According to Global Survey of Senior Executives,' July 14, 2004.

[2]   The Free Dictionary, www.thefreedictionary.com

[3]   Gold Wire Technology, "Gold Wire: Survey Shows Security Still Top Concern," April 13, 2004.

[4]   CobiT Steering Committee, IT Governance Institute, *COBIT Control Objectives,* 3rd ed., July 2000.

[5]   CobiT Steering Committee, IT Governance Institute, *COBIT Executive Summary,* 3rd ed., July 2000.

[6]   CobiT Steering Committee, IT Governance Institute, *COBIT Framework,* 3rd ed., July 2000.

[7] CobiT Steering Committee, IT Governance Institute, *COBIT Management Guidelines*, 3rd ed., July 2000.

[8] Cosgrove, Lorraine, "CSOs Prioritize Security Spending for 2003," *CSO Online*, CSO Research Reports, January 7, 2003.

[9] Martin, James A., "Security Spending on the Rise," *iQMagazine*, September/October 2003.

[10] Ernst & Young, "Global Information Security Survey 2003," No. FF0224.

[11] United States General Accounting Office, Accounting and Information Management Division, *Information Security Risk Assessment: Practices of Leading Organizations, A Supplement to GAO's May 1998 Executive Guide on Information Security Management*, GAO/IAM-00-33, November 1999.

[12] Federal Trade Commission, Standards for Safeguarding Customer Information; Final Rule, 16 CFR Part 314, *Federal Register*, Vol. 67, No. 100, May 23, 2002. www.ftc.gov/os/2002/05/67fr36585.pdf

[13] Federal Trade Commission, Standards for Privacy of Individually Identifiable Health Information; Final Rule, 45 CFR Parts 160 and 164, *Federal Register*, Vol. 67, No. 157, August 14, 2002. http://www.hhs.gov/ocr/hipaa/privrulepd.pdf

[14] International Organization for Standardization, International Electrotechnical Commission, *Information Technology — Code of Practice for Information Security Management*, ISO/IEC: 17799. First Edition 2000-12-01.

[15] *An Introduction to Computer Security: A NIST Handbook*, NIST Special Publication 800–12, October 1995. http://csrc.nist.gov/publications/nistpubs/800-12/800-12-html

[16] American Institute of Certified Public Accountants, *Service Organizations: Applying SAS No. 70, as Amended: AICPA Guide*, 2004.

[17] ASIS International, *The General Security Risk Assessment Guideline*, November 13, 2002. http://www.asisonline.org/guidelines/guidelinesgsra.pdf

[18] *Risk Management Guide: Recommendations of the National Institute of Standards and Technology*, NIST Special Publication 800-30, July 2002. http://csrc.nist.gov/publications/nistpubs/800-30/sp800-30.pdf

Chapter 2

Information Security Risk Assessment Basics

It is the aim of this book to provide an extensive discussion of information security risk assessment. As such, you will find detailed information, discussion, and advice on all elements of the information security risk assessment. Many of the sections of this book will provide a rather detailed discussion of a single element of information security risk assessment. However, before we get into this type of discussion, it seems useful to provide a brief overview of the information security risk assessment process.

For the purpose of this book, the information security risk assessment process is defined as "an objective analysis of the effectiveness of the current security controls that protect an organization's assets and a determination of the probability of losses to those assets." There are many methods available and currently in use. Depending on the specific security risk assessment employed, a security risk assessment may have any number of steps or phases, but the overall process is largely similar in all these methods. The generic phases of a security risk assessment are as shown in Figure 2.1.

2.1 Phase 1: Project Definition

As with many projects, the success of the security risk assessment project relies not only on the skill and experience of the team assigned to the security risk assessment but also on the effectiveness of the project management. A key

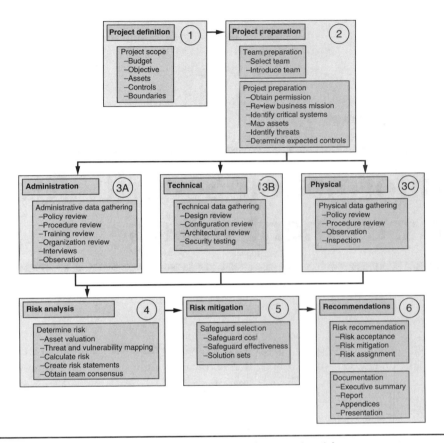

Figure 2.1   Security risk assessment process. The security risk assessment process comprises the following phases: project definition, project preparation, administrative data-gathering, technical data-gathering, physical data-gathering, risk analysis, risk mitigation, and recommendations. These phases are described in more detail in the remaining chapters of this book.

component of project management is arriving at an agreement as to the scope and content of deliverables. Within the project definition phase, the project is properly scoped and documented.

The scoping of any project includes a clear understanding of the cost and timeframe of the engagement. The security risk assessment team leader needs to ensure that the project budget and time constraints are well understood. Documentation of this understanding is captured in the project plan and in the contract, if this is outside support. A project plan not only documents the budget and time constraints but breaks down the overall project into manageable tasks and allocates resources to those tasks.

Beyond the budget and time constraints of the project, scoping of a security risk assessment can be more complex than the scoping of some other projects. Unique variables to the security risk assessment process include the objective of the assessment, the assets and controls to be covered, and the boundaries of the assessment. Obtaining clarity on the security risk assessment objective is necessary to understand the customer needs. For example, a security risk assessment performed for contract compliance has a different objective than a security risk assessment performed for program review. The team must also seek clarity on the boundaries of the assessment through an identification of the assets, systems, and other boundaries of the project. Each of these tasks is discussed in greater detail in Chapter 3.

2.2 Phase 2: Project Preparation

Based on the scope of the security risk assessment project identified in phase 1, the team leadership needs to ensure that adequate preparations are performed prior to entering the data-gathering phase. Preparation includes team preparation and project preparation.

Team preparation comprises the selection of the security risk assessment team and the introduction of the team to the organization to be assessed. Many factors go into the proper selection of the security risk assessment team, including objectivity, expertise, and experience. Introduction of the team to the customer includes formal letters of introduction as well as a request for permission and access. Each of these tasks is discussed in greater detail in Chapter 4.

2.3 Phase 3: Data Gathering

The data-gathering phase is typically performed on site and results in the collection of information concerning the effectiveness of the current administrative, physical, and technical security controls. The security risk assessment team will review the administrative controls through the collection, review, analysis of available policies and procedures, and observation and interviews with staff. The physical security controls will be assessed through techniques such as observation, testing, and analysis. The technical security controls will be reviewed through technical analysis, testing, and review of logs. The data-gathering phase is the most comprehensive of all of the phases and is discussed in more detail in Chapter 5.

2.4 Phase 4: Risk Analysis

The risk analysis phase involves a review of the data gathered and an analysis of the resulting risk to the organization. During this phase the security risk assessment team must determine asset values, system criticality, likely threats, and the existence of vulnerabilities based on the data gathered. Furthermore, the team must calculate the risk to the organization for each threat/vulnerability pair. The calculation and presentation of these risks can vary greatly, depending on the security risk assessment method being used.

Several elements of the risk analysis phase are considered key concepts within security risk assessments. These include assets, threats, vulnerabilities, and security risk.

2.4.1 Assets

The first element to be considered and discussed in an information security risk assessment is the assets of the organization. Assets are the items considered valuable by the organization. Later in this book we shall discuss classes of assets, valuation of assets, and grouping of assets, but for now it is important to understand that assets are the information and resources that have value to the organization. Examples include buildings, equipments, personnel, organization reputation, business documents, and many other tangible and intangible items.

Assets are an important element of a security risk assessment for several reasons. First, the enumeration of assets helps to scope the security risk assessment. Scoping of the security risk assessment will be discussed later as well, but for now consider the following example. If an organization has commissioned a security risk assessment and has dictated that the buildings and equipment are not among the assets within the scope of the security risk assessment, then a review of the physical security controls protecting the buildings and equipment would not need to be performed. In this way, the enumeration of assets helps to scope the security risk assessment.

Second, the valuation of assets helps to determine the countermeasures employed. A countermeasure is simply an activity, technique, or technology that reduces the possible loss to an organization's assets (see Table 2.1). While the selection of countermeasures can be somewhat involved, it is clear that we should not spend more on the countermeasure than the possible reduction in the organizational loss. Later in the book we shall discuss both asset valuation and countermeasure selection.

2.4.2 Threat Agents and Threats

The next elements to be considered and discussed in an information security risk assessment are the threats and the threat agents. A threat is an event with an undesired impact. A threat agent is the entity that may cause a threat to happen. Threats and threat agents are inextricably linked in that it is the threat agent that causes a threat to happen. In a later chapter we shall discuss threat classes, threat environments, and threat analysis. The basics of threats and threat agents are presented here as a primer on the topic. Threat agents include Mother Nature and

Table 2.1   Asset Summary. Assets are those items the organization wishes to protect. The enumeration and valuing of the assets scopes and guides the security risk assessment.

Definition	Resource, data, or other item of value to the organization	
Key concepts	Asset enumeration	A listing or grouping of assets under assessment. Asset enumeration helps to scope the information security assessment.
	Asset valuation	The placement of a relative or dollar value on each asset. Asset valuation s useful in determining potential loss and countermeasure selection.

mankind. Examples of threats include earthquakes, fires, theft, insertion of malicious code, accidental disclosure, and many others.

The main reason that threat agents and threats are important elements of the information security risk assessment is that they help to determine the scope of the vulnerabilities of the system being assessed. To begin a security risk assessment we must understand the threats from which we plan to protect the assets. It is rather naïve to believe that something undesired will never happen and it is equally naïve to believe that you can possibly anticipate or even list every possible threat. However, we can describe the threat environment of the target system. This approach helps the security risk assessment team to consider those threats that are most likely to impact the target of the security risk assessment and to ignore those that are least likely to impact the target of the security risk assessment.

For example, an information security risk assessment being performed on an organization in Austin, Texas, would not need to consider the threat of earthquakes, snow blizzards, or perhaps even hurricanes. However, it would need to consider flooding, tornadoes, and severe thunderstorms. In this example the threat agent is Mother Nature and we consider some of her threats valid and others not valid for this portion of the country.

2.4.2.1 Threat Agents

Threat agents are the catalyst of the threat. A threat agent is the entity that causes a threat to happen. A list of possible threat agents is provided below for illustrative purposes:

- Nature — Any number of natural disasters could affect the support systems relied upon by your organization's information system. If the threat is a natural threat, such as storms or floods, then "nature" can be considered the threat agent.

- Employees — Organizations entrust their personnel to perform their duties accurately and consistent with the polic_es of the organization. A major threat to organizations is the threat that an employee could make a critical mistake in data entry, release proprietary data, or decide to defraud the organization.

- Malicious Hackers — Information systems that are networked with other systems or even the Internet expose themselves to millions of potential hackers. Even those systems that do not provide a public interface, such as the Internet, are still exposed to hackers through social engineering, modem connections, or physical attacks.

- Industrial Spies — The value of proprietary information to the competition should not be under-estimated. Industrial espionage is a significant threat to most organizations and can result in loss of profits, competitive advantage, or even the business itself.

- Foreign Government Spies — Foreign spies could perform espionage for the purpose of advancing the capabilities of a foreign government, restricting our government's abilities, or could even include foreign-sponsored industrial espionage.

2.4.2.2 Threats

A threat is an undesired event that may result in the loss, disclosure, or damage to an organizational asset (see Table 2.2). A partial set of threats is listed below:

- Errors and Omissions — Occasionally, mistakes made by authorized employees, users, developers, and testers can be made during data entry, operations, or in system or application development. These errors and omissions can lead to the lack of data and system integrity, system stability, and even disclosure of sensitive information.

- Fraud and Theft — The threat to the information system could be for the purpose of fraud or theft. Information systems are targets of fraud and theft because they directly or indirectly protect assets of value. For example, financial systems directly protect the assignment of funds to accounts, whereas inventory systems indirectly protect equipment through inventory tracking. Each of these types of systems can be the target of those attempting to steal from or defraud a corporation.

- Sabotage — Those authorized by the organization to access the organization's information systems and assets must be trusted to uphold the trust placed in them. However, sometimes this trust is misplaced. Such misplaced trust leads to sabotage. Sabotage may include the physical

Table 2.2 Threat and Threat Agent Summary. Threats and threat agents are the actions and entities the organization would like to avoid. Threats and threat agents are determined by the physical geography and mission of the organization.

Definition	Threat	An event with an undesired impact
	Threat agent	The entity that may cause a threat to happen
Key concepts	Threat environment	Determining the physical, geographical, and other aspects of the organization's system helps to determine the scope and extent of applicable threats

damage to facilities or equipment, destruction of processes, the deletion of data, or the loss of data integrity.

- Loss of Physical and Infrastructure Support — The physical and infrastructure support provides the required services for an organization's information systems, such as power communication, and transportation. Many threats, both natural and human, endanger the ability of the support structure to supply the required services to the information system. Threats in this category include power failures, winter storms, labor strikes, and terrorist attacks,

- Espionage — Proprietary information is a highly valued asset of the organization. Proprietary information is also highly valued by the competition. The act of gathering proprietary data for the purpose of aiding another organization is referred to as "espionage." Espionage is performed by foreign governments and competitive organizations.

- Malicious Code — The connectivity of systems and the introduction of new software and data from other sources increases the threat that an organization's information system may become infected with malicious software. Malicious software could be a virus, Trojan horse, worm, logic bomb, or other software that does not perform as intended.

- Disclosure — Information systems contain vast amounts of data that is sensitive to the organization and to individuals. The concern that data about an individual could be disclosed to someone unauthorized is referred to as "privacy." The concern that data about the organization could be disclosed is referred to as "confidentiality." Both the personal privacy threat and the organizational confidentiality threat are major concerns.

2.4.3 Vulnerabilities

A vulnerability is a flaw or oversight in an existing control that may possibly allow a threat agent to exploit it to gain unauthorized access to organizational assets. In later chapters we shall discuss in detail how to find, describe, and rate vulnerabilities within an organizational system. For now it is important to understand the relationship of vulnerabilities to other elements of the information security risk assessment and the importance of the vulnerability in this effort.

Vulnerabilities are important elements of a security risk assessment because they are instrumental in determining existing and residual risk. Without vulnerabilities there would be no risk. However, we know there is no such thing as a system without vulnerabilities, so it is the task of the security risk assessment team to assess the vulnerabilities in the existing system and those vulnerabilities that are likely to still exist if the safeguard recommendations are implemented. When assessing vulnerabilities in the system, it is useful to categorize the vulnerabilities according to administrative, physical, and technical areas.

Administrative vulnerabilities are those vulnerabilities that exist in policies, procedures, or security activities. Examples include missing acceptable use policies, gaps in termination procedures, or the lack of independence in security testing.[1] Physical vulnerabilities are those vulnerabilities that exist in the physical, geographical, personnel, or utility provisioning controls. Examples include holes in the fence line, location in a flight path, lack of background checks for sensitive positions, and lack of redundant power supplies. Technical vulnerabilities are those vulnerabilities that exist in the logical controls in the organization's system. Examples include misconfigured routers, backdoors in programs, and weak passwords (see Table 2.3).

2.4.4 Security Risk

A security risk is the loss potential to an origination's asset(s) that will likely occur if a threat is able to exploit a vulnerability. In this book we shall discuss various ways to assess, reduce, and report security risk. Security risk (and residual security risk) is the key element of the information security risk assessment because it is the culmination of all the other assessments, calculations, and analysis. Security risk is the key measurement that the organization's management really cares about; the rest of the stuff is just a way to get to the key measurement of security risk.

There are many key factors to consider when discussing security risk, but the most important factor of security risk to consider right now is the manner in which the security risk is derived and presented. There are many ways to derive and present security risk, but all of these approaches can be described as quantitative or qualitative.

The quantitative approach to deriving and presenting security risk relies on specific formulas and calculations to determine the value of the security risk.

Table 2.3 **Vulnerability Summary. Vulnerabilities are a weakness or absence of a security control. These vulnerabilities can exist in administrative, physical, or technical controls.**

Definition		A flaw or oversight in an existing control that may possibly allow a threat agent to exploit it to gain unauthorized access to organizational assets
Key concepts	Administrative	Gaps in policies, procedures, or security activities, e.g., missing acceptable use policies, gaps in termination procedures, or the lack of independence in security testing
	Physical	Gaps in physical, geographical, personnel, or utility provisioning controls, e.g., holes in the fence line, location in a flight path, lack of background checks for sensitive positions, and lack of redundant power supplies
	Technical	Gaps in the logical controls in the organization's system, e.g., misconfigured routers, backdoors in programs, and weak passwords

A quantitative approach to determining and even presenting security risk has the advantages of being objective and expressed in terms of dollar figures. However, such quantitative calculations can be rather complex and accurate values for the variables in quantitative formulas may be difficult to obtain.

The qualitative approach to deriving and presenting security risk relies on subjective measures of asset valuation, threats, vulnerabilities, and ultimately of the security risk. A qualitative approach to determining and presenting security risk has the advantages of being easy to understand and in many cases provides adequate indication of the organization's security risk. However, a security risk measurement derived from such qualitative measures is, indeed, subjective and may not be trusted by some in management positions (see Table 2.4).

2.5 Phase 5: Risk Mitigation

Based on the risks defined in the risk analysis phase, the team must develop recommendations for safeguards to reduce the identified risks to an acceptable level. The safeguard selection process involves mapping safeguards to threat/ vulnerability pairs, determining the reduction of risk, determining the cost of the safeguard, and grouping safeguards into solution sets.

Several elements of the risk mitigation phase are considered key concepts within security risk assessments. These include safeguards and residual risk.

Table 2.4 Security Risk Summary. Security risks are a measurement of the likelihood that the organization's assets are susceptible. Security risk assessment methods can be either quantitative or qualitative.

Definition		The loss potential to an origination's asset(s) that will likely occur if a threat is able to exploit a vulnerability
Key concepts	Quantitative risk	A method of determining and presenting security risk that relies on specific formulas and calculations to determine the value of the security risk
	Advantages:	Objective; security risk expressed in terms of dollars
	Disadvantages:	Security risk calculations are complex; accurate values are difficult to obtain
	Qualitative risk	A method of determining and presenting security risk that relies on subjective measures of asset valuation, threats, vulnerabilities, and ultimately of the security risk
	Advantages:	Easy to understand; provides adequate indication of the organization's security risk
	Disadvantages:	Subjective; may not be trusted by some in management positions

2.5.1 Safeguards

Next we consider the security controls, or safeguards, put in place to protect the organization's assets from reasonable threats. A safeguard or countermeasure is a technique, activity, or technology employed to reduce the risk to the organization's assets. A safeguard may prevent, detect, or minimize the potential loss to an organization's assets. For this reason, safeguards are generally categorized as preventative, detective, or corrective measures. Preventative measures are controls that are designed to deter undesirable events from happening. Examples include access controls, door locks, and security awareness training. Detective measures are controls that identify conditions that indicate that an undesirable event has happened. Examples of detective measures include audit logs, security testing, and intrusion detection systems. Corrective measures are controls designed to correct the damage caused by undesirable events. Examples of corrective measures include security guards, termination policies, and file recovery. Note that safeguards (also referred to as controls) may be classified as being in multiple categories, such as security guards, which can be considered a preventative, detective, and corrective measure.

Safeguards are an important element in information security risk assessments for two reasons. First, all existing safeguards must be considered when determining the present vulnerability of the organization's system. If the security risk assessment

Table 2.5   Safeguard Summary. Safeguards protect the organization's assets from the risks of threats.

Definition	A technique, activity, or technology employed to reduce the risk to the organization's assets	
Key concepts	Preventative	Controls designed to deter undesirable events from happening, e.g., access controls, door locks, and security awareness training
	Detective	Controls that identify conditions that indicate that an undesirable event has happened, e.g., audit logs, security testing, and intrusion detection systems
	Corrective	Controls designed to correct the damage caused by undesirable events, e.g., security guards, termination policies, and file recovery

team fails to consider all the safeguards in place to protect the organization's assets, then the security risk assessment results will be inaccurate and will likely error on the side of overestimating the risk. Such errors can be costly, as decisions for implementing additional security measures should be based on the results of security risk assessments.

Second, safeguards are an important element of security risk assessments because the final report should recommend safeguards to be implemented to bring the residual risk within tolerance levels of the senior management of the organization. Safeguard recommendations are key to the results of a security risk assessment and must be carefully considered (see Table 2.5).

2.5.2 Residual Security Risk

Residual security risk is the security risk that remains after implementation of recommended safeguards. The objective of security risk management is to accurately measure the residual security risk and keep it to a level at or below the security risk tolerance level.

Residual security risk is an important element of information security risk assessments for several reasons. First and foremost, residual risk is the security risk that the organization will inherit when safeguards are implemented. It is important that the organization's management fully understand the concept of residual security risk and be comfortable with staffing and budgeting decisions that determine the residual security risk level.

Second, the security professional and the organization's management must clearly understand that there is no such thing as 100 percent security (or 0 percent residual security risk). Even if the organization implements every one of the information security professionals' recommendations, the organization still has some residual

Table 2.6 Residual Risk Summary. Residual risks are the leftover risks to the organization's assets after safeguards have been applied.

Definition	The security risk that remains after implementation of recommended safeguards	
Key concepts	Static risk	The security risk that will always exist
	Dynamic risk	Security risk that may be reduced through the implementation of safeguards

security risk to its assets. It may be useful to introduce two security risk concepts: static security risk and dynamic security risk. Static security risk is the security risk that will always exist. As mentioned above, no matter what controls you put into place, something can still go wrong — a trusted employee may decide to violate your trust, a determined and skillful hacker may decide to target your system exclusively for months, Mother Nature may unleash her power at one of your sites. If these are concerns for your organization, then you should implement the appropriate safeguards to reduce their chance of success, but also realize that there always remains some possibility that these attacks may be successful — that is, static security risk.

Dynamic security risk is that security risk for which something can be done. Because we can do something about dynamic security risk, it is worthy of study and discussion. That is the topic of the rest of this book. For the remainder of this book when referring to dynamic security risk we shall simply use the term "security risk" (see Table 2.6).

2.6 Phase 6: Risk Reporting and Resolution

The final phase of a security risk assessment is the risk reporting and resolution phase. During this phase, the security risk assessment team develops a report and a presentation to the project sponsor that clearly identifies the risks found and the safeguards recommended. The final risk assessment report should provide clear information for the executive, management, and technical personnel. The executive management of the assessed organization must then determine the resolution of the identified risks. The risk resolution element within this phase is considered a key concept within security risk assessments.

2.6.1 Risk Resolution

At the conclusion of a security risk assessment project, the senior management of the assessed organization must determine the resolution of each of the

Table 2.7   Risk Resolution Summary. Safeguards protect the organization's assets from the risks of threats.

Definition	Risk resolution is the decision by senior management of how to resolve the risk resented to them	
Key concepts	Risk reduction	The reduction of risk to the organization to an acceptable level through the adoption of additional security controls or improvement of existing controls
	Risk acceptance	The deliberate decision by senior management to accept an identified risk based on the business objectives of the organization
	Risk transference	The contractual transfer of risk to another organization through outsourcing or insurance

identified risks. In other words, the senior manager must decide to reduce the risk, accept the risk, or delegate the risk to someone else.

A security risk can be reduced by implementing additional security controls or even by improving existing security controls. Suggestions for risk-reducing safeguards for each identified risk should be documented in the final report. Along with these recommendations should be cost and effectiveness estimations to assist in the senior manager's decision.

A security risk can be accepted if the senior manager believes that it is in the best interest of the organization to accept the risk rather than to accept the cost burdens of implementing additional safeguards. The acceptance of this risk must be performed by a senior manager of the organization, because this decision impacts the organization as a whole and not just a single department or project.

Lastly, a security risk can be transferred to another organization such as an outsourcing company or an insurance agency. The transfer of security risk is a contractual agreement that clearly spells out the risk and the burden accepted along with the conditions and limitations of such an agreement (see Table 2.7).

Note

1.   Administrative security controls comprise policies, procedures, and security activities. Often the term "administrative" has a bad connotation among security engineers. Those that come from a technical background may tend to think that "administrative" means paperwork, but this is not the case. Administrative security controls include controls that require technical skills such as risk assessments, security testing, and code review.

References

[1] *Common Criteria for Information Technology Security Evaluation, Version 2.1,* CCIMB-99-031, August 1999.

[2] Krause, Micki, and Tipton, Harold F., *Handbook of Information Security Management,* 1997.

Chapter 3

Project Definition

A security risk assessment can mean many things to many people. Within the context of this book, a security risk assessment is defined as "an analysis of the effectiveness of the current administrative, physical, and technical controls that together protect an organization's assets." Various regulations, guidelines, and other information sources sometimes call the security risk assessment by another name. Terms used include security audit, risk assessment, security testing, and so on. Other times a "security risk assessment," is used to mean something different than what we describe in this book.

Realizing the confusion surrounding these terms, it is important that the security risk assessment project is well defined prior to project initiation. Definition of a risk assessment project requires knowledge of the budget, objective, scope, and level of rigor of analysis expected. Each of these areas is discussed in the following sections. But first a quick discussion of how to ensure a successful security risk assessment.

3.1 Ensuring Project Success

Performing a security risk assessment is a project and, as such, anyone seeking to be an effective member of a security risk assessment team should understand how such a project is run successfully. Moreover, the leader of the security risk assessment team needs to be able to plan, track, and ensure the success of the risk assessment project.

3.1.1 Success Definition

Success cannot be achieved until we define the meaning of success. For a risk assessment project, success is defined as achieving customer satisfaction, quality technical work, and project completion within budget.

3.1.1.1 Customer Satisfaction

The customer of a risk assessment includes the "sponsor" of the risk assessment and additional stakeholders within the organization being assessed. Each of these stakeholders has a unique point of view and a distinct definition of what they expect from a successful security risk assessment.

3.1.1.1.1 Identifying the Customer

Regardless of whether the risk assessment is performed by internal resources or is contracted out to a security consulting firm, the primary customer of a risk assessment is the individual responsible for commissioning the risk assessment. If the risk assessment is performed by a contracted security consulting firm, the project sponsor should be explicitly stated in the contract. If not explicitly stated, consider the project sponsor the most senior official who will be at the final briefing. For internal risk assessments, the project sponsor is the department manager or director who commissioned the project.

Project Sponsor — The project sponsor is the person internally responsible for the success of the project. If this is a contracted effort, then the project sponsor is typically the signature authority for the project. Either way, the project sponsor will define the success of the project in terms of the quality of the technical work and completion of the project within time and budget constraints.

The technical quality of the work can be ensured through careful selection of project members and following the guidelines in this book. The completion of the project within budget can be ensured through following the guidelines in Chapter 12.

The secondary customer for the risk assessment project includes any other stakeholder in the process. These stakeholders are numerous and play a vital role in the ultimate acceptance of the risk assessment and in turn customer satisfaction. Each of these secondary customers is listed and discussed below.

Security Officer or Security Team — The most senior security officer in the organization may be a chief security officer, with a staff, visibility, and a security budget, or it may be a systems administrator who enjoys the security aspects of setting up the network. Regardless of their position within the corporation, the most senior security officer will be very interested in the security risk assessment project. These people can be either the biggest critic or the most ardent supporter of the security risk assessment. Typically, the senior security officer will be a supporter of the security risk assessment effort and may even be the project sponsor.

The most senior security officer will be concerned that the security risk assessment is properly scoped, accurate, and performed by professionals with the appropriate experience and credentials. Many of these concerns can be addressed through proper negotiation and development of the statement of work. The accuracy of the security risk assessment can be ensured through careful data gathering, testing, analysis, and review. The professionalism and credentials of the security risk assessment team can be addressed through the presentation of résumés, past performance descriptions, and certifications.

Be aware that the most senior security officer will likely have their own set of security controls that they are trying to get adopted within the organization. The security risk assessment can point out the specific benefits of implementing these controls from a risk-based approach. Therefore, the security risk assessment may be able to give the senior security officer the support they need for upcoming projects or the security risk assessment may recommend other projects with a larger return on investment (ROI) than the ones currently planned. Be careful to ensure that you gain the necessary information from the security team, but remain objective and credible by forming your own opinions and recommendations.

Business Unit Managers — Organizations divide responsibility for corporate governance among business units. These units may take on various names such as groups, departments, or divisions. Here they are referred to simply as business units. The business unit will have a single individual in charge — sometimes referred to as the division chief, director, or even department head. Here we shall refer to them as the business unit managers. The business unit manager will be concerned with several factors, including proper understanding of the business unit, accurate identification of risks, clarity and usefulness of recommendations, and cost of recommendations.

- Understanding the Business Unit — The risk assessment team will need to ensure they offer the opportunity for an interview with each of the business unit managers. This interview will give them a chance to explain the business unit functions and to voice concerns about existing risks. Granting the business unit manager an opportunity to explain and voice these concerns will help to ensure their acceptance of the results.
- Accurate Identification of Risks — The business unit managers are likely to be among the sharpest critics of risk results that affect their business unit. This should not be surprising, as risk results and their recommendations will affect their budget. The risk assessment team should take the necessary steps to ensure that risk findings are accurate. These steps include the

interview with the business unit manager mentioned above, interviews with other representatives for the business unit, and the ability for each business unit manager to review draft findings of the risk assessment.

- Clarity and Usefulness of Risk Recommendations — A risk assessment that simply states that the organization is at a certain level of risk is of little value. The most valuable component of a risk assessment is a prioritized list of actions that may be taken to reduce the risk. Unclear, high-level, or ambiguous recommendations like "increase security staff" offer little guidance to those who need to act on these recommendations. Risk recommendations need to be clear, unambiguous, and ultimately useful to the customer.

- Cost of Risk Recommendations — Clearly, business unit managers would rather hear that the actions recommended are cheap and easy. But that might not always be the case. The project team cannot and should not artificially reduce cost estimates of the recommendations for reducing risk. Although it may lead some segments of the customer population initially to be disappointed in the results, ultimately an underestimate of recommendation costs would lead to a greater disappointment. The risk assessment team should be straightforward and as accurate as possible when stating the cost of a risk recommendation.

Compliance Officer Legal Department — In many organizations a risk assessment is a legal requirement. Organizations with a legal requirement for obtaining a risk assessment include healthcare entities, financial institutions, and government agencies, but could include others as well. In these cases, the individual within the corporation responsible for compliance with these laws or contractual obligations would certainly be interested in the method and results of the risk assessment.

Risk Assessment Method — The organization compliance officer will be concerned that the risk assessment will meet the legal or contractual obligations. Some customers may have strict requirements as to the risk assessment methodology. These requirements will typically state that the risk assessment must follow certain guidelines or methods which are spelled out explicitly in the governing law or in the contract. The risk assessment project manager should be familiar with the governing law affecting the customer and should ask specifically for contracts that have specific requirements for a security risk assessment.

Risk Assessment Team — Although most governing law and contracts will not explicitly call for a specific risk assessment methodology, there are some indirect requirements on the objectivity and credentials of the risk assessment team. Several governing laws call for an objective review by security professionals.

While not stating exact requirements for these terms, the following guidelines could be applied.

Objective Review — Objectivity requires the lack of real or perceived conflict of interest. Conflict of interest arises when the risk assessment team has a stake in the outcome of the assessment. Namely, a conflict of interest occurs when the risk assessment team includes members who have designed, operate, or are in charge of portions of the security program. This includes any element of the security program that is to be assessed; for example, security policies, security awareness programs, security architecture, system hardening, audit log review, physical access control, logical perimeter controls (firewalls, routers), and managed security services. Anyone representing or involved in these functions will have a vested interest in how well they are perceived. This vested interest and the interest in uncovering all flaws that present a risk to the organization are at odds and culminate in a conflict of interest.

To some, the exclusion of these members from the risk assessment team may seem inappropriate or overkill. After all, these members know the systems better than anyone and can identify possible risks with great efficiency. It is for this reason that these members must clearly be involved in the risk assessment process. They should be interviewed, consulted, and could even be included in many of the discussions that lead up to the findings of the risk assessment. However, they should not be a "voting" member of the risk assessment team. In the end, those who make the final recommendations must be objective or the validity and credibility of the risk assessment is questionable.

Security Professionals — The risk assessment team needs to be composed of members who understand the concepts to be applied in a risk assessment, bring a measure of expertise to the project, and will act in a professional manner.

An understanding of the concepts in a risk assessment is required simply to be a productive member of the team. Without such an understanding, a team member may find themselves lost in the process, misinterpreting results, and unable to be a productive member of the team.

Some measure of expertise is required from each member of the team. The team will require members who can draw from experience to provide reasonable measurements of threat frequency, impact, and overall risk. Furthermore, the team should include members with different areas of expertise so that the scope of the assessment may be covered. Depending on the scope, the risk assessment team requires experts in the areas of physical security, security testing security policies and procedures, disaster recovery plans, and other areas.

Each member of the risk assessment team will need to act in a professional manner. This includes the proper respect for the customer. Even more importantly, professional behavior requires the ethics necessary to ensure that information uncovered during the assessment will not be misused. Members of the risk assessment team will uncover vulnerabilities in the customer's system. These vulnerabilities could include external exposure to company sensitive information, account names and passwords, and other vulnerabilities that could pose a severe risk the customer's organization if this information is not properly handled and controlled.[1]

Technicians, Operators, and Administrators — These are the people in the organization who are relied upon to maintain and operate security controls. The network administrator is relied upon to apply up-to-date security patches to affected systems; the systems operator maintains user account information; the network engineers set the firewall rules that implement the security policy. All of these people within the organization have a vested interest in the perceived quality of their work. A risk assessment that results in findings that point out gaps within their area of responsibility may be seen as unjust or unkind. Risk assessment team members must understand that care must be taken to ensure that all findings are accurate and worded appropriately. Properly worded findings clearly indicate the problem, its potential impact, and how to fix it, and do not point fingers or place blame. Failure to recognize this population, ensure their concerns are addressed, and to carefully word findings could result in an unsatisfied customer. Understand that these people are not typically the direct customer, but the direct customer is influenced by them. Moreover, a risk assessment team should always strive to be fair and accurate.

3.1.1.2 Quality of Work

The success of the security risk assessment project will be based in large part on the quality of the technical report. After all, this is the project deliverable and it will far outlast any other tangible evidence that such a project ever occurred.

Most consumers of a security risk assessment will judge the success of the project based on what they see as a result. The result seen by most security risk assessment consumers is the final security risk assessment report. The importance of the real quality of work and the perceived quality of work reflected by this document must be well understood by the entire security risk assessment team.

Information security engineers sometimes lose sight of the objective of their activities. They sometimes give the technical activities of their project precedence and leave little time to complete a quality report for delivery to the project sponsor.

Sidebar 3.1 What Do We Sell?

I have been known to ask seemingly obvious questions at staff meetings in hopes of uncovering some greater truths. One such question provided our group a useful insight into the needs of our customers and the r perceived value in our services. The following question was posed at one such meeting:

"What do we sell?" I asked

The first answer was rather expected and went down the list of services we offer such as policy development, security risk assessments, security tra ning, and other services.

"No, what do our customers want to buy?" I asked, hoping the slight rephrase would spark some creative thought.

This rephrased question elicited more of the same descriptions with only slight changes to the titles we gave them.

"Let's try this another way," I said. "Our customers don't want a security policy, they don' want a security risk assessment; they don't even want security training."

"But they buy our services? Why would they buy them if they don't want them?," answered the team.

"Because our services are a means to an end," I explained. "Our customers want..."

"Our customers buy our services because they want confidence that they are secure, or knowledgeable, or compliant," the enlightened audience interrupted.

BINGO

It is important to understand that although we, as information security professionals, may be very excited about our techniques, methods, and tools, our customers' expectations do not center on these. Their expectations center on providing confidence that they are doing the right thing.

> The takeaway from this slightly offbeat discussion is that the quality of the security risk assessment project is not solely reliant on the quality of the technical work but also heavily reliant on any element that may influence the confidence of the project sponsor. It is for this reason that correct formatting and spelling are just as important as adequate security testing.

This is unfortunate, short-sighted, and in the end will not accomplish the goal of either party. In the pursuit of obtaining the best configuration for your scanners, getting the most up-to-date threat estimates, and determining the precise words for acceptable use policy statements given the organizational culture, information security engineers forget that the consumer of the information security risk assessment really does not care about such details. This is not to say that consumers do not care about quality work, of course they do. It is just that the consumer does not generally care about how the quality work gets done, just that it is quality.

For example, consider having a house built. This process involves a great many professional trades to design your house, install systems, and build to the specifications. The typical consumer of a newly constructed house judges the quality of the house on the result of inspections and a walk-through. Although it is important for the electrician to use the appropriate tools, supplies, and electrical code, the consumer only sees the exposed electrical components (e.g., switches, lights, etc.) and the inspection certificate that the system meets the electrical code. If the system did not meet the expectations of the consumer, it does not matter how great the electrician's tools or techniques were, the consumer would be dissatisfied.

Now consider the final security risk assessment report. If the final report contains the name of a previous company the consultant did work for (i.e., a "cut and paste" error), the consumer of the report is likely to lose confidence in the entire project. At this point it does not matter how good the tools, techniques, and tests were. Many information security engineers would defend this work by saying, "That is just a typo — the results are still right." This engineer would be technically correct, but fail to see the importance of the delivery of a quality report.

In general, all consumers care that the work they have performed is done by professionals and in the quality of the work, but they do not generally care about the details of the tools, methods, and techniques that go into the work. As consumers we expect that professionals keep up with the latest trends and obtain the appropriate tools for the job. We do not expect to have to be experts in the activities that we outsource.

3.1.1.2.1 Quality Aspects

The consumer of a security risk assessment report includes the "sponsor" of the risk assessment and additional stakeholders within the organization being assessed. Each of these stakeholders has a unique point of view and a distinct definition of what they expect from a successful security risk assessment.

General Quality Expected in Any Report — The following is a discussion of the quality aspects that are expected in any report, whether the report is technical or otherwise. These general quality aspects include grammar, format, audience, and understanding of the topic. Each of these is discussed briefly below.

- Grammatically Correct — Any correspondence that ever goes to a customer is a representation of the author and the organization associated with the author. A formal project deliverable such as a report, or even a draft report, must be grammatically correct. What the author may consider a small grammatical error may or may not change the meaning of the sentence but it will make an impression on the reader. As unfair as it may seem, that impression may have as much weight in customer satisfaction as the underlying analysis. Furthermore, grammatical errors involving the customer's name, interviewees' names, systems names, and the like are likely to make an even less favorable impression.
- Visually Pleasing — Without even changing the words, a report can be vastly improved during document production and the formatting process. Improvements in the formatting of the report will make the report look professional. Reports that look like they have been put together in a hurry do not convey professionalism. Moreover, it is likely that the acceptance of the conclusions of such a report will be subtly affected. When a report looks professional, it also looks more authoritative. The security risk assessment team should appoint one member of the team to produce the report. The report producer should be familiar with techniques to create a professional report. This text does not cover such a topic in any detail, but you should expect the report producer to be familiar with the following:
- Elements of a Professional Report
  - Selection of a font.
  - Common treatment of tables, figures bullets, etc.
  - Appropriate styles for headings.
  - Spacing between paragraphs, graphics, and headers and footers.
  - Proper use of headers and footers.
  - Generation of a table of contents and table of figures.
- Addresses Its Intended Audience — As discussed earlier in this book, the security risk assessment report is intended for several different audiences.

These audiences will have differing levels of familiarity with the project and differing levels of technical expertise. For this reason, the report must be written for several different audiences.

- Executive Summary — The executive summary is written for the audience that wants to know the bottom line. An executive summary should be short and to the point. For a security risk assessment it should answer the following question: "What are the security risks to my organization, and what should we do about it?"
- Technical Appendices — Technical details and supporting documentation to the security risk assessment report belong in an appendix. The more technical readers of the report will want the details of the vulnerability scan or a list of the user groups with short passwords. Examples of typical appendices to a security risk assessment report are as follows:
  - Vulnerability Scan Report — the results of a vulnerability scan run on the systems being assessed.
  - Evidence — a list of evidence used to draw conclusions. This would include interviews, test results, worksheet calculations, etc.
  - References — a list of sources of information and guidance used in the security risk assessment.
  - Solution descriptions — additional descriptions on proposed solutions. This could include product literature or a review of available solutions.
  - Calculations — mathematical calculations supporting the findings.
  - Understanding of the topic — It is important that the reader of the report realizes that the security risk assessment team not only knows how to perform a security risk assessment but has a grasp of the relevant background necessary for performing the work. The introduction of the report can be used to reiterate relevant background information, including a description of the organization and the need for the security risk assessment.

General Quality Expected in Technical Reports — Technical reports have their own unique requirements and the audience reading a technical report has additional expectations. Technical reports, such as a security risk assessment, are expected to contain technical data and draw conclusions based on an assessment of the technical data. For this reason it is important to ensure that the technical data presented in the report is accurate, the conclusions are clear, and the approach for deriving the conclusions is presented.

- Technically Accurate — Technical reports are based on technical data. Any inaccuracies in the data could lead to incorrect conclusions. It is important that the technical members of the security risk assessment team review all technical data to ensure its accuracy. This includes removal of false positives in vulnerability scanning, and ensuring account names, system names, and IP addresses are correct.

- Approach Described — The security risk assessment approach used by the team should be described in the final report. This has several benefits. First, it gives the report credibility. If the report references and follows a well-known or well-developed approach for performing security risk assessments, then the customer will be less likely to question the methods employed to determine the conclusions. Second, a description of the approach will allow the customer to follow the process and the logic of the analysis more closely, which will allow the customer to provide a better review of the draft report and a better understanding of the process.

- Clearly Presented Conclusions — The conclusions of a technical report are the most important element. These are likely the items that will be implemented. It is important that these conclusions be well articulated so that the implementer of the conclusions will know what is expected. For example, it is not very useful to simply recommend that the organization develop security policies. This advice provides little insight or direction and is an indication that the security risk assessment team may not clearly understand how to write security policies themselves. A better recommendation would be a description of the security policies that are currently missing and perhaps an outline of the basic structure for each.

Quality Expected in Security Risk Assessment Reports — A security risk assessment report is a specific type of technical report with its own unique quality requirements. A security risk assessment report is expected to provide a clear and accurate identification of the security risk to an organization's assets. Furthermore, the security risk assessment report is expected to contain adequate and relevant evidence to support its findings, clear and relevant recommendations, and clear compliance results for relevant information security regulations. For this reason it is important to ensure that the technical data presented in the report is accurate, the conclusions are clear, and the approach for deriving the conclusions is presented.

- Clear and Accurate Identification of Risk — The identification of risk is the basic objective of the security risk assessment. Therefore, it is not surprising that customers would expect an identification of risk as part of the security risk assessment report. However, it is important to convey that risk in a meaningful way to the customer. The description of the residual security risk can be presented in a quantitative or qualitative manner, depending on the overall approach of the security risk assessment. In either case the residual security risk should be presented in a context that is understandable by the customer. As such, a description should accompany the residual risk statement, such as a range for quantitative risk approaches and a managerial description for qualitative risk approaches.

- Adequate and Relevant Evidence — The results of a security risk assessment are recommendations for changes at an organization. Prior to those changes being implemented, the organization will likely scrutinize elements of the security risk assessment report to ensure that the recommendations are well founded. A quality security risk assessment report will contain adequate and relevant evidence for its conclusions and recommendations.
- Clear and Relevant Recommendations — Hopefully many of the recommendations from the security risk assessment report will be implemented. Most organizations will have set aside resources to implement the recommendations of the security risk assessment, but these recommendations cannot be implemented if they are not clear and they are not likely to be implemented if they are not relevant to improving the organization's security risk. The security risk assessment team must ensure that all recommendations are based on relevant data and solid analysis. If it is unclear why the recommendations would improve the security posture of the organization, then the recommendations have not been clearly articulated. Also, the security risk assessment team should include cost and effort estimations for implementing each of the recommendations. Organizations typically require such estimations prior to moving forward with a project.
- Clear Compliance Results — For those organizations operating within regulated industries (e.g., healthcare, energy, government), an analysis as to their compliance with the regulation is useful, if not a requirement of the security risk assessment project.[2] If such an analysis is performed, the security risk assessment report should contain a table that clearly indicates those areas that meet the regulations and those that do not.

3.1.1.3 Completion within Budget

The biggest success factor of any project is whether or not it is completed on time and within budget. The project leader of the security risk assessment team must manage the project carefully to ensure that the project is completed within the time allotted and with the resources granted. Any project not completed within time or budget constraints is in danger of being canceled or completed too late to have an impact. Moreover, a project with significant overruns is typically an indication of the project team's inexperience.

The goal of completing within budget is not limited to outside consultants performing a security risk assessment. This goal applies equally to internal security risk assessment projects. In either case, the project has been granted a limited amount of resources (e.g., time, money) and must be completed within those constraints. Project leaders of security risk assessments must ensure that they meet this most important quality aspect of their project.

3.1.2 Setting the Budget

One of the biggest gating factors for scoping a risk assessment is how much is in the budget for the risk assessment. If no such line item exists in the budget, consider how much you plan on spending. Exact figures are not required here, but there is a huge difference in the scope and rigor of a $450,000 risk assessment and a $45,000 risk assessment. The fact is the more time that the team spends reviewing the security controls, the more rigorous the risk assessment will be. So if you plan on spending over $250,000 on a risk assessment, then you would expect (and demand) more rigor than if you wanted to keep the cost down to less than $50,000.

In addition to the rigor of analysis, the amount of money you plan to spend on the risk assessment will also be affected by the size of the organization, their geographical separation, the complexity of the security controls, and the threat environment in which your organization operates.

- Organization Size — A small organization, up to 500 employees, is likely to have many factors that simplify a security risk assessment. The organization structure is likely to be relatively simple and centrally located. This brings down the cost/effort in obtaining interviews with key personnel and gaining approval for testing and access to information A small organization is also likely more centralized and to have less complex controls, which may reduce the effort required to assess their effectiveness. A larger organization is more likely to have a more complex organizational structure, and decentralized and complex controls.
- Geographic Separation — If your organization has just one location, then the effort to gather the information required to perform the security risk assessment is significantly reduced. An organization with multiple sites and geographically separated systems and key personnel will require additional funds for travel and information gathering
- Complexity — The more complex the security controls, the more effort is required to assess their effectiveness. An organization with physical access controls that include perimeter barriers, armed guards, biometrics, a CCTV system, zoned areas, smart-card badge access, and multiple types of intrusion detection is going to require a little effort to effectively review. An organization with a more simple physical security control that includes locked doors and visitor control will clearly require less effort.

- Threat Environment — Certain organizations operate within a higher risk environment than others. For example, a high-profile and controversial national lobbying organization will clearly be exposed to a greater number of serious threats than the headquarters of a nationally franchised sandwich shop. A security risk assessment for an organization existing within a more serious threat environment will require more careful consideration of the threats. An organization existing within a less serious threat environment is likely to be affected by the standard array of threats that affect most organizations.

The other factor to consider for scoping a risk assessment is how much is in the overall information security budget. If an organization has limited funds for improving information security, then it is important to allocate those resources efficiently. This sounds rather obvious, but it remains overlooked by many organizations. Consider an organization that spends nearly its entire information security budget in a given year on a widely scoped and rigorous security risk assessment and has little or no budget left to fix anything. A main benefit of a security risk assessment is to provide guidance for risk-based spending, so that ultimately the security risk to the organization is lowered to a reasonable level. If the entire budget is spent on a security risk assessment, the organization may be unable to implement any of the recommendations. The result is that the organization is more aware of their risks but their assets are in the same danger as before.

A better approach is for the organization to determine a percentage or ratio of the budget that should be spent on the security risk assessment (see Figure 3.1). As with many elements of establishing and maintaining an information security program within an organization, there is no well-known or accepted ratio or percentage. Furthermore, it is not recommended that such a ratio or a percentage be the only factor in determining how much to spend. However, an organization should carefully review their budget allocation if they are spending more than 25 percent of their security budget on a security risk assessment.

3.1.3 Determining the Objective

A security risk assessment can provide many possible benefits: a basis for risk-based spending, a periodic review of the security program, and a part of a system of checks and balances for sensitive tasks. Understanding and documenting the objective of a specific security risk assessment helps to focus the project on meeting the needs of the organization. The core of a security risk assessment remains an analysis of the effectiveness of the current security controls that protect an organization's assets. This is the objective of the security risk assessment.

> Security Risk Assessment Objective — accurate analysis of the effectiveness of current security controls that protect an organization's assets.

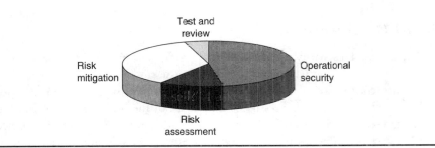

Figure 3.1 Security spending ratios. The exact spending ratios for elements within a security program will differ greatly between organizations. However, the relative spending ratios shown here are likely to be applicable to most organizations.

Most organizations simply want an objective review of their controls. This may be provided by an independent team of security professionals who understand the risk assessment methodology, possess the proper experience and credentials, and are provided the resources to adequately perform the assessment.

3.1.4 Limiting the Scope

The scope of the security risk assessment is the boundary of the security controls and assets included in the review. The definition of what is "in" and "out" of the scope of the assessment may be rather easy in some organizations but more difficult in others. In either case, the project sponsor and the security risk assessment team should carefully and clearly define the scope of the assessment in terms of the security controls to be reviewed, the assets to be protected, and the system boundaries of the security risk assessment target.

Every security risk assessment is limited: limited by budget, limited by time, and so forth. Project members of a security risk assessment will constantly find themselves reaching the limitations of the project. After all, could we not all do more in-depth analysis, more insightful recommendations, and more accurate risk measurements given unlimited time and money? But, no matter how much time or budget or skill possessed by the security risk analysis team, if a security risk exists outside the boundaries of the security risk assessment, it will not be documented in the security risk assessment.[3] The single biggest limitation of a security risk assessment is the definition of the system being assessed.

The boundaries of a security risk assessment are determined by the sponsor of the security risk assessment. Identifying the security risk assessment boundaries is essential for the security risk assessment team to ensure that neither underscoping nor overscoping occurs.

3.1.4.1 Underscoping

Underscoping of a security risk assessment is a dangerous practice that may happen all too often. It occurs when the security risk assessment team does not address all security concerns of the sponsor. The term "underscoping" is from the perspective of the security risk assessment team and not the project sponsor. In other words, the security risk assessment team is not addressing the needs of the project sponsor because some of the organization's assets and relevant threats are not assessed within the security risk assessment.

Underscoping typically results in high-risk items left unaddressed and eventually exposure of the organization's assets. Consider the following common scenario: An officer of a financial institution recognizes that his organization is legally required to comply with the Gramm-Leach-Bliley Act (GLB Act) (see Appendix). The GLB Act clearly requires a security risk assessment among other information security requirements. The organization hires Fly-By-Nite Security[4] to perform what they call a security risk assessment. The Fly-By-Nite Security only knows how to run a vulnerability scan and have found that these services sell much better when they call them security risk assessments. The officer of the financial institution is unknowingly underscoping his security risk assessment by declaring (again unknowingly) administrative, physical, and most other elements of technical controls out of bounds for this assessment.

Although the example above is a little extreme, similar problems can exist simply from dismissing other elements of a security risk assessment without ensuring that they are covered elsewhere. For example, it is relatively common in many organizations for physical security to be considered beyond the bounds of a security risk assessment. If the physical security controls are reviewed as a part of a separate risk assessment, there is little to be worried about. However, if the physical security of an organization is ignored by all risk assessments within the organization, then serious breaches in the security of multiple systems could occur. What good is writing the perfect firewall ruleset if a thief can walk away with the box?

3.1.4.2 Overscoping

Overscoping of a security risk assessment is dangerous as well. Overscoping occurs when the security risk assessment team assesses threats, vulnerabilities, or risks that are outside the bounds of the security risk assessment. The term "overscoping" is from the perspective of the security risk assessment team and not the project sponsor. In other words, the security risk assessment team is assessing organizational assets and threats that are beyond the needs of the security risk assessment sponsor. If a project sponsor fails to clearly indicate the bounds of the security risk assessment, the team may perform activities that end up wasting time and money. Another danger of overscoping is that the security risk assessment team may overstep its authority to test elements of a system that is not covered under the security risk assessment. Such out-of-bounds behavior could, by itself, be a serious breach of security. Consider the following out-of-bounds activities allowed by the practice of overscoping:

- Example 1: What's In A Name? — Fly-By-Nite Security is hired by the XYZ organization to test the security of its website. Fly-By-Nite Security obtains permission from XYZ to perform security testing, but the XYZ organization fails to properly scope the test and simply asks for a "zero-based" review. When Fly-By-Nite Security performs its research, it finds www.xyz-org.com and www.xyz_org.com. When performing the security testing of the above websites, Fly-By-Nite unknowingly performed security testing on both the XYZ organization and the XYZ Manufacturing Company. Depending on the level of testing performed, Fly-By-Nite could end up on the wrong end of a lawsuit or criminal prosecution.

- Example 2: Take Out the Trash — Fly-By-Nite Security is again hired by the XYZ organization but this time to perform a security risk assessment at their physical location. The project manager believed that the assessment would only cover the information security systems, but the industrious Fly-By-Nite employees diligently searched the trashcans for sensitive information, checked the security of the doors to sensitive areas and reviewed the visitor and escort procedures. The security risk assessment sponsor was disappointed that the Fly-By-Nite team spent so much time "off task", since physical security is controlled by another department altogether and they just completed an assessment the month before. Although this behavior did not trample on another organization's assets, it still wasted time and money.

3.1.4.3 Security Controls

An organization may have implemented a wide variety of security controls to protect its assets. These security controls can range from policies and procedures to lighting and fences to firewalls and anti-virus solutions. Rather than list these controls one after the other, it is useful to group these controls into the categories of administrative, physical, and technical. These groupings provide a common approach to define or limit the scope of the security risk assessment.

3.1.4.3.1 Administrative Security Controls

These are defined as policies, procedures, and activities that protect the organization's assets. Policies include the information security policies such as acceptable use policy, system monitoring policies, and security operations policies. Procedures include emergency response procedures, computer incident response procedures, and procedures for hardening and testing the security of servers for example. Activities include any activity performed to ensure the protection of the organization's assets. These could include "technical" activities such as audit log review or penetration testing or "nontechnical" activities such as exit interviews for terminated employees. Administrative controls should be within the scope of any security risk assessment. An assessment that does not include these types of controls should be referred to as security testing instead as it would not give an accurate measurement of the risk to the organization's assets.

3.1.4.3.2 Physical Security Controls

Physical security controls are those controls that are associated with the protection of the organization's employees and facilities. These protection measures include facility perimeter controls such as fencing, lighting, gates, and access controls, surveillance such as guards and closed-circuit television (CCTV), facility protections such as seismic bracing and fireproofing, and personnel protection such as evacuation procedures and patrolled parking lots.[5]

3.1.4.3.3 Technical Security Controls

Technical security controls are those mechanisms that logically protect the organization's assets, such as routers, firewalls, anti-virus solutions, logical access controls, and intrusion detection systems. A security risk assessment should consider the capabilities of the technical security controls, their current configuration, and their arrangement within the system to provide protection of assets (i.e, system architecture).

3.1.4.4 Assets

An organization has numerous assets of value that warrant protection. Assets are defined as the resources by which the organization derives value. These can include hardware, software, systems, services, documents, capital equipment, personal property, people, goodwill, trade secrets, and many other elements of the business process. Although it is clear that many factors create value for an organization, it is not always easy to define its assets. An attempt to simplify the enumeration process includes discussing both tangible and intangible assets.

3.1.4.4.1 Tangible Assets

Tangible assets are those assets that you can "touch." These assets include hardware (or equipment), systems, networks, interconnections, telecommunications, wiring, furniture, audit records, books, documents, cash, and software. However, the number one tangible asset is always people (employees, vendors, customers, guests, visitors, and others). These assets tend to be easier to list because they are visible and perhaps even accounted for in auditing records or assets tracking systems.

3.1.4.4.2 Intangible Assets

Intangible assets are those that you cannot "touch." These assets include employee health and safety, data, customer and employee privacy, image and reputation of the organization, goodwill, and employee morale. These assets tend to be rather difficult to list or enumerate as they are not visible or accounted for. Nonetheless, an organization must seek to protect these intangible assets as well.

3.1.4.5 Reasonableness in Limiting the Scope

As discussed before, not all security controls or assets may be within the scope of the security risk assessment. Although, as security professionals, we should typically like to see the security risk assessment process not being hindered by a smaller scope than is warranted, there are a variety of adequate reasons for limiting the scope of a security risk assessment.

Many organizations rely on other entities to supply some of their infrastructure components. These supplied components could be physical security within a shared tenant building, or an outsourced managed security service. If the security risk assessment team or the customer decides that an assessment performed by another team that covers the supplied component meets their needs, they may decide to adopt the findings of that report or to place the supplied components outside the scope of the security risk assessment.

In the example below, some of the network components and the procedures for clearing individuals are considered outside the scope of the security risk assessment. For this example, the customer determined that the clearance process for personnel with SECRET clearances was outside the scope of the evaluation for an information system on a single military base. Furthermore, the customer decided that the system boundary did not include the MILNET or the firewalls connecting the MILNET to the information system being assessed — these components were considered part of another evaluation.

Many other scope combinations and limitations are common in the industry. Common security risk assessment scopes include geographic limitations, functional limitations, and technology limitations. In this case, many customers would assume that the scope of the assessment would include all information system assets such as information systems and data. This customer should also consider if the organization's reputation and goodwill should be considered as well.

3.1.5 Identifying System Boundaries

It should now be clear that the failure to properly scope a security risk assessment can have disastrous consequences. One important element of scoping a security risk assessment effort is to identify the system (or systems) being assessed. An information system is any process, or group of related processes, under a single command or management control that reside in the same general operating environment. The information system comprises the processes, communications, storage, and related resources necessary for the information system to operate.

Although a security risk assessment is typically limited to a single business unit, the information systems within that business unit may cover one or many information systems. Each information system to be assessed should be properly identified by explicitly stating its physical and logical boundaries.

3.1.5.1 Physical Boundary

Identifying the physical boundaries of an information system (or systems) to be assessed limits the scope of the security risk assessment. Such a limitation is appropriate as security risk assessments should be limited to those resources under the control of the project sponsor. Besides, a system without boundaries cannot be assessed.

The physical boundaries of an information system properly identify those elements within the scope of the evaluation and those outside of the scope of evaluation (see Figure 3.2). Physical boundary elements include the following:

- Workstations
- Servers
- Networking equipment
- Special equipment
- Cabling
- Peripherals
- Buildings
- Individual rooms or floors within buildings.

3.1.5.2 Logical Boundaries

Identifying the logical boundaries of an information system (or systems) to be assessed also limits the scope of the security risk assessment. A limitation in scope based on logical boundaries is also appropriate as security risk assessments should be limited to those system functions under the control of the project sponsor.

The logical boundaries of an information system properly identify the functions of the systems within the scope of the evaluation and those functions outside

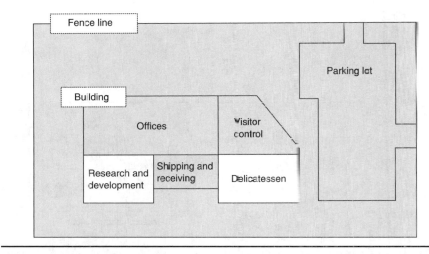

Figure 3.2   Physical system boundaries. It is important to properly identify the physical elements that are inside and outside the security risk assessment boundary. This diagram shows the physical elements inside the physical boundary by shading the covered elements.

the scope of evaluation. The determination as to the inclusion or exclusion of system functions in the scope of the security risk assessment must be carefully considered.

By default, the logical boundaries of a security risk assessment should be inclusive of all functions within the information systems identified (see Figure 3.3). A reasoned approach for excluding certain functions should be executed. Specific reasons for the exclusion of system functions should be documented by the project sponsor or the security risk assessment team and the identification of these functions should be included in the security risk assessment report. Specific reasons for the exclusion of system functions should accompany this discussion. The project sponsor and the security risk assessment team should refrain from excluding important system functions and should only exclude functions for good reason. Below are some possible reasons why a system function may be excluded from a security risk assessment:

- Function Is Not Security-Relevant — Some system functions (or applications) are not relevant to a specifically targeted security risk assessment. Such nonrelevance should not be confused with nonimportance. For example, a word-processing application or a custom application for creating and submitting timecards may not be security-relevant and can be safely ignored in a security risk assessment. Most word processors operate on behalf of the user who called the program and not in a privileged state. In this case, the worst the word processor can do is mangle your document, but it cannot breach the confidentiality of a document owned by another if

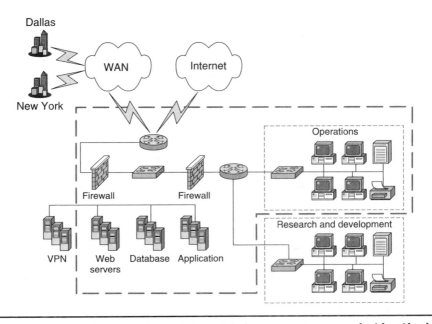

Figure 3.3   Logical system boundaries. It is important to properly identify the logical elements that are inside and outside the security risk assessment boundary. This diagram shows the logical elements inside the logical boundary by a dashed line the covered elements.

such access is restricted. In the same manner, a custom timecard application running with user privilege would be restricted from breaching confidentiality of other files as well. However, be careful in your analysis if either of these programs are relied upon to enforce a security function, such as the integrity of the timecard file; in that case the function of the application would be considered security-relevant.

- Function Is the Subject of Another Assessment — Even security-relevant functions may be excluded from a specific security risk assessment if they are the subject of another risk assessment. This happens often in larger organizations in which multiple security risk assessments are performed on subsets of all of the organization's information systems. For example, if all applications rely on the services provided by an organization's internet data center (IDC) (e.g., power, Internet connectivity, backup, firewall, IDS), then it may be beneficial for the organization to have a security risk assessment on the IDC itself. The results of the IDC risk assessment would then be shared with the business unit managers in charge of each of the applications. The applications may be the subject of another security risk assessment, but in this case it would not be necessary to reperform the assessment on those services provided by the IDC.[6]

- Analysis of the Function Is Beyond the Skills of the Assessment Team — This sounds like something you would typically like to avoid. But it is not as bad as it seems. It is not uncommon for security risk assessments to be scoped according to the rigor requested by the organization. Scoping of the risk assessment can include security-relevant functions that require specific skills not within the experience of the security assessment team For example, many security risk assessments do not include the code review or penetration testing of Web applications. It is clear that many Web applications (if not all) are security-relevant. However, the skills required to review code for common errors is not possessed by all security risk assessment teams. It may be beneficial to "carve out" that portion of the assessment and get the experts in.
- Physical or Environmental Control Makes the Function Non-Security Relevant — Ensuring that security functions are enforced does not always have to be satisfied by logical means. Physical or environmental controls may adequately enforce security functions and therefore obviate the need for analysis of that function. For example, protection of the confidentiality and integrity of information while in transit on the internal local area network (LAN) is certainly an important security function. However, if the internal LAN is physically protected (e.g., encased in pressurized conduit), then other logical controls to protect that information in transit are not required and therefore not relevant to the assessment.

3.1.6 Specifying the Rigor

Any team of security engineers could spend as little as a week and as much as six months assessing the ability of the organization's security controls to protect its assets. A quick assessment that lasted only a single week would be forced to review the security controls with less rigor while a security risk assessment scheduled for six months could afford to perform a more in-depth review of the existing security controls.

An organization and the security assessment team will need to determine the appropriate rigor for the security risk assessment. While available budget could certainly limit the extent of the risk assessment, it is not necessary to simply spend the available money — in fact from the point of view of the risk assessment team hired to perform the risk assessment it is unethical. The determination of rigor should instead be based on the maturity of the security program.

If an organization would not be surprised if the security risk assessment resulted in the listing and description of many high-risk items, then it is not ready for the "white-glove test." A less rigorous risk assessment on a less than mature security program will result in nearly the same recommendations. Therefore it is unwise and wasteful to spend money or perform a risk assessment that simply increases the certainty of what is probably already known within the first several weeks of the risk assessment. For example, if an internal vulnerability scan of a representative sample of workstations reveals that none of them is hardened, then it is unnecessary to continue to perform vulnerability scans on the remaining workstations. The conclusion that hardening policies are nonexistent or ineffective is already formed and additional vulnerability scanning adds nothing to the analysis.

3.1.7 Sample Scope Statements

As discussed above, the creation of a proper scope statement is an important step in defining the security risk assessment project. A proper scope statement will specify the budget, objective, target system(s), and the rigor of the assessment. Table 3.1 shows an example scope statement that provides the information necessary to properly define a security risk assessment project.

3.2 Project Description

Once the project is properly defined in terms of budget, objective, rigor, and scope, the project should be properly described in the project contract or description.

3.2.1 Project Variables

Each of the variables listed above influences each other. It is not possible to perform the most widely scoped risk assessment in the most rigorous fashion for the lowest price. The level of rigor and scope of the assessment, as well as the objective of the assessment, all influence the price and vice versa.

The customer should decide on the appropriate "values" for these project variables for their needs. Herein lies the problem. Many customers are obtaining a security risk assessment from an outside vendor because they are not experts in information security and they want an outside opinion. So, if they are not experts, how are they supposed to know the appropriate values for these project variables? The typical answer is "Let the experts tell you."

To the customers in this situation I have the following advice: "Buyer beware." Be careful of sole source bids. Obtain several bids from several different companies. These bids should explain as best as they can the level of rigor for the assessment.

3.2.2 Statement of Work

The statement of work (SOW) is a portion of the contract that specifies the work to be performed. These may be as simple as a single paragraph or as complex as a multiple-page document covering the expectations and the bounds of a security

Table 3.1   Sample Scope of Work Statement. A statement of work for a security risk assessment should clearly define the threats, assets, controls, and tasks of the security risk assessment.

The scope of the assessment includes all the physical premises at 1313 Mockingbird Lane, the automated information systems (AISs) located on premises, the employees of ACME, all users of the AISs located on the premises, and all policies and procedures governing AIS users and ACME employees. Examination of proximate facilities and systems will only be done in reference to ACME.

The security risk assessment includes consideration of risks related to the following:

Threats

- **Natural disasters**, including fire, flood, earthquake, windstorm, and snow/ice storm.
- **Authorized personnel**, including insufficient or unqualified personnel, insufficient personnel training or supervision, and malicious insider activity.
- **Unauthorized personnel**, including hackers, script kiddies, competitors, thieves, and vandals.
- **Malicious software,** including viruses, worms, Trojan horses, and backdoors.

Assets

- **Personnel**, including ACME staff and guests.
- **Computer systems**, including databases system software, hardware, network communications, and application software for existing and new implementations.
- **Data**, including data in transit and storage; hard copy or soft.
- **Equipment**, including capital equipment, laptops, and office equipment.

Controls

- **Existing countermeasures**; safeguards already in place to address risks.
- **Security awareness and communication**, including insufficient security awareness and communications, unclear assignment of security roles and responsibilities, and insufficient security plan documentation.
- **Data controls**, including insufficient controls for data integrity, data retention and backup (short-term and long-term), system access, and system logging/auditing.
- **Maintenance controls**, to include those for preventative maintenance, hardware failures, and remedial maintenance.
- **Physical and logical access controls.**
- **Systems architecture**, including previous analyses of architecture in regard to security.
- History of security and disaster incidents at the facility and the surrounding area.
    The security risk assessment analysis shall include a review of the effectiveness of security controls, including the following tasks:
- Policy and procedure review.
- Organizational structure review.
- Social engineering.
- Wardialing.
- Vulnerability scanning.
- No penetration testing.
- Application vulnerability scanning (but not application penetration testing or code review).

risk assessment. Regardless of the length or complexity of the SOW, it should document the parameters of the security risk assessment to be performed. At a minimum, these parameters should include the service description, scope of the assessment, and description of the deliverables.

3.2.2.1 Specifying the Service Description

A security risk assessment should be clearly defined in the statement of work. There should be no confusion as to whether this service is a vulnerability scan, penetration test, compliance audit, or a security risk assessment. Using our definition above this service should be defined as:

> an objective analysis of the effectiveness of the current security controls that protect an organization's assets and a determination of the probability of losses to those assets.

A more complete service description would include the more detailed definition of the security risk assessment. This can best be accomplished by briefly describing the elements of a security risk assessment. By adding the following sentence, the definition of a security risk assessment becomes even clearer:

> Such analysis shall consist of an identification of tangible and intangible assets under protection, an identification of the threats to and vulnerabilities of the current system controls, an analysis of the threat/vulnerability likelihood, the impact of the threat to the identified assets, and recommendations for security controls to mitigate the risks.

3.2.2.2 Scope of Security Controls

The statement of work should further describe the scope of the risk assessment by clearly stating if administrative, physical, and technical controls are included in this assessment. Physical boundaries are typically defined by building address. If various elements of the physical controls are handled by different organizations, it may be necessary to provide further refinement and identification of the physical controls to be reviewed. For example, if an organization is located within a shared facility, the building grounds, security force, and building entry control may not be under the control of the organization seeking the assessment. Furthermore, this organization may not be able to grant sufficient access for the security risk assessment team to adequately assess the adequacy of these controls. Either the organization should obtain permission and adequate access for the security risk assessment team, or they should request the organization that does control the building's physical security controls to obtain and share an objective security risk assessment covering those elements.

Administrative boundaries are typically defined by a description of the policies and procedures covered by the assessment. The complete set of policies that impact the administrative security controls within an organization can very often be owned by various departments within the organization. For example, a complete set of security policies will likely include policies from human resources, legal, help desk, network administration, business development, and operations. Moreover, many policies and procedures may be implicit, that is, practiced but not documented. It is important to specify all policies and procedures to be considered in the assessment.

Technical boundaries are defined as the systems, communication devices, and networks that are to be assessed. These boundaries are typically defined by system and network names. Often systems or system components are determined to be outside the boundaries of a risk assessment by the organization. Reasons for ignoring portions of the systems can range from recent reviews, to control by another organization, to future rollout. Be sure to clearly identify all technical elements as either within scope or out of scope. For example, modems, VPN pool, wireless networks. The technical boundaries of the system are best described in a well-labeled system diagram.

3.2.2.3 Specifying Deliverables

The deliverables for a security risk assessment always include the security risk assessment report. Other deliverables may be various drafts of the report. An SOW can go to great lengths to describe a security risk assessment report, but it simply contains four major elements. To be valuable to the customer, security risk assessment reports should clearly document the risk assessment process, results, recommendations, and evidence.

The security risk assessment report should describe the process or methodology used in the risk assessment. The description of the process should be no more than a few pages. The risk assessment methodology description provides the reader with the confidence that an adequate methodology was used and gives them a roadmap to understanding of the results. Many risk assessment results may seem coded. For example, the risk assessment may conclude that there exist 8 level I risks and 14 level II risks. Without a description of how these risk levels were determined and what they mean, the risk assessment report is less useful.

The security risk assessment report should also have a section that clearly presents the results. This section should be understandable by the senior manager and the technical readers. The results section should include a title or short description of the risk, an indication of its likelihood and impact, a resultant level of the risk, and a recommendation for mitigating the risk.

The recommendations in the security risk assessment report should be described in enough detail that those who decide to implement them understand what is requested. This is not to say that the recommendations should provide step-by-step instructions for implementing the change, just enough that it is clear. For example, instead of saying "Improve logical perimeter security," state "Perimeter security should be improved through the addition of firewalls on all external interfaces and the development of a DMZ architecture."

Many times the results of a security risk assessment are questioned by the organization who commissioned the assessment. The security risk assessment team should keep careful notes and collect evidence to defend its findings. Evidence includes documents, interviews, and the results of inspections and testing. Evidence notations need not be elaborate. A simple notation such as "interview with Bob Smith, system administrator, on March 16, 2005" should do fine.

Sidebar 3.2 Negotiation

Coming to an agreement of terms and documenting the agreement for a security risk assessment effort requires negotiation skills. Negotiation skills can be learned in many different forums including business school and professional education. Describing these skills is beyond the scope of this book, but the major elements required to adequately negotiate are described here:

- *Understanding the customer's needs* — Negotiation is a process of discovering the needs of others and modifying the arrangement in an attempt to meet everyone's needs. Negotiation cannot even start until the customer's needs are understood. The possible needs for a security risk assessment are numerous and should not be assumed. It is far too easy to assume that a customer simply wants a security risk assessment to identify the possible security risk to the organization's assets.
- *Identifying next-best alternatives* — An important concept in negotiations is being aware of the other party's next-best alternative. The next-best alternative for the contracting organization is typically your competition or even an "in-house" effort. Understanding the market and the competitive advantages of the competition is essential to the consulting firm in contract negotiations. The next-best alternative for the contractor is typically other consulting work. Having a good understanding of the consulting firm's utilization rate,

current backlog, and sales pipeline is useful to the contracting organization in contract negotiations.

- *Finding win-win solutions* — If the negotiating parties are able to discuss the needs of each organization, many "win-win" situations can occur. Negotiating parties often assume that the other party's desires are in conflict with their own. If the negotiators are able to open up the discussion, many discoveries regarding mutual and complementary needs can be uncovered. For example, after some open discussion, many parties find that the concerns of each party are not solely focused on money. Issues such as time to start and complete the project, individuals assigned to the project, details of the report, and ability to follow up with assessor long after the report is complete typically come up. These issues are important to the customer organization and typically easy for the consulting organization to give.
- *Giving a little more than was negotiated* — Even after a negotiated contract, the consulting organization should strive to give more than is expected. Look for opportunities to impress the customer by taking on additional research, providing links for more information, comparing results to named competitors or industries, or other items that may be especially appreciated.

3.2.2.4 Contract Type

The direction of the negotiation depends directly on the type of contract. Contracts can be either firm-fixed price or time and materials. The difference between these two types of contracts is a matter of who is taking the risk.

3.2.2.4.1 Time and Materials Contract

In a time and materials contract the risk belongs to the contracting organization. The contracting organization and the contractor come to an agreement as to an estimated number of hours required to complete the risk assessment. If the risk assessment comes in at the estimated amount of time then all is fine. If the risk assessment takes more time than expected, then the contracting organization can decide whether or not they would like the contractor to continue or not. If the risk assessment takes less time than expected, then the contracting organization pays less than expected. The risk and reward (less likely) all belong to the contracting organization.

Variations and other measures exist, such as a "not to exceed" limit, but the time and materials contract still places the risk on the contracting agency. That is because the real deliverable here is hours. If the contractor delivers hours toward the development of the risk assessment report, then, according to the contract, they should be paid even if the report is not quite finished. Time and materials contracts are well suited for tasks where it is difficult to define the task upfront or if there may be considerable unknowns. It is a rare case when a security risk assessment is best suited for a time and materials contract.

3.2.2.4.2 Firm-Fixed Price Contract

In a firm-fixed price contract the risk belongs to the contractor. The contractor and the contracting organization come to an agreement as to the description of the project and the price to be paid when the project is complete. If the risk assessment is completed for the effort expected, then all is fine. If the risk assessment takes more effort than expected, then the the contractor must continue to expend effort until the project is complete to the satisfaction of the contracting organization within the definition of the contract. If the risk assessment takes less effort than expected, then the contractor still gets paid the originally agreed price. The risk and reward all belong to the contractor.

In a firm-fixed price contract the description of the deliverables is very important. The completion of the project is completely defined by the description of the deliverables. Because the scope and level of rigor for a security risk assessment are so difficult to describe, most contracting organizations do not want to own the risk in the contract. Therefore, most security risk assessments are performed as a firm-fixed price effort. Both parties would be well advised to carefully describe the deliverables in the contract. To clarify understanding here, it is recommended that both parties review a sample deliverable from a previous similar effort.

3.2.2.5 Contract Terms

First, let us assume that the security risk assessment is a firm-fixed price contract. Negotiation is the process of determining the needs of each party and coming to an agreement that comes as close as possible to meeting the needs of both parties. In order to negotiate, you must first understand the other party's needs and their next-best alternative.

3.2.2.5.1 Determining Needs

The contracting organization wants a quality risk assessment performed by an objective and experienced team that results in an accurate risk assessment report with clear and effective recommendations. The contractor wants to be fairly compensated for their work. From a contractor's point of view, they are just as happy to perform a three-week-long risk assessment as they are a six-month-long risk assessment.[7] As you can see, the needs of the contractor are rather simple. Given an accurate description of the risk assessment required by the contracting organization, the contractor simply wants to be compensated for the effort required to complete the task. The definition of the scope, rigor, and overall level of effort of the risk assessment are all in the contracting organization's court.

The contracting organization should clearly describe the scope of the risk assessment. The remaining factors of rigor and overall level of effort can be difficult to describe. Most requests for proposals (RFPs) that go out fail to address the level of effort or rigor expected. As stated before, a description of the security risk assessment that only mentions the scope of the project can be interpreted in many ways. A team could spend as much as six months on a rigorous assessment and as little as a few weeks on the same project at a much higher level. The level of rigor required by the contracting agency should depend on their needs and their budget, both discussed earlier in this section.

The most direct way to describe the level of rigor is to simply state how long you think it would take a team to perform the assessment. For example, "The level of rigor on the assessment should be consistent with a team of three experienced professionals spending four weeks gathering data, interpreting the results, and producing the report." Of course, not all teams will take the exact same amount of time, but at least now both the contracting organization and the bidders are all in the same ballpark. This will provide a much better understanding of needs and make negotiation much smoother.

3.2.2.5.2 Determining Next-Best Alternative

Many approaches to better negotiation discuss the benefits of understanding the next-best alternative available to the other party. Understanding the next-best alternative for both the contracting organization and the contractor can help to ensure a smooth negotiation process.

The next-best alternative to a contracting organization is the "next-best" contractor. The "next-best" contractor is likely very close in terms of quality and price to the preferred contractor. Contractors should be aware that there are many qualified companies waiting in line to take the job if negotiations break down. However, there are some exceptions that must be explored when determining the value of the next-best contractor:

- Familiarization — The preferred contractor may stand out above the crowd if they possess a unique familiarization with the contracting organization's systems, or technology deployed. Familiarization is both an advantage and a disadvantage and as such may either increase the value of the familiar contractor or actually decrease their value. On the one hand, a familiar contractor is able to spend less time and effort in learning the organization's systems or specific technology. This ability will allow the contractor to perform a similar security risk assessment for a little less money than an otherwise equally qualified competitor. On the other hand, the familiar contractor may no longer be independent and possibly lose the ability to be objective. A contractor that has developed the systems to be assessed or who sells the technology being used fails to be objective. If familiarity with the systems comes from actually developing them, or if familiarity with the installed technology comes from being a vendor for the technology, then the case for loss of objectivity seems rather clear. A contractor, no matter how well-meaning, cannot objectively review their own work or technology upon which they rely for their financial reward. If, however, familiarity with the systems and technology comes from other experience with the client or the technology, then the contractor could successfully argue that they can remain objective. To the extent that the preferred contractor remains objective despite this familiarization, that contractor could be a much better choice than the next-best alternative.

- Expertise — Contractors possessing expertise within the organization's industry, with the specific security risk assessment requirements, or with the activities to be performed with the security risk assessment, have a distinct advantage when it comes to delivering the best value to the organization.
  - Industry Expertise — Many industries, such as healthcare, energy, financial, and E-commerce, have specific concerns, terminologies, and practices that are unique to that industry. A familiarization with these aspects of the industry will allow the contracting organization to more efficiently and effectively serve the organization. The contractor with industry expertise will be able to comprehend system functions and connections more easily since it will seem familiar. The contractor will also find it easier to interview key personnel and anticipate their concerns since the contractor has experience discussing the concerns with other industry leaders. Lastly, the contractor with industry experience is likely to be able to discuss and present the findings of the security risk assessment to those within an industry that the contractor has worked with before, because the contractor is able to correctly use the industry terminology and avoid terminology within the information security industry that may be used in a different context within the industry.
  - Regulation and Requirement Experience — If the security risk assessment is being performed to meet specific requirements or regulations, a contractor who has had experience with those regulations or requirements may be able to provide security risk assessment services better than other similarly qualified individuals. Specific regulations

such as HIPAA, the GLB Act, Sarbanes-Oxley, 21 CFR Part 11, and others may have similar wording associated with the requirement for a security risk assessment, yet each of these regulations has its own unique set of expectations based on interpretations of the requirements, case history, and the current expertise and expectations of the auditors.[8] A contractor who has experience in the regulation will not need to spend copious amounts of time coming up to speed on the regulations and other requirements that affect the requirements for the security risk assessment. Furthermore, a contractor with experience in specific regulations, such as HIPAA or the GLB Act, will already be familiar with how these requirements are being interpreted within the industry, the depth of analysis accepted by reviewers, and the scope of the requirements on the various system components and controls.

- Security Risk Assessment Activity Expertise — There are many different techniques, methods, and activities that may be performed within a security risk assessment in order to determine the overall risks to the system. Depending upon the customer requirements, some of these aspects may be required within a specific security risk assessment. Key aspects include security risk assessment methods such as OCTAVE, FRAP, and CRAMM;[9] techniques such as interviews, physical walk-throughs, and use of checklists; and activities such as social engineering, penetration testing, code review, architectural analysis, and organizational structure review. For those security engineers who have no experience with specific security risk assessment methods, techniques, or activities, the learning curve for these is likely to be steeper than for those security engineers with previous experience with these aspects.

The next-best alternative to the contractor is not to take the job. A contractor may choose to refuse to contract with the organization requiring a security risk assessment if there appear to be unreasonable expectations. Since most security risk assessments are performed as a firm-fixed price contract, the contractor can end up spending a lot of hours attempting to obtain sign-off on a project with unreasonable expectations. Professional and experienced contracting organizations would sooner walk away from such a project than risk poor customer satisfaction or an unprofitable project that utilizes key resources.

3.2.2.5.3 Negotiating Project Membership

Occasionally, the contracting organization may find it necessary to specify the team that will be performing the assessment. This is typically a result of getting burned in a "bait and switch" routine.

For example, consider the following scenario. A large consulting firm sends around its "big guns" to present proposals to clients. The clients become enamored by the skill, experience, and depth of knowledge possessed by the presenter. Then when it comes time for the project to begin, the large consulting firm sends out recently indoctrinated graduates to perform the project. The "big gun" presenter only plays a review role in the project. The result is a mismanaged, low-quality project that goes over budget and underdelivers on quality.

A good way to avoid this problem is to specify the qualities, experience, or credentials of the individuals on the project. Occasionally, the contracting organization may even require that named individuals be assigned to the project. Specifying named individuals can ensure a quality project but it may unnecessarily tie the hands of the contractor. Remember that the contractor may have several bids out as once and experiences turnover from time to time. A more preferred method of ensuring quality personnel is to allow substitution of named individuals with similar credentials and experience or upon approval of the contracting organization.

Notes

1. One way of ensuring the professionalism of the team members is to select members with relevant professional credentials. Among the most respected credentials relevant to performing a security risk assessment are the CISSP and the CISA.

2. Such analysis can be a considerable effort on the part of the team, so such a discussion as to inclusion of compliance review in the security risk assessment should have been settled in the negotiation phase. Compliance analysis is sometimes called "gap analysis."

3. That is not to say that if a security risk is noticed it should not be reported — it should. In fact, some security risks are required to be reported, such as the discovery of child pornography. However, the security risk assessment report should not contain such reported risks that are outside the boundaries of the security risk assessment.

4. Fly-By-Nite Security is a completely fictitious name used throughout this book to make examples and discussions more readable. Any resemblance of this company to a real company (by name or practice) is completely unintentional. However, if this name does resemble your company name, I would have to question your marketing intelligence.

5. The alert reader will have noticed several overlaps within physical security controls, such as fireproofing protecting both the buildings and the employees. Such overlaps are welcome as these security control measures can reduce the risk for more than a single threat or asset.

6. This is pretty much what is done in a SAS (Statement of Accounting Standards) No. 70 audit. SAS 70 audits are performed on service organizations that provide internal controls for systems that may affect the financial statements of other organizations, for example, an IDC that houses an application that takes

orders over the Internet. The IDC may have hundreds of customers, who all have the same concerns about the security controls that protect their applications. If the IDC has a SAS 70 audit performed once, it can share the results of the audit with all customers for their use in their own audits.

7.   It could be argued that the contractor would prefer to get a larger contract and thus prefer the longer effort, but let us just assume that there is enough work out there to keep them busy.

8.   Not all regulations have associated auditors. For example, there are no auditors directly associated with the Health Insurance Portability and Account-ability Act (HIPAA). Some vendors of HIPAA training would like you to believe so, but it is not true.

9.   Although there may be very good reasons for specifying or preferring specific security risk assessment activities or techniques, contracting organizations should resist specifying a risk assessment method unless it is absolutely necessary. Contractors familiar with a specific security risk assessment method are sometimes drawn to requiring this same method within an RFP. A more flexible RFP that allows the proposing security engineers to describe the methodology they believe is most appropriate is likely to yield far better results.

References

[1]   *Guide for Developing Security Plans for Information Technology Systems*, NIST Special Publication 800-18, December 1998. http://csrc.nist.gov/publications/nistpubs/800-18/Planguide.PDF

[2]   *Security Self-Assessment Guide for Information Technology Systems*, NIST Special Publication 800-26, November 2001. http://csrc.nist.gov/publications/nistpubs/800-26/sp800-26.pdf

[3]   *Guide for the Security Certification and Accreditation of Federal Information Systems*, NIST Special Publication 800-37, May 2004. http://csrc.nist.gov/publications/nistpubs/800-37/SP800-37-final.pdf

Chapter 4

Security Risk Assessment Preparation

Prior to the security risk assessment team arriving on site at the customer location, there are a number of activities to be performed to ensure an efficient project. These activities include introducing the assessment team to the organization, obtaining permission for testing and data gathering, and reviewing available information.

4.1 Introduce the Team

The introduction of the security risk assessment team to the customer organization is important in establishing a good start for the project. Introducing the security risk assessment team, contact information, and credentials of individual team members to the customer organization provides the customer confidence in the professionalism of the effort to come. In some cases the customer organization may have already been introduced to the team. For example, the security risk assessment team may have presented to the customer organization during the bidding and negotiation process. In many cases, however, the members of the security risk assessment team are unknown to the customer organization. Either way a letter of introduction should be used to formalize the start of the security risk assessment project.

Sidebar 4.1 Open Communications versus Cover Story

Occasionally a security risk assessment team is asked to perform its work under the cover of an unrelated project. The unrelated project is purely a distraction from the main purpose of the assessment. This type of security risk assessment is meant to provide the security risk assessment team a better view of the actual security controls and current operations without the influence or suspicion of the current personnel. Although this type of assessment may be necessary during an investigation of a suspicious employee, it is of little use in a general security risk assessment. Security risk assessments described in this book depend on the involvement and support of current personnel, and their opinions and information relayed during interviews is an essential element of data gathering. The "undercover" security risk assessment would be unable to depend on the involvement and support of current personnel and would result in a completely different type of assessment.

4.1.1 Introductory Letter

The form and content of an introductory letter may vary a little, but there are several key elements that must be contained within this letter. Key elements of the introductory letter include primary points of contact for both the customer and the security risk assessment team, a reference to the statement of work, a start date and projected end date for the project, a date for the on-site portion of the assessment, data requested at this time, and access required for the on-site visit.

- Points of Contact — The introductory letter should provide points of contact for all security risk assessment team members as well as contracting officers, and management responsible for oversight of the project.
- Reference to the Statement of Work — The letter should also reference the specific contract and statement of work that contains the detailed requirements for the project.
- Start Date and End Date — The letter should inform the organization to be assessed of the desired or selected dates to begin the project, perform on-site data gathering, and complete the project.
- Data Requested at This Time — The security risk assessment team should request any available information to reduce the amount of time required

on site. Information that would prove useful includes system diagram, policies, procedures, previous risk assessment reports, and so on.

- Access and Other Requirements For On-Site Assessment — Lastly, the introductory letter should list the on-site requirements for the team so the sponsor may begin preparations. On-site team requirements typically include desks, phones, whiteboards, physical access, logical access (accounts required), and access to a point of contact while on site.

The introductory letter should be addressed to the primary point of contact as specified in the statement of work.

4.1.2 Pre-Assessment Briefing

It is always better to let people know what to expect rather than surprise them. A pre-assessment briefing can help to set the expectations of the organization to be assessed and also to listen to their concerns and adjust the security risk assessment approach accordingly. A pre-assessment briefing should cover the following topics:

- Introduction — The briefing should provide an introduction of the assessment team (or several representatives) to the organization, a review of the assessment objective, a schedule of the on-site assessments, and the final briefing.
- What to Expect — The presenter should let the members of the assessed organization know what to expect. The best way to improve the usefulness of the security risk assessment results is to make the following expectations known:
  - Not a Score Card but a Planning Tool — The organization being assessed should understand that the security risk assessment is not a scorecard. The finding of a high risk posture should not be an indication that people are not doing their jobs. Instead it should be received as an indication of the need for an increased budget and staff for security. Such increases in staff or other changes such as improvements to existing controls require planning. A security risk assessment is the first step in the planning process.
  - First Step in Risk Management Process — The audience should be introduced to the risk management process and told where a risk assessment fits in that process. Risk assessments are the input into the determination of security controls, but periodic testing and operational controls play an important role as well.
  - Many Findings — There will likely be many findings. The organization should not be surprised (or disappointed, shocked, depressed, etc.) at the amount of findings yielded by the security risk assessment.

The process is such that many items will be listed; some will be major findings and some minor, but the amount of findings is less important than the overall risk level.

- Not Always a Quick Fix — Some findings will be operational in nature and will require a quick fix. For example, a finding of obvious vulnerabilities in an externally available Web server will require immediate patching. Other findings will be tactical or strategic in nature and will require longer-term planning to fix.
- What the Team Needs to Know — The presenter should give the members of the assessed organization a forum to provide information to the assessment team that will likely impact the assessment. The presenter may want to ask open-ended questions to encourage the organization to share information. Information that would be useful includes special events during the on-site schedule, procedures for access, past experiences with assessments, possible architectural changes, and plans for additional security controls.

4.1.3 Obtain Proper Permission

Prior to gathering data, the security risk assessment team must obtain the proper authorization for certain data-gathering activities. These activities include monitoring of user communications and access to information systems.

4.1.3.1 Policies Required

First, if the security risk assessment will include or possibly include the monitoring of user communications, then the security risk assessment team must ensure that their activities do not violate the Electronic Communications Privacy Act of 1986. The ECPA protects the electronic privacy of an individual and prohibits the monitoring of e-mail, voicemail, and cell phone conversations. These protections extend to users of the organization's information and telecommunication systems and the security risk assessment team is precluded from accessing these communications without the proper authority and treatment.

For practical purposes, most security risk assessments need not monitor or even sample employee e-mail, voicemail, or cell phone conversations. The only reason to monitor or sample such conversations is to ascertain if there is a risk to the organization's information systems through the use of these communication methods. The risks are as follows:

- Authorized users could be sending unauthorized information (e.g., sending sensitive information to a competitor).
- Authorized users could be receiving unauthorized information or files (e.g., executables with malicious code).

In either case, a review of the current security controls in place would give the security risk assessment team adequate information to ascertain the risk. For example, if the organization does not have content filtering and anti-virus protection on the mail server, then the chances are pretty high that these things could happen.

In the event that the security risk assessment team feels that it really needs to monitor these communications in order to sample data and obtain a more accurate assessment of the risk, then the following business processes must be confirmed. Failure to confirm these business processes could result in a violation of the ECPA.[1]

- The organization must have an existing policy that states the organization's rights to monitor communications.
- The policy must be applied according to procedures that ensure that monitoring will be employed only to ensure availability and quality of the service and not to single out any individual without due cause

4.1.3.2 Permission Required

If the security risk assessment team plans to access or attempt access to the organization's information systems, then the security risk assessment team must ensure that they obtain the proper authorization. Proper authorization includes explicit written permission by the system owner. Caution must be exercised here, since the determination of the owner is not always a straightforward task. First, ensure that the security risk assessment is being done with the permission of the system owner. The system owner should be independently verified through a trusted source.

For example, in 2002 Veridyn was asked to perform penetration testing for a financial institution in a foreign country. The contract and the standard permission forms were signed and we had even confirmed that the IP addresses given to us indeed belonged to the financial institution in question. However, we had yet to confirm that the parties we were dealing with actually represented the financial institution. In order to confirm that we had the authority of the bank and the IP address owner, we independently obtained the name of the entity that owned the IP addresses (our customers) and a point of contact for the financial institution. We contacted the financial institution and received a confirmation that our customers indeed represented the financial institution in this testing effort. Then we got it all in writing.

Next, consider the case when there are multiple owners of the information systems or the intermediate systems connecting you to them. For example, your customer's Web site may be hosted at a Web hosting facility. The Web site in question may even be running on a shared server. The security risk assessment team may have already obtained permission from the owner of the Web site but not the owner of the system that hosts the Web site. Furthermore, the security risk assessment team would be remiss if they proceeded to run a battery of vulnerability and penetration tests against the Web site, possibly disturbing or disrupting the other sites on the shared server. The security risk assessment team must ensure that they have the permission of the owner of all of the systems they will need access to in order to test the systems.

Because of this concern, outsourcing organizations many times obtain their own security risk assessment on their environment and systems and share the results with their customers. This allows their customers to accept the results of a security risk assessment performed by another organization. Customers who accept these results will save themselves the hassle of performing security testing and analysis on the outsourcing organization, provided they trust the objectivity and quality of the security risk assessment performed.[2]

In the case of the shared server, or in fact most outsourced environments, the security risk assessment team should consider using the results from a previously conducted security risk assessment. Before simply accepting the results of the previous security risk assessment, the team should consider the objectivity of the security risk assessment team that performed the assessment, the quality of their work, and the extent to which the systems and their environment may have changed. In the event that the security risk assessment team still feels the need to test these outsourced systems, the team should obtain explicit permission to test from the owner of the outsourced systems.

4.1.3.3 Scope of Permission

Organizations should not be asked to give outright permission for access to everything at all times. Security testing permission should only be requested and granted for specific systems, at specific times, and for a specific purpose.

The permission form should specify the IP addresses and phone numbers (if wardialing or social engineering) to be included in the test. The tests should be restricted to a specified time window. If possible, the time window should not be selected such that the organization can be ready and waiting for the test. We suggest a window of at least seven days, especially if the testing window is restricted to several off hours for each of those days. Lastly, the type of testing should be described (e.g., vulnerability testing, penetration testing, social engineering, wardialing).

4.1.3.4 Accounts Required

The security risk assessment team must specify to the sponsor the number and type of accounts that will be required. The accounts required for any particular security risk assessment are dependent on the processes to be used by the security risk

Table 4.1 Example of Required Accounts. The security risk assessment team will require multiple accounts with various privileges and access to properly gather information for the assessment.

Account Required	Privileges	Need
Guest account	User privileges only	User security functions
Privileged account	Administrator privileges	Administrator security functions
Network component account	Read access	Read configuration files
Network access	Network media access	Vulnerability scanning, network sniffing

assessment team and the permissions that the customer will grant. An example of the accounts that should be requested is provided in Table 4.1.

4.2 Review Business Mission

Before attempting to assess and report on the risks to an organization and its assets, the security risk assessment team must first acquire a basic understanding of the organization, its mission, its objectives, and its critical systems. The security risk assessment team will never develop as complete an understanding of the organization as the organization's executives, but there must be a basic understanding of the corporate mission, structure, businesses, and culture. The security risk assessment team must determine the business mission of the organization to have a basic understanding of the business assets, potential risks, and the impact of risks on those assets.

4.2.1 What Is a Business Mission?

Every organization has a reason for existing outside of making money. Making money is a potential side effect of performing the mission well. Sometimes it can be difficult to determine the business mission. Other times it is clearly stated and available. In either case the security risk assessment team is looking for the answer to three simple questions:

1. Who is the customer? — The basic starting block for understanding a business is to understand the customers they serve. For example, consider the magazine publishing industry. A surface-level understanding of the business tells you that the readers and subscribers are the customers. However, the revenue generated from subscriptions and newsstand purchases typically only covers the cost of printing and distribution.

The real customers of the magazine publishing industry are the advertisers and the customers of "nonadvertising marketing."[3] Understanding that these customers are the real customers of the magazine publishing industry will give the team members to a better understanding of the assets, critical systems, and acceptable levels of risk for each of those assets.

2. What does the organization offer the customer? — Find out what they sell, how they make money, what the product is. The business mission is not always clear, but if you want to find out how that mission is defined, follow the money. Business missions are defined by the various services or products offered by the organization. Ask about business units, organization charts, and the sources of revenue for the organization.

3. What makes the organization different from its competitors? — Even within an industry familiar to members of the assessment team, the assessed organization may have several unique characteristics that set it apart. Simply ask senior management how they differentiate themselves from competitors. For example, an organization may be the low-cost provider of E-commerce for certain items. In this case you would expect them to accept more risk than most of their competitors. Although this organization would need to meet minimum standards set by regulations and customers, it is unlikely that they would want to expend a lot of resources to implement additional controls unless these controls had other clear benefits.

The business mission statement typically identifies the customers and how the organization plans to serve them.

Beyond those simple elements, look for how this company sees itself as different from its competitors. There are only two ways to differentiate yourself: (1) offer a better product or service; (2) offer a cheaper price. A better product or service can take on many forms. Better could mean higher quality (e.g., reliable, respected, fast) or more convenience (e.g., better integrated, easy ordering process). A cheaper price could mean less cost initially or less cost in the long run. In either case, the security risk assessment team is looking for the company to fall into one of three tiers of security need (see Table 4.2). In most cases it becomes rather obvious into which tier a client falls, based on a cursory review of the business mission. Because of the need to differentiate one organization from its competitors, few companies are "on the fence" when it comes to these categories.[4]

4.2.2 Obtaining Business Mission Information

To the extent possible, the security risk assessment team should attempt to obtain the business mission prior to visiting with the organization. A review of public and provided information may produce the knowledge necessary to understand the organization's business mission. Public information available to the security risk

Table 4.2 Business Mission and Security Need. A governing information security principle is that security needs are based on business objectives. Below is a simplified illustration of how business mission can affect the level of security required within an organization.

Security Level	Business Mission Elements	Security Need
Tier 1	• Cutting-edge organization • High-quality provider • Critical systems with critical data assets • Sensitive customers	Low risk acceptance • High availability • Defense in depth • Redundancy • High security culture • Cutting-edge security mechanisms • First-rate security organization
Tier 2	Average • Just do what is right	Average risk acceptance • Standard security practices
Tier 3	• Cost leader • Minimalist • Bare bones	High risk acceptance • Minimal security practices

assessment team includes the organization's Web site, annual reports, and press releases. Other information that may contain statements relevant to the organization's mission includes introductory letters from the organization's chief executive officer, internal memorandums, or corporate training material. Any of these sources should yield a statement as to the customers served and the products or services offered.

The security risk assessment team leader should perform the basic research necessary to identify the organization's business mission. This proposed mission statement should be reviewed by and approved by the customer organization and appropriately modified.

4.3 Identify Critical Systems

The customer organization is likely to have multiple information systems within the scope of the security risk assessment. Each of these critical systems must be considered independently as they will have unique critical assets, missions, data, procedures, controls, and data owners. Once these systems have been identified, the security risk assessment team may find some overlap between the systems in terms of some of these aspects. For example there may be a single data owner for two or three systems supporting a business function. However, it is still important to identify these individual critical systems if there are any unique aspects.

Information systems are defined by their boundary of resources and characterized by their function, data, authorized users, and data owners. For example, a customer organization may have the information systems listed in Table 4.3 defined as part of the security risk assessment.[5]

4.3.1 Determining Criticality

The security risk assessment team should seek to obtain an understanding of the criticality of the various information systems to the success of the organization. This is part of understanding the organization's mission.

The criticality of information systems is determined by their support for business objectives. More specifically, critical systems are those systems that automate critical business functions. Criticality assignments and criticality prioritization is a difficult task, especially for a security risk assessment team that may not have adequate representation from all the business units of the organization. However, this should not be a problem. There are three approaches for determining the criticality of systems for a security risk assessment described in this book.[6]

- • Approaches for determining system criticality:
    1. Reuse information from other assessments.
    2. Determine critical systems quickly.
    3. Determine critical systems laboriously.

4.3.1.1 Approach 1: Find the Information Elsewhere

Many organizations may have already performed business continuity planning (BCP). As part of a BCP effort, they would have already identified and prioritized critical systems within the organization. The security risk assessment team can reuse this information provided it is still considered up-to-date and relevant by the organization. Furthermore, the BCP documentation is likely to have additional information that can be used elsewhere, such as likely threats, asset valuation, and other aspects that can be used in other phases of the security risk assessment.

4.3.1.2 Approach 2: Create the Information on a High Level

If a BCP is available, by all means use it, but if the security risk assessment team must take on the process of identifying critical systems, sometimes only a high level of information is required. It is enough for most security risk assessment methods to simply identify those systems that are critical, important, and of moderate importance. There is no need to determine a prioritization of these systems and a measurement of how long they can be down before the organization is in danger of going out of business.[7]

Table 4.3 Sample Critical System Identification. Critical systems must be identified and treated uniquely as they have unique functions, data, users, and data owners.

System Name	Functions	Data Owner	Data	Authorized Users	Boundary of resources
E-mail	Provide e-mail services	Dir. of IT	Personal Company confidential Company sensitive	Employees and contractors	E-mail server, e-mail client, e-mail archive
GSS	General office automation support	Dir. of IT	Personal Company confidential Company sensitive	Employees and contractors	Individual workstations with operating system and applications
Claims	Claims processing	Privacy Officer	Protected Health Information (PHI)	Customer service agents	Custom applications, data store, remote access

4.3.1.3 Approach 3: Classifying Critical Systems

The information technology (IT) infrastructure of many organizations can be rather complex, making the identification of critical systems a daunting task. It is important to divide the organization's IT infrastructure into manageable parts. A security risk assessment should not be attempted on the whole system for complex IT infrastructures.

Even given the assumption that a security risk assessment is to be performed on a manageable sized network and infrastructure, the task of identifying critical systems can be difficult. One approach to simplify this process is to classify the systems. The following classification is well documented in several NIST publications and is intended for government agencies, but it should work well for most organizations. Minor modifications have been made to the NIST text, but the general concepts are largely the same.

4.3.1.3.1 Determine Protection Requirements

These requirements are derived from the need for protection among the three elements of the security policy, namely, confidentiality, integrity, and availability. The following scale may be used for rating the protection requirements of the systems:

- High — A critical concern for the system or major financial loss (greater than $1 million), or requires legal action up to imprisonment for correction.
- Medium — An important concern but not necessarily paramount in the organization's priorities or could cause significant financial loss ($100,000 to $1 million) or require legal action for correction.
- Low — Some minimal level of security is required, but not to the same degree as the previous two categories, or would cause only minor financial loss (less than $100,000) or require only administrative action for correction.*

4.3.1.3.2 Determine Mission Criticality

The next step is to determine the mission or business criticality of each system. Criticality is defined as the extent to which the system is integral to carrying out the mission of the organization. The following NIST definitions are useful for providing guidance for the criticality assignments of the identified systems:

- Mission Critical — These systems are those that would preclude the organization from accomplishing its core business functions if they fail. A system should be considered critical if it meets any of the following criteria:
  - Supports a core business function.
  - Provides the single source of mission-critical data.
  - May cause immediate business failure upon its loss.

- Important — These systems are those whose failure would not preclude the organization from accomplishing its core business functions in the short term, but would if the system is not repaired in the mid or long term (three days to one month). A system should be considered important if it meets any of the following criteria:
  - Serves as a backup source for data that is critical.
  - Would have an impact on business over an extended period of time.
- Supportive — These systems are those whose failure would not preclude the organization from accomplishing its core business functions, but would affect the effectiveness or efficiency of day-to-day operations. A system should be considered supportive if it meets any of the following criteria:
  - Tracks or calculates data for organizational convenience.
  - Would only cause loss of business efficiency and effectiveness for the owner.

4.3.1.3.3 Define Critical Systems

The final phase in the process of identifying critical systems is to define each system as a general support system (GSS), major application (MA), or application.

- Applications — These systems are defined as "the use of information resources to satisfy a specific set of user requirements" [1].
- Major Applications — These systems are defined as "an application that requires special attention to security due to the risk and magnitude of the harm resulting from the loss, misuse, or unauthorized access to or modification of the information in the application" [1]. Applications are considered a major application if they have been determined to be "critical" or "important" or if they have been determined to be supportive but have at least one of the protection requirements rated as medium or high.
- General Support Systems — These systems are defined as "an interconnected set of information resources under the same direct management control which shares common functionality". General support systems provide support for the applications that reside on them. The criticality of a GSS is based on the highest criticality of any application or major application that resides on the GSS.

4.4 Identify Assets

A key step in preparing for a security risk assessment is to identify the assets to be protected. The identification of assets is a necessary precursor to understand the overall risk to those assets.[8]

The depth and rigor of the asset identification process should be commensurate with the depth and rigor of the overall security risk assessment. Asset identification can be a rather easy exercise of listing the items requiring protection based on available checklists and engineering judgment, or it can be an involved process requiring an inventory of capital equipment, a traceability matrix of system resources, a review of legal documents, and an attempt at listing all intangible assets such as the organization's reputation.

Sidebar 4.2 Futility of Listing Assets

No matter how hard you try you can never list all of the assets, tangible and intangible. There are too many factors that go into creating value for an organization. Unless you are an auditor you really should not even try to list them all. First, it is extremely time-consuming to attempt to put together a list of everything that brings value to the organization. The time spent compiling a list of office equipment or trade secrets or workstations leaves less time for the remainder of the security risk assessment. Moreover, such a list is simply not very useful to the security risk assessment effort. When assessing the risk to data and programs on workstations from malicious software, is it really important if there are 43 workstations or 435 workstations? Does it really matter what general office software is installed?*

An effective security risk assessment recognizes the assets under consideration in relative terms only, because the purpose of asset scope is to scope the security risk assessment to the areas intended to be assessed. For instance, because physical security is typically separated from information security, many security risk assessments are performed without regard to the safety of people or building structures. So, rather than attempting to list all physical assets, simply note that building structures and facility utilities and protection mechanisms are outside of the scope of this security risk assessment.

These were intended to be rhetorical questions, but for those readers not yet convinced the answer is "no" to each of these questions. Of course it matters if the workstations are protected and if the general office software is up-to-date with security patches, but it is a waste of time to create a complete list of all such assets. This is a security risk assessment and not an asset audit.

4.4.1 Checklists and Judgment

Listing assets based on checklists and judgment will yield an adequate identification of the critical assets of the organization. For many security risk assessments this is good enough, as the organization would be unwise to spend its entire budget on a security risk assessment. A security risk assessment team can efficiently develop a relatively good list of assets by reviewing general lists of assets and using judgment to apply the list to the organization they are reviewing. Consider the general asset list in Table 4.4.

4.4.2 Asset Sensitivity/Criticality Classification

Assets are, by definition, those items that require protection. It is useful to categorize or classify assets to organize asset protection requirements, and the vulnerability assessment of assets. There are three approaches for classifying or categorizing assets described below:

- Approaches for asset classification:
  1. Reuse information from other assessments.
  2. Determine critical systems quickly.
  3. Determine critical systems laboriously.

4.4.2.1 Approach 1: Find Asset Classification Information Elsewhere

Some organizations may have already performed an activity in which assets have already been classified. Types of activities that may have classified assets include previous security risk assessments, asset inventories, security policies, or system documentations. The security risk assessment team can reuse this information provided it is still considered up-to-date and relevant by the organization.

4.4.2.2 Approach 2: Create Asset Classification Information Quickly

If there are no documents or previous activities that have already classified the organization's assets, the security risk assessment team must take on the process of classifying assets, but only a high level of information may be required.

It may be enough for most security risk assessment methods to simply identify basic classes of information. For example, most organizations have many different reasons for protecting data (e.g., personal data on employees, proprietary data about product pricing, security data regarding protective measures), but it may be enough for the security risk assessment to simply determine if information is sensitive or not. Sensitive data requires protection and public data does not.

This may be an oversimplification for some organizations, especially those that must comply with information security regulations such as the Health Insurance

Table 4.4 General Asset List. It may be impossible and certainly futile to exhaustively list every asset in an organization for a security risk assessment. However, the security risk assessment team should endeavor to account for the general assets and asset classes as they affect the organization's security posture. Below is a list of general assets to aid the security risk assessment team in identifying a reasonable set of assets to review.

Asset Category	Subcategory	Examples
Information	Sensitive	• Employee applications • Employee records • Facility plans • Intellectual property • Account passwords • Pricing information • System vulnerabilities • Financial data • Contingency procedures
	Protected	• Medical records • Financial inquiries • Health insurance applications • Bank statements • Credit reports • Prescriptions
	Public	• Web site • Marketing materials • SEC filings
Equipment	Network	• Cabling • Hubs • Switches • Routers • Bridges • Subnets • Firewalls • IDS appliance • Modems
	Computing	• Servers • Workstations • Laptops
	Telecomm.	• Cabling • Switches
	Transportation	• Vehicles • Trucking
	Special purpose	• Check printing • Product manufacturing

(*Continued*)

Table 4.4   (Continued)
General Asset List

Asset Category	Subcategory	Examples
	Maintenance	• Tools • Spare parts
Inventories	Material	• Raw material • Partial assemblies
	Finished goods	• Products
Personnel	Staff	• Executives • Managers • Security personnel • Employees • Field personnel
	Outsiders	• Contractors • Temporary workers • Vendors • Visitors
	Contractors	• Cleared contractors • Escorted contractors
	Temporary workers	• Front office worker • Sensitive position
Services	Movement	• Equipment • Personnel
	Training	• Staff • Outsiders
	Infrastructure	• Power • Communication • Water • Cooling • Fire suppression
	Research and development	• New product research • Optimization
Facilities		• Headquarters • Field offices • Utility buildings
Financial resources		• Checks • Accounts • Cash

Portability and Accountability Act (HIPAA) or the Gramm-Leach-Bliley (GLB) Act. Healthcare organizations seeking to comply with HIPAA also need to know whether or not information assets contain Protected Health Information (PHI). Similarly, financial institutions seeking to comply with the GLB Act also need to

Table 4.5 Sample Asset Classifications. For many organizations assets may be easily classified into relatively few categories, thus making asset classification a relatively simple task.

Classification	Description	Examples
Sensitive assets	Assets that contain any form of sensitive information including personal information on employees, configuration information of security controls, and company proprietary information	Employee applications, account passwords, pricing information
PHI or customer assets	Assets that contain PHI or customer information • Customer information — any record containing nonpublic personal information about a customer of a financial institution • Protected Health Information — individually identifiable health information	Medical records, financial inquiries, health insurance applications, bank statements, credit reports, prescriptions
Public assets	Assets that contain neither sensitive information nor PHI or customer information	Web site, marketing materials, SEC filings

know whether or not information assets contain customer information (see Table 4.5).

4.4.2.3 Approach 3: Create Asset Classification Information Laboriously

Another approach for categorizing assets is in terms of critical, important, and supportive. Similar definitions to those used by NIST for system criticality definitions can be used here as well. Using those definitions and applying them to assets, we derive the following definitions:

- Critical Assets — Assets that would preclude the organization from accomplishing its core business functions if they are not protected. Critical assets are those that meet any of the following criteria:
  - Required by a critical system.
  - Backup is not provided elsewhere.
- Important Assets — Assets whose compromise would not preclude the organization from accomplishing its core business functions in the short

term, but would if the assets are not restored. Important assets are those that meet any of the following criteria:

- Serves as a backup for other critical data.
- Would have an impact on business over an extended period of time.
- Supportive Assets — Assets whose compromise would not preclude the organization from accomplishing its core business functions, but would affect the effectiveness or efficiency of day-to-day operations. Supportive assets are those that meet any of the following criteria:
    - Tracks or calculates data for organizational convenience.
    - Would only cause loss of business efficiency and effectiveness for the owner.

4.4.3 Asset Valuation

One of the key steps to performing a security risk assessment is to determine the value of the assets that require protection. Asset valuation is an important element of business accounting and planning within the organization and may be performed for many reasons. These reasons may include compliance, contingency planning, insurance, legal claims, records management, budgeting, information classification, or criticality assignment. Within a security risk assessment, asset valuation is performed for information classification and criticality assignment. Asset valuation is a required element in determining critical systems and the impact on the organization if the asset is lost or compromised.

There are many approaches to determine the value of an organization's assets. These approaches range from simple binary decisions to complex quantitative valuation. There are seven asset valuation approaches discussed below (see also Table 4.6) to give the reader an overview of the possible techniques that could be applied to any given security risk assessment. Choosing the asset valuation technique that best fits any particular security risk assessment depends upon the budget, time, and regulatory requirements of the assessment effort. The asset valuation techniques are presented in order of rigor starting with the least rigorous and therefore less costly to apply approach.

- Qualitative asset valuation approaches
    1. Binary Asset Valuation
    2. Classification-Based Asset Valuation
    3. Rank-Based Asset Valuation
    4. Consensus Asset Valuation

4.4.3.1 Approach 1: Binary Asset Valuation

A binary asset valuation involves a simple decision for each asset: yes or no? This type of asset valuation is applicable to situations in which specific security controls are required for strictly defined data. For example, within the HIPAA regulation,

Table 4.6 Asset Valuation Techniques. Many asset valuation techniques are available to the security risk assessment team. Choosing the appropriate technique requires an understanding of the various techniques and the project requirements of the security risk assessment.

Technique	Description	Comments
Binary	Determination if data belongs to a protected class	• Easy to apply • Applicable in regulated industries
Classification	Data is classified as high, medium, or low	• Easy to apply • Generally applicable to any organization
Ranking	Each asset is ranked against all other assets	• Relatively easy to apply • Results in an ordered list of assets
Consensus	Consensus estimate by a group of experts	• Works well with small groups • Not scientific, difficult to replicate results
Cost valuation	Based on economic principle of substitution	• Quantitative valuation • Replacement cost
Market valuation	Based on economic principles of competition and equilibrium	• Quantitative valuation • Market value
Income valuation	Based on economic principle of expectation	• Quantitative valuation • Expected income

electronic Protected Health Information (e-PHI) is a protected class of data and must comply with specific requirements within the HIPAA regulation. A HIPAA-based security risk assessment requires the identification of PHI and non-PHI data.

4.4.3.2 Approach 2: Classification-Based Asset Valuation

An extension of the binary approach for asset valuation is the classification-based approach. In this approach, assets are classified as one of several value classifications. For example, all critical assets can be considered of high value, important assets have a medium value, and supportive assets have a low value. This approach is the classic qualitative approach. It is a more general application of the binary approach, in that it is more flexible and can distinguish between multiple classifications instead of just one. Another example of classification-based asset valuation is shown in Table 4.7.

4.4.3.3 Approach 3: Rank-Based Asset Valuation

The ranking approach to asset valuation requires that each asset is ranked in value against all other assets. For example, if the security risk assessment team has

Table 4.7 Classification-Based Asset Valuation. Assets may be classified in one of several asset classifications that indicate their qualitative value. For many organizations the qualitative approach to asset valuation provides adequate asset valuation with less effort than quantitative asset valuation approaches.

	Asset Impact/Criticality Rating Criteria
Criticality Level	Description
Critical	Indicates that compromise of the asset would have grave consequences leading to loss of life or serious injury to people and disruption to operation of a critical business function
High	Indicates that a compromise of the asset would have serious consequences that could impair the operation of a critical business function
Medium	Indicates that compromise of the asset would have moderate consequences that would impair the operation of a critical business function for a short time
Low	Indicates little or no impact on human life or the continuation of the operation of critical business functions

identified 50 assets within the organization, then each asset will be ranked between 1 and 50. This requires a little more analysis and discussion than the binary or classification-based asset valuation techniques, but it provides the security risk assessment team with more information as well.

4.4.3.4 Approach 4: Consensus Asset Valuation

Another approach to determining the value of an organization's assets is to gain a consensus estimate by a group of experts. The Delphi method, which involves the use of at least three experts and a facilitator, is the most popular technique for gaining consensus. The Delphi method was developed by the RAND Corporation in 1969 and continues to be the standard for consensus-based estimation. This method works well for small groups of experts, but tends to be labor-intensive as the number of experts increases. Other criticisms of the method are that it lacks scientific rigor and it is difficult to replicate the results.

4.4.3.5 Approaches 5–7: Accounting Valuation Approaches

In many security risk assessment efforts it may be enough to simply assign a relative or qualitative value based on the asset classification. Notice that assigning a value in a qualitative security risk assessment approach can be done at the same time (and with the same effort) as assigning a classification to the asset. Many qualitative methods therefore skip asset valuation because a value is inherent in the classification of the data.

However, assigning a value to an asset may be a more complex process. For security risk assessments that implement quantitative methods in the calculation of risk, assets must be assigned a monetary value. There are three quantitative approaches for determining the valuation of an asset discussed below:

- Quantitative asset valuation approaches:

    5. Cost valuation — base the value of the asset on replacement or alternative costs.
    6. Market valuation — base the value of the asset on the market value.
    7. Income valuation — base the value of the asset on the expected income from the asset.

4.4.3.6 Approach 5: Cost Valuation

This approach to determining the value of an asset uses the economic principle of substitution. The principle of substitution states that businesses strive for efficiency by substituting current arrangements for another arrangement that will get the job done better for the same amount of money or produce the same results for less money.

Applying this principle to asset valuation, an asset is valued at the cost of a substitute that performs the same job. For example, consider placing a value on intellectual property such as a security risk assessment training class. Under the cost valuation approach, the class material would be valued the same as a similar class. If you can contract a firm to produce a similar training class for $50,000, then this specific security risk assessment class is worth $50,000.

4.4.3.7 Approach 6: Market Valuation

Another approach to determining the value of an asset is market valuation. This approach is based on the economic principles of competition and equilibrium, better known as the law of supply and demand. The law of supply and demand states that (1) the greater the supply of courseware for sale, the lower the price is set, and (2) the greater the demand for similar courseware, the higher the price is set. Lower prices bring more customers; high prices drive some away. The equilibrium is set at a market clearing price, meaning that a price is reached such that the amount of buyers and sellers is equal.

Applying this principle to asset valuation, an asset is valued at the price someone is willing to pay for it. Using the same example, if nobody is willing to pay $50,000 for the class materials and ownership, but they are willing to pay $45,000, then the class material is worth $45,000.

Table 4.8 Sample Asset Valuation — Income Approach. The value of educational materials for a security risk assessment class is used below to demonstrate the the income approach to asset valuation. Based on the assumptions documented below, such class would be valued at over $100,000.

	Assumptions	
Useful life of materials	Class is based on general principles and does not require updates	5 years
Expected income from classes per year	• 5% royalty • 24 classes per year • 10 students per class • $2000 per student	Revenue: 24*10*2000 = $480,000 Royalty Income: 5%* revenue = $24,000
Present value of expected income	Rate of return = 6%	$101,096.73

4.4.3.8 Approach 7: Income Valuation

The last approach covered in this book for determining the value of an asset is income valuation. This approach is based on the economic principle of expectation. This principle states that the value of an asset is equal to the expected incomes from that asset.

Applying this principle to our example, the security risk assessment class materials should be valued at the expected incomes to be received. For example, if you were to license the materials to a training company that could sell 24 classes per year with an average of 10 students, a course price of $2000, and get a 5 percent royalty, then the class materials would be valued at over $100,000[9] (see Table 4.8)

4.5 Identifying Threats

The next step for the security risk assessment team in preparing for a security risk assessment is to identify the threats to the system to be considered. The identification of the threats is important because it bounds the assessment to the actions that can be performed by those threats. For example, if a security risk assessment team is told by the assessed organization to only consider human and not nature threats, then the assessment is bounded to those threats that can be performed by humans. Furthermore, if the security risk assessment team is told to only consider external threats, then the assessment team would not look at insider threats.

The examples above are simple cases of identifying the threats since the threats were treated in broad terms. A more in-depth review of the threats applicable to an assessment will show that there are a great many possible threats to the organization's assets. To provide some structure to the multitude of possible threats, threats are discussed in terms of their components.

4.5.1 Threat Components

A threat is commonly described as an event with an undesired impact on the organization's assets. The components of a threat include the threat agent and the undesirable event.

4.5.1.1 Threat Agent

A threat agent is an entity that may cause a threat to happen, such as an earthquake or a disgruntled employee. Threat agents can be organized according to their type (i.e., human, natural, technological) and further broken down into categories (i.e., insider, outsider, associate, fire, weather, vibration, wildlife, biological, infrastructure, system). Table 4.9 provides a list of possible threats organized by their type and category.

4.5.1.2 Undesirable Events

An undesirable event is what is caused by a threat agent. The event is considered undesirable if it threatens a protected asset. Such events include destruction of equipment, disclosure of sensitive information, and unavailability of resources. Undesirable events can be organized according to their type (health, physical exposure, logical exposure, and resource availability) and further broken down into subcategories (e.g., sicken, endanger, injure, and kill). Table 4.10 provides a detailed breakdown of possible event/asset pairs.

   The depth to which a security risk assessment team should identify undesirable events and asset pairs depends on the expected rigor of the overall assessment. If additional depth of analysis is required during the threat identification stage, the security assessment team should further break down the subcategories into specific assets. For example, instead of treating all information as a single asset, the team could further subdivide this asset into critical, important, and supportive assets.

4.5.2 Listing Possible Threats

The next action for the step of identifying threats is to actually list the threats that are considered for the specific security risk assessment. In some cases, the list of threats to be considered may have been bounded during the project definition phase; for example, only external threats are to be considered. In other cases the breadth of threats to be considered is wide open. In either case the security risk assessment team must now consider the depth to which these threats will be

Table 4.9 Threat Agents by Type and Category. There are many different approaches for identifying threats to an organization's assets. One approach is to first consider the threat agent and then consider the action the threat agent can take. This table lists the various threat agents from human, nature, and technology.

Human	Nature	Technology
Insider	Fire	Infrastructure
Executive	Heat	Internal
Management	Smoke	Power
Sensitive position	Toxic fumes	Water
Employee	Weather	HVAC
Security force	Rain	Gas
Outsider	Lightning	Telecomm
Terrorist	Flood	Internet
Hacker	Hurricane	Network
Ex-employee	Monsoon	Electronic interference
Competitor	Tsunami	External
Building crew	High winds	Power
Associate	Tornado	Water
Business associates	Volcano	Gas
Customer	Extreme heat	Telecomm
Vendor	Extreme cold	Internet
Visitor	Snow/Ice	DNS
	Solar flare	Electronic interference
	Humidity	System
	Vibration	Hardware
	Earthquakes	Software
	Landslides	Application
	Wildlife	
	Insects	
	Rodents	
	Birds	
	Biological	
	Virus	

identified. For example, is it enough to simply consider the threat agents of internal and external humans and nature or is it required to further specify the types of internal and external humans along with the types of natural events?

Based on the degree of rigor and depth at which the security risk assessment team must identify assets, the following two approaches are covered here:

- Approaches for listing threats:
  1. Checklist and judgment.
  2. Threat statement generation.

Table 4.10 Undesirable Events and Protected Assets. Threat agents can be paired with potential hazards and protected assets to create threat statements. This table represents an example of how to pair undesirable events and protected assets.

		Protected Asset						
Hazard		Personnel	Information	Services	Equipment	Inventory	Facilities	Financial Resource
Health	Sicken	X						
	Endanger	X						
	Injure	X						
	Kill	X						
Physical	Damage		X	X	X	X	X	
	Breach		X				X	
	Steal				X	X		X
	Destroy		X	X	X	X	X	X
Logical	Damage		X	X				
	Expose		X	X				
	Release		X					
	Destroy		X	X				
Availability	Slow		X	X	X	X	X	X
	Deny		X	X	X	X	X	X

4.5.2.1 Checklists and Judgment

Review a checklist of threats and exercise judgment in selecting appropriate threats. Listing threats based on checklists and judgment will yield an adequate identification of the threats to an organization's assets for some security risk assessments. For many security risk assessments this is good enough, as the organization would be unwise to spend its entire budget on a security risk assessment. A security risk assessment team can efficiently develop a relatively good list of threats by reviewing general lists of threats like those in Table 4.9 or other sources of threat listings. The team can use judgment to apply the list to the organization they are reviewing.

4.5.2.2 Threat Agent and Undesirable Event Pairing

Another more rigorous approach to identifying threats to an organization's assets is to create a list of threat agents and possible undesirable events they may cause. This list could be quite extensive as a single threat agent possesses the ability to cause any number of a multitude of undesirable events. Therefore it is important that the security risk assessment team adopts a disciplined approach to listing the threats. One such approach, threat agent and undesirable event pairing, is explained below.

Once threat agents and undesirable events are identified, the security risk assessment team can identify the appropriate pairings of these to threat components. A pair is simply the logical association of a threat agent and a possible undesirable event that the threat agent may cause.

Given a list of threat agents, there are some undesirable events that these threat agents may possibly cause and some that they could not. For example, a human being could cause undesirable events in any category (i.e., health, physical exposure, logical exposure, and resource availability). On the other hand, severe weather can cause undesirable events within the health, physical exposure, and resource availability categories, but cannot cause a logical exposure. Table 4.11 provides a mapping of threat agents and undesirable event pairs.

Sidebar 4.3 Limitation of Checklist-Based Approaches

Checklists are an incredibly useful tool and are in fact highlighted throughout this book with example checklists for many security risk assessment tasks. However, it is appropriate to provide severe warnings regarding the use of checklists as well. The following guidelines regarding checklists should be understood by any security professional considering their use:

- Checklists are a memory aid — No security risk assessment team member should rely on checklists to tell them what to look for and how to look for it. Checklists instead are an aid to the memory of information security professionals who understand the concepts contained within the checklist.
- Checklists help to ensure accuracy and completeness — Many of the tasks involved with performing a security risk assessment can be simplified and to some extent improved through the use of tools or checklists. The purpose of these tools and checklists is to simplify computationally complex tasks, to ensure complete coverage, to organize and present the wealth of information and findings. Risk assessment tools can perform risk calculations and prepare well-organized reports. Checklists can be used as a guide and a reminder to provide a complete and accurate analysis. On larger security risk assessment projects, these tools and checklists can be vital to the project's success.
- Checklists can drive the results instead of guiding the engineer —The information security professional must use caution not to let the tools or the checklists "run" the assessment. In the end, a security risk assessment is filled with subjective analysis and relies on professional judgment. Checklists can be relied upon to the detriment of creativity and keeping your eye out for the usual or new.
- Checklists should be generated by senior people — Senior information security engineers or experts within a key aspect of information security are best suited for the creation or modification of checklists.
- Don't rely solely on checklists — A team member who relies too heavily on a checklist will find that their skills of observation, investigation, and perception can weaken. An overreliance on a checklist or a checklist-based approach for security risk assessments can lead to tunnel vision and a breakdown in the analytical process required for effective security risk assessment.

Checklists have received a bad reputation in some circles because of negative customer experiences. Checklists can be misused, as in the case of when a consultancy provides intensive training on the use of checklists to new recruits followed by letting them loose on the customer with little or no supervision.

Table 4.11 Threat Agents and Undesirable Event Pairs.
Threat agents, such as humans, nature, and technology, can
create a number of different undesirable events. This table
provides a matching between threat agents and possible
undesirable events.

	Undesirable Event			
Threat Agent	*Health*	*Physical Exposure*	*Logical Exposure*	*Resource Availability*
Human				
• Insider	×	×	×	×
• Outsider	×	×	×	×
• Associates	×	×	×	×
Nature				
• Fire	×	×		×
• Weather	×	×		×
• Vibration	×	×		×
• Wildlife	×			×
• Biological	×			
Technology				
• Internal			×	×
• External			×	×
• System			×	×

4.5.3 Threat Statements

Threat components (threat agents and undesirable events) can be combined with assets to create threat statements (see Figure 4.1). The creation of threat statements is a way to more clearly express the threats to be considered and countered during the security risk assessment process.

Threat statements can be further refined with the addition of intention of human threat agents. Human threat agents can cause undesirable events on purpose or accidentally. Therefore, two threat statements can be generated for each threat statement created that involves a human. one for the intentional cause of an undesirable event and one for an accidental cause of an undesirable event (see Table 4.12).

4.5.4 Validating Threat Statements

The final action for the step of identifying threats is to validate the list of threat statements developed in the previous section. Among the threat statements that can be generated, only a portion of them are worthy of considering for any specific

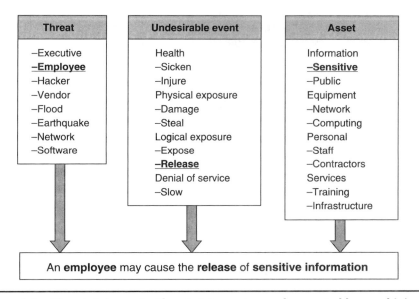

Figure 4.1 Threat statements. Threat statements may be created by combining a threat agent, undesirable event, and an asset. Threat statements are a way to clearly express the threats to be considered during a security risk assessment.

Table 4.12 Multiple Threat Statements. Multiple threat statements may be created from a single threat statement if the intention of the threat agent is considered.

Threat Statement A	*An employee may cause the release of sensitive information*
Threat statement A1	An employee may accidentally cause the release of sensitive information
Threat statement A2	An employee may purposefully cause the release of sensitive information

security risk assessment. Consideration for the appropriateness of a threat statement should be based on the threat environment of the organization being assessed. A security risk assessment should take the approach of validating only those threat statements that appear to be most likely, ignoring threats that appear to be a remote possibility.[10]

The security risk assessment team is expected to use their experience, judgment, and common sense when assessing the validity of threat statements. Team members who are experienced in information security will have specific experiences with actual breaches at other organizations and can project the relevance of these past experiences to the current project. Judgment and common sense are built on the lessons learned from previous experience. Each of these attributes should be relied upon to determine reasonable threat statements. For example, a security risk assessment should probably include the following threat statement:

"An employee may accidentally cause the release of sensitive information."

However, the threat statement below may be considered beyond remote and thus dropped from consideration:

"A volcanic eruption may destroy critical equipment."

4.5.4.1 Factors Affecting Threat Statement Validity

That being said, the last threat statement above may be appropriate for some areas of the world. For example, organizations residing near Mount St. Helens in Washington State should consider the threat statement reasonable and thus include it. In fact the security risk assessment team should consider a variety of factors when determining the validity of possible threat statements.

- History — It is hard to argue against the history of an organization. If considering whether or not it is likely that an executive laptop would ever be misplaced or stolen, simply ask the assessment sponsor if there is any history of this occurring. If so, then a threat statement concerning the loss of an executive laptop is certainly valid. (Of course, it may be valid even if there is no history of it happening.)
- Environmental Factors — Another important factor to consider in the validation of threat statements is the environment in which the organization resides. These factors include geography and climate, size and configuration of the facilities, and the social and political environment.
  - Geography and Climate — The geography and climate of the organization's facilities affect the validity of possible threat statements. Geography and climate can have an impact on the likelihood of natural threats occurring. For example, ice, snow and extreme cold are not applicable in too many locations in the southern part of the United States. Also, natural disasters such as hurricanes, tornadoes, and earthquakes are more likely in some areas of the country and rather remote in others. In addition to affecting the likelihood of natural disasters, geography can affect infrastructure threats as well. Facilities located in certain areas of the country are more susceptible to power outages, electronic interference, and water shortages.
  - Facility Size and Configuration — The size and configuration of the organization's facilities can also affect the validity of possible threat statements. The size of the buildings and their configuration can have an impact on the likelihood of natural and human threats occurring.

Key aspects of facility size and configuration include construction material used in the buildings, the intended use of the facilities, square footage, working population during all shifts, number of visitors, number of cars parked on the premises, and to what extent the structures may be below grade level. As many of these factors increase (e.g., number of visitors, number of employees, number of cars parked, square footage), so does the organization's susceptibility to various threats. For example, a large facility with hundreds of visitors a day is more likely to have a valid threat of unescorted visitors breaching physical security than a smaller facility with few visitors.[11]

- Social and Political Climate — The social and political climate of the organization's facilities affects the validity of possible threat statements. Social and political climate can have an impact on the likelihood of human threats occurring. Factors here include proximity to emergency and policy services, local crime rates, and the stability of the local government. For example, facilities located in areas of a city with high crime rates should certainly consider any human threat statements regarding the safety of their employees from crime and theft of equipment.

- Business Factors — The last important factor to consider in the validation of threat statements is business factors. These factors include visibility of the organization, the type of services performed, the value of the equipment on the premises, and the value of the inventories.

  - Visibility — Some businesses may be more of a target than others. Organizations that provide services or produce products that may be considered controversial (e.g, research labs, world trade groups, clinics, political position organizations, pharmaceutical companies) should seriously consider all human-based threats targeted at any protected asset such as employees, services, and financial resources.

  - Services Performed — Some services performed are more dangerous or susceptible to threats than others. Organizations that deal with hazardous chemicals, weapon manufacturing, or send their employees abroad need to consider all threats related to such activities.

  - Value of Equipment and Inventories — Organizations that house valuable equipment and inventories such as computer chips, financial instruments, and other assets need to consider threats related to theft of assets.

4.6 Determine Expected Controls

By this stage in a security risk assessment the team should have a good understanding of the business objectives, assets to be protected, and relevant threats to those assets. This information is adequate to determine high-level security requirements for an organization. Although traditional security risk assessment does not include a step for developing security requirements, this type of analysis has always been performed (perhaps unconsciously) by many information security professionals.

Consider the following scenario. During the data-gathering phase of a security risk assessment, team members are surprised to find that a major pharmaceutical company has no security force on the premises. This is instantly written up as a vulnerability because it is clear to the team members that the value of information assets and the prevalence of industrial espionage within this industry warrants that physical security be strong.

Now consider the reason this vulnerability was identified. Was the identification of this vulnerability a weakness in existing controls? Or should it be considered the absence of an expected control? Some security risk assessment approaches are now formally recognizing this practice of expecting specific security controls within various risk situations. Specifically, a recently released guideline by the National Institute of Standards and Technology, (NIST) recognized four risk situations and listed expected security controls for each [2]. Table 4.13 shows expected security controls for various types of systems from the NIST guideline.*

Members of the security risk assessment team may have additional expectations based on their experience. These expectations will ultimately impact the identification of vulnerabilities in the assessed system. Additional expectations may include any of the following security controls, depending on the threat environment of the organization to be assessed:

- Security Policy Expectations — Every organization is expected to have adequate information security policies. Depending on the size and industry of the organization, many security engineers would expect the following security policies documented, approved, distributed, and updated.
  - Senior Management Statement
  - Acceptable Use Policy
  - System Development and Deployment
  - Security Maintenance
  - Security Operations
  - Security Monitoring
  - Business Continuity Planning
- Security Organization Expectations — Every organization should have some type of security organization. At a minimum, the role of the security officer should be described and assigned. In larger organizations, the effectiveness of the security organization can only be achieved if the organization has the proper authority, adequate resources, and a skilled staff.
- Security Procedure Expectations — In larger organizations, security procedures should be expected. The accuracy and consistency of security activities must be ensured through the development of and adherence to

Table 4.13 Expected Security Controls. The NIST guideline lists expected security controls for SOHO, enterprise, high security, and custom systems.

Environment	Description	Example Systems	Expected Controls
Small office/home office (SOHO)	Informal computer installation used for home or small businesses	Home office Small business	• Firewall appliance • Personal firewalls • Security updates • Anti-virus software • Malicious filtering on Web and e-mail • Disable unnecessary applications • Encrypt wireless traffic • System connection restrictions • User privilege restrictions • Resource-sharing restrictions • Backup and recovery procedures • Physical security procedures
Enterprise	Managed environments consisting of centrally managed workstations and servers protected from the Internet	Medium to large businesses	• Segmented internal networks • Centralized system management • Centralized security application management • Automated update management • Restricted access to printers • Centralized backup and recovery

High security	An environment that is at a high risk of attack or data exposure. Security takes precedence over usability. Environment includes limited function computers and highly confidential information	Banking systems Healthcare systems	• Single-function servers • Removal of unnecessary services and applications • Host-based firewall applications. • Limited users • Strong authentication • Restricted and encrypted remote access • Intrusion detection monitoring • Regular vulnerability scans • Skilled administrators
Custom	Specialized systems in which function and degree of security do not fit other environments	Legacy systems	• Varies widely

security procedures. These procedures should cover the initiation and continuous refining of the security organization and the program and initiatives it institutes. Expected elements include account, system, and code maintenance, configuration management, security testing, interconnections with other organizations, security data management, and incident response. The lack of documented procedures for any of these security activities could be considered a vulnerability in most medium- to large-sized organizations.

If the security risk assessment team (or the security risk assessment methodology) decides to include the step of determining expected controls, then these controls should be documented as the expected security program for the organization. Organizations within some regulated industries, such as the federal government, healthcare, and banking, will have some of these expected controls documented in the form of requirements. Do not confuse the required security activities in these regulations with the expected elements of a security program. Many regulations provide only a baseline of minimum standards; your security risk assessment team may determine that additions to the standards baseline are required.

Notes

1. This is not legal advice. You should consult with your own legal counsel on these matters.
2. A common security risk assessment obtained by outsourcing organizations is the SAS No. 70. This is a Statement of Accounting Standards (SAS) that specifies the security control objectives of the organization and their ability to enforce them. Security risk assessment teams reviewing the results of a SAS No. 70 review should pay special attention to the security control objectives as they can include or exclude any condition the audited organization wishes. Also be aware that SAS No. 70 risk assessments are typically more expensive than a standard risk assessment and are not required.
3. Nonadvertising marketing consists of the selling or renting of subscription lists.
4. The reader must be careful not to apply these categories with too much rigor. Again, this is a technique for gaining an understanding of a business mission and is meant to encourage a conversation between senior organization management and the security risk assessment team.
5. Clearly an in-depth understanding of a business or agency cannot be reduced to such simplistic terms. The understanding required by the security risk assessment team is not the same level of understanding required by those that have a fiduciary responsibility to the organization. An understanding of these key elements of the business, however, provides a level of understanding of the business objectives necessary to properly define the security requirements for the organization.

6. Throughout this book, examples and more in-depth descriptions of security risk assessment processes are provided to give the reader a better understanding of the process. This is not an attempt to create yet another security risk assessment process, nor an attempt to exhaustively survey all available methods. Instead this book is intended to provide the reader with practical advice for performing security risk assessments no matter what methodology is employed.

7. Within the business continuity planning process a business impact assessment (BIA) is performed. The BIA determines critical systems, assets required, and the maximum time down (MTD), which is defined as the maximum amount of time a critical business function can be interrupted without threatening the company's ability to survive.

*A more recent NIST Publication, NIST SP 800-60, provides updated and more detailed guidance on identifying "impact levels" for information systems in the areas of confidentiality, integrity, and availability. For Federal information systems this classification system is required. For others it is yet another example of how to determine protection requirements.

8. The identification of assets is also covered in section 3.2. The earlier discussion of asset identification was in relation to defining the project and scoping the assessment. Such lists of assets will tend to be on a high level such as "information assets only." In this section we discuss the identification of all such assets. For example, the security risk assessment team may be expected to develop a complete listing of all information assets.

9. The value of the class materials is based on a calculation of the present value of expected payments over five years. The present value function discounts expected payments using a discount rate of return.

10. Of course the relative possibility of threat statements is a subjective measure here. Furthermore, the security engineer must be careful not to exclude less likely threat statements that may be associated with wide-open vulnerabilities and large impacts. For example, just because a fire may only happen once in 20 years on average, does not mean that this threat is remote and should be ignored. Threats that should be ignored include those obvious ones such as the threat of a volcanic eruption in Austin, Texas.

11. One could also argue the opposite, that a larger facility that must deal with visitor control on a daily basis is more likely to have strong procedures and a culture of challenging visitors without badges or escorts, while a smaller facility with fewer visitors may be complacent. This is where engineering judgment comes in. The security risk assessment team must consider all relevant input in determining the validity of a threat statement. Again, this is another reason that checklist and tool-based security risk assessment approaches without expertise typically fail to accurately measure security risk.

12. A more recent NIST Publication, NIST SP 800-53, provides additional guidance/requirements for selecting controls based on the impact values for confidentiality, integrity, and availability. These controls encompass management controls (risk assessment, planning, system acquisition, assessment), operational controls (personnel, physical, contingency planning, configuration

management, maintenance, system integrity, media protection, incident response, and awareness), and technical controls (access controls, audit, and communication protection).

References

[1] *Management of Federal Information Resource*, The Office of Management and the Budget, Circular A-130, July 2, 1993.

[2] *The NIST Security Configuration Checklists Program*, NIST Special Publication 800-70, August 12, 2004. http://csrc.nist.gov/checklists/index.html

[3] *Guide for Developing Security Plans for Information Technology Systems*, NIST Special Publication 800-18, December 1998. http://csrc.nist.gov/publications/nistpubs/800-18/Planguide.PDF

[4] ASIS International, *Protection of Assets*, 2004.

[5] *Guide for Selecting Automated Risk Analysis Tools*, NIST Special Publication 500-174, October 1989. http://csrc.nist.gov/publications/nistpubs/500-174/sp174.txt

[6] Dalkey, N. C., "The Delphi Method: An Experimental Study of Group Opinion," Rand Corporation, RM-5888-PR, 1969.

[7] *General Support Systems and Major Applications Inventory Guide*, NIST Publications, July 2002. http://csrc.nist.gov/fasp/FASPDocs/risk-mgmt/GSSMA-Inventory-Guide.doc

[8] Guide for Mapping Types of Information and Information Systems to security categories, NIST special Publications 800-60, June 2004.

[9] *Energy Infrastructure Risk Management Checklists for Small and Medium Sized Energy Facilities*, Department of Energy, August 19, 2002.

[10] Milton, Thomas J., Rabe, James G., and Wilhoite, Charles, *Economic Analysis of Intangible Assets and Intellectual Properties*, 1999.

[11] Marshall, Alfred, *Principles of Economics*, 1920.

[12] *Guideline for Information Valuation* (GIV), Information System Security Association (ISSA), 1993.

[13] Recommended Security Controls for Federal Information Systems, NIST special Publication 800-53, February 2005.

Chapter 5

Data Gathering

No matter what security risk assessment method or tool is used, the data-gathering process is an essential step in the process. The scope of the data-gathering phase depends on the results of the project definition phase to define the system boundaries, controls, and assets to be reviewed, and the project preparation phase to ensure that the team's time on site collecting data will be effective and efficient. By the time the security risk assessment team begins the data-collection process, the necessary definitions and preparations have been completed.

Sidebar 5.1 Data Gathering: Tools versus Experience

One of the core activities performed during security risk assessments is the gathering of data. Data Gathering involves the discovery of vulnerabilities in existing security controls through examination and observation. By reviewing the security controls in their operating environment against the security requirements of the organization, the security risk assessment team is charged with identifying areas of weakness. Some security risk assessment tools and methods attempt to ensure the thoroughness of this effort through checklists and questionnaires. Although such tools and methods can help to guide this effort, there is no substitute for experience.

An experienced security engineer possesses two critical skills required for an effective data-gathering effort:

- **Application of information security principles.** The discovery and identification of vulnerabilities can be a complex process that involves the application of information security principles to situations not previously encountered. No matter how many times the team members have reviewed other organizations' security controls, there always seems to be something new. This may be new controls or simply a new application of an existing control. In these cases the security risk assessment team cannot fall back on a questionnaire or a checklist, but must assess the effectiveness of the security control based on well-understood security principles such as defense in depth, default deny all, and separation of duty. The application of these principles can often guide the assessment of new controls and result in a reliable conclusion. An over-reliance on checklists, questionnaires, and tools can leave the security risk assessment team flat-footed and unsure of the next step when they encounter anything new.
- **Observation techniques based on experience.** A good security engineer can probably spot 80 percent of the administrative and physical vulnerabilities in your organization by walking around the building and hanging out in the lounge. Such a cursory review of the administrative and physical security controls can later prove rather accurate because the security engineer knew what to look and listen for. This skill becomes developed over the course of years of experience in reviewing other organizations, finding flaws, and expanding observational skills based on that experience. Although checklists, questionnaires, and tools can help to guide the observations, experience proves much more flexible, efficient, and accurate.

Those attempting to perform security risk assessments based solely on the possession of a security risk assessment process description, checklists, and a few weeks' training should reconsider their approach. A better approach would be to contract out the security risk assessment to an objective and experienced team. Alternatively, the security risk assessment team could be bolstered by the inclusion of one or more experienced security engineers.

Performing a security risk assessment using a checklist without an appreciation for how the checklist was developed and the principles reflected in it, is doing so without an understanding of the security risks in the system. Is that not the whole reason for the security risk assessment in the first place?

Depending on the breadth of the scope of the security risk assessment, the data-gathering phase can cover administrative, physical, or technical controls or any combination. Depending on the rigor of the scope of the security risk assessment, the data-gathering phase can provide in-depth analysis of security controls or a rudimentary review. In either case, two important approaches can be utilized, no matter what the breadth or depth of the assessment, or even despite the security risk assessment methodology employed.[1] These two approaches are sampling and the RIIOT method of data-gathering.

5.1 Sampling

Any testing other than complete testing is referred to as representative testing or sampling. If less than 100 percent of the population is tested, then this is sampling. If the selection of a random sample is performed correctly, the testing is practically just as accurate as complete testing. Sample testing is performed when there is time, budget, geographic, or other constraints that preclude complete testing.

Before sampling techniques are presented, some key statistical terms and concepts need to be introduced. These concepts are required within the area of sampling and sample selection, but many concepts within security risk assessments require a working knowledge of statistics and data analysis and this knowledge is generally useful to any security risk assessment team member. Below are some key terms and concepts that the security risk assessment team member should understand:

- Population — A population is the entire set of items being studied, for example, all the marbles in a bag, all the invoices in a given year, all the people voting in an election, or all the network components in a network.
- Sample — If it is impossible or simply too costly to gain information regarding every element of a population, then we try to gain an understanding of the population based on a representative sample of the population. For example, in a poll regarding early voting conducted prior to the 2004 election, the Gallup organization sampled 1866 registered voters.

The poll showed that 21 percent planned to vote early and 77 percent planned to vote on Election Day. With a population of over 120 million voters, the Gallup organization was able to claim a 3 percent margin of error with a 95 percent certainty [www.gallup.com].

Sidebar 5.2 Sample Size

It is surprising to most people that the size of a sample selected from a population can be such a small percentage of the population yet still allow for accurate predictions regarding the entire population. For example, most political pollsters make predictions on the voting public based on 1200 to 1800 voters.

There is a specific formula that can be used to determine the sample size (*n*) required based on the population (*N*), the confidence level desired (*P*), and the expected number of deviations within the population (*x*):

$$n = N\left[\frac{1-P}{X}\right]$$

The table below provides the results of such a calculation for the confidence levels 99%, 95%, and 90%, and for sample sizes ranging from 1200 to 1800 voters.

	Sample size			
Confidence level	*1200*	*1400*	*1600*	*1800*
99% confidence	3.7%	3.4%	3.2%	3.0%
95% confidence	2.8%	2.6%	2.5%	2.3%
90% confidence	2.4%	2.2%	2.1%	1.9%

The objective of sampling is to make a statement regarding characteristics of the population based on testing a portion of it. A surprising degree of accuracy regarding the population can be gained using mathematical methods to select a random sample and performing testing on the sample. Some even argue that sampling provides a more accurate measurement of the population, because it can be shown to have a high degree of confidence and sampling the entire population can lead to mistakes because of the tediousness of the process.

- Accuracy — The accuracy of a sampling technique can be measured and reported. The mathematical terms used to indicate accuracy are as follows:
  - Standard Deviation — This is a dispersion measurement, that is, the distance of all values from the arithmetic mean (average). The actual formula for standard deviation is

$$S = \sqrt{\frac{\sum (X - \overline{X})^2}{n}}$$

This formula measures all samples and their distance from the mean. In order for larger distance from the mean to count more, the differences are squared.
  - Confidence Level — This is an accuracy measurement, that is, the probability that the results of the sample testing are representative of the testing for the overall population. Specifically, the confidence level is the probability that any given element of the population will fall close to the average number (i.e., within a number of standard deviations). If a sample is a representative sample (i.e., a random sample) and the data exhibits a normal (i.e., bell-shaped) distribution, then we can assume the following:
    - ~68 percent of the observations are within one standard deviation of the mean.
    - ~95 percent of the observations are within two standard deviations of the mean.
    - ~99.7 percent of the observations are within three standard deviations of the mean.

    In many polls and surveys the confidence level itself is not implicitly expressed, but it should be at least above an 90 percent confidence level. The results of the polls and surveys are typically expressed as "plus or minus" a specific measurement. For example, "58 percent of those polled will vote for candidate X, plus or minus 3 percent." The specific measure (3 percent in this case) is two standard deviations from the mean measurement (in this case 58 percent) if the confidence level is 95 percent.

5.1.1 Sampling Objectives

Sampling techniques can be used for several different objectives. Depending upon the objective of the test, different sample techniques are more appropriate than others.

- Discovery (Exploratory) Sampling — Discovery sampling is used to uncover fraud or find a single instance of an infraction, error, or irregularity. Such a discovery would typically call for a more intensive investigation.

- Unit Sampling — Unit sampling is used when the tester wants to determine a characteristic or value of the population within a degree of confidence. This type of sampling is meant to answer the "How much?" or "How many?" questions regarding the population, for example, the value of inventories, or error rates of controls.

5.1.2 Sampling Types

There are two basic types of samples: probability samples and judgment samples. *Probability samples* are selected at random through the use of a random technique such as a random number table. *Judgment samples* are selected by any other technique and are based on the selector's judgment. It is impossible to draw statistically relevant conclusions about characteristics of the population based on judgment samples, because these samples are not statistically representative and contain bias. For this reason, the remaining sampling techniques are all probability samples.

- Simple Sampling — This sampling technique involves the use of a random selection of sample units from a population. For example, if you were to select 20 random employees from a company of 2000 by using a random number generator to generate 20 numbers between 1 and 2000 and selected 20 employees associated by their employee number.
- Systematic (Interval) Sampling — This sampling technique is based on a systematic approach to selecting sample units from the population. For example, to choose 20 employees from a company of 2000, a systematic approach could (a) divide the population into 100 sampling intervals, (b) select a random number between 1 and 100 (e.g., 37), or (c) choose the employee associated with the first random number and every 37th employee in each interval (i.e, 137, 237, 337, etc.). Systematic sampling is a simple approach that approximates random sampling and can be used if the order of the population has no relevance to the characteristics of the data being measured. For example, if you were measuring the salary or time at the company, it is clear that low-numbered employees will have been with the company longer and more likely that very low employee numbers correspond with higher-level positions and therefore are more likely to earn more salary.
- Stratified Sampling — This sampling technique is based on the grouping of similar sample units into strata. This technique is useful when there is a potentially large variation between strata but a small variation within each stratum. Stratified sampling allows the observer to make different observations about each stratum.
- Cluster Sampling — This sampling technique selects clusters of sample units from the population to create a representative sample. Cluster

sampling provides convenience for the surveyor in terms of proximity of sample units. For example, if it was determined that a vulnerability scan must scan 10 percent of the 500 IP addresses within a network, it would be easier to scan 5 groups of 10 IP addresses than 50 individual IP addresses.[2] On the other hand, such a restriction in selection may skew the randomness of the sample if the proximity of IP addresses has relevance to the characteristic of the population being measured.

- Multistage Sampling — This sampling technique combines cluster sampling and simple sampling. Cluster sampling is used to determine the clusters of sample units and simple sampling is used to determine sample units within the cluster. The Gallup organization uses multistage sampling in the typical Gallup poll.

5.1.3 Use of Sampling in Security Testing

Sampling can be an excellent technique for gathering representative security test data about a large number of network components. If the sample is selected correctly, then testing a small sample of the population can provide the security tester with the information regarding the network that's required for the security risk assessment. Proper selection of the sample, however, can be difficult and should only be undertaken by someone with an understanding of the basic principles of statistical sampling. Several approaches for selecting a security test sample are described below.

5.1.3.1 Approach 1: Representative Testing

Within many information systems there exist several components that are replicated many times. For example, in many information systems a user workstation is created for each user in a department and is identical in terms of connectivity, operating system, configuration, and applications. Except for the data stored on the system, these systems are the same. If an information system consists of 20 file servers, 5 Web servers, 3 e-mail servers, and 800 workstations, a representative sampling approach would select to test a representation from each group (e.g., 4 file servers, 2 Web servers, 3 e-mail servers, and 50 workstations).

The advantage of representative sampling is cost savings and a reduction in repetitive data. Time and money are conserved through reducing the number of machines that would be tested. Repetitive data is reduced since it is highly unlikely that a scan of the other 750 workstations would yield any different security risk findings.[3]

The disadvantage of representative sampling is that in cases where the system components are different, the lack of testing may indeed miss a security risk finding. For example, if one of the file servers is dedicated to external users and it was not the file server chosen for scanning, some significant security risk findings could be overlooked.

5.1.3.2 Approach 2: Selected Sampling

Selected sampling is the technique of choosing areas of the infrastructure to test based on a belief that they may contain vulnerabilities. Since it is not possible to test all areas of the infrastructure or all components within the information system, the assessor would choose the test sample based on the perceived likelihood that these specific components may contain vulnerabilities. For example, out of the 50 workstations to test within an information system, the assessor selectively samples the following 30 workstations:

- 10 workstations from the IT department.
- 5 workstations from the R&D department.
- 5 workstations from those who work on the night shift.
- 5 workstations from the help desk.
- 3 workstations for executive administrators.
- 2 workstations used as guest computers.

The advantage of selective sampling includes the same advantages of representative sampling, namely, cost savings and a reduction in repetitive data. An additional (possible) advantage of selective sampling is that the selected sample may be more likely to identify vulnerabilities that may have been overlooked through other sampling techniques. This last advantage is true only if the sample is selected wisely.

The disadvantage of selective sampling comes into play if the sample is not selected wisely. The assessor should be careful to choose areas that are likely to contain vulnerabilities, but should also balance that with the recognition that vulnerabilities can turn up in unexpected places. If you only look for them in expected areas you are not likely to uncover them.

5.1.3.3 Approach 3: Random Sampling

Random sampling is a technique of choosing areas to test based on a random selection of test subjects. In true random sampling there is no bias toward or away from any area. The advantage of random sampling is that the test sample is unbiased and results from the sample can be used to make statistical conclusions.[4] The disadvantages of random sampling include the difficulty of choosing a truly random sample. To correctly choose a random sample the selection process must be free of bias. This activity requires an understanding of statistics and survey principles, a skill that may not be present on the security risk assessment team.

5.2 The RIIOT Method of Data Gathering

During the data-gathering phase the security risk assessment team will apply various techniques such as document review interviews, observation, design review, and physical and technical testing. This phase of the security risk assessment process is at the heart of the process and involves volumes of data, scores of activities, and many hours of effort. The data-gathering phase is perhaps the most labor-intensive phase of the security risk assessment process and covers all of the organization's security controls within the boundaries of the project. Despite the complexity of this phase of the security risk assessment process, few tools or methods have been developed that assist in the planning, performance, and coordination of these activities.[5]

The RIIOT approach to data-gathering is a method for attacking the problem of gathering data on a wide variety of controls using a seemingly endless number of tools and techniques. The RIIOT method simply breaks down the process of data-gathering into one of five different approaches. Within any given security risk assessment or any given area of assessment, some combination of these approaches may be taken to obtain data.

5.2.1 RIIOT Method Benefits

The value of breaking the task of data-gathering into the RIIOT approaches is as follows:

- Organization — The RIIOT approach helps to organize the data-gathering effort. This organization is useful within the data-gathering, analysis, and presentation steps of the security risk assessment process.
- Project Management — The RIIOT approach enables the definition and management of multiple tasks within the data-gathering phase. Each approach can be assigned to different resources and progress can be tracked individually.
- Coverage — The RIIOT approach helps the planners of the security risk assessment data-gathering effort to ensure that there is appropriate coverage of the threats and safeguards. An approach that uses only one of the RIIOT approaches without consideration for other approaches of gathering data is likely to fail to uncover key vulnerabilities.

5.2.2 RIIOT Method Approaches

The RIIOT method comprises five different approaches to data-gathering and can be applied to the administrative, physical, or technical areas. The RIIOT method approaches are as follows:

- Review Documents — The security risk assessment team reviews documents regarding the rules, configurations, layouts, architectures, and other elements of the security controls. All available and relevant documents may be reviewed and can include policies, procedures, network maps, site layouts, backup schedules, and security awareness training slides.

- Interview Key Personnel The security risk assessment team interviews key personnel to determine their ability to perform their duties (as stated in policies), their implementation of duties not stated in policies, and observations or concerns they have with current security controls.

- Inspect Security Controls — The security risk assessment team members inspect specific implemented security controls such as visitor control, configuration files, smoke detectors, and incident response handling. These controls can be inspected against industry standards, specific checklists of common vulnerabilities, or by using experience and judgment.

- Observe Personnel Behavior — The security risk assessment team members will observe the behavior of users, the security protective force, visitors, and others during the course of the assessment. These observations can provide keen insight into the effectiveness of the security controls in place.

- Test Security Controls — The security risk assessment team members will test specific security controls such as firewalls, servers, open-door alarms, and motion sensors. Almost all security risk assessment methods currently account for this approach. Testing involves the use of vulnerability scanners for logical security controls, but also specific methods for physical controls such as the shuffle test for motion sensors.

Each of the RIIOT approaches is described in more detail below. Additional guidance for performing each of these RIIOT approaches is contained within each section.

5.2.2.1 Review Documents or Designs

The first approach in the RIIOT data-gathering is reviewing documents or designs. The process of reviewing documents to gather data for the security risk assessment involves knowing which documents to request and how to review the documents for adequacy. The process of reviewing designs to gather data for the security risk assessment involves an understanding of basic design principles and how to recognize their application, or lack of application.

But first the member of the security risk assessment team assigned to review documents or designs must have an appreciation for the importance of security documentation. Reviewing information security documents and designs may be considered a "desk job," meaning that it can be performed without reviewing the IT infrastructure or the facilities. However, it is useful for this review to be performed on site (or at least followed up on site) so that the effectiveness of these policies can be ascertained. For now the review of these documents and designs only concerns the existence of statements and not whether or not those statements are being followed.

5.2.2.1.1 The Importance of Security Documents

Many security engineers come to the profession through a steady succession of accomplishments from a technology-centric discipline, for example, systems administration, or programming. Perhaps because of this experience, many information security engineers fail to understand the importance of documents — policies and procedures. Before discussing the review of documents provided by the organization to be assessed, it is useful to stress the importance of policies and procedures in the establishment and governance of a security program. The absence of solid, complete, and articulate security policies can be the root cause of many security vulnerabilities.

Security policies and procedures are the cornerstone of information security and the most important element of the security program for any organization. Without security policies we may have strong security mechanisms implemented, but the policies they attempt to enforce will be a mixture of guesswork and confusion. Although the tenets of information security (confidentiality, integrity, availability) seem rather straightforward, the application of these tenets can be quite complex (see Sidebar 5.3). Effective information security policies can clarify the security objectives of the organization and ensure that security controls are enforcing a clear security policy.

Sidebar 5.3 Do We Really Need Security Policies: Isn't Security Just Common Sense?

While advising an Internet start-up with more money than time, I was pressured to skip the normal approach of designing security from the ground up. The customer was adamantly opposed to the process step of creating security policies prior to advising on the selection of security mechanisms for a soon to be released health insurance information Web service. After much discussion, the customer agreed to a short ten-minute conversation regarding the importance of a security policy prior to first step.

The conversation was brief and illustrative of the importance of these documents. Below is an approximation of the conversation as it happened:

Customer: OK, so why do we need a security policy? This stuff is rather simple and my programmers are ready to get started.

Consultant: I'm not sure the security policy is that simple at all. In fact, I believe that, without making the access control rules clear, your programmers will likely implement a solution that violates several federal and state laws.

Customer: Oh come on. It couldn't be simpler. If it is your information or your family's then you can see it and if it isn't you can't. Write that down — that's your policy — are we done?

Consultant: Hold on a minute. Let me ask a few clarifying questions to ensure I understand.

- What if you are legally separated from your spouse but still paying their medical bills, could you view their records then?
- What if you are given legal guardianship for a child, can you view their records prior to when you retained guardianship?
- What if you had an eighteen-year-old daughter enrolled in an out-of-state college but still under your health insurance; in what states are you allowed viewing of her health records for treatment at school? Does it matter where you live vs. where the service was performed?
- What if you pay cash for a treatment or test and don't claim insurance coverage; can the insurance company request to view those records or results?

Customer: Uh, I don't know.

Consultant: I don't know either, but we can start compiling this information, determining the attributes we need in the record to determine access, and decide if we want to limit this service to certain states.

At this point the customer decided that he needed to rethink his entire business process and ultimately decided to change the direction of the company to supplying information to doctors on medical procedures. It is not that such a business should not be tackled but that it should be well planned. It is important to identify the assumptions, obstacles, and requirements of the endeavor during the planning stage in order to properly plan and budget the project. Ignoring this type of planning does not make obstacles go away; it only postpones them until they surface painfully.

A security policy is not only a statement of the organization's security rules, but also a plan for behavior of the organization's systems and personnel. Organizations that create and install information systems or create departments and assign responsibilities without first planning the security with a set of security policies will soon learn of the painful surfacing of security issues.

5.2.2.1.2 Documents to Request

The security risk assessment team should request any document that may contain information relating to an administrative security control. It would be great if every organization had neatly titled documents that led the team directly to a description of a security control or policy; however, this is seldom the case. The team must be clear in its request for information by specifying the documents it requires through examples and a description of its contents. The assessed organization may find it necessary to provide multiple documents to cover the contents of what may typically be a single document. For example, many organizations have a single acceptable use policy that is given to all employees upon hiring. However, some organizations have multiple documents covering what is typically contained in a single acceptable use policy (e.g., e-mail use policy, software use policy, network use policy). Prior to arriving on site, the security risk assessment team should request all documents relevant to security controls at the organization.

5.2.2.1.3 Policy Review within Regulated Industries

Many organizations within regulated industries may have policies developed for them or dictated to them from others, especially federal government agencies. In these cases it may not be necessary to review security policies as they have already been crafted by another entity and considered adequate for the threat environment of that organization. For example, within the federal government the Federal Information Security Management Act (FISMA) provides minimum security standards for federal agency information systems. The FISMA is itself a policy that requires annual risk assessments, the appointment of a security official, and mandatory adherence to NIST guidelines, among many other requirements. The point here is that the policies for a federal agency have been developed outside that particular agency. In this case, the security risk assessment team should have a member familiar with federal agency information security requirements.

Other regulated industries may have portions of what is required for information security policies. For example, both HIPAA and the GLB Act require annual security awareness training. This is considered a security policy element. However, neither of these acts provides a security policy covering acceptable use policy statements. The security risk assessment team should have a member familiar with the information security requirements for the specific industry, including what these regulations do and do not cover in terms of providing security policy.

5.2.2.1.4 RIIOT Document Review Technique

The following guideline provides the RIIOT technique for reviewing information security documents. The RIIOT technique can be used with any set of security document requirements, standards, or guidelines. The technique simply provides structure and process to an otherwise loosely structured process. Figure 5.1 depicts the RIIOT technique for reviewing documents. The technique is described in more detail below:

- Review Documents for Clarity — The security risk assessment team members should read through all policy documents to determine if they are clear and understandable. The team member must be sure to review the document from the perspective of the intended audience and not from their own perspective. For example, when reviewing security awareness training material, consider that the intended audience is not likely to have a technical understanding of the security controls they are asked to use. The assessors should use experience and judgment to determine if the governance and guidance is clear and free from unknown acronyms and technical jargon, and unambiguous.
- Review Documents for Content — The security risk assessment team members should analyze the document of each policy and procedure document. Concentration on this task is on the completeness and correctness of the documents, and consistency between governance and guidance.
  - Completeness — The assessor should review the documents for set completeness and internal completeness. The set completeness review ensures that the document set includes the entire set of policies i.e. Acceptable use policy business cataloging security testing, etc. The internal completeness review ensures that all of the appropriate areas are addressed within each document. Appropriate areas are defined based on the threat environment, business objectives, and criticality of assets for the specific organization. The assessor can start with a

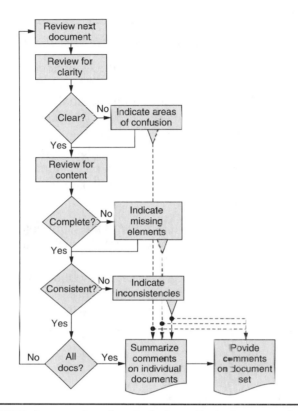

Figure 5.1   RIIOT document review technique. Each cocument is reviewed for clarity to the intended audience, completeness as measured against a standard, and consistency with other documents. Comments are provided on the complete documentation set and the individual documents.

checklist but should modify the checklist to meet the needs of the specific security risk assessment. Table 5.1 provides an example of using a template of expected elements in a completeness review.

- Correctness and Consistency — The assessor of the security policies should also review the documents with an eye on the correctness and consistency of the policies. The team member should ensure that policy statements are technically feasible, consistent with applicable regulations, and consistent with other policies and procedures.
- Indicate Coverage of Expected Elements — The assessor should review each document provided by checking off expected elements as they are located. Be sure to record where each element was found and in what document.
- Record Gaps — The team member should then compile a report showing the difference between the organization's current document set and the expected document set. This report should be organized according to the organization's document set and not the expected document set (see Figure 5.2).

Sidebar 5.4 Evidence Tracking and Recording

It is important to collect and retain the evidence for all data gathered during a security risk assessment. Evidence is used to support the claims made during the analysis portion of the security risk assessment process. Although this may sound like a lot of extra work, proper evidence collection and tracking does not place an undue burden on the project. Instead, collecting and tracking evidence properly can actually reduce the effort required to perform a security risk assessment.

- Easy to do if you do it while you are gathering data.
- Provides better data upon which to make judgments. It is easier to assess the value or certainty of data if you know how you got it, i.e., somebody said this as opposed to we found this vulnerability.
- Provides a way to avoid arguments with the customer.

5.2.2.2 Interview Key Personnel

The second approach in the RIIOT data-gathering is interviewing key personnel. Interviews are conversations guided by a member of the security risk assessment team with key staff members in order to gain additional information on security controls and input on the security risk assessment process. The objectives of conducting interviews include the following:

- Confirmation of threat identification, asset valuation, and critical system identification.
- Confirmation of security procedure execution.
- Measurement of security awareness among staff.
- Identification of vulnerabilities in the area of the interviewee's expertise.

Interviews can provide an incredible amount of information in a short amount of time. However, information gained during the interview should be considered as a single data point regarding vulnerabilities. Some findings from interviews are considered "hearsay" and should be confirmed through follow-up activities. Other findings, such as a lack of security awareness, can be considered "direct evidence." The process of conducting interviews to gather data for the security risk assessment involves selecting the interviewer(s), preparing for the interview, and the interview process itself.

Sidebar 5.5 Interviews: Limitations

It is essential that the security risk assessment team understand the limitations of the interview process. Information gathered during an interview should be considered as a way to identify areas for further study. Findings should not be based solely on the interview process.

This is a significant difference from other types of data-gathering. Findings such as the absence of an acceptable use policy, lack of separation of duty in the security organization reporting structure, and vulnerabilities found in the Web server, can all stand on their own as a security risk assessment finding. No further corroboration is needed since the finding is self-evident.

Findings resulting from an interview, however, should be followed up through additional data-gathering activities. The reason such findings cannot stand on their own is that both the interviewer and the interviewee are fallible.

The interviewer can make mistakes through misinterpretation of the questions or the answers provided, or through misreporting what was said. Many security risk assessments are performed by teams with relatively little experience. In these situations, the likelihood that a question or the answer provided is misinterpreted is greatly increased. Even experienced information security professionals can misinterpret what is said by the interviewee.

The interviewee can make mistakes as well. It is quite typical that the interviewee is unfamiliar with many of the terms used within the interview process, or the interviewee may have a different understanding of the question than the interviewer does. In these cases the answer provided may not be accurate. Also, interviewees tend to be eager to please and will attempt to answer questions as much as they can. This process leads to guessing and "filling in the blanks." Again, this can result in inaccurate answers.

There are some security risk assessments that rely solely on questionnaires and interviews. The results of these risk assessments are completely contingent on the accuracy of the interview process and should be viewed with the appropriate degree of skepticism. In order to remove skepticism from your security risk assessment process, it is necessary to corroborate interview results with other data-gathering activities.

Table 5.1   Expected Elements Completeness Review Example. Each document that covers any of the business continuity expected elements is indicated in the chart. Once all documents have been reviewed, overlap and gaps can be more readily detected.

Policy Area	Expected Elements	Business Continuity	
		Relevant Policy	*Comments*
Responsibilities	Responsibility assigned	Security group charter BCP initiative document	Security group charter and BCP document have inconsistent roles assigned
Disaster recovery	Recovery strategy Recovery procedures Plan administration		
Business continuity planning	Business continuity strategy Business impact analysis Emergency response procedures Crisis management Plan administration Plan maintenance and testing	Latest risk assessment Physical security handbook PR handbook	Handbook covers physical threats only Media handling well covered

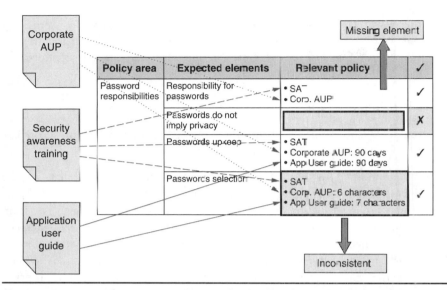

Figure 5.2 RIIOT document review method. All policies should be reviewed for content and mapped to an expected elements table. Once all documents are mapped the completed expected elements table can be used to note missing elements and inconsistent policies.

5.2.2.2.1 Selecting the Interviewer

Interviews should not necessarily be conducted by anyone on the security risk assessment team. Performing one-on-one interviews is a difficult process and requires skills of perception, tact, and experience. This is true in almost all interview situations, but is especially true during a security risk assessment. Interviews conducted within the security risk assessment process can be difficult for a number of reasons:

- Cynicism or suspicion on the part of the interviewee.
- Use of unfamiliar terms and jargon (on the part of both parties).
- Difficulty in correctly recording information.

The security risk assessment team should carefully consider the selection of team members who will conduct these interviews to ensure that the data-gathering process goes well. A good interviewer must be able to put the interviewee at ease, use familiar terms and seek clarification for unfamiliar terms, and be able to fluidly explore topics and possible findings. Although some of these skills can be taught, others are more prevalent among people with certain character traits. Furthermore, the greatest teacher is experience.

> **Warning:** Among all the other criteria for selecting interviewers, the security risk assessment team must also be careful to ensure that the

interviewer can be objective and free from conflict of interest concerns. One such concern is the relationship between the interviewer and the interviewee. The interviewer must not interview co-workers, superiors, or subordinates.

5.2.2.2.2 Preparing for the Interview

To conduct a successful and fruitful interview, the interviewer must prepare properly. Preparation involves the following items:

- Determine Interview Subjects — Based on the areas that require investigation, the security risk assessment team must select the subjects and business function areas that they would like to investigate. The team must carefully consider project time constraints and even and adequate coverage of all relevant areas when developing a list of interview subjects.
- Determine Interviewing Team — Following the advice of the previous section, the security risk assessment project leader must select appropriate team members to conduct interviews. Interviews should be conducted as one-on-one meetings, or at most a two-on-one meeting, to reduce suspicion and increase the candidness of the interview conversations. The security risk assessment team will need to determine the most effective number of interviewers for their specific environment. The benefit of having multiple team members is to have a witness to the information and therefore provide more robust observations. The benefit of having a smaller interview team is the reduced effort required to conduct the interview and more candid responses that may be ellicited. Since recording of information can be a burden on the interviewer and distract from the flow of the conversation, the team should consider the inclusion of a transcriber in the interview process. If a transcriber is used, they should strive to limit their interference in the interview process by sitting away from the conversation and quietly recording the responses of the interviewee.
- Review Relevant Documents — The objective of this activity is to obtain an understanding of the interviewee's position, responsibilities, concerns, and likely questions. Proper preparation for an interview includes the review of information relevant to the interviewee's function within the organization. Just as a potential employer reads a candidate's résumé prior to conducting an interview, the assessment team's interviewer must familiarize themselves with the security controls and functions relevant to the interviewee and their position within the organization. Relevant documents include, but are not limited to, security policies and procedures, business function descriptions, job descriptions, and organization charts.
- Determine Objective of the Interview — Although all interviews are designed to gain additional information on security controls, the specific objective of individual interviews can vary greatly. These objectives should

be determined by the security risk assessment team for each interview. The points below can be used as a guideline for interviewing different positions:

- Staff Members — The objective of these interviews is to determine the security awareness of the general staff within the organization.
- Key Personnel — The objective of these interviews is to confirm execution of documented procedures and draw out perceived vulnerabilities.

- Determine the Type of Interview to Be Conducted — There are several types of interviews that are appropriate for use within the security risk assessment. Each of these types has its own benefits and drawbacks. These interview types include the following:
  - Guided Interview — This type of interview is based on a standard set of questions. The advantage of this type of interview is that the answers can be more easily standardized and summarized. If the interview team plans to perform a lot of evaluations, this technique may be valuable.
  - Fixed Response — The interview technique consists of questions for which there are "yes," "no," or numbered answers. This technique may be used effectively in interview efforts that involve numerous responses and therefore require the compilation of many responses to draw conclusions. The interviewer should construct the interview questions to use consistent questions for each respondent and use common scales and definitions.
  - Conversational Interview — This type of interview has no set format and can be useful in obtaining a wide variety of information. The ability to put the interviewee at ease can elicit responses and information that may not have been forthcoming using other interview techniques.
  - Open-Ended Interview — This type of interview is based on a set of open-ended questions. These questions do not solicit "yes" or "no" answers but ask the interview subject to discuss an issue. These interviews are also effective at getting the interview subject to talk more about information security issues and reveal more information than the standard guided or fixed response interviews.

5.2.2.2.3 Conducting the Interview

The interview itself can result in an incredible amount of information if it is conducted properly. There is a lot of advice concerning how to conduct a successful interview. Below is a compilation of that advice as it applies to the security risk assessment process.

- Establish a Productive Environment — The forum for the interview should allow for a distraction-free conversation. The best approach is to acquire a small conference room reserved for the interviews. When interviews are conducted within the interviewee's office they may be interrupted by phone calls and other distractions.

- Put the Interviewee at Ease During the Introduction — The quality and quantity of responses from the interview subject can be greatly increased by putting them at ease during the interview introduction.
    - The interviewer should introduce themselves to the interview subject and explain the purpose of the interview.
    - It should be made clear that the security risk assessment, and therefore the interview itself, are planning tools and not report cards.
    - The interviewer should explain the degree of confidentiality they can provide for information obtained during the interview and the intended use of the information. If no confidentiality can be promised — don't. The decision to provide confidentiality has the tradeoff of the advantage of additional information gathered and the disadvantage of not being able to link findings to specific evidence.
    - The interviewer should explain the format and timeframe of the interview. Make it clear that the interview subject will have time at the end of the interview to ask any questions of the interviewer. If the interviewer is using a transcriber, the transcriber should be introduced. If the interviewer plans to use recording equipment during the interview, permission needs to be obtained. Lastly, the interviewer should leave contact information so that the interviewee can provide additional information at a later time if something comes to mind.
- Use Various Question Types to Elicit Required Response — The interviewer should be familiar with the different types of questions and use them appropriately to control the interview and guide the interview subject into providing relevant information.
    - Knowledge Questions — This type of question seeks to gather specific knowledge from the interview subject. The objective is to better understand security controls for which adequate documentation may not exist.

        Example: "Please explain your process for applying security patches to production systems."

    - Behavioral Questions — These questions ask the interview subject to indicate their behavior in certain situations. The objective of this type of question is to determine actual behavior and an understanding of how security controls are implemented and operated.

        Example: "Please explain the steps performed the last time a security patch was applied to a production system."

- Opinion Questions — These questions ask the interview subject their opinion on certain matters. The objective is to solicit their perspective or judgment regarding a specific security control

    Example: "Do you believe that your security patch management process is effective?"

- Arrange Question Order — The interviewer should arrange the questions in an order that will result in the most effective interview session. Considerations for question arrangement include:
    - Ask Fact-Based Questions First — These questions are easy to answer and can break the ice. Getting the interview subject to start talking early on can lead to better and more in-depth answers for questions later in the interview.
    - Start with the Familiar — Questions regarding present behaviors should be asked first before moving on to questions regarding past or future behaviors. Bouncing around a timeline can become confusing and lead to inaccurate responses.
- Carefully Word Questions — The interviewer should spend some time ensuring that the wording of the questions is in line with the objective of the interview. Considerations for interview question wording include:
    - Use Standard Terminology — The questions should be free of terminology that is not well understood by both parties. The interviewer should be on the lookout for perceived misunderstandings and have a standard set of definitions available.
    - Use Straightforward Questions — The questions and their delivery should be neutral, nonjudgmental, and nonleading.
- Elicit Candid Responses — Although it may not be obvious, the behavior of the interview team can greatly influence the candidness of responses from the interview subject. The following behaviors of the interview team should be considered:
    - Show Limited Emotion — Don't show emotion when asking questions or hearing answers. Security risk assessment team members may find it difficult not to show surprise, disappointment, empathy, or even amusement. Also be careful not to emphasize the note-taking process.
    - Show Appreciation — Nonverbal communication such as head nodding and an occasional "uh-huh" can keep the conversation going.
    - Be Patient — Just prior to revealing insightful information, many respondents pause sometimes for what seems to be a long time. Wait — own the silence, be comfortable with the pause — the good stuff is coming.

- Provide Transitions — When moving from one topic to another, be clear that your questioning has changed direction. For example, "Moving on to…."

Sidebar 5.6 Interviewing: Tricks of the Trade

Performing interviews effectively can be a complex process. The difference in results from an experienced and skilled interviewer and an inexperienced interviewer can be quite substantial. Although much of this skill will come in time as more interviews are performed, the following tricks of the trade are offered as a jumpstart to those who may structure and perform interviews as a part of a security risk assessment:

- *Test questionnaires and checklists.* If your interview process involves a pre-test questionnaire or a checklist for the interviewer, it is a good idea to perform a pilot test of the interview aide. A pilot test will help determine the clarity and coverage of the questions and lead to the development of the better questionnaire and interview process.
- *Dress like the interview subject.* If you will be interviewing executives you should wear a suit. If you are interviewing staff members you should wear business casual. Dressing reasonably alike puts the interviewee somewhat at ease.
- *Beliefs vs. behaviors.* Beliefs and behaviors often do not match. Someone may hold a certain belief but practice differently. For example, someone may state they believe in ethics and integrity but illegally download songs. Here are some approaches to get to the bottom of how people actually behave:
  - Ask a hypothetical question. Example: "If someone was to steal a check and pay themselves, how would this behavior be detected?"
  - Ask about specific behaviors. Examples, pick a specific security patch and ask about when the patch was applied, ask if they have ever challenged an unescorted visitor, ask if they have ever seen the telephone closet open.
- *Probing.* If the interviewee defines or defends behavior based on an existing policy or on orders of another,

ask if they always do what is in the policy. You
will likely get a "no." Then follow up by asking for a
specific instance where a policy was not followed.

5.2.2.2.4 Documenting the Interview

The results of the interview must be recorded for evidence and for sharing
with the rest of the security risk assessment team. The interviewer or transcriber
should be certain to record the name, position, and contact information of the
interviewee as well as the time, date, and location of the interview. Notes should
be compiled and reviewed by the interview team as soon as possible. It is suggested
that you schedule occasional breaks from interviews for his purpose. If this is not
possible, notes should at least be reviewed and compiled by the end of the day.

5.2.2.2.5 Flexibility in the Process

Recall that the interview is a data-gathering tool and is designed to confirm under-
standings of security controls, measure security awareness, or identify additional
areas to review. The team's understanding of these controls becomes more astute as
the security risk assessment progresses, therefore the interview process must be
flexible and fluid.

Flexibility is required because the team's understanding of the security controls
is still incomplete. The topics covered and the questions asked in the interview
should depend on the findings from these other activities. Following a questionnaire that was developed prior to digesting available information can be ineffective
and make the interviewer and the team seem inexperienced. For this reason, the
team and the interviewer need to be flexible when developing a set of questions
for each of the key personnel to be interviewed.

Fluidity is required because the interview process is an interactive process.
The interviewer should react (not emotionally) to the answers to the questions
and modify lines of questions accordingly to gain the most useful knowledge for
the assessment.

5.2.2.2.6 Questionnaire Preparation

The development of a set of interview questions depends heavily on the security
risk assessment method, scope, and budget being applied. Many security risk
assessment methods (at least those that depend heavily on questionnaires and
surveys) have a predeveloped set of questions to be asked. When performing a

security risk assessment without a predeveloped set of questions, the security risk assessment team will need to develop their own set.

Specific questions should be developed based on the approach, style, and format of the interview process. The interviewer should also consider the security controls for which there is a lack of information. For example, if the security risk assessment team is unable to find an adequate termination procedure, the interview of the human resources director, the facilities manager, and the IT director should include questions regarding protection of assets upon termination of employment. Table 5.2 provides some sample topics that should likely be covered for different key personnel.

5.2.2.3 Inspect Security Controls

The third approach in the RIIOT data gathering is inspecting security controls. Inspections are performed when security testing would be infeasible, ill-advised, or out of scope. For example, it is appropriate for the security risk assessment team to inspect a fire control system (i.e., examine the controls in place) but not to test it (i.e., light a fire in a trashcan and see how long it takes for a Halon discharge).

Many security controls, especially physical security controls, do not lend themselves well to the testing process. The testing of some security controls could possibly disrupt the organizational mission; if security testing were your only option, vulnerabilities within these security controls may go unnoticed. For this reason it is important for the security risk assessment team to consider using the inspection approach of the RIIOT method. A security risk assessment that skips the inspection stage because it is inappropriate to test the security controls can leave out significant vulnerabilities in the security controls protecting the organization's assets and therefore result in an inaccurate measurement of risk.

The objective of the "inspect security controls" approach is to verify the information gathered during the document review and interview approaches. Specific inspection techniques will be discussed in the administrative, physical, and technical data-gathering sections (chapter 6, 7, and 8). The following steps provide general guidelines for the inspection approach:

- List Security Controls — Obtain or create a list of the security controls under review. Such a list can be requested, obtained during the interview process, or compiled through observation during a site tour. The list of security controls should list the security control, specific model number or configuration information, its objective, interfaces to other security controls, and the point of contact for further information.
- Verify Information Gathered — The information gathered in the security controls list, interviews, and other RIIOT approaches can be confirmed

Table 5.2   Sample Interview Questions for Key Personnel. Each document that covers any of the business continuity expected elements is indicated in the chart. Once all documents have been reviewed, overlap and gaps can be more readily detected.

System Development Staff Interview Questions		
Objective	Key Topics	Example Questions
Determine existence and adequacy of security controls within system development	• Separation of duty	Who develops system (or new code) and who is responsible for putting it into production?
	• Define security requirements	How are security requirements defined and what groups are involved in the development? How are they documented?
	• System security plan	How is assurance gained for systems with security requirements? For example, system documentation, threat assessment, vulnerability assessment, penetration testing, etc.
	• Operations plan	How are the required security activities (e.g., audit procedures, backup, monitoring) and security requirements for operating the system conveyed to those who will operate the system?
	• Plan approval	Who approves the system requirements, system security plan, and operations plan?
	• Accreditation decision	Who decides to "turn the system on?" Who "owns" the risk? Is this a formal and documented process?

Table 5.3 Sample Inspection Checklist. When inspecting security lighting systems, the assessor should inspect their ability to control sabotage, single points of failure, and access to critical components.

Security Lighting Inspection Checklist		
Objective	*Key Topics*	*Example Questions*
Determine existence and adequacy of security controls within lighting system	Sabotage	Tour areas critical to lighting systems to determine susceptibility to sabotage Switchyards Transformers Circuit breakers Power lines Engine generators UPSs
	Single point of failure	Inspect lighting system to determine if security lighting systems have any single points of failure Single lighting circuit Power supply on a single circuit breaker Single power grid
	Access control	Inspect access controls on areas containing lighting system components

through inspection. Security risk assessment team members will find that many of the procedures, mechanisms, and other security controls mentioned in documents and interviews may not operate as described or even be completely missing.[6]

- Determine Vulnerabilities — The goal of the inspection is to ensure that vulnerabilities of the security controls are discovered. The security risk assessment team should have at least one member who has experience and knowledge with the security controls to be inspected. Those with experience can likely determine vulnerabilities without the aid of checklists or other guidelines. However, a guideline or checklist is useful to both experienced and inexperienced members of the inspection team. A sample inspection checklist for the security control lighting system is provided in Table 5.3.
- Document and Review Findings — Preliminary findings of the inspection should be documented in as much detail as possible. Include dates and times of inspection and what characteristics or vulnerabilities were observed. The documented findings should be reviewed with the point of

contact for each security control to provide them with a chance to clarify any possible misinterpretations.

5.2.2.4 Observe Behavior

The fourth approach in the RIIOT method for data-gathering is observing the behavior of the organization. The process of observation involves gathering information on the actual implementation of the security controls and determining if they are uniformly applied and effective. For example, the assessor may have already confirmed that a policy and procedure exists that says that unbadged visitors will be challenged. Furthermore, your interview subjects confirmed that this policy is enforced. Now simply walk around in a new area without your badge and observe if anyone challenges you. This is essentially an analysis of the effectiveness of policies and procedures based on observation.

As with many data-gathering activities during a security risk assessment, there are no complete set guidelines on how to perform observation. Observation is a process in which the assessor observes behavior and situations and then develops a judgment regarding the observed behavior. Keen and useful observations to the security risk assessment process are more likely to come from more experienced team members, because they have more experience from which to draw observations and comparisons. However, other team members may naturally have a keen sense of observation. These members can prove just as useful in data gathering through the use of observation.

> **Advice:** Team up less experienced members with more experienced members during the observation stage in order to develop the experience and observation capabilities of all members.

5.2.2.4.1 Observation Guidance

I once described the process of observation as "you walk around and look for stuff." Although that does not sound overly helpful, it is actually rather descriptive of the high-level process for gathering data through observation in a security risk assessment. A lower-level description of the process is difficult, because the observation process is flexible and based on specific circumstances and environments. However, a few examples of observations may illustrate the concept:

- Policy and Procedures — Observation of behavior to confirm or disprove that policy and procedures are followed. Examples include passwords posted on monitors, visitors walking around unchallenged, and changes not being documented.
- Physical Security — Observation of behavior of personnel and condition of controls to confirm or disprove that physical security requirements are

met. Examples include gaps at the bottom of a fence, unlocked telephone closets, and unlit parking lots.

- Security Awareness — Observation of behavior and knowledge of personnel to confirm or disprove security awareness assumptions and requirements. Examples include social engineering, quizzing on policies, and unauthorized downloading.
- Media and Hard Copy Disposal — Observation of behavior to confirm or disprove that media and sensitive information disposal requirements are met. Examples include borrowing used floppies and examining trashcans near fax machines.

The areas above provide some guidance as to the areas of observation. Chapters 6 through 8 provide additional observation guidance based on administrative, technical, and physical controls.

5.2.2.5 Test Security Controls

Security testing of information systems within the scope of the security risk assessment is performed to identify the vulnerabilities of those systems. The inclusion of security testing in a security risk assessment is essential to identify the existence of these vulnerabilities and to provide this information to the organization so that they may address these vulnerabilities. It is important to understand both the abilities and limitations of security testing performed as part of a security risk assessment.

Depending on the type of security testing performed and the depth of testing, security testing can reveal many vulnerabilities that exist in systems protecting sensitive information. The results of a security test, however, only show the presence of known vulnerabilities at the time of testing. Security testing does not show the absence of any vulnerability. Furthermore, it must be recognized that the results of the security test are only accurate for the specific instance in which the test was performed. Almost immediately the system and the threat environment begin to change. As these aspects of the system change, the results of security testing are less relevant.[7]

It is with this background that the information security professional must recognize that security testing is a tool employed by the security risk assessment team to identify possible vulnerabilities in the system and organizational processes. For example, consider a system in which a security test reveals that the information system is susceptible to a well-known buffer overflow attack and an effective patch has been available from the vendor for over three months. This finding would reveal (1) the system has a vulnerability that must be patched and (2) the procedures for implementing patches are ineffective.

5.2.2.5.1 Security Testing Documentation

It is important to carefully and fully document all aspects of the security testing effort. Since the security risk assessment team will be testing a live system, several elements require diligence in the security test documentation effort:

- System Changes — Elements affecting the system security test can change during the security risk assessment engagement. Hopefully, the team is working with a stable system and architectural changes are not performed during the test process. However, other changes such as users logged on, load to the system, emergency patches, and many other factors that may occur or change during the test effort, can change test results. Careful documentation can help to determine the relevance of the test results and recreate the test if necessary.

- Troubleshooting — When you are part of the security team performing tests on a live system, you must be aware that your team will be the first one blamed if anything goes wrong anywhere near the time or place you are testing. Be prepared to work with the assessed organization to help them determine the root of any problem. Detailed test documentation can save a lot of time and headaches when dealing with this situation. Also consider that from time to time your security tests may have actually been the catalyst for causing errors or system crashes. Even seemingly benign security tests such as a port scan can exercise some interfaces that have never been previously tested. In the case of custom-made applications a simple security scan may cause delicate and untested applications to fail. Documentation comes in handy here in helping to resolve the problem.

All security tests should have documentation that, at a minimum, includes the following elements:

- Time and Date — Record the time each test started and completed.
- Tools Used — Identify the tools (or commands) used in each test.
- Tester — Document the name of the tester for each test.
- System — Document the systems and interfaces tested
- Results — Indicate the results of the tests.[8]
- Comments — If anything usual or unexpected happened, include that in your notes as well.

5.2.2.5.2 Coverage of Testing

The complexity of an information system, the vastness of its interfaces, and the multitude of variables involved makes comprehensive or exhaustive testing impossible. There is no conceivable way to completely test an information system. Therefore any security testing effort is going to be less than complete. But that does not mean that testing should be considered inadequate. In fact, through thoughtful selection of the testing coverage, security testing can be performed effectively and efficiently.

There are several approaches for ensuring proper coverage in performing security testing. The approaches covered here include representative testing, selected sampling, and random sampling. Each has it own unique approach, advantages, and disadvantages. Each of these techniques may be used in isolation or in combination with each other.

Complete Testing — A security testing effort may attempt to test all components of an information technology infrastructure. This approach is referred to as complete testing.[9] The term "complete" here refers not to the rigor of the testing method but instead to the number of network components included in the test. For example, if an information technology infrastructure is composed of 550 workstations, 10 Web servers, 5 file servers, 2 e-mail servers, 4 database servers, 3 application servers, 4 firewalls, and 10 routers, then all 588 network components would be tested.

The advantages of complete testing are rather obvious — complete testing provides security vulnerability information on all network components. This complete coverage allows the security risk assessment team to make reasonable conclusions regarding the network components, because all components were tested. When the network is relatively small (e.g., less than 200 servers) and the testing method is relatively simple (e.g., vulnerability scanning), it usually makes sense to perform a complete test.

Complete coverage for security testing has disadvantages as well. Clearly, complete security testing can be expensive and time consuming when the network is relatively large (e.g., over 500 servers) or when the testing method is more complex (e.g., ad-hoc penetration testing).

5.2.2.5.3 Types of Security Testing

Security testing can be used toward many different objectives, such as testing that established procedure (such as system hardening or account maintenance) was followed information accuracy testing to identify possible vulnerabilities, (vulnerability testing) or to determine the system's resistance to attack (penetration testing). Each of these testing types is useful within the process of a security risk assessment.

It is important to understand the distinction between these security testing types and objectives as not all security risk assessment will employ all three types. For example, a security risk assessment with a low level of rigor is unlikely to perform penetration testing. The security risk assessment team needs to understand where a vulnerability assessment leaves off and a penetration test begins. Each of these testing types is described below.

Information Accuracy Testing — Information accuracy testing is performed to confirm the accuracy of data gathered within other stages of the assessment. Much of the data gathered within a security risk assessment could be considered "hearsay" or uncorroborated information. This is not to say that we believe the information was purposefully misleading, just that interviews can result in inaccurate information, network diagrams can be out of date, and policies may not be strictly implemented. The objective of information accuracy testing is to corroborate information obtained during other data-gathering activities. Several examples of how information can be corroborated or corrected are given below.

- Interviews — During an interview the subject may, by nature, be eager to please and rather than state that they do not know the answer, they guess at an answer. At other times, terminology gets in the way. The interviewer and the interviewee can be using the same terms but have different meanings associated with the terms. For example, when asked, an interviewee may state that passwords are never sent in the clear. The interviewee may truly believe this statement because he has just finished a project on the upgrade of a legacy system that had passwords embedded in batch commands. Now that those commands are removed, he believes that passwords are never sent in the clear.[10] However, it may be shown through a packet-sniffing test that they are indeed still sent in the clear. The interviewee is not being dishonest, he just does not understand the implication of the implemented authentication protocols and protected communication paths.
- Network Diagrams — Network diagrams are a representation of the logical arrangement (connectivity) of the network components. These diagrams are useful during a security risk assessment to determine information flow, external and internal interfaces, and the architectural design of the network. As the network architecture can be in a constant state of change, the accuracy of a network diagram must be verified.
- Policies and Procedures — The organization may have a strict policy that every desktop must receive daily anti-virus updates. However, there may be some users within the organization who have figured out how to defeat the automatic updates ("because they slow down the machine too much") or other users who are not connected to the Internet every day, but do receive e-mail every day.

5.2.2.5.4 Vulnerability Testing

The objective of vulnerability testing is to identify the vulnerabilities that exist in the currently deployed systems without causing a breach to the security of the system the security control is protecting. Within technical security controls this is referred to as vulnerability scanning, because the use of tools allows for a quick scan of the system to identify any obvious vulnerabilities. Vulnerability testing can be applied to physical security controls as well. For example, a vulnerability test of a badge-access activated entrance could entail the timing of the door mechanism to properly close. A long time to close would indicate a vulnerability that could allow an intruder without a badge to gain entry.

5.2.2.5.5 Penetration Testing

The objective of penetration testing is to exploit the vulnerabilities found during vulnerability testing. Penetration tests may lead to a breach in security. Applying penetration testing to the physical security control in the previous example (the door that takes a long time to close), the assessor would attempt to actually gain access through utilizing this vulnerability.

5.2.3 Using the RIIOT Method

As security controls are typically divided into the administrative, physical, and technical areas, and different techniques and even skill sets are used to collect data in these areas, the team typically divides the data-gathering process along the same lines. Chapters 6, 7, and 8 provide the reader with an overview of the threats and safeguards relevant to each of these areas. These chapters also provide a discussion of how the RIIOT approach can be applied to administrative, physical, and technical data-gathering.

Notes

1. Just to remind the reader, this book is not intended as a stand-alone method for performing security risk assessments. Instead it is intended as a companion document to those performing any security risk assessment.

2. Perhaps a better example of a cluster sample is a geographic example. For example, if your population is every convenience store within a national chain of convenience stores, it may be too burdensome to perform a site survey on every store. Instead you may choose to perform an audit on every store within 15 counties throughout the nation.

3. It is important to understand that the objective of security testing is to discover the possible security risk findings and not necessarily all missed patches on a workstation. It does not really matter if you find 8, 11, or 14 missed patches on a workstation, the security risk finding is the same: "Workstations are not

adequately patched." Scanning more workstations is unlikely to change that finding.

4.   The foundation for and application of statistical principles and techniques is beyond the scope of this book.

5.   For those not familiar with security risk assessment approaches, it may seem hard to believe that there are not a huge number of tools and methods already out there to help. In fact there are a large number of risk assessment tools and methods available (see Chapter 13), but few, if any, provide much guidance at all on the data-gathering step of the process. For example, OCTAVE provides a very detailed process for performing a security risk assessment (down to how many hours each step is likely to take), but when it comes to the data-gathering step of the process (Process 6: Evaluate Selected Components), users of the method are given little more advice than to run the latest version of a vulnerability tool.

6.   One should not get too cynical here. Key personnel are typically charged with being aware of many activities outside their direct control. The delegation of these duties relieves them of daily observances of specific security controls and leads them to rely on the observation of others or, in the absence of information, to create a belief that such controls are actually there. This is why we inspect.

7.   Security testing is a tool that should be used by the organization continually throughout the system development life cycle, including the operations and maintenance phase.

8.   The results of any system testing are bound to be one of the most referenced documents after the security risk assessment. That is because it likely contains vulnerabilities in operational systems that need to be fixed right away. In order to make the report more useful, the security risk assessment team should offer the report in softcopy format and include several views of the testing results, for example, vulnerabilities sorted by IP address, vulnerabilities sorted by severity, and summary data such as average number of high severity vulnerabilities per type of computer.

9.   As mentioned above, it is impossible to completely test all interfaces of all components for all conceivable conditions within a testing effort. In fact all testing is in essence a partial test.

10.   Removing plaintext passwords from a batch file was certainly a badly needed security improvement, but it does nothing to ensure that passwords are not sent in the clear. In fact, the imbedded passwords may have been protected from eavesdropping by implementing an encrypted tunnel between the application and the database, for example.

References

[1]   Albright, S. Christian, Winston, Wayne L., and Zappe, Christopher, *Data Analysis and Decision Making*, Duxbury Press, 1999.

[2]   *IS Auditing Guideline: Audit Sampling, Information Systems Audit and Control Association*, November, 1999.

[3] Kennedy, Mary, "A Guide to Interview Guides," Teacher Education Doctoral Students, Digital Advisor for Research Projects. http://ed-web3/educ.msu.edu/digiatladvisor/ResearchFiles/InterviewGuide.htm

[4] McNamara, Carter, "General Guidelines for Conducting Interviews." www.mapnp.org/library/evaluatn/interview.htm

Chapter 6

Administrative Data Gathering

Each of the next three chapters is dedicated to the topic (or security risk assessment phase) of data gathering. The topic of data gathering is a large one and encompasses many activities and security controls. This large topic has been divided into three groups: administrative (Chapter 6), technical (Chapter 7), and physical (Chapter 8), to facilitate the use of this book and to provide security risk assessment team members with target guidance on their area of review.

In the previous chapter, the RIIOT approach was introduced as a method of organizing, describing, and managing the data-gathering effort. The bulk of the next three chapters is dedicated to the description of how to gather data in the respective areas of administrative, technical, and physical. However, the ability to gather data efficiently is based on experience and understanding of the threats and security controls within a particular area. While this book cannot give the reader experience in these areas, it can provide a primer on the threats and safeguards in each of the areas. Therefore, each of the next three chapters will have a similar format of a discussion of threats and safeguards, followed by the RIIOT method for data gathering.

6.1 Threats and Safeguards

The definition of threats, threat agents, and threat statements were covered earlier. Administrative threats specifically are covered here as an approach to introducing administrative data gathering. This section, on threats and safeguards, is intended as a primer or introduction to security threats in the administrative area.[1]

A member of a security risk assessment team requires a basic understanding of the threats and safeguards within the administrative security area to be an effective member of the team. There are numerous administrative security threats; some of the more frequent administrative threats are discussed here and listed in Table 6.1.

Table 6.1 Administrative Threats and Safeguards. Administrative threats include errors, omissions, fraud, waste, abuse, negligence, excessive privileges, and many more threats to the organization's assets. Administrative safeguards are policies, procedures, and activities that may reduce these threats.

Area	Class	Threat	Safeguard
Human resources	Recruitment — unqualified/ untrustworthy personnel	• Errors • Omissions • Fraud • Waste • Abuse	• Application • Job requirements • Reference checks • Employment checks • Accuracy checks • Credit checks • Clearance procedures
	Employment — unqualified personnel	• Errors • Omissions	• Employment policies • Training and education • Job description • Job requirements • Annual reviews
	Employment — untrustworthy personnel	• Fraud • Waste • Abuse	• Acceptable use policy • Monitoring • Two-man control • Job rotation • Clearance refresh • Ethics training • Sanctions policy • Separation of duty • Job rotation
	Termination — untrustworthy personnel	• Fraud • Waste • Abuse	• Termination procedures • NDA, NCC • Out-briefing
Organizational structure	Senior management	• Negligence	• Risk management • Assign duties • Understand responsibility

(Continued)

Table 6.1 (Continued)
Administrative Threats and Safeguards

Area	Class	Threat	Safeguard
	Security program	• Incomplete • Inadequate • Inefficient • Ineffective	• Assign duties • Authority, visibility • Budget • Risk analysis • Review of security activities
	Security operations	• Fraud • Waste • Abuse	• Assign duties • Security operations policies • Maintenance procedures • Separation of duties • Dual control • Least privilege • Monitoring
	Audit	• Fraud • Waste • Abuse	• Internal audit • Third-party review • Security risk assessment
Information control	User error	• Social engineering • Errors • Omissions	• Security awareness • Job training • Job rotation • Policy and procedures • Monitoring • Double key data entry • Two-man control
	Sensitive information	• Disclosure	• Criticality analysis • Information labeling • Review of access controls • Media destruction
	User accounts	• Disclosure • Excessive privilege	• Account creation procedures • Review of access controls • Account termination procedures • NTK • Separation of duty
	Asset control	• Theft	• Asset inventory • Asset tracking
Business continuity	Contingency planning	• Disclosure • Unavailability	• Business continuity strategy • Business impact analysis • Disaster recovery plan • Crisis management • DRP testing and maintenance • Data backup

(Continued)

Table 6.1   (Continued)
Administrative Threats and Safeguards

Area	Class	Threat	Safeguard
	Incident response program	• Disclosure • Subversion • Fraud	• Incident response plan and procedures • Incident response training • Availability of experts
System security	System controls	• Disclosure • Subversion • Fraud	• Operating procedures • Server hardening • Vulnerability scanning • Scheduled and emergency patches • Remote maintenance • Remote access • Security review/ approval
	Applications security	• Disclosure • Subversion • Fraud	• Coding standards • Code review • Penetration testing
	Change management	• Errors • Fraud	• Configuration items • CI protection • Change control • Status reporting
	Third-party access	• Disclosure • Unavailability	• Contractual obligations • Minimum security requirements • Review of third-party security

6.1.1 Human Resources

Organizations need to protect their assets from unqualified or untrustworthy personnel. Employees, through purposeful or accidental behavior, may expose sensitive assets to disclosure, compromise integrity of information, or block availability of critical systems.

6.1.1.1 Recruitment

Prior to hiring an individual to become an employee within an organization, the human resources department has many opportunities to provide safeguards that may avoid or deter employee error or abuse. These safeguards include hiring procedures, job requirements, and a series of possible background checks that may be performed on the applicant. Each of these safeguards is briefly described below:

- Application — The application must collect the appropriate information and consent from each applicant to enable proper reference, background, and employment checking. Furthermore, the application will provide information on the applicant's experience and skill set that is intended to meet the requirements of the job description.

- Job Requirements — The hiring manager for each position must pay careful attention to the description of the job duties and employee requirements. The specific duties and requirements recorded in the job description are what the human resources manager will use to screen candidates. An inaccurate description of the job requirements can lead to the hiring of an inadequate employee.

- Reference Checks — These checks include both professional and personal references who can attest to the skills, experience, and work ethic of the applicant. You should generally expect that such checks will come back quite positive because the applicant provided the names of whom to call. Nonetheless, such checks do provide some assurance that the applicant possesses the characteristics required for the position.

- Employment Checks — When called concerning a reference check, employers are only expected to provide information concerning the date of hire, date of termination, and job title. If the applicant has signed a "hold harmless" agreement with the previous employer, additional information may be provided. Although employers may provide this information without such an agreement, it is unlikely.

- Accuracy Checks — These checks provide an assurance that all the information provided on the application is accurate. Such checks cover employment dates, salary histories, education, professional affiliations, and other data that may be confirmed. Significant errors within the application could simply be a mistake but may also indicate either carelessness or deceit.

- Credit Checks — Credit checks provide a measure of the financial well-being of the prospective employee. This could provide insight into the candidate's dependability. In the case of sensitive government jobs, this could provide insight into the susceptibility the candidate may have to blackmail. A credit check may be conducted by ordering a credit check on the employee. Such a check may be performed only if the employee is informed that a credit check will be issued and signs a consent form to be provided to the credit reporting agency.

- Background Checks and Clearance Procedures — Employers may access arrest and conviction records that are available as public information. The use of these records to make hiring decisions, however, varies from state to state. If the practice is legal within the governing jurisdiction, background checks can provide an immediate measure of the applicant's integrity. Within the federal government, additional checks will be performed to determine if the applicant is eligible for the required clearance.[2]

6.1.1.2 Employment

Once an individual becomes an employee, the potential for errors, omissions, fraud, waste, and abuse can impact the security of the organization's assets. There are many approaches to safeguarding the organization from the potential of such losses. Some of these are briefly described below:

- Employment Policies — The proper behavior of an employee begins with the organization making the expected behavior clear. Policies such as acceptable use of equipment, noncompete agreements, and nondisclosure agreements define the security responsibilities and the sensitivity of organizational assets. These policies should be reviewed and signed as a part of the employment process.
- Training and Education — Many mistakes made by employees are a matter of improper training and education. Programs such as security awareness training, process training, and regulation education help to ensure that employees understand their security responsibilities and how to carry them out.
- Job Description — The description of a job is not simply a human resources paperwork exercise. The job description itself is a security safeguard. An employee's expectations and limits of authority should be captured in the job description. Expectations set out the specific duties that must be performed and the duties for which the employee is responsible. Limits of authority document the need-to-know of the individual in the specific job position. For example, expectations may include annual testing of the DRP plan; limitations may include account activation but not audit log review. Ensuring that these duties are performed and privileges are not exceeded is a primary security concern.
- Job Requirements — Covered in the section above.[3]
- Annual Reviews — The strength of the security measures set up during job description and job requirements is tested during an annual review. The annual review provides a measurement of the ability of the employee to meet the expectations of the position. Additionally, the supervisor should use the annual review as a method to review the job description and ensure that the job description properly identifies all of the duties performed in that position.
- Acceptable Use Policy — The nature of work requires the use of the computer equipment, the corporate network, and possibly the Internet for

electronic communication. "Acceptable use" addresses employee use of the organization's resources for accessing the information, transmitting or receiving electronic mail, general use of software, and system access. This policy communicates and documents the responsibilities and limit of privileges for employees.

- Monitoring — To further enforce the organization's security policies and procedures, the organization may employ monitoring procedures or automated monitoring equipment. Monitoring includes all activities that provide oversight of the employee's ability to follow stated security policies. These activities include supervision, review of the use of information resources such as e-mail, and automated Web surfing behavior monitoring. As the laws in each state differ with regard to monitoring employee communications, the monitoring approach should be reviewed by the organization's legal department.[4]
- Dual Control — This safeguard is applied to sensitive tasks and requires both individuals' approval before action is taken. This provides accountability and reduces fraud, waste, and abuse.
- Two Man Control — This safeguard employs the use of two employees to review and approve the work of each other. This provides accountability and reduces fraud, waste, and abuse
- Separation of Duty — This is a concept that states that no single sensitive task should be able to be executed by a single individual from beginning to end. This concept may also be applied to any implementation task and requires that someone other than the implementer review the work.
- Job Rotation — This safeguard requires that employees perform a variety of job functions within a single department. Job rotation forces others' work to be reviewed and performed by their peers, thus reducing the chance for collusion and helping to prevent fraud. Job rotation has a side benefit of providing "bench strength" within a single department, because more than one person can perform critical duties.

The concepts of two-man control, dual control, separation of duty, and job rotation all help to reduce opportunities for fraud, waste, and abuse. Figure 6.1 illustrates the distinction between these concepts.

- Clearance Refresh — For those positions that require government clearance for access to sensitive information, the clearance process must be reperformed periodically.
- Ethics Training — Providing courses and training in ethics to the workforce is an effective way to ensure that employees understand the expectations of their ethical behavior. Ethics training should be customized to situations that apply to the employees and should be consistent with documented guidance and policies.

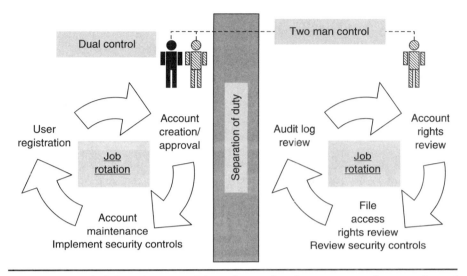

Figure 6.1   Administrative oversight safeguards. The concept of separation of duty states that one group should be responsible for reviewing another group's work. Job rotation requires that employees rotate positions within a department. Dual control requires two operators to perform a single function. Two-man control designates another individual to review the work of an operator.

- Sanctions Policy — All employee security policies should have specific and clear implications if violated. A sanctions policy provides the policy and procedures for the organization's actions upon violation of security policy. The sanctions policy should include, at a minimum, policies for documentation of incidents, definitions of prohibited actions, applicable policies and laws, and escalation procedures for incidents.

6.1.1.3 Termination

When it becomes clear that an employee will no longer be employed at the organization, the termination procedures must be handled appropriately to avoid a breach in security. The potential for fraud, waste, and abuse can be rather high, especially with disgruntled employees who have had access to sensitive information and critical systems. There are many approaches to safeguarding the organization from the potential of a security breach in the event of an employee termination. Some of these are briefly described below:

- Termination Procedures — The organization should have a clear set of procedures to be followed upon an employee's termination. These procedures need to be tailored to the organization, because they will be dependent upon the industry, environment, and business structure. Some examples of items that should be included within termination procedures include the return of capital equipment and security access cards, termination of accounts, and the turnover of duties.

- Nondisclosure Agreements and Noncompete Clauses — Upon termination the employee should be reminded of any nondisclosure agreements that have been signed with the former employer and any partners. A nondisclosure agreement identifies sensitive information (i.e., trade secrets, customer lists) and the restrictions on its dissemination. A noncompete clause specifies the restrictions placed on the future employment of the individual (e.g., restrictions on doing business with customers or even competing in the same industry).[5]
- Out-Briefing — An out-briefing is a formal process during a nonhostile termination that can gather information from the terminated employee that could be used to improve the work environment or reduce vulnerabilities. Out-briefings are also performed to remind the employee of the contracts still in place (e.g., NDAs, NCCs) and their responsibility for continuing obligation.

6.1.2 Organizational Structure

The structure of the organization plays a large role in the ability of the organization to effectively enforce security controls. The organization of departments, responsibilities, and reporting structures within the organization can affect the most basic of security controls. From security regulations compliance responsibilities, to security activity coordination, to security activity execution, the effectiveness and efficiency of security controls can be thwarted by weak organizational structure controls.

6.1.2.1 Senior Management

All security starts at the top. It is senior management that is ultimately responsible for the security of an organization. It is senior management that will be held accountable by the organization's stakeholders and for violation of laws and regulations. It is senior management that determines the organizational structure in which the security program and activities operate. If senior management does not establish an effective organizational structure for the security program, then the effectiveness of all other security controls is in question.[5]

Specifically, the threats to the organization's assets that can be most attributed to senior management include the threat of an incomplete security solution, inadequate personnel and controls, inefficient methods of detection and enforcement, and an ineffective security program. The following safeguards can help to lessen the likelihood or impact of these threats:

- Risk Management — Risk management is the process of understanding, mitigating, and controlling risk through risk assessment, risk mitigation, operational security and testing. As mentioned earlier, the objective of security risk management is to accurately measure the residual security risk and keep it to a level at or below the security risk tolerance level. Only senior management has the ability to define the organization's tolerance for security risk.
- Assign Duties — The senior management of the organization needs to determine the organizational structure most appropriate to enabling the risk management process. The structural decisions are implemented through an assignment and placement within the organization, establishment of roles and duties, and the granting of budget and staff.
- Understand Responsibility — It is imperative that senior management understand their security responsibilities and ensure that delegated duties are understood as well. Senior management needs to have an operating knowledge of the security regulations and controls within their industry and cannot simply delegate such responsibility. For example, the administrator of a hospital is not implementing this safeguard (understanding responsibility) if security duties have been completely delegated to the systems administrator. The hospital administrator needs to understand the components of the HIPAA regulations (and others) and understand that specific security activities and controls are required, many of which are likely outside the control of the systems administrators (e.g., business associate contracts).

6.1.2.2 Security Program

The security program is functionally responsible for the oversight, governance, and direction of the security controls within the organization. A well-structured, staffed, and funded security program can offer many security advantages to the organization. Specific elements of an effective security program are described below:

- Assign Duties — The security program must clearly assign duties to the members of the program. Duties include anything from running vulnerability scans, to creating security policies, to running the security awareness program. A clear and complete assignment of duties, coupled with annual reviews that measure individuals on how well they met their responsibilities, can provide effective safeguards against many threats to the organization's assets.
- Authority and Visibility — The security organization must have the ability to perform its activities effectively. Since security reaches across many

departments, it can sometimes be difficult for the security team to be noticed or for the security team to effect changes and enforce policy. The security team must be given the proper authority and visibility within the organization to effect changes and enforce policies.

- Budget — The security team will undoubtedly require an expenditure of money to implement some of its functions or acquire security technology. If the security budget is determined by another department (e.g., information technology), then the security team is in effect controlled by that other organization and loses its credibility and effectiveness to deliver the most cost-effective solutions.

- Risk Analysis — The security team should continually perform risk analysis on the security of the organization's assets. Based on available information (e.g., latest security risk assessment, scan, password cracking, and the latest incident), the security team must be able to articulate the security risk to the organization to senior management and other stakeholders. Furthermore, the security team should periodically report the security state of the organization to senior management and others.

- Review of Security Activities — If the security team is responsible for performing certain security activities, the principle of separation of duty dictates that someone else review the security team as to their effectiveness and adherence to policies and procedures. This can be performed by internal audit teams or as a part of a security risk assessment performed by an independent consultancy.

6.1.2.3 Security Operations

The security operations team is typically responsible for the implementation and maintenance of technical security controls such as account and access controls, firewalls, and anti-virus software. Since these duties involve the direct control of security safeguards, they are targeted at the prevention of errors and omissions as well as fraud, waste, and abuse. Some safeguards that may be applied to security operations are described below:

- Assign Duties — The security operations team must have clearly assigned duties to the members of the team to ensure complete coverage and enforcement of separation of duties principles. Duties include account creation, account maintenance, file access controls, role definitions, and audit log reviews. A clear and complete assignment of duties, coupled with annual reviews that measure individuals on how well they met their responsibilities, can provide effective safeguards against many threats to the organization's assets.

- Security Operations Policies — Policies and procedures regarding the way in which the security operations team performs its functions help to ensure that individuals behave in a manner that benefits the organization. Policies are the foundation of security operations activities, because the policies define the expected behavior. Procedures further provide guidance as to how activities should be performed. The organization should have security operations policies that cover the activities of system or security administrators, such as account creation, server hardening, and file backups.

- Maintenance Procedures — These procedures provide additional guidance for those activities required to maintain security controls. Maintenance activities include account maintenance, software maintenance, and access control maintenance. The modification of the parameters of these security controls must be carefully managed; maintenance procedures provide clear guidance and help to reduce errors and omission.
- Separation of Duties — Covered in the section above.
- Dual Control — Covered in the section above.
- Least Privilege — The concept of least privilege states that each employee should be given the least amount of privilege they need to perform their duties. Security operations must practice this concept when creating accounts and establishing access control rules. This concept can also be applied to the accounts of the security operations personnel themselves. For example, there is no reason for everyone in security operations to have all (or root) privileges.
- Monitoring — Covered in the section above.

6.1.2.4 Audit

The audit function provides oversight for sensitive tasks and protection of organizational assets. Audit functions include the safeguards of internal audit, third-party review, and security risk assessments. The key to a successful audit function is to ensure that auditors are not involved in the development of what is to be audited, auditors have access to all records, and senior management must be formally required to respond to audit findings.[7]

- Internal Audit — The internal audit function is an in-house team of auditors that can review security controls and accounts. For those organizations large enough to have an internal audit team, security risk assessments are typically performed or commissioned out of these offices. This team should also have a direct report to a C-level executive, generally the CEO, board, or CFO.
- Third-Party Review — If the organization has allowed outside organizations to connect to their network or share sensitive information, then the security boundary for the protection of the organization's assets has effectively increased to include that organization as well. A third-party audit is a security audit performed on a third party to ensure that they are

properly safeguarding the organization's assets. These audits are typically bounded by specific requirements documented in a business associate contract. Third-party review can be conducted directly by the assessing organization, conducted by hired external security experts, or the assessing organization can accept the audit reports of other qualified security experts.

- Security Risk Assessment — The security risk assessment is an objective analysis of the effectiveness of the current security controls that protect an organization's assets and a determination of the probability of losses to those assets.

6.1.3 Information Control

Information is one of the most valuable assets of the organization. Adequate security controls should be placed on sensitive information to ensure that it is protected. Various controls and safeguards exist, including controlling user accounts, restricting user error, controlling assets, and protecting sensitive information.

6.1.3.1 User Accounts

A user account contains a user's attributes such as name, sensitivity level, and account expiration. The user account provides the user access to organizational critical resources and files and should therefore be strictly controlled. The following safeguards can assist in ensuring that security is preserved through user accounts:

- Account Creation Procedures — The organization should have strict account creation procedures in place. These procedures should include approval from the information or system owner, a review of accesses required, and a notification to the information or system owner once the account is created.
- Review of Access Controls — Access controls include user accounts, file attributes, and access control rules. These attributes and rules need to be reviewed periodically to ensure that the current configuration reflects the intention of the information or system owners. The following schedule is suggested:
  - Review all accounts every 180 days.
  - Review all sensitive accounts every 90 days.
- Account Termination Procedures — Covered in the section above.
- Need-to-Know — The principle of need-to-know (NTK) states that each person shall have access to the minimal amount of information necessary to perform their duties. This principle is closely aligned with the concept of least privilege. The difference between these two safeguards is that NTK is with respect to access to information while least privilege is with respect to

capabilities. The implementation of NTK in handling access to information reduces the chances of disclosure.

- Separation of Duty — Covered in the section above.

6.1.3.2 User Error

Many controls and safeguards discussed so far have dealt with ways to stop fraud, waste, and abuse, but even well-meaning employees can breach the security of the organization's information through accidental means. The administrative controls discussed below are some of the ways to restrict user error as it would impact the security of the organization's information:

- Security Awareness — Covered in the section above.
- Job Training — The best way to ensure a lack of mistakes on the part of the user is to properly train them to perform their job. Assessors should be careful not to confuse education and experience with job training. Each organization has its own specific environment, policies, and ways of doing things. Job training ensures that the user knows what is expected and how to perform their duties.
- Job Rotation — Covered in the section above.
- Policy and Procedures — For each position within the organization there is a specific set of activities that are expected to be performed. If these activities are sensitive and can affect the security of the organization's assets, then the assessor should expect there to be some policies and procedures in place to ensure that the activities are performed in a manner that enforces the security policy of the organization.
- Monitoring — Covered in the section above.
- Double Key Data Entry — This is a data entry method in which each transaction is entered twice. The first data entry and the second data entry are checked for consistency with each other. This control helps to reduce errors and fraud.
- Two-Man Control — Covered in the section above.

6.1.3.3 Asset Control

Asset control involves the explicit control and tracking of individual organizational assets. This includes both tangible assets and intangible assets. Organizations that employ asset control can easily keep tabs on critical assets, control theft of equipment, and handle assets according to their sensitivity.

- Asset Inventory — An asset inventory is a list of all of the assets of the corporation. This list typically has many fields such as location, type of asset, asset owner, and serial number. For smaller organizations such lists could be created manually, but large organizations will likely use an asset inventory system such as bar codes, asset tag, or even Radic Frequency IDentifications (RFID). The asset inventory can be used as data to improve other security controls as well such as termination procedures (ensure that all capital equipment is returned) and visitor control (ensure that visitors do not leave with an organization asset).

- Asset Tracking — Once an inventory has been created and the assets have identifiers (e.g., serial numbers or asset tags), then an asset tracking system can be used to monitor all organizational assets. These systems assist the organization in controlling their assets through checking them in and out, tracking the destruction of sensitive material, and managing their inventory.

6.1.3.4 Sensitive Information

All data is valuable to the organization, but some data is more critical and sensitive than other data. The organization should identify this information and provide additional controls to protect it from disclosure.

- Criticality Analysis — Among the information and resources controlled by the organization, some are more critical than others The organization can identify critical assets by analyzing the critical systems and the assets and resources required by those critical systems. The labeling of assets as critical allows the organization to more effectively track, control, and protect those assets, thus ensuring their availability for critical systems.
- Information Labeling — All information is valuable to the organization, but some of the information is more sensitive than others. Sensitive data, however, is likely to be treated in a less strict manner than intended if the organization fails to properly classify and label sensitive information. The organization should create and implement a data classification scheme that takes into account the various levels of data sensitivity within the organization. For example, the organization may consider a scheme that dictates different controls for public, personal, partner-proprietary, and sensitive data.
- Review of Access Controls — The access controls for sensitive information should be reviewed more frequently than those controls for less sensitive information. For example, the access control lists (ACLs) for the payroll database should be reviewed more frequently than the ACLs for a user's home directory.
- Media Destruction — Whenever a computer, hard disk, or magnetic media is to be disposed, transferred, or sold, it must be done in a way that ensures the confidentiality of the data. To ensure that media that leaves the control of the organization contains no sensitive information, extra efforts

must be applied to remove any content. These efforts are referred to as sanitization:

- Sanitization of Data — All information must be erased or overwritten. Specifications for sanitization call for repetitious overwriting a specific number of rounds. Sanitization standards depend on the organization, its environment, and any regulations it may fall under. Typical standardization standards include a provision for three (3) to seven (7) rounds of overwriting of the complete media, including BIOS.
- Sanitization of Hard Drives — There are generally three acceptable methods for the sanitization of hard drives: overwriting, degaussing, and physical destruction. The method used for sanitization depends on the operability of the hard drives. Operable hard drives that will be reused are overwritten. If the hard drive is to be removed from service, it is preferable to physically destroy or degauss the hard drive.
- Sanitization of Other Media — The risk of disclosure of sensitive information lies outside of computer hard drives. Specific attention should be paid to floppy disks, tapes, CDs, DVDs, optical disks, and volatile and nonvolatile memory components. These devices must be erased, degaussed if possible, or physically destroyed.

6.1.4 Business Continuity

Business continuity is the field of preparation planning undertaken by organizations to ensure that they remain a viable entity if and when a disaster impacts their critical systems. The possibility that a disaster will impact at least one critical system within an organization is rather large. In fact, a recent study cited 40 percent of the companies surveyed as having experienced a disaster in the past three years that took out a critical system. Of these, 38 percent experienced downtimes that lasted a minimum of eleven hours and up to three days [4].

Business continuity planning is the process of identifying critical systems, identifying reasonable threats, and creating a long-term strategy for reducing the impact of interruptions to the business and stabilizing critical business functions.

6.1.4.1 Contingency Planning

The contingency planning process includes the business continuity planning (i.e., long-term strategy) and the disaster recovery planning (i.e., near- and mid-term strategies) to handle specific situations:

- Business Continuity Strategy — A business continuity strategy is a plan to minimize the impact of realized risks on critical resources. The business continuity strategy is based on an analysis of the threats and critical systems (e.g., BIA), a determination of alternative site requirements, and approval, implementation, and training of the plan.

- Business Impact Analysis — A business impact assessment (BIA) provides a measured impact assessment on business operations from a disastrous event. The steps involved in a business impact assessment are first to establish priorities for which systems to bring up first in the event of a disaster, and second to allocate the appropriate resources to those systems during an actual disaster.
- Disaster Recovery Plan — A disaster recovery plan (DRP) documents the business continuity process and provides a written plan in the event of an emergency. The disaster recovery plan should contain emergency response guidelines for specific disaster scenarios such as a computer virus outbreak, an internal hacker, a tornado, and an epidemic.
- Crisis Management — The procedures for crisis management should be contained with the disaster recovery plan; however, they are called out here since they are often left out of that document. Crisis management is a public relations program that proactively handles external agencies (e.g., emergency services, weather bureaus) and stakeholders (e.g., employees, key customers) in crisis situations.
- DRP Testing and Maintenance — A disaster recovery plan is not considered viable until it has been successfully tested. DRP testing verifies the adequacy of the team procedures and the compatibility with backup facilities, and provides training for team members. Any inadequacies discovered in the testing phase or because of changes in the environment are handled within the scope of DRP maintenance.
- Data Backup — Data required for critical systems on both the system level and the user level must be performed periodically. Backup tapes of sensitive or critical information should be stored in a secure and separate location, but retrieval capability must be consistent with required recovery times. The ability to restore data must be performed periodically as well.

6.1.4.2 Incident Response Program

An effective incident response program is essential to the organization to limit the potential for disclosure of confidential information, subversion of critical systems, or the perpetration of fraud because of security incident. Incident response programs include a response plan for each type of considered incident, incident response procedures to be followed by the organization's personnel in charge, incident response training, and the availability of experts when needed.

- Incident Response Plan and Procedures — An incident response plan and procedures provide the direction and authority to the incident response team for identification, containment, and recovery capabilities.

- Incident Response Training — All members of the incident response team should be well trained in the policy and procedures for incident response and reporting. Training should include how to recognize an incident, who to notify in a given scenario, how to contain the damage, and how to recover the critical functions of the system.
- Availability of Experts — In the event of an actual disaster the capabilities of the incident response team may not be adequate for certain situations. For example, the incident response team may have determined to pursue prosecution of an employee. If the incident response team does not have a staff expert in evidence collection, analysis, and court presentation of evidence, it may be wise to retain the services of experts in this field. Such arrangements should be made ahead of time during the planning, and not reacting, process.

6.1.5 System Security

The organization must protect its information systems from unscheduled changes, third-party access, system-level vulnerabilities, and application-level vulnerabilities. Any of these threats to the organization's information systems could lead to disclosure or corruption of sensitive information, subversion of network systems, or fraud.

6.1.5.1 System Controls

The organization's information systems can be further protected from rogue applications and unauthorized users through a set of system controls. These controls include policy, procedures, and security activities that discover, reduce, and avoid vulnerabilities with the organization's information systems:

- Operating Procedures — The system operating procedures establish the responsibilities of the system operations staff. These responsibilities include the protection of diagnostic ports, controlling changes to the system, maintaining operator logs, and creating emergency procedures.
- Server Hardening — System operators shall ensure that all systems have the latest approved patches, unused services are disabled, unused software is deleted, and any other known vulnerabilities of the system are addressed. This process is referred to as server hardening.
- Vulnerability Scanning — Since the systems operations personnel are responsible for hardening the systems, they should also perform a check of their work by running vulnerability scanners against the hardened machines.[8]
- Scheduled and Emergency Patches — The systems operations personnel are expected to test and apply all scheduled patches that have gone through the

normal approval process. Additionally, the systems operations personnel shall apply all emergency patches; these patches may have been approved on an emergency basis by someone who normally has less authority.

- Remote Maintenance — Systems operations personnel are not always trained or cleared to work on all systems and software that is a part of the organization's information systems. In the cases where systems or software is worked on by other personnel, this maintenance is sometimes performed remotely. The organization should ensure that this remote connection does not significantly degrade the security of its systems. Several remote maintenance safeguards and things to look for are listed below:
  - Modem Protection — The modem by which the remote personnel gain connectivity should have access controls such as dial-back modem or two-factor authentication. Additionally, the modem may be turned off when not in use and plugged in when needed if maintenance access is few and far between.
  - Access Controls — The passwords or other authentication used to gain access remotely should be issued to a single person within the maintenance company's staff. It is important to be able to trace audit events back to a single individual instead of to a company. These authentication attributes should follow good security practices, for example, strong passwords, changed every 90 days.
- Remote Access — Many organizations find the need for their systems operations personnel or regular users to gain access remotely. Provided the organization implements appropriate safeguards this practice should not lessen the security protections on the organization's assets. Here are a few additional safeguards that may be implemented for employee remote access:
  - Remote Access Policy — Employees must be informed of the responsibilities and security safeguards that accompany remote access. This can be added as a rider to an acceptable use policy.
  - Strong Authentication — Users' authentication credentials should be based on at least two factors, for example, a password and a token device.
  - Use of Home Computers — Organizations must determine if employees shall be allowed to access the network using home computers. This is a dangerous practice as Virtual Private Network (VPN) and other clients must reside on the system to gain access, and other family members share the same computer.
- Security Review and Approval — The systems operations personnel play an important role in implementing security controls for the information systems. However, the organization must implement policies and procedures that ensure that changes to the security-relevant aspects of the system are reviewed and approved by others. This increases oversight and reduces the chance of fraud, waste, and abuse.

6.1.5.2 Application Security

Until recently, application security has been largely ignored by companies protecting their assets, but applications have not been ignored by hackers. Even though Web applications sit behind a firewall and perhaps even behind hardened operating systems, they are still vulnerable. This is because firewalls and hardened operating systems are not designed to restrict all access to Web applications (i.e., port 80 HTTP). Furthermore, exposed Web applications are likely to have errors. It has been estimated that close to 90 percent of Web applications contain major security holes. Below are a few security controls that may be employed to reduce the risk in applications:

- Coding Standards — The adoption and practice of secure coding standards within an organization is one approach to ensure that insecure code is not developed. Secure coding standards include guidance in terms of secure principles to be implemented and dangerous practices to be avoided. If the organization produces its own application code, the assessors should expect to see secure coding standards documented, taught, and adhered to.
- Code Review — Application code review is one approach to ensure that applications are devoid of inherent vulnerabilities. Code review is typically an expensive alternative but perhaps the best way to ensure a rigorous analysis of the security capabilities of the code. Code review can be assisted by the use of software tools, but is still a semimanual activity. Organizations with experienced, skilled, and independent staff could perform a security code review in-house, but many security code reviews are performed by outside firms.
- Penetration Testing — Performing security testing of applications can also be called penetration testing. This activity involves the rigorous analysis of the application and an ad-hoc attempt to subvert the security controls of the application. Penetration testing should not be confused with vulnerability scanning, which is simply a search for obvious flaws. Penetration testing goes further by examining the design of the system, its interfaces, and its environment. Just like secure code review, organizations with experienced, skilled, and independent staff could perform a security code review in-house, but most penetration testing activities are performed by outside firms.

6.1.5.3 Configuration Management

An information system infrastructure is a complex and evolving system. Changes to the system affect its ability to effectively enforce the security policies and therefore protect the organization's assets. The process of managing the changes to the system and its components is referred to as configuration management. More specifically, configuration management is the process of identifying configuration items, controlling their storage, controlling change to configuration items, and reporting on their status.

- Configuration Items — Configuration items (CIs) are unique work products that are individually controlled, tracked, and reported on.
- CI Protection — Configuration items must be protected from unauthorized changes. Without protection of the CIs, a configuration management system cannot function.
- Change Control — There must exist a process by which changes to configuration items are reviewed, approved, and controlled.
- Status Reporting — Configuration management systems must be able to report the status of any configuration item and its history of changes. Moreover, the reporting feature must be capable of generating a version of the system based on the correct version of each of the configuration items.

6.1.5.4 Third-Party Access

Despite any efforts the organization makes to secure its infrastructure, vulnerabilities can be introduced to the system through third-party access to the infrastructure or sensitive data. The organization must take precautions to ensure that the security posture of the system is equally protected by those given access outside of the organization itself. A few safeguards that help to protect the system from third-party access are listed below:

- Contractual Obligations — Prior to granting access or disclosing sensitive information to a third party, the organization should legally bind the third party to providing adequate measures to safeguard the system and sensitive information.
- Minimum Security Requirements — Any legal agreement stating that adequate precaution must be taken should also list what precautions are considered adequate. These precautions should include the minimum security requirements necessary to ensure the security of the system. The assessment team should expect to see requirements for user authentication, agreement to the acceptable use policy, use of personal firewalls and anti-virus software, and other safeguards on the third parties' systems that gain access to or house the sensitive information.
- Review of Third-Party Security — The third-party access contract should also contain a clause that allows the organization to review the security controls of the third party to ensure compliance with the contract and minimum security requirements. Review of these controls could be performed through external vulnerability scans, physical inspection, review of others' reports on the security of the third party's system, or through a security risk assessment on the third party.

6.2 The RIIOT Method: Administrative Data Gathering

As introduced in Chapter 5, the RIIOT method of data gathering can be applied to any security risk assessment technique and helps to ensure a more complete and well-managed data-gathering process. The RIIOT method is applied to any area of security controls by reasoning about the most appropriate approach for gathering data on each security control under review. Applying the RIIOT method to the administrative area shows that a majority of the data-gathering techniques to be applied to administrative security controls will be document review and key personnel interviews. Table 6.2 provides suggested reasonable approaches to gathering data for each of the security controls described in this chapter.

The sections below describe approaches and provide a discussion for each of the RIIOT methods for data gathering within the administrative security controls area. These discussions are intended to provide an approach to be used by security risk assessment teams, and not specific answers to questions that may arise during a security risk assessment.

Table 6.2   RIIOT Method of Data Gathering for Administrative Controls. The application of the RIIOT method to administrative controls indicates that data gathering in this area will focus mainly on document review and personnel interviews.

Controls	Review Documents	Interview Key Personnel	Inspect Controls	Observe Behavior	Test Controls
Application	×	×			
Job requirements	×	×			
Reference checks	×	×			
Employment checks	×	×			
Accuracy checks	×	×			
Credit checks	×	×			
Clearance procedures	×	×			
Employment policies	×	×			
Training and education	×	×		×	
Job description	×	×			
Job requirements	×	×			
Annual reviews	×	×			
Acceptable use policy	×	×		×	
Monitoring	×	×		×	
Two-man control		×	×		
Job rotation	×	×			
Clearance refresh	×	×			

(Continued)

Table 6.2 (Continued)
RIIOT Method of Data Gathering for Administrative Controls

Controls	Review Documents	Interview Key Personnel	Inspect Controls	Observe Behavior	Test Controls
Ethics training	×	×		×	
Sanctions policy	×	×			
Separation of duty	×	×		×	
Termination procedures	×	×			
NDA, NCC	×	×			
Out-briefing	×	×			
Risk management	×	×			
Understand responsibilities	×	×		×	
Assign duties	×	×			
Security team structure	×	×		×	
Security team budget	×	×			
Risk analysis	×	×			
Review of security activities	×	×			
Security operations policies	×	×			
Maintenance policies	×	×		×	
Dual control	×	×	×		
Least privilege	×	×		×	
Internal audit	×	×			
Third-party review	×	×			
Security risk assessment	×	×			
Security awareness	×	×			
Job training	×	×		×	
Policy and procedures	×	×		×	
Double key data entry	×	×		×	
Two-man control	×	×		×	
Criticality analysis	×	×			
Information labeling	×	×	×	×	×
Review of access controls	×	×			×
Media destruction	×	×		×	×
Account creation procedures	×	×		×	×
Account termination procedures	×	×			×
NTK	×	×			×
Asset inventory	×	×	×		
Asset tracking	×	×	×		
Business continuity strategy	×	×			
Business impact analysis	×	×			
Disaster recovery plan	×	×			
Crisis management	×	×			
DRP testing and maintenance	×	×			

(Continued)

Table 6.2 (Continued)
RIIOT Method of Data Gathering for Administrative Controls

Controls	Review Documents	Interview Key Personnel	Inspect Controls	Observe Behavior	Test Controls
Data backup	×	×			×
Incident response plan and procedures	×	×		×	
Incident response training	×	×		×	
Availability of experts	×	×			
Operating procedures	×	×			
Server hardening	×	×			
Vulnerability scanning	×	×			
Scheduled and emergency patches	×	×			
Remote maintenance	×	×			
Remote access	×	×			
Security review/approval	×	×			
Coding standards	×	×	×		
Code review	×	×			
Penetration testing	×	×			
Configuration items	×				
CI protection	×				
Change control	×		×		
Status reporting	×				
Contractual obligations	×	×		×	
Minimum security standards	×	×			
Review of third-party security	×	×			

6.2.1 Review Administrative Documents

As demonstrated in Table 6.2, gathering data on nearly every administrative security control involves the review of documents. The bulk of the document review will be a review of policies and procedures. The remaining document reviews will include a review of coding standards, information security policies, security awareness training, and various security work products.

6.2.1.1 Documents to Request

Using the RIIOT document review technique, the security risk assessment team should determine the set of documents to be reviewed. In many cases the team will be able to review all documents obtained through information requests. In other

Table 6.3   Administrative Documents to Request. The security risk assessment should attempt to obtain and review as many relevant administrative documents as possible within the data-gathering stage of the security risk assessment. This table provides a sample list of documents to request, but it is by no means exhaustive.

Document Type	Sample Titles
Policies	• Acceptable/Appropriate use policy • Password policy • Security plan/program • Employee manuals/handbook • Human resources manual • Audit policy • Physical security policy
Procedures	• Concept of operations (ConOps) • Operations manual • Hardening procedures/guidelines • Security checklists • Disaster recovery procedures • Termination procedures • New account activation form • Disposal of equipment form
Contracts	• Service-level agreements • Business associate agreements
Training materials	• Security awareness training • Security briefings • Security posters

cases, because of time or budget constraints, the team will need to narrow the evidence reviewed to determine the strength of administrative security controls (see Table 6.3).

6.2.1.2 Review Documents for Clarity, Consistency, and Completeness

All documents reviewed should be reviewed based on clarity, completeness, and consistency:

- Clarity — Determination of clarity depends on the intended audience. If the intended audience is considered technical, then the level of technical content within the document would be expected to be higher than in a document intended for a more general audience.

Table 6.4 Expected Element Tables. A sample of elements to be expected within the various security policies is provided in Tables 6.5 through 6.12.

Security Policy	Expected Elements Table
General security policies	Table 6.5
Senior management statement	Table 6.6
Acceptable use policy	Table 6.7
System development and deployment policy	Table 6.8
System and network security maintenance policy	Table 6.9
System security operations policy	Table 6.10
System and network security monitoring policy	Table 6.11
Business continuity policy	Table 6.12

- Consistency — A measurement of the consistency of the documents will be determined once all documents have been reviewed. If more than one document covers a specific area or control and provides conflicting guidance or policy, then those policies can be said to be inconsistent.
- Completeness — Lastly, completeness will be determined based on the security risk assessment team's expectations for a given document. The expectations, or expected elements, could be dictated from a regulation or they could be based on the team's experience.

As discussed in the previous section, it is important to create a checklist or table of expected elements for each document or policy area.[9] Expected elements are simply a listing of all the things a reasonable security engineer would expect to find in a complete document. For example, a complete account creation approval form would be expected to have the following elements: name of requester, name of user, approval, user name to be used, date of request, group access, and account privileges.

In order to assist those performing security risk assessments, the set of expected element tables is listed in Table 6.4. These tables are an illustration of how to construct and use lists of expected items in security documents. However, the team must understand that not all documents are required for all environments, not all expected elements are necessary for all security controls, and not all documents provided will be as neatly titled as the documents discussed here.[10]

6.2.1.2.1 General Information Security Policies

In general, the information security policies should be well organized, documented, approved by management, and distributed to the appropriate staff. The organization of the security policy set can take many forms. It is suggested that

Table 6.5   General Security Policy Expected Elements. All security policies are expected to be organized, documented, approved, and distributed to the audience intended.

Policy Area	Expected Elements	Relevant Policy	√
Organized	Organized in a logical manner to promote their use and distribution		
Documented	Policies must be documented and revised as appropriate		
Approved	The appropriate authority must approve policies		
Distributed	Policies must be made accessible to appropriate personnel		

the policies be organized by audience first and subject matter second. For example, all of the policies regarding expected behavior of employees can go into a single manual because it is intended for the same audience. The single manual should be well organized to promote readability and usability (see Table 6.5).

6.2.1.2.2 Senior Management Statement

All organizations should have a high-level statement of policy that acknowledges the importance of computing resources and organizational assets, provides support for the information security program within the organization, and commits management to authorize and ensure the implementation of an effective security program. This may seem like window dressing to some, but it provides the basis for all conversations regarding the implementation of information security controls. If an organization has a problem producing such a document, this may be indicative of much larger problems (see Table 6.6).

Table 6.6   Senior Management Statement Expected Elements. The senior management of the organization is expected to document their understanding and support for the security function within the organization.

Policy Area	Expected Elements	Relevant Policy	√
Senior management statement	Acknowledgement of importance Statement of support Commitment of authorization and funding		

6.2.1.2.3 Acceptable Use Policy

The acceptable use policy covers the use of the Internet, network, e-mail, and software. This document provides the basis for the following security controls:

- Informing users of their security responsibility.
- Informing users of the organization's right to monitor.
- Informing users of prohibited activities and items.
- Informing users of prohibited behavior and expected behavior.

Not only is it essential to cover all policy elements, but the employee must sign and date the policy (see Table 6.7).

Table 6.7 Acceptable Use Policy Expected Elements. The acceptable use policy is intended for all network users and should cover network use, software use, and e-mail use.

Internet and Network Use		
Policy Area	*Expected Elements*	*Relevant Policy* √
No expectation of privacy	No expectation of privacy No privacy in communications Monitoring of computer usage	
Security measures	Virus detection Blocking inappropriate content (optional)	
Prohibited activities	Inappropriate or unlawful material Prohibited uses Waste of computer resources Illegal copying Games and entertainment software	
Password responsibilities	Responsibility for passwords Passwords do not imply privacy Password upkeep Password selection	
Security responsibilities	Accessing the Internet Accessing others' files Accessing other computers or networks Computer security responsibility Employee's duty of care	
Policy scope	Compliance with applicable laws and licenses No additional rights	

(*Continued*)

Table 6.7   (Continued)
Acceptable Use Policy Expected Elements

Internet and Network Use			
Policy Area	Expected Elements	Relevant Policy	√
	Other policies and guidelines		
	Amendments and revisions		
	Disclaimer of liability		
Employee signature	Name, signature, date		

Software Policy Statement			
Policy Area	Expected Elements	Relevant Policy	√
Prohibited activities	Copy, install, provide to a third party		
	Download		
	Modify, reverse-engineer		
Policy scope	Compliance with applicable laws		
	and licenses		
	No additional rights		
	Other policies and guidelines		
	Amendments and revisions		
Employee signature	Name, signature, date		

E-mail Use Policy			
Policy Area	Expected Elements	Relevant Policy	√
No expectation	No expectation		
of privacy	Waiver of privacy rights		
Prohibited activities	Inappropriate or unlawful		
	material		
	Prohibited uses		
	Waste of computer resources		
	Communication of trade secrets		
	Spamming		
	Spoofing		
	Initiation or forwarding of		
	chain mail		
Password	Responsibility for passwords		
responsibilities	Passwords do not imply privacy		
	Password upkeep		
	Password selection		
Security	Accessing others' files		
responsibilities	Accessing other computers		
	or networks		
	Computer security responsibility		

(Continued)

Table 6.7   (Continued)
Acceptable Use Policy Expected Elements

E-mail Use Policy		
Policy Area	*Expected Elements*	*Relevant Policy* √
Security measures	Virus detection	
Encryption software	Use of encryption software	
	Export restrictions	
Miscellaneous	Attorney-client communications	
	Standard footers	
	Large file transfers	
	Retention policy	
Policy scope	Compliance with applicable laws and licenses	
	No additional rights	
	Other policies and guidelines	
	Amendments and revisions	
Employee signature	Name, signature, date	

Table 6.8   System Development and Deployment Expected Elements. The security function within the organization should be involved in the system development process.

Policy Area	*Expected Elements*	*Relevant Policy* √
Responsibilities	Responsibilities assigned	
System description	System description	
	Threat assessment	
	Architecture description	
	Security requirements	
	Information owners identified	
System evaluation	Security test	
	Penetration test	
	System management evaluation	
System acceptance	Risk assessment	

6.2.1.2.4 System Development and Deployment

The system development and deployment policy dictates the controlled development and deployment of systems to ensure that the organization's security posture is not reduced. This policy should cover system description, system evaluation, and system acceptance (see Table 6.8).

Table 6.9   System Maintenance Expected Elements. The system maintenance policy should cover situations such as system patching, application maintenance, remote maintenance, and change management.

Policy Area	Expected Elements	Relevant Policy √
Responsibilities	Responsibilities assigned	
Scheduled patches	Operating system maintenance	
	Emergency patches	
	Version updates	
Application maintenance	Scheduled patches	
	Emergency patches	
	Version updates	
Remote maintenance	Remote maintenance access	
	Modem management	
Change management	Configuration items	
	Change control	
	Change approval	
	Version control	

6.2.1.2.5 Security Maintenance Policy

The security maintenance policy dictates the system and network security maintenance process. This policy should cover operating system maintenance, application maintenance, remote maintenance, and configuration management of the system (see Table 6.9).

6.2.1.2.6 Security Operations Policy

The security operations policy dictates the security operations process. This policy should cover security control administration, security auditing and review, data backup, and virus protection of the system (see Table 6.10).

6.2.1.2.7 Security Monitoring Policy

The security monitoring policy dictates the system security monitoring process. This policy should cover monitoring of the security posture, monitoring for system vulnerabilities, incident response, and periodic risk assessment of the system (see Table 6.11).

6.2.1.2.8 Business Continuity Planning

There should be policies in place that dictate the business continuity process. This policy should cover disaster recovery and business continuity planning (see Table 6.12.).

Table 6.10 System Security Operations Expected Elements. The system security maintenance process policy is expected to contain policies for the administration of security controls, auditing and audit log review, and data backup.

Policy Area	Expected Elements	Relevant Policy	√
Responsibilities	Security responsibility assigned		
Security control administration	Account maintenance		
	Separation of duties		
	Perimeter security		
Security auditing and audit review	Audit policy		
	Audit log review		
Data backup	System backup plan and procedures		
	Laptop backup plan and procedures		
	Backup storage plan and procedures		

Table 6.11 System Security Monitoring Expected Elements. The system security monitoring policies should cover areas such as security posture monitoring, vulnerability monitoring, incident response, and periodic risk assessments.

Policy Area	Expected Elements	Relevant Policy	√
Responsibilities	Responsibility assigned		
Monitor security posture of system	Audit log review		
	Network device log review		
	Security incident reporting		
	Virus checking		
Monitor system vulnerabilities	Monitor threat environment (CERT, BugTrac)		
	Periodic vulnerability scans		
Security incident response	Reaction		
	Response		
	Recovery		
Periodic risk assessment	Periodic risk assessment		
	Periodic security assessment		

6.2.1.3 Reviewing Documents Other Than Policies

Although security policies may be the most numerous documents the security risk assessment team reviews, they will not be the only ones. Other documents to review within the administrative data-gathering task include code review

Table 6.12   Business Continuity Expected Elements. The business continuity policy is expected to contain statements concerning disaster recovery and business continuity planning.

Policy Area	Expected Elements	Relevant Policy	√
Responsibilities	Responsibility assigned		
Disaster recovery	Recovery strategy		
	Recovery procedures		
	Plan administration		
Business continuity planning	Business continuity strategy		
	Business impact analysis		
	Emergency response procedures		
	Crisis management		
	Plan administration		
	Plan maintenance and testing		

guidelines, work products from security activities, security procedures, and security awareness training.

6.2.1.3.1 Coding Standard Review

A coding standard is a set of rules and guidelines that programmers are expected to follow to increase the quality and security of the code produced. Any organization that writes applications should have a coding standard and associated training. The absence of a coding standard greatly increases the likelihood that produced code will contain material security flaws. The security risk assessment team should ask for and review the organization's coding standards for clarity, completeness, and consistency. The security coding standard review guideline in Table 6.13 provides a baseline for the review.

6.2.1.3.2 Security Work Product Review

Security work products are the output of a security-relevant activity. For example, signed acceptable use policy forms are a work product of security awareness training. The review of security work products differs greatly depending upon the security activity. Regardless, all work products should simply be reviewed as evidence that a security activity is performed regularly and completely.

The review of information security procedures should follow the review of policies. Procedures are the "next level down" from the security policies in that they provide guidance or instructions on how to implement security policy statements.

Table 6.13 Coding Standard Expected Elements. The security coding standard should cover secure coding principles, good practices, and warnings.

Policy Area	Expected Elements	Relevant Policy √
Principles	Least privilege	
	Fail-safe default	
	Economy of mechanism	
	Least common mechanism	
	Open design	
	Role separation	
Good practice	Strip symbols from binary files	
	Use program wrappers	
	Self-limit resource consumption	
	Sanity check input	
	Use true random functions in encryption routines	
	Plan maintenance and testing	
	Use static links	
	Use return codes	
	Use privilege bracketing	
Warnings	Do not hardcode passwords	
	Do not echo passwords	
	Do not store sensitive data unencrypted	
	Do not transmit sensitive data unencrypted	
	Do not invoke shells or command lines from within an application	
	Do not use filenames (use file descriptors)	
	Do not rely on IP address as authentication	
	Do not create files in world writable directories	
	Do not make time of use/time of check errors	
	Do not make race condition errors	

6.2.1.3.3 Information Security Procedure Review

The same approach as described for reviewing information security policies can be applied here:

- Review Documents for Clarity — The procedures should be useful to their intended audience without the need to research terms, definitions, and jargon.
- Review Documents for Content — The assessor should judge the content of procedures based on their completeness (coverage of the topic area) and the correctness and consistency with the policy it references. One approach

Table 6.14 Policy and Procedure Association Example. The termination procedures implement the termination policy statements.

Policy statement	*Employee Termination*: All access and privileges to system and facility resources must be removed immediately upon termination of employment.
Termination Procedures	*Notification*: Human resources will ensure that all appropriate parties are notified and review nondisclosure and noncompete agreements with the terminated individual.
	Logical Access: Operations will terminate access to all accounts associated with the terminated individual.
	Physical and Communication Access: Facilities will terminate all physical access (return of badge, revocation of access codes, lock and combination changes) and communication access (cell phone, e-mail, voice mail).
	Duties: The supervisor will turn over duties to another individual and notify appropriate partners of the termination of employment.

to creating security procedures is to create one or more security procedure steps for each policy statement. The security procedures would then provide a mapping of procedures to security policy statements making a completeness and consistency argument.

The assessor can use this mapping technique to review the adequacy of the procedure content. There should be a one-to-many mapping from the security policy statement to the security procedure statements. For example, a security operations policy should have a security policy statement covering the termination of individuals. The associated security procedures should provide guidance (or requirements) on how to implement the policy statements See the example in Table 6.14.

Not all security policies are expected to have associated security procedures. For example, the acceptable use policy typically has no need for more detailed procedures implementing the policy. However, policy statements covering system hardening, account creation and termination, and incident tracking and reporting could certainly use more detailed description of how the policy statement will be enforced.

6.2.1.3.4 Security Awareness Training Review

The security risk assessment team, or a member of the team, should review the security awareness training material for completeness, correctness, and

Table 6.15 Security Awareness Expected Elements. The security awareness program should cover areas such as physical security, technical controls, and requests for information.

Policy Area	Expected Elements	Relevant Policy √
Physical security	Lock rooms and cabinets with sensitive information Proper disposal of sensitive material Challenge unbadged visitors	
Technical controls	Use password-protected screen savers Use strong passwords Change passwords regularly Protection of sensitive information (encryption)	
Request for information	Recognizing fraudulent attempts Reporting attempts to security hotline Referring requests to appropriate personnel	

effectiveness. The completeness of the security awareness training depends on the acceptable use policy and the threat environment for the assessed organization. A baseline set of topics that should be covered would include education on physical and technical security controls as well as how not to be a victim of social engineering. All employees should understand the value of sensitive information and how to recognize and report attempts to gain access to such information. Table 6.15 provides a baseline checklist for reviewing security awareness training.

6.2.2 Interview Administrative Personnel

Data gathering for administrative security controls also involves interviewing key personnel. The security risk assessment team can interview key personnel regarding nearly any aspect of administrative security controls. It is important that the security risk assessment team carefully plan the topics to cover, whom to interview, and what questions to ask.

6.2.2.1 Administrative Interview Topics

It is rare that the team has the luxury of interviewing personnel on every aspect of the security controls, so the team must prioritize topics and even specific questions to optimize the effectiveness of the interview process. A few key points to consider:

- Give Precedence to Questions Concerning Key Security Controls — The team may have discovered that the organization relies heavily on several key security controls. For example, the incident reporting and response process may be instrumental to the maintenance of the security posture. In this case, the interview of key personnel should include probing questions as to the effectiveness and maturity of this process.
- Get a Second Opinion — When asking about key security controls, obtain information from several parties involved in the process to compare views of the process effectiveness.
- Do They Walk the Walk? — Ask for specific steps involved in key processes. Specifically, ask what steps were followed recently so that you may compare those steps to the documented policy or process.

6.2.2.2 Administrative Interview Subjects

The security risk assessment team should interview those personnel best able to provide information regarding the topics they have selected to cover. Recalling that it is best to obtain several points of view on key processes, the team should also seek to interview those in various roles associated with key processes. Although the specific selection of who to interview will depend largely on the organization's structure and the security risk assessment team's selected topic, the roles listed below should be considered:

- Users — The security risk assessment team should always interview a few representative users. If possible, these users should be picked at random or at least the selection should be largely influenced by the security risk assessment team. Users can provide insight into the effectiveness of security awareness training, efficiency of security controls, and actual processes that are practiced.
- Human Resources Manager — Many administrative controls involve the human resources manager. Controls such as applications, job requirements, employment checks, accuracy checks, credit checks, clearance procedures, employment policies, training, job descriptions, job requirements, annual reviews, sanctions policies, and termination procedures are typically created by and administered by the human resources department.
- Senior Management — One of the principles of information security is that senior management is ultimately responsible for security. This principle is founded in the fact that senior management is in control of the budget, the organizational structure, and the ultimate decision to accept or reduce risk. A security risk assessment must include interviews with senior

management to determine their risk tolerance and establish their role in risk management.

- Security Staff — Of course, the interview process must include interviews with those who perform the security activities such as system hardening, incident response, and account creation. The security risk assessment team should be looking for adherence to policies and procedures or evidence of good practices that do not happen to be documented. Be sure to include open-ended questions such as "What suggested safeguards are you hoping will come out of this security risk assessment?"

6.2.2.3 Administrative Interview Questions

Prior to any interview, the security risk assessment team (or interview team) should prepare a set of interview questions to ask each interview subject. To give the team an idea or example of such a set of questions, Tables 6.16, 6.17, and 6.18 provide a baseline set of questions that may be used, modified, or extended. These baseline interview questions cover the topics of incident response, security operations, and the security program.

6.2.2.3.1 Incident Response Interview Questions

The incident response questions in Table 6.16 can be asked of anyone involved in the incident response process. The questions cover the planning, detection, response, recovery, post-recovery, and reporting phases of incident response. If the organization has few incident response processes and does not clearly define these stages, the team should switch to a more open-ended interview that allows the interviewee to describe the current process by walking through a sample or the most recent incident.

6.2.2.3.2 Security Operations Interview Questions

The security operations questions in Table 6.17 can be asked of several representatives of the security or systems operations groups. The questions cover the system operations, server operations, file operations, user operations, and emerging threats. If the organization has few processes, the team should switch to a more open-ended interview that allows the interviewee to describe the current process by walking through patch management, account management, and system file management.

6.2.2.3.3 Security Program Interview Questions

The questions regarding the security program in Table 6.18 can be asked of several representatives of the security program group and to the person to whom that

Table 6.16   Incident Response Interview Guideline. The interviewer should structure the interview to determine the processes in place within each of the incident response phases and the extent to which these processes are followed.

Objective	Sub-topic	Suggested Questions
Determine existence and adequacy of security controls within incident response area	Planning	• Under what circumstances would you pursue prosecution? • Who are the members of the incident response team? • How will the team communicate if the primary communication method is suspected of being compromised? • What credentials does anyone on the team have for computer forensic investigation?
	Detection	• Give an example of an event in which you would need to pull the CEO out of a board meeting? • Would someone on the night shift be able to make the same determination?
	Response	• How do you go about deploying the team (specifically)? • Under what circumstances does a system owner's permission need to be granted? How is that documented? • Describe the process for evidence collection. • How do you determine the cause of the breach?
	Recovery	• How are compromised systems restored? • How do you validate that the systems have been restored?
	Post-recovery	• How is evidence protected?
	Reporting	• What does an incident report look like? • To whom would you report the following incidents: theft of trade secrets (FBI), imported child pornography (U.S. Customs Service)?

group reports. The questions cover security awareness, policy development, risk assessment, security review, coordination and promotion, and program updates. If the organization has few processes, the team should switch to a more open-ended interview that allows the interviewee to describe the current processes by walking through training, the budgeting process, and how new security controls are selected and implemented.

Table 6.17 Security Operations Interview Guideline. The interviewer should structure the interview to determine the processes in place within each of the security operations areas and the extent to which these processes are followed.

Objective	Subtopic	Question
Determine existence and adequacy of security controls within system development	System operations	• What types of changes can be performed without approval or documentation? (None) • How are hard drives disposed of? Do you ever give systems away to employees or charities? How are they sanitized? • What is your backup plan? What about for laptops? Where are the tapes stored? Do you test your backups?
	Server operations	• What guidance do you use or produce for system hardening? • What changes do you have to make to that guidance for some of your systems?
	File operations	• How do you control access to library code? • Is there an owner for every file?
	User operations	• How are changes in privileges tracked? • What happens if a user forgets his password? • Are user accounts ever reviewed? How often? By whom?
	Emerging threats	• How do you learn about new vulnerabilities in your systems? • How do you determine your reaction? • How do you test your possible solution?

6.2.3 Inspect Administrative Security Controls

Data gathering for administrative security controls also involves inspecting administrative security controls. Recall that inspection differs from testing in that inspection is performed when testing is inappropriate or infeasible. Inspection involves the review of the security control and aspects of it such as configuration or arrangements.

For the most part, the approach for performing a security control inspection includes the listing of the security controls under review, verifying information

Table 6.18   Security Program Interview Guideline The interviewer should structure the interview to determine the processes in place within each of the security program areas and the extent to which these processes are followed.

Objective	Subtopic	Question
Determine existence and adequacy of security controls within information security program	Security awareness	• Do you have a list of all users who need training and have received it? • Where are the records kept? Do these records include a signature of the student and the instructor?
	Policy development	• When were the policies last updated? How long did it take to get them approved? • How were users informed of their change? New signatures?
	Risk assessment	• How often are risk assessments performed? • By whom? What is their relationship to the organization or any of its security controls? Did they recommend products? Did you buy them?
	Security review	• Do you think that other departments are following the policies you set for them (operations, monitoring, development)? Would it surprise you if I told you they were not? • Do you have any annual or periodic report on the security posture of your organization?
	Coordination and promotion	• Who is the security liaison within the development organization? (follow up by reviewing that person's job description.) • What is your role in the BCP/DRP process? (Not leading it or sole member.)
	Program updates	• To what extent do you research new security initiatives? What are you likely to recommend next? What did you recently block or not recommend and on what basis? • Describe your role as a security liaison in another project

gathered, determining vulnerabilities, and documenting the results. Each of these phases is discussed within the context of administrative data gathering.

Special consideration must be paid, however, to the review of the security organization itself. This "inspection" is much more involved than the inspection of other security controls because it covers many activities, documents, roles, and even organizational structure. The inspection of the security organization is covered at the end of this section.

6.2.3.1 Listing Administrative Security Controls

The relevant security controls to be inspected include only those that lend themselves to inspection. In the case of administrative controls, this includes the following:

- coding standards;
- asset and inventory tracking;
- information labeling;
- change control;
- two-man control; and
- dual control.

Of course, only those controls actually implemented by the organization can be inspected. The list of administrative security controls to be reviewed for a specific organization comprises any of the controls that the organization has stated are in place. Statements regarding administrative controls in place could have come from interviews or provided as part of the document review process. The team should obtain a point of contact for each of these controls.

6.2.3.2 Verify Information Gathered

Information gathered regarding administrative security controls should be confirmed through the inspection process. Team members should use various methods to confirm the existence of each of these security controls.

- Coding Standards — Although a document called "coding standards" or something similar may exist, this does not mean that coding standards are in place. The security risk assessment team should be looking for evidence that these standards are carried out. Ask the point of contact for any work products from the coding standard process (i.e., peer review process documents, completed code review checklists for the most recently approved module) or ask to see a portion of the code produced and inspect it yourself for adherence to the coding standards.
- Asset and Inventory Tracking — If there is a policy in place that requires that all assets be tracked, then members of the team should check to see if all assets they come across are tagged. This does not need to be an exhaustive search. Instead the inspection can be done throughout the time the team spends on site. The inventory tracking system can be spot checked

by tracing the disposition of a few assets. The inventory tracking system should be able to locate any item number in the inventory or produce a transfer or destruction document.

- Information Labeling — If the organization has instituted an information labeling program or has an information labeling policy, then the assessment team should inspect the administrative controls for their effectiveness in enforcing this policy. Inspection can be in the form of inspecting various documents or media containing sensitive information for the proper label. During the course of the on-site assessment the team will come across many documents and media that contain sensitive information. The team merely needs to be cognizant of the information labeling policy and determine if it is being followed. Specific documents that the team is likely to review include previous audit reports and internal documents.

- Change Control — If a change control process is in place, the team should read available documentation to become familiar with the process. Then the team members should select several recent changes to the system, including at least one you know about through other data-gathering processes. Ask to see the documents that walk through the process of change control for these selected changes.

- Two-Man Control and Dual Control — If the organization has policies and procedures in place for two-man or dual control, the assessment team should inspect these controls to determine their effectiveness. Inspection of these controls can be accomplished through an understanding of the policies and job descriptions and then a review of any evidence of separation of duties. For example, if dual controls are in place for the creation of an account, the security assessment team members can review audit logs for the account application and account creation activities. If both activities are performed by unique individuals, then dual control could be deemed to be effective in this case.

6.2.3.3 Determine Vulnerabilities

During inspection of the security controls, the security risk assessment team should look for vulnerabilities. Administrative security controls are policies, procedures, or activities and not physical or logical controls. Therefore the inspection process of these controls simply involves the determination of their effectiveness. If the controls are determined to be ineffective, then they have a vulnerability.

Work products of each of the administrative security controls (that lend themselves to inspection) can be inspected to determine if a vulnerability exists:

- Coding Standards — If instances are found where the code does not conform to coding standards or the code review does not take place, then the coding standards and coding procedures are ineffective.

- Asset and Inventory Tracking — If instances are found where assets or inventory cannot be tracked or accounted for, then the asset and inventory tracking policy and procedures are not effective.
- Information Labeling — If the team is able to find instances of information (media or documents) that do not have the proper labels, then the information labeling procedures are not effective.
- Two-man and Dual Control — If the team finds instances where the two-man or dual controls are not being enforced, then these procedures are not effective.

When the team finds any of these policies or procedures lacking, it is also important to determine the reason for the ineffectiveness of the policy. The team will need to use judgment to determine the root cause of the failures. Possible root causes are lack of sufficient training, lack of leadership, lack of sanctions, culture or morale, lack of clarity in the document, insufficient time or resources to complete reviews, or lack of skills among the staff.

6.2.3.4 Document and Review Findings

As with all findings, the security risk assessment team must be sure to carefully record their findings in the area of administrative controls through inspection. The team should include dates, evidence, team member names, and the vulnerabilities observed. These findings must be reviewed with the entire team and the point of contact for the control to give them a chance to clarify any misunderstandings.

6.2.3.5 Inspect the Security Organization

One of the most important administrative data-gathering exercises the security risk assessment team can perform is assessing the effectiveness of the information security organization. The team must review the organization's security staff and the way in which the security staff is organized and reports within the organization. The security staff, after all, is the team responsible for the selection, application, and maintenance of the security controls within the organization. The composition and placement of this team within the assessed organization greatly affects the security posture of the organization.

The rise of threats to information assets and the development of information security regulations have led to a much greater appreciation for a strong information security capability within the organization. The way in which this capability is implemented in the organization can take many forms. Some organizations have created security teams while others have appointed Chief

Table 6.19 Security Organization Inspection Guideline. The security risk assessment should inspect the effectiveness of the security organization through a review of the organizational structure, budget and resources, and roles and responsibilities.

Security Program Area	Expected Elements
Organization	Visibility
	Objectiveness
	Authority
Budget and resources	Adequate resources
	Resources distributed based on a risk model
	IT security part of capital planning process
	Cost-effective solutions
Roles and responsibilities	Responsibilities assigned
	Skills
	Staffing

Security Officers (CSOs) or Chief Information Security Officers (CISOs). Despite the form the security risk assessment team requires an approach for measuring the effectiveness of the information security capability of the organization.

There are no hard-and-fast rules or numbers to follow when it comes to measuring the effectiveness of the information security capability of the organization, but the application of information security and business management principles can yield useful guidance.

6.2.3.5.1 Organization

The information security organization is functionally responsible for the security posture of the organization and the protection of the organization's assets. Execution of the security activities and other elements of an effective security program needs to be coordinated through a security organization and staffed by knowledgeable and experienced security professionals. Such an organization must have the proper organizational placement, adequate resources, and appropriate responsibilities consistent with its mission.

The regular and routine practice of risk reduction must be ensured through efficient operation of the security program. The principles by which any information security organization may be measured are listed in Table 6.19.

The importance of information security and the protection of the organization's assets are certainly understood within most organizations today. However, the proper placement and structure of the information security organization is not. It is useful to understand that information security can be divided into operations and oversight, see Table 6.20.

- Security Operations — This function is responsible for the operations and maintenance of technical security mechanisms. This includes tasks such as server hardening, firewall ruleset maintenance, account maintenance, security patch application, and intrusion detection system maintenance.
- Security Oversight and Direction — Security oversight is responsible for the overall information security program. This includes development of policies and procedures, security awareness training, and periodic review of security operations.

The placement, structure, and authority of the security organization can greatly influence its effectiveness. To be most effective, a security organization must have a direct reporting line to an officer or the company. Although almost any information security professional will agree that information security needs to report to (or be) a C-level position, few understand why. See Sidebar 6.1 for an explanation.

Sidebar 6.1 Why Security Should not Be Part of the IT Department.

One of the most important elements of a security program within an organization is the placement of the security personnel within the organization. There are a few key elements of information security that need to be considered for the organizational placement of the security department:

- Information security (IS) is a multifaceted concern. An information security department needs to consider the threats to the organization's assets no matter what the source. Therefore, the IS department will be working with many other departments such as legal, human resources, executives, department heads, and information technology (IT).
- The information security program develops information intended for C-level executives. Such information includes risks to the organization, tradeoffs between usability and security, tradeoffs between departments, and cost of adhering to contracts and regulations.

- The information security program is only effective if it is unbiased and protected. C-level executives need the information that the IS department can produce so that they can make informed decisions. If that information is tainted, swayed, or suppressed, then the organization is in danger of making decisions with the wrong information or without any information.

An information security department has three basic functions: governance and oversight, audit, and operations. The functions of the information security department can be divided across multiple organizations. In fact, such a separation increases the objectivity of the governance and audit functions. However, under no circumstances should the governance and oversight functions be inside the IT department. These functions must report directly to (or be) a C-level executive

C-level executives, and not department heads, are trusted to make risk decisions for the organization. Furthermore, the IT department is the center of many security-relevant tradeoffs and decisions. Placing the IS department inside the IT department effectively confirms that each tradeoff will likely side with the budget and schedule constraints of the IT department and will not adequately consider the ramifications to the overall business.

The governance and oversight element of the security organization needs to be placed appropriately within the organization for it to be effective. The important aspects of the organizational placement of the governance function of the security organization are visibility, objectiveness, and authority. Without these three aspects the security organization is likely to fail in its mission.

- Visibility — In order to be effective, an information security organization must have visibility into all functions of the organization that can affect the overall security posture of the organization. If the security department is seen as "an IT thing," then it is likely that the security organization will be ineffective at controlling security risk in areas such as human resources, facilities, legal, and other business areas.
- Objectiveness — An information security organization must be objective. This principle is a long-standing one in any function that provides oversight, audit, or compliance. The principle states 'You can't check your

Table 6.20 Security Organization Structure. The effectiveness of the security organization can be enabled or disabled by its placement within the security organization.

Security Organization	Functions	Reporting Requirement
Security governance and oversight	Overall internal security office. Overall security program including interface with other departments. Provide advice and guidance to other departments, create policy and awareness training, and periodically review security operations. Be in charge of resolving incidents. Report security posture to more senior management.	"C-level" executive, CIO, CFO, CEO, or even be a CSO or CISO itself and report to the CEO or board of directors. You could (should) have physical security reporting to the CSO.
Security audit	Oversight for overall security program. Perform independent periodic risk assessment and security program review.	This should be internal audit (if not reporting to CSO) or an outside firm.
Security operations	Account maintenance, firewall and IDS configuration, operating system patching, anti-virus configuration and operations, etc.	It seems reasonable that this function reports to director of IT, although the security audit and governance should periodically review for compliance.

own work." Consider the security department that both hardens systems and provides the vulnerability scanning to ensure that the systems are hardened correctly or, worse, designs the network security model and provides the review of the network security architecture.[11]

• Authority — The information security department should also be given proper authority to provide oversight of the organization's security controls. Specific authority may include representation on the change control board and reporting to a C-level executive.

6.2.3.5.2 Budget and Resources

The information security organization must have adequate budget and resources in order to ensure the development and maintenance of an appropriate security posture for the organization and the protection of the organization's assets. The key aspects of appropriate budget and resources are discussed below:

- Adequate Resources — The information security department must have adequate resources to get the job done. As there are no hard-and-fast rules as to what constitutes "adequate" resources, the security risk assessment team member must use interviews, observation, and judgment to determine the adequacy of the organization's information security resources. However, here are a few of the things to look for:
  - Does the security department have control of its own budget?
  - What percent of the overall IT budget is the security budget?
  - How many staff members are on the security team compared to IT?
  - How much does the company spend on legal costs as compared to information security costs?
  - How does the organization compare with its peers?
  - Are resources distributed based on a risk model?
  - Is information security part of the capital planning process?

6.2.3.5.3 Roles and Responsibilities

Lastly, the information security organization needs to formally recognize the roles and responsibilities of the team. These roles and responsibilities should be documented. The security risk assessment team member should review the current job descriptions of the information security staff to determine if the roles and responsibilities are appropriately assigned and documented. Again, there are no hard-and-fast rules as to what constitutes "appropriate" assigning of roles and responsibilities, so the security risk assessment team member must use interviews, observation, and judgment to determine the adequacy of the organization's information security resources. The assessor can use the following questions and observations as a guideline:

- Does each staff member within the security organization have an accurate job description?
  - Are all of the responsibilities of the security organization assigned to individuals?
  - Does the description specify the qualifications required for each position?
  - Does the description specify the expectations and boundaries of the role?
- Are the staff members qualified and properly trained for their positions?
- Are there an adequate number of staff members to get the job done?

6.2.4 Observe Administrative Behavior

The process of gathering data through observation is a subtle one. With a few exceptions, this process is passive and depends on team members being aware of the organization's policies and procedures and keeping an eye out for opportunities to confirm or disprove the organization's adherence to policies and procedures. Although some observations can be active in nature, such as placing a control badge in your pocket and seeing if anyone challenges you. More experienced team members will find observation to be second nature and a side effect of being on site.

With a little guidance and teamwork these observations can be recorded from most team members and add additional data points to the data-gathering process. Table 6.21 provides some guidance for observing the behavior of the organization's staff to determine the strength of some of the administrative controls. The security risk assessment team is encouraged to review Table 6.21 and add or modify table elements to suit its own needs and experiences.

6.2.5 Test Administrative Security Controls

The last phase of data gathering for administrative security controls in the RIIOT method is testing. Testing of administrative controls is the process of invoking conditions that should trigger the administrative controls and reviewing the response against the policies, procedures, and good practice. This type of data gathering provides excellent insight into the actual effectiveness of the controls, but it can only be applied in a limited fashion.

The administrative controls that lend themselves to testing include information labeling, media destruction, and account and access controls. An approach for testing each of these controls is presented below. The security risk assessment team is encouraged to adopt, modify, or add to these test methods.

6.2.5.1 Information Labeling Testing

Testing the procedures for information security labeling requires that the security risk assessment team perform activities that cause the information labeling procedures to come into in effect (i.e., cause sensitive documents to get created). There are typically many activities that will cause a sensitive document to get created during a security risk assessment. In the event that the security risk assessment team has not performed any activities that would cause the creation of sensitive information, the team can simply ask for a document to be created that contains sensitive information.

Any one of the following events is likely to cause the assessed organization to create a sensitive document:

- Request SMTP strings for internal testing.
- Request minutes of change management control board meetings.

Table 6.21 Administrative Controls Observation Guideline. The security risk assessment team should be prepared to observe the behavior of the security staff, key personnel, and general employee population as a check against policies, procedures, and training.

Administrative Control	Claim	Observation Test or Procedure Check
Ethics	All employees exhibit ethical behavior	General observations from being on site: • Did any members of the team witness or overhear any unethical behavior?
Separation of duty	• No sensitive transactions are performed by a single person • Security controls are independently reviewed	Identify critical transactions requiring separation: • Development/production • Key generation/key delivery • Design and implementation/audit • PO creation/PO payment • Associate transactions with accounts or individuals • Check of conflicts of interest
Understanding responsibilities	All personnel understand their responsibilities	General observations from being on site: • Did personnel generally understand what they were responsible for? • Were there any noticed gaps or overlaps in responsibilities?
Security team structure	Security program has the authority and visibility they need to accomplish their job	General observations from being on site: • Did the security organization have the access and authority it needed to do their job? • Were any areas inappropriately excluded from the security risk assessment?
Least privilege	All personnel have the minimum privileges they need to perform their job	Did personnel have more privilege than necessary? • Did anyone log in as root? • How many administrators have root access? • Who had access to audit logs?

(Continued)

Table 6.21 (Continued)
Administrative Controls Observation Guideline

Administrative Control	Claim	Observation Test or Procedure Check
Job training	All personnel have the proper training and skills to perform their duties	Was there anyone who did not have adequate skills or training to do their job? • Were the available security tools being used to their full extent? • Did internal reviews, scans, and audits expose obvious vulnerabilities?
Policy and procedure	All policies and procedures are followed	Were there any obvious breaches to security policies? • Were acceptable use policies followed? • Were visitor control policies followed? • Was change management policy followed? • Did you see any passwords on monitors or other areas (e.g., under keyboards or phones)?
Double key data entry	Sensitive data is entered twice to ensure accuracy	Ask to observe the data entry process: • Were the data entry procedures followed? • Did you witness any mistakes being caught?
Two-man control and dual control	Sensitive tasks are performed by more than a single person	Ask to observe the sensitive process: • Does the process really require two people? • What would happen if a single person attempted to perform the whole process alone?
Information labeling	All sensitive information is labeled	Find instances of unlabeled or improperly labeled information: • Check all documents reviewed for proper labels • Witness documents being created (perhaps as part of the security risk assessment). Were the documents properly labeled?
Media destruction	All sensitive information is removed from media released from control	Ask to witness media destruction methods: • Were the media destruction procedures followed?

	• Query the inventory tracking system for disposed systems — check methods of disposal. • Check media destruction area or store rooms for unused media. Double-check stored media against the inventory tracking system for inaccuracies. Check to see if processes are followed: • Check trash bins near fax machines or user work areas. Is there any sensitive information in them? • Check storage areas for older systems and system parts. Have all of these systems and parts been properly sanitized?
Account maintenance • No group IDs • No dormant accounts • No weak passwords	• Ask to see a list of accounts for selected network components. Look for the following as good candidates: 　• Equipment requiring remote maintenance 　• Help desk functions • Any group accounts associated with the equipment? • Do these accounts conform to policies? Sufficiently strong passwords? Passwords changed and not shared?
Contractual obligations All business partners with access to sensitive information properly protect information	Ask for list of contractors and list of signed contracts: • Were there any contracts that had significant modifications to the standard contractual obligations? • Do all contractors have a contract with the important elements of contractual security obligations? • Have any audits on the contractors been performed?
Security awareness and acceptable use policy All staff follow guidance	Perform security walk-throughs. Be aware of: • Recorded passwords in workspace • Sensitive conversations in public areas • Sensitive information left on printers or in waste baskets

(Continued)

Table 6.21 (Continued)
Administrative Controls Observation Guideline

Administrative Control	Claim	Observation Test or Procedure Check
	Staff understands how to recognize and guard against social engineering	Perform social engineering (optional): • Attempt to gain sensitive information or access through social engineering methods
	All staff is security aware	Ask some questions within the interviews to test security awareness: • Ask for information you should not receive • Ask who they would contact if they noticed a security breach
Incident response	Incident response policies and procedures are followed	Ask for a walk-through of the last incident response: Ask for documentation of the response. Check against the policy. Also recall an incident from an interview or other source and ask to see where that incident was documented
Hiring and termination	• References are checked for all employees	• Randomly select some employees and ask your HR contact to verify that references were checked for that person.
	• Background checks are performed for sensitive positions	• Randomly select some employees with sensitive positions and ask your HR contact to verify that background checks were performed for that person.
System monitoring	• Violations of the acceptable use policy are monitored and reported	• Attempt to violate the acceptable use policy by going to some forbidden Web sites. Ask to see the monitor logs later that day.
	• Attempts to circumvent security are monitored and logged	• In conjunction with your external security testing, review system monitoring effectiveness.
Data backup	Backups are performed for critical data	• Ask to witness data backup procedures on a test system • Ask to witness any backup or restore procedure that is scheduled while you are on site.

- Request latest incident handling report.
- Create contractual documents for an independent security risk assessment.

The security risk assessment team can then simply check that the document was created according to the associated procedures. The team should specifically check for the proper label in the proper place and format.

6.2.5.2 Media Destruction Testing

Testing the media destruction controls requires that the security risk assessment team perform activities that cause the destruction of media that could possibly contain sensitive information. This can be a follow-on activity from the information labeling testing, since that task involves the creation of sensitive information. The approaches for TRASHINT and sanitization testing methods below should be considered.

6.2.5.2.1 Approach 1: TRASHINT

This approach involves a simple test of the disposal and destruction procedures for sensitive information. The security risk assessment team should be familiar with the information labeling and sensitive information and media disposal and destruction procedures. With those procedures in mind, the team should look for any deficiencies in the practice of the procedures. The TRASHINT (short for Trash Intelligence) approach tests these controls by looking for improper disposal of sensitive information or media.

- Where to Look — During a TRASHINT testing exercise the security risk assessment team should search candidate areas for the possible presence of sensitive information. Sensitive information could be just about anywhere but the following places are good candidates:
  - Trash Receptacles — Check trash bins for sensitive information, especially those near fax machines, sensitive areas, and shredding bins.
  - Shredding Bins — Check for shredding bins that have not been properly secured.
  - Out in the Open — Check for sensitive information left in unsecured areas. Places to look include desk tops, executive floors, conference rooms, and outside security control areas.
  - Outside Trash Receptacles — Check for unsecured outside trash receptacles. No need to scrounge through coffee grounds, but the team should look for boxes or stacks of paper or special forms.
- What to Look For — Sensitive information is typically quite easy to spot. Look for any papers with sensitive information labels or with

clearly sensitive information. Clearly sensitive information includes credit information, salary information, customer lists, personal data, and the like.

- What to Do With It — Prior to participating in the TRASHINT exercise, the security risk assessment team must all be briefed as to the protocol for handling sensitive information. The protocol should be developed specifically for the assessed organization's needs and approved by the organization. As a baseline protocol, the following is suggested:
  - Trash — If the sensitive information was found in the trash or discarded in an open area (e.g., hallway), then it should be collected, labeled, documented, and returned to the assessed organization.
  - Unsecured Shredding Bins — If the sensitive information is found in any container that is normally secured (or should be), then the information may be reviewed but should not be removed.
  - Workspace — If the sensitive information is discovered on someone's workspace when it should have been secured, then the information may be reviewed but should not be removed.
  - For those situations in which the material is not to be removed the team should consider documenting the evidence by taking a digital picture.

6.2.5.2.2 Approach 2: Sanitization Test

The sanitization test requires that the security risk assessment team have tools to check the effectiveness of the assessed organization's sanitization methods. The security risk assessment team should be familiar with the media disposal and destruction procedures. With those procedures in mind, the team should collect samples of sanitized data, test the media for proper sanitization, and document the results.

- Collection of Samples — Samples of media that should be sanitized can be collected from store rooms, recycle bins, or work areas dedicated to this task. The team should seek only those devices that are believed to have completed the sanitization process.
- Test Media for Residual Data — The assessment team can test the data sanitization measures to assess their effectiveness. The tests should start with simple read attempts, but could progress to low-level attempts to read data residuals with the use of tools. These tools can vary from the quality assurance option in data sanitization tools, to disk recovery tools and data forensic tools.
- Document Results — The security risk assessment team needs to document the results of the attempts to read data from sanitized media. Any findings will be referenced as evidence in the final risk assessment report. It is important to record what data was captured and the effort and toil the team required in gaining access to the data.

6.2.5.3 Account and Access Control Procedures Testing

Whether a policy exists or not, the security risk assessment team should review the account provisioning procedures and the account maintenance procedures during the data-gathering stage of the security risk assessment. Accounts on the systems within the organization represent the allowed accesses and privileges of users within the system. These security controls are central to the enforcement of any security policy. The following approaches are offered as examples of performing an account review.

6.2.5.3.1 Approach 1: Process Test

This approach involves a simple test of the account provisioning process. Prior to the on-site portion of the security risk assessment, the team will have requested accounts for the team members. At this stage the team can simply ask to see documented evidence on those requests and evidence of the account provisioning process that was followed. For example, if the organization has a policy and specific forms and signatures that must be obtained prior to account provisioning, then the security risk assessment team would expect to find evidence that this policy and procedure were followed in this case as well. If no such policy or procedure exists, the team would document the process and note any deficiencies.

While all organizations are likely to have slightly different processes for account provisioning, the security risk assessment team should look for the following elements of the process as a minimum:

- Account Provisioning Approval Form — This should include the name of the requester, the reason for the request, the accesses or privilege levels requested, the signature of the approver, and an indication that the candidate user has completed security awareness training.
- No Access Prior to Approval — The assessors (or any guest) should be denied access to information systems until approval is granted.

6.2.5.3.2 Approach 2: Process Audit — Sample

Another approach the security risk assessment may use is a process audit in which the team samples elements of the account provisioning and maintenance program. Sampling is performed to gather some evidence quickly and efficiently on the account process. Sampling should be performed consistent with the team's sampling policy (see section 5.1). Samples should be selected and reviewed in each of the account provisioning phases:

- Phase 1: Account Creation — This phase covers the creation of accounts for new staff members and guests. As mentioned in the first approach, accounts created should follow the documented policy. Expected elements of the policy include an account provisioning form which includes the requester's name, request type, privilege level, approval signature, and signature of account holder indicating security awareness training has been completed.

- Phase 2: Account Maintenance — This phase covers changes in account status, for example, an increase in privileges for an existing account. To audit this activity, the assessor should ask for a list of personnel who recently changed positions within the company. The assessor should then ask for the documentation that was used to ensure that the process of changing accounts or increasing the privilege of the current account was performed appropriately.

    Another activity that could be performed during this phase is to review a list of all account status changes for the last two months. This list should be reviewed with the information owners to determine if such a change was appropriate for each person listed in the report.

- Phase 3: Account Removal — Lastly, the termination of accounts must be handled appropriately. A discussion on expected policy elements was covered earlier in the book. The assessor should obtain a list from human resources on recent departures. Based on time available, the assessor should choose a number of terminations and walk through the termination procedures to determine if they were followed. Another approach to reviewing account terminations is to review the account provisioning for the last guest or last set of auditors who no longer should have access. Then follow the same procedures as described above.

6.2.5.3.3 Approach 3: Process Audit — Complete

The last approach for reviewing account maintenance is much like the previous approach, process audit — sample, but it should be performed in a complete manner. This means that during the account creation phase, all current accesses should be audited for the completion of an account provisioning form. Also, all changes and terminations should be reviewed. Other than simply being more complete, this approach is basically the same as the second approach. However, there is one activity that should be performed during the complete process audit that has not yet been discussed: the zero-based review.

- Zero-Based Review — When accounts are reviewed at random, or even when monthly changes are reviewed completely, some accounts can still slip through the cracks. Sometimes accounts are held open for the expected return of an employee. At other times, key personnel responsible for elements of the process are absent. A zero-based review is a review of all accounts on each critical system. The account review is simply a printout of all accounts on a system reviewed by the owner of the system. It may also be useful to cross-check the access list with human resources to ensure that all staff indicated on the access list are still employed and all contractors should have current access.

6.2.5.4 Outsourcing and Information Exchange

The security policies, procedures, and organizational structures we have discussed so far all have to do with the organization being assessed. But when the assessed organization outsources a critical function or shares sensitive information with another organization, then the security risk assessment must review the security controls being applied to those critical functions and sensitive data outside of the organization.

Almost all security risk assessment will be bounded such that the security risk assessment team would not be expected to travel to the other location and perform a security risk assessment there.[12] However, there are several actions that should be performed by the security risk assessment team to gather data on the outsourcing and information exchange actions of the organization.

6.2.5.4.1 Outsourcing Review

If an organization has outsourced any of its critical functions, it may be difficult for the security risk assessment team to gather data regarding the adequacy of security controls within that outsourced function. The following approaches for obtaining appropriate data should be considered.

(a) Approach 1: Review Contracts — The security risk assessment team member could simply review the contracts covering the outsourcing of the critical function. The assessor should look for the following elements in the contract:

- Is there a service-level agreement associated with the outsourced function?
  - Are reasonable and relevant security metrics defined?
  - Are these security metrics measured and reported?
- Is there a business associate agreement or other contractual agreement covering the sharing of sensitive information?
  - Does the organization have the ability to terminate the contract upon a material breach or violation of the outsourcing organization's obligations?
  - Does the contract specify appropriate safeguards for reasonably protecting the sensitive information and organizational assets from breaches of security?
  - Is the outsourcing organization required to report material security incidents that may impact the security of the organization's sensitive information and protected assets?

- Does the organization have the right to audit or test the outsourcing organization's ability to provide adequate security?

(b) Approach 2: Review Available Assessments — Many organizations that are in the business of performing critical business functions for other organizations (e.g., service organizations) or receiving sensitive information from other organizations (e.g., business partners) commission independent reviews of their security controls. The final report from these reviews is intended to be shared with organizations that must trust the security controls of the service organization or business partner.

If such a report is available, the security risk assessment team can simply review the results of the report. However, the assessor should also be careful to ensure that the report is recent, positive, and performed by someone knowledgeable and objective.

- Recent — An assessor cannot expect that the outside assessment be completed within the last 30 days, but a report more than a year old is probably no longer relevant. The assessor should use judgment to determine the extent to which there may have been significant changes in the business functions or threat environment and determine how recent a report should be to provide a measure of assurance that the service organization appropriately protects sensitive information and protected resources.
- Positive — The report should be rather clear as to the findings of the adequacy of the security controls. To be sure, the report will not make statements regarding "complete" or 100% security. The assessor should be looking for acceptable risk or adequate measures. Furthermore, the assessment report is likely to contain recommendations along with a timeline. The assessor should ask the sponsoring organization to follow up with the service organization to see if the recommendations have been implemented.
- Knowledgeable and Objective Author — If the assessment report is authored by the service organization itself then this is not considered an assessment, instead it is a statement. Such a report may still be useful in documenting the claimed security controls, but this does not provide a measurement of their adequacy because the author would not be capable of providing an objective review. Moreover, the author of the document must demonstrate expertise and knowledge of security testing and security risk assessment methods. The assessor should expect to see the author's credentials, indication of experience, or an explanation and citation of the methodology that was used to perform the assessment.

(c) Approach 3: Review Questionnaire Responses — A third approach would be to engage the service organization in communicating their claimed security controls through the use of a questionnaire or a phone interview. This questionnaire should solicit many of the same questions and report elements discussed in the other approaches. The following questionnaire may be appropriate for many service organizations.

- Does your organization have an information security policy?
- Does your organization maintain a firewall at the boundary of your network?
- Do you regularly apply security patches?
- Does your organization maintain anti-virus software?
- Do you protect stored and transmitted sensitive data through encryption?
- Are access controls used within your information systems?
- Is each person assigned a unique identification on the system?
- Are audit controls in place to associate security-relevant actions with a person or entity?
- Have default passwords and security parameters been overwritten?
- Are the security controls regularly tested?
- Is access to sensitive data and critical systems physically protected?

At the conlusion of the interview the answers should be compiled, approved, and signed by the service organizations.

Notes

1.   For those who are experts in this field or have a checklist they are comfortable with, you may skip this section without losing any context for the rest of the chapter.

2.   The details of government clearance procedures are beyond the scope of this book.

3.   Many safeguards apply to more than one threat, thus safeguards to threats can be a one-to-many relationship. To avoid repeating the same information regarding any of these safeguards, the book simply refers back to previous sections that covered the safeguard.

4.   Federal laws governing the monitoring of communication include the Electronic Communications Privacy Act of 1936 (US Code title 18). The law requires that organizations monitoring communications do so only if employees are informed of monitoring, there exists a policy and procedure for monitoring, the monitoring is a part of business, and it is applied equally to all employees. Organizations that do not follow these guidelines may be in violation. (This is not legal advice — merely an interpretation from a nonlawyer.)

5. There seems to be a lot of lore and rumor regarding noncompete clauses. The stories typically told to departing employees from friends and well-wishers are that the NCC "won't hold up in this state." The thought is that NCCs are not enforceable; however, these are legal contracts and often retain some if not most of their enforcement even through the courts. Those who have signed such clauses should seek legal counsel prior to engaging in any activities that may violate such a contract.

6. Senior management is typically defined as the "CXO," meaning a Chief something Officer. For example, CFO, CEO, COO, and CIO are all considered senior management. Senior management does not typically include directors, managers, and team leaders. These latter positions have specific responsibility within a specific operating environment and do not have fiduciary responsibilities or provide general knowledge and direction for the company. A typical mistake made by organizations is to place the security function as a branch within information technology (see Sidebar 6.1 for a more detailed discussion).

7. Even though the resources that perform security operations can also technically perform these audit functions, such an action is considered as checking you own work and not as audit. Do not confuse the two. Audit is a review of controls or accounts by an independent and objective party. Those who performed the original process or created the accounts are involved with the process and cannot be objective and certainly do not provide a safeguard against fraud, waste, and abuse.

8. It is expected that those performing the audit function would run similar tools as well, but this does not mean they are performing the same function. The system operators are performing checks to ensure quality of workmanship, while the audit function is performing checks to detect violations of policy and to reduce the opportunity for fraud, waste, and abuse.

9. Many experienced security consultants will be tempted to simply review documents and provide comments on discovered security deficiencies but fail to spot missing key elements. It is for this reason that the discipline of completeness review using a table of expected elements is recommended to improve the review process.

10. For a more complete discussion of how to use the "review documents" approach, refer to section 5.2.2.1.

11. The reader should realize that, of course, it is a good idea to check your own work. For example, you would expect that those who harden systems would run a vulnerability scanner to double-check their work. However, this is no substitute for oversight. Furthermore, the reader should be aware that some security oversight controls are in place to reduce the chance of fraud. For these reasons it is important that the security department be objective.

12. If a security risk assessment team was expected to review the security controls at the other location, then the entire risk assessment process could be repeated for that location and the results fed back into the original security risk assessment.

However, this would be unusual and it is more appropriate to consider these two as separate security risk assessments.

References

[1] Hass, Anne, Configuration Management Principle and Practice, December 30, 2003.
[2] *NCSA Secure Programming Guidelines*, National Center for Supercomputing Applications, 1997. www.ncsa.uiuc.edu/General/Grid/ACES/security/programming
[3] Graff, Mark. *Secure Coding: The State of the Practice, 2001*
[4] Pfenning, Art, IT Needs to do better at planning for the worst, *InternetWeek*, October 8, 2001.
[5] Williams, Jeff, Security Code Review — The Best Way to Find and Eliminate the Vulnerabilities in Your Web Applications, August 2002, unpublished White Paper.
[6] Aleph One, Smashing the Stack for Fun and Profit, *Phrack Magazine*, issue 49, article 14, November 8, 1996.
[7] *National Industrial Security Program Operating Manual (NISPOM)*, DoD 5220.22-M, January 1995. http://www.dss.mil/isec/nispom_0195.htm
[8] *Plain English Guide to Hiring*, U.S. Small Business Administration. www.business.gov
[9] National Institute of Standards and Technology, *Recommended Security Controls for Federal Information Systems*, NIST Special Publication 800-53, Final Draft, January 2005. http://csrc.nist.gov/publications/drafts/SP-800-53-FinalDraft.pdf
[10] *Audit IT Examination Handbook*. Federal Financial Institutions Examination Council, August 2003. www.ffiec.gov/ffiecinfobase/booklets/ausit/audit.pdf
[11] *Financial Institutions and Customer Data: Complying with the Safeguards Rule*, Federal Trade Commission. http://www.ftc.gov/bcp/conline/pubs/buspubs/safeguards.htm
[12] *Tools to Manage Technology Providers' Performance Risk: Service Level Agreements*, Federal Deposit Insurance Corporation http://www.fdic.gov/regulations/information/btbulletins/brochure2.html

Chapter 7

Technical Data Gathering

7.1 Technical Threats and Safeguards

Threats, threat agents, and threat statements were covered earlier. Technical threats specifically are covered here as an approach to introducing technical data gathering. This section, on threats and safeguards, is intended as a primer or introduction to security threats in the technical area.[1]

A member of a security risk assessment team requires a basic understanding of the threats and safeguards within the technical security area to be an effective member of the team. There are numerous technical security threats; some of the more frequent technical threats and safeguards are discussed in Table 7.1.

7.1.1 Information Control

Information is one of the most valuable assets of the organization. Adequate technical security controls should be placed on sensitive information to ensure that it is protected. Various controls and safeguards exist, including restricting user error, protecting sensitive information and controlling user accounts.

7.1.1.1 User Error

Many controls and safeguards discussed so far have dealt with ways to stop fraud, waste, and abuse, but even well-meaning employees can breach the security of the organization's information through accidental means. The technical controls

Table 7.1 Technical Threats and Safeguards. Technical threats include disclosure, modification, denial of service, and many more threats to the organization's assets. Technical safeguards are logical controls that may reduce these threats through prevention, detection, or correction.

Area	Class	Threat	Safeguard
Information control	User error	• Social engineering • Errors • Omissions	• Monitoring technology • Audit logs
	Sensitive/Critical information	• Disclosure • Modification • Denial of service	• Logical access controls • Checksums • Encryption • Anti-virus system
	User accounts	• Disclosure • Excessive privilege	• Single sign on systems • Two-factor authentication • Identity management systems • Automated password policies • Password crackers • Password generators
Business continuity	Contingency planning Incident response program	• Disclosure • Unavailability • Disclosure • Subversion • Fraud	• Data backup technologies • RAID • Forensic analysis tools
System security	System controls	• Disclosure • Subversion • Fraud	• Logical access controls • Vulnerability scanning tools • Patch management systems • Screen savers • Personal firewalls • Anti-virus • Anti-SPAM • Spyware removal

Category	Subcategory	Threats	Controls
Architecture	Applications security	• Disclosure • Subversion • Fraud	• Penetration testing tools
	Change management	• Errors • Fraud	• Digital signatures • Configuration management systems
	Topology	• Design flaws • Denial of service	• Defense in depth • Network segmentation • Security domains • Redundancy • Evaluated products
	Transmission	• Eavesdropping	• Link encryption • Traffic flow security • Secure protocols
	Perimeter network	• Disclosure of internal structure • Network attacks	• DMZ segmentation • NAT/PAT
Components	Access control	• Disclosure of internal structure • Network attacks • Denial of service • Network attacks	• Application-level FW • Session-level FW • Packet filter FW • Callback modems
	Intrusion detection		• Host IDS • Network IDS
Configuration	System settings	• Network attacks	• System hardening • No default shared keys
	Configuration	• Application-level attacks	
Data	Storage	• Disclosure • Modification	• File encryption
	Transit	• Disclosure • Modification	• Network encryption • Virtual private network • E-mail encryption

discussed below are some of the ways to restrict user error as it would impact the security of the organization's information:

- Monitoring Technology — Monitoring technology includes any technical device or program that can monitor a user's behavior on the organization's information system. Monitoring technology could focus on the user's Web-surfing habits, e-mail sent or received, or any keystroke. Universal Resource Locator (URL) monitoring (or blocking) can report on user Web-surfing habits or even block such behavior. E-mail monitoring systems can monitor the information received or sent by the user or even block certain e-mails. Keystroke monitoring can record and report on individual keystrokes at a specific user's machine.

- Audit Logs — Audit log files contain data recorded by the system at the time of a security-relevant event. The data contained in these logs should include, at a minimum, the following information: identification, time, event, success/failure. Additional information, such as performance metrics, warnings, and location, could be supplied in audit logs for certain events. The system events that produce audit logs are typically configurable and should strike a balance between performance impact and the availability of detailed audit data.

7.1.1.2 Sensitive and Critical Information

All data is valuable to the organization, but some data is more critical and sensitive than other data. The organization should implement technical security controls to protect it from disclosure or modification and to ensure its availability.

- Logical Access Controls — Logical access controls are used to enforce the organization's intention of how control to critical and sensitive files may be accessed by users. These controls can be implemented through many different means, such as permission bits, access control lists (ACLs), capability lists, and passwords.[2] These types of logical access controls provide access control based on the identification of the user and the controls placed on the file. Some highly secure systems may employ the use of mandatory access control features, which control access to sensitive files based on the user's clearance and the file's sensitivity.

- Checksums — Checksums and cryptographic checksums provide a method for detecting unauthorized modifications to sensitive files. This service is provided by computing and separately storing a numeric value based on the contents of the file. The file's integrity is determined by recomputing the numeric value and comparing it against the stored value. If the values do not match, the integrity of the file has been compromised.

- Encryption — Specifically, encryption is the transformation of plaintext into another unrecognizable form. However, the term "encryption" is generally used to describe the application of one or more cryptographic techniques to ensure confidentiality, integrity, authentication, or non-repudiation. Encryption technology can be applied to sensitive and critical information to ensure its confidentiality and integrity.
- Anti-Virus Systems — The extensibility of an organization's networks and the possibility of the introduction of malicious code make an anti-virus system an essential component of technical security controls. Anti-virus systems can be deployed at the network or workstation level. Both network- and host-based anti-virus systems depend on the diligent practice of signature updates and active scanning.

7.1.1.3 User Accounts

A user account contains a user's attributes such as name, sensitivity level, and account expiration. The user account provides the user access to organizational critical resources and files and should therefore be strictly controlled. The following technical safeguards can assist in ensuring that security is preserved through user accounts:

- Single Sign-On (SSO) Systems — A single sign-on (SSO) system is a networkwide system for user authentication based on client/server technology. Instead of having to remember an identification and password pair for every system on the network, a user of an SSO can simply remember a single identification and authentication pair (typically more than just a password). Such a system provides the benefits of consolidating authentication within the enterprise and encouraging better user habits because they only have to remember one password.
- Two-Factor Authentication — Two-factor authentication, also called strong authentication, is the practice of requiring at least two forms of authentication information from a user prior to confirming their identity.[3]
- Identity Management Systems — Identity management systems identify individuals and provide systemwide access control. Identity management is a step beyond single sign-on in that it provides a single identity for each individual (e.g., John M. Smith) and associates all of that user's system identities (e.g., jsmith, smithjm, admin003) to that single individual.
- Automated Password Policy Enforcement — Many operating systems have password policy enforcement controls as a built-in function of the system. These controls allow the administrator to define password policies such as minimum length, expiration date, and password complexity. The system will then enforce these policies for the user accounts under the control of the administrator.

- Password Crackers — User passwords are stored in a one-way encrypted form on the system. An administrator with access to the file containing these encrypted passwords (e.g., the password file) can use a program that tries to determine users' passwords by one-way encrypting candidate passwords and comparing the results to the data stored in the password file. Password crackers can use dictionaries of probable passwords or they can perform the cracking through a brute-force attack. Password crackers can be used as a method of testing the strength of user-selected passwords and informing those with weak passwords to choose a more secure password.
- Password Generators — Left to their own devices, many users are not good at selecting security passwords. Password generators can be implemented within the password reset routine to assist users in creating strong passwords for their use. There are many types of password generators. One such type provides pronounceable passwords made of up three- to four-letter combinations, such as "val-ton-mar" or "byt-mem-att."

7.1.2 Business Continuity

Business continuity is the field of preparation and planning undertaken by organizations to ensure that they remain a viable entity if and when a disaster impacts their critical systems. Business continuity planning is the process of identifying critical systems, identifying reasonable threats, and creating a long-term strategy for reducing the impact of interruptions to the business and stabilizing critical business functions.

7.1.2.1 Contingency Planning

The contingency planning process includes the business continuity planning (i.e., long-term strategy) and the disaster recovery planning (i.e., short- and mid-term strategies) to handle specific situations.

- Data Backup Technologies — Critical data should be backed up to ensure its availability immediately following a disaster. Depending on the recovery time objective (RTO) for the data or the system the data supports, there are many different backup technologies that may be appropriate. Simple solutions include traditional full and incremental tape backups stored on or off site. More complex solutions include journaling and remote backup.
- Redundant Array of Inexpensive Disks (RAID) — A redundant array of inexpensive disks (RAID) is a technology used for redundancy and performance improvement. RAID technology combines several physical disks and integrates them into a logical array. There are many RAID levels that provide various levels of performance and redundancy improvements.

7.1.3 System Security

The organization must protect its information systems from unscheduled changes, system-level vulnerabilities, and application-level vulnerabilities. Any of these threats to the organization's information systems could lead to disclosure or corruption of sensitive information, subversion of network systems, or fraud.

7.1.3.1 System Controls

The organization's information systems can be further protected from rogue applications and unauthorized users through a set of technical system controls. These technical controls include logical controls and devices that discover, reduce, and avoid vulnerabilities within the organization's information systems.

- Logical Access Controls — Covered in the section above.
- Vulnerability Scanning Tools — Vulnerability scanning tools are used to gather information about possible vulnerabilities within the target system. These tools can provide both network mapping (listing available hosts and their open interfaces) and vulnerability scanning (providing an automated mapping of available hosts and ports to known vulnerabilities).
- Patch Management Systems — Keeping up with the latest vendor security patches can be a complex task, especially in a larger enterprise. Patch management systems provide an automated method for testing and tracking the application of vendor patches to workstations and servers within a security domain.
- Screen Savers — Password-protected screen savers provide default protection of a user's workstation if it is left unattended for a preset period of time.
- Personal Firewalls — Personal firewall is a software application designed to protect a single workstation from Internet-based attacks. Personal firewalls protect a single system's security by inspecting and controlling Internet connections to and from the workstation.
- Anti-Virus — Covered in the section above.
- Anti-SPAM — SPAM is defined as unsolicited broadcast commercial e-mail. Such e-mail can be more than a mere nuisance to information systems. SPAM can waste individuals' time by causing them to have to sort through it to get to legitimate e-mail. Furthermore, SPAM can cause denial of service by hogging storage or bandwidth resources. Anti-SPAM (or SPAM filter) systems use various techniques to identify and eliminate SPAM.
- Spyware Removal Tools — Spyware is defined as software that gathers information on the user's Internet surfing habits without the user's permission or knowledge. Information gained is then sent or shared with others over the Internet connection, usually for the purposes of directed

advertising, but spyware could collect and send any information available from the interception and viewing of Internet connection sessions. Spyware removal tools search for installed spyware tools on user systems and remove the identified malicious programs. The effectiveness of spyware removal tools is based on the definitions file, which should be updated regularly.

7.1.3.2 Application Security

Until recently, application security has been largely ignored by companies protecting their assets, but applications have not been ignored by hackers. Even though Web applications sit behind a firewall and perhaps even behind hardened operating systems, they are still vulnerable. This is because firewalls and hardened operating systems are not designed to restrict all access to Web applications (i.e., port 80 HTTP). Furthermore, exposed Web applications are likely to have errors. Below are a few technical security controls that may be employed to reduce the risk in applications:

- Penetration Testing Tools — Penetration testing is a methodical and planned attack on a system's security controls to test the adequacy of security controls in place. Some of the penetration testing is done "by hand," but there exist many available tools, both commercial and shareware, that help to automate the process. The use of these tools can greatly increase the rigor of an application security review.
- Source Code Review — Source code review is a process of manually inspecting the code for custom developed web applications. The review searches for security weaknesses such as insecure coding practices and security breaches such as the insertion of Trojan horses and backdoors. Source code review is the most rigorous and complete methods for improving the security of custom developed applications.

7.1.3.3 Change Management

An information system infrastructure is a complex and evolving system. Changes to the system affect its ability to effectively enforce the security policies and therefore protect the organization's assets. Below are a few technical security controls that may be employed to help enforce strict change management:

- Digital Signatures — A digital signature is a cryptographic verification that a file or message was created or sent by a specific user or entity. Using asymmetric cryptography (e.g., RSA, *El Gamal*), a user digitally signs the file or message with his private key. The recipient of the message can be sure of the authenticity and integrity of the message if he can verify the message using the sender's public key. Digital signatures are mentioned here as a technique of verifying the authenticity and integrity of a workflow message for change management. For example, imagine a change management process for changes to the firewall ruleset that is based on an e-mail from key personnel within the organization. Such e-mails could be easily spoofed and the change management process could be bypassed. Incorporating digital signatures into critical workflow processes helps to ensure the security of the process.

- Configuration Management Systems — Configuration management systems implement change control or specific work products such as code, test suites, and user documentation. The implementation of a configuration management system formalizes and controls the process of change management to ensure that changes to the system are properly reviewed, documented, and implemented.

7.1.4 Secure Architecture

Much of the security in an information system is reliant upon the structure and services provided by the underlying architecture. Secure architectures are important because the lack of an adequate security architecture limits (or even negates) the security provided by other security mechanisms. The organization must ensure that the information system architecture is free from design flaws and protects itself from denial of service attacks, network attacks, disclosure of the internal network structure, and eavesdropping.

7.1.4.1 Topology

One of the key aspects of the secure system architecture is the topology of the network. A network topology is the physical and logical arrangement of the network components. Safeguards that can be applied within the network topology area are discussed below:

- Defense in Depth — Defense in depth is a security engineering principle which states that critical assets should not rely on single mechanisms for their protection. Applying this concept to security network topologies means that there should be multiple controls in the network to protect critical assets from compromise. For example, we would expect to see perimeter firewalls and internal firewalls on network segments, strong authentication, access controls, and audit log and review. These safeguards together provide a defense in depth for critical files stored within the network.
- Network Segmentation — A network segment is a subset of a larger network bounded by networking devices such as routers, switches, bridges, or gateways. By dividing a network into segments or groups of computers, the organization can gain performance and security by limiting the traffic

on the network segment to the traffic sent or intended for computers on the network segment.[4]

- Security Domains — A security domain is a logical grouping of computers on a network in which there exists a trust relationship among all those computers. For example, you may set up a security domain for the accounting group that includes all of the accounting group's computers and printers. By creating multiple domains and carefully implementing trust relationships between domains, the network architect can reduce the risk of unauthorized access and disclosure.

- Redundancy — When critical applications or systems rely on a resource for their security, the failure of such a component could be devastating. The absence of redundancy in such critical components is called a single point of failure. It is important to implement network architecture redundancies for critical components such as networkwide authentication servers, firewalls, and Internet connectivity.

- Evaluated Products — The U.S. Government, specifically the National Security Agency (NSA) and the National Institute of Standards and Technology (NIST), long ago recognized that trusted computer systems or information assurance products for which we rely on the provision of security services need to be analyzed beyond the simple interface tests that may be performed in a laboratory. Furthermore, to truly analyze the ability of these systems to enforce a security policy, in-depth analysis would need to be performed by skilled evaluators with access to vendor design documentation. The National Information Assurance Partnership (NIAP) oversees the Common Criteria Evaluation Scheme within the United States and licenses laboratories to perform these evaluations. Once a product has been evaluated it is placed on the validated products list (VPL) (http://niap.nist.gov/cc-scheme/vpl/vpl-type.html).

7.1.4.2 Transmission

The transmission of data across the network may be secured through the use of link encryption, traffic flow security, and secure protocols.

- Link Encryption — Link encryption is implemented through intelligent switching nodes to set up encrypted links within a network. This provides confidentiality and traffic flow security on the link and is completely transparent to the user. Link encryption is implemented at layer 2 of the OSI model (e.g., L2F, PPTP L2TP) or layer 3 of the OSI model (e.g., IPSEC).

- Traffic Flow Security — If an eavesdropper is able to gain information about the messages sent to and from your network, this may give him relevant information about your operations. It is not always necessary for an eavesdropper to decrypt the messages in order to gain information. For example, consider the fact that all stations send messages to station A. This may indicate that station A is headquarters or at least a critical component of the network. Traffic flow security masks the ultimate source and destination addresses for packets and can even mask the fact that any information was sent across a network segment at all (e.g., filling dead spots with noise).

- Secure Protocols — A network protocol is a set of rules used by endpoints of a connection to communicate. Many protocols, such as HyperText Transfer Protocol (HTTP), File Transfer Protocol (FTP), and Password Authentication Protocol (PAP), are inherently insecure because they do not provide basic security services such as confidentiality. Use of secure protocols, such as HyperText Transfer Protocol + Secure Sockets Layer (HTTPS), Secure File Transfer Protocol (S-FTP), and Challenge Handshake Authentication Protocol (CHAP), will ensure confidentiality of the communication.

7.1.4.3 Perimeter Network

The perimeter of the organization's network is that part of the network directly exposed to untrusted users, such as the Internet or a modem bank. The protection of the network from these untrusted users is imperative and can be accomplished within the network architecture through DMZ segmentation and Network Address Translation (NAT).

- DMZ Segmentation — The organization's critical assets can be better protected by separating Internet-accessible devices, such as the Web server, FTP server, and e-mail server, from the rest of the organization's network. This architectural component is called a demilitarized zone (DMZ), named after the military term for creating a buffer area between two enemies (see Figure 7.1).
- Network Address Translation — Network Address Translation (NAT) allows a local area network (LAN) to use two sets of Internet Protocol (IP) addresses for each communication between the LAN and the Internet. An internal LAN computer is assigned a unique IP address used by the NAT box for communication between the NAT box and the LAN computer. The NAT box translates that address into an externally routable IP address for communication between the NAT box and the Internet. NAT technology provides the following benefits:
  - Internal Structure Masked — By using NAT technology the internal structure of the network is masked from eavesdroppers.
  - Extends IP Address Space — The one-to-many mapping of external IP addresses to internal addresses means that a LAN with more than 256 hosts could use a C-class network.

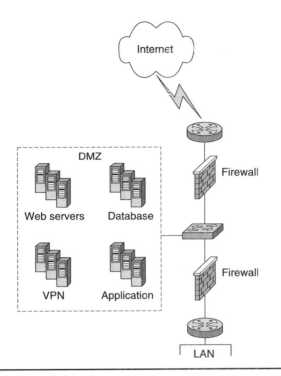

Figure 7.1   A demilitarized zone (DMZ) is a secure network architecture configuration in which publicly accessible services are separated from the rest of the network by employing firewall technology.

- Port Address Translation — Port Address Translation (PAT) is a type of network address translation that provides a service similar to NAT through the use of port numbers.

7.1.5 Components

The components of an organization's network can provide security services to protect the critical resources. Components provide access controls and data security. Also discussed in this section is the proper configuration of components.

7.1.5.1 Access Control

Logical access control provides mechanisms that restrict the access to critical resources to only those authorized to have access. Components that provide access control include firewalls and callback modems.

- Application-Level Firewall — Application-level firewalls, also called proxy firewalls, are a type of firewall that processes data packets for specific applications. These packets are intercepted, analyzed, and may be sent to the intended host. The advantage of an application-level firewall over other firewalls is that because there is no direct communication between the external and internal host, there is no direct access granted to the internal network. Application-level firewalls can also proxy applications like strong authentication services.

- Session-Level Firewall — A session-level firewall, also called circuit level gateways and stateful inspection firewalls, is a type of firewall that creates virtual circuits for permitted and established sessions between an external and internal host. The advantage of a session-level firewall over other firewall types is that since it retains state information about established connections, it can be much faster than other firewalls.
- Packet-Filtering Firewall — A packet-filtering firewall is the simplest type of firewall. This firewall uses access control lists (ACLs) to determine permitted traffic flows based on the source and destination IP address and port. These firewalls can be inexpensive and relatively quick. However, they cannot provide protection against spoofing, cannot proxy applications like strong authentication, and audit logs are rather limited.
- Callback Modem — A callback modem is an intelligent modem that requests a user identification and password for attempted connections, and then hangs up. If the user identification and password pair is a match, then the callback modem calls the phone number associated with that account. Callback modems provide access control protection over dial-in ports to the network or to critical equipment.

7.1.5.2 Intrusion Detection

Intrusion detection systems (IDSs) provide protection against attacks to the information system based on the attack definitions or behavior anomalies as detected by the IDS. These systems provide an additional defense against attacks that may go unnoticed by other protection methods such as firewalls and audit log review.

- Host-Based IDS (HIDS) — Host-based intrusion detection systems (HIDS) (Figure 7.2) are installed locally on host machines such as laptops, workstations, and servers. These IDSs inspect packets sent to the host for the potential of malicious attacks. HIDS are deployed in areas in which specific host-level assets and attacks are the concern.
- Network-Based IDS (NIDS) — Network-based intrusion detection systems (NIDS) (Figure 7.3) are installed on the network. The NIDS device has a network interface card (NIC) and is set up in promiscuous

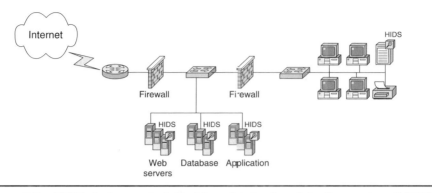

Figure 7.2 HIDS deployment. A host-based intrusion detection system (HIDS) inspects packets sent to the host. HIDS are deployed as software agents running on the host.

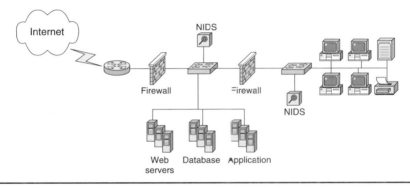

Figure 7.3 NIDS deployment. A network-based intrusion detection system (NIDS) analyzes network traffic. NIDS are deployed as network devices running in promiscuous mode.

mode, meaning that it will analyze all traffic within its deployed network segment.

7.1.6 Configuration

Technical safeguards are designed to enforce a security policy over a defined set of critical assets, but the effectiveness of these safeguards can be limited or eliminated if the safeguards are not configured properly. Specific implementation and installation advice and guidance should be sought from the vendor of the device. A high-level discussion of safeguards aimed at ensuring that technical controls are properly configured is presented below.

7.1.6.1 System Settings

A system component must be properly configured to enforce the security policy intended. Specific safeguards that may be implemented to ensure a proper configuration include system hardening, and ensuring that default shared keys are not used.

- System Hardening — System hardening is the term used to describe the process of securely configuring an operation system, application, or component. Elements of most system hardening processes include the removal of default passwords and accounts, the deletion of services and ports not used, and the setting of security parameters to meet the needs of the environment.
- No Default Shared Keys — Many secure protocols (e.g., IPSec/IKE, WEP) rely on a preconfigured shared key to initialize the secure communication between entities. Attackers armed with the knowledge of the default shared keys can compromise the secure communication. Organizations should ensure that no default shared keys are used.

7.1.7 Data Security

The security of the data itself can be further protected through safeguards that apply to both data in storage and data in transit.

7.1.7.1 Storage

When sensitive data is stored it may be susceptible to attacks from others sharing the workstation or network, stealing a laptop, or finding a lost flash memory device. Technical safeguards such as file encryption can help protect the confidentiality and integrity of the data.

- File Encryption — Individual files may be encrypted through the use of bulk encryption programs that can store an encrypted version of sensitive information and delete the plaintext file.

7.1.7.2 Transit

When sensitive data is transmitted across the network it may be susceptible to eavesdropping attacks. Technical safeguards such as network encryption virtual private networks, and e-mail encryption can help protect the confidentiality and integrity of the data.

- Network Encryption — Communication sessions can be encrypted to ensure the confidentiality and integrity of the network communication.[5]

- Virtual Private Network — A virtual private network (VPN) provides remote users with a secure connection to one of the organization's servers sitting on the edge of the organization's local area network (LAN) over an otherwise public network. To the user this seems as if it is a point-to-point connection from the user's computer to the organization's LAN.
- E-mail Encryption — E-mail encryption is a form of end-to-end encryption that is implemented at layers 6 and 7 of the ISO model. End-to-end encryption allows users to select messages for encryption across the entire transmission. The advantage of end-to-end encryption is that the data is not susceptible to attacks at the intermediate nodes. However, a user must specify transmissions for encryption — this is not performed automatically.

7.2 The RIIOT Method: Technical Data Gathering

As introduced in chapter 5, the RIIOT method of data-gathering can be applied to any security risk assessment technique and helps to ensure a more complete and well-managed data-gathering process. The RIIOT method is applied to any area of security controls by reasoning about the most appropriate approach for gathering data on each security control under review. Applying the RIIOT method to the technical area shows that a majority of the data-gathering techniques to be applied to technical security controls will be document review and testing controls. Table 7.2 provides suggested reasonable approaches to gathering data for each of the security controls described in this chapter.

7.2.1 Review Technical Documents

As demonstrated in Table 7.2, gathering data on nearly every technical security control involves the review of documents. The bulk of the document review will be a review of manuals and diagrams. The remaining document reviews will include a review of hardening guidelines, network maps, technical policy statements, and various security work products.

7.2.1.1 Technical Documents to Request

Using the RIIOT document review technique, the security risk assessment team should determine the set of documents to be reviewed. In some cases the team will be able to review all documents obtained through information requests. In most cases, because of time or budget constraints, the team will need to narrow the evidence reviewed to determine the strength of technical security controls (See Table 7.3).

7.2.1.2 Review Technical Documents for Information

It is important to create a checklist to guide the review of each document.[6] A checklist is simply a listing of all the things a reasonable security engineer would expect to find in a reviewed document. In order to assist those performing security risk assessments, checklists for document review are provided in Table 7.4.

Tables 7.2, 7.3, and 7.4 are an illustration of how to construct and use checklists for the review of technical security documents. However, the team must understand that not all documents are required for all environments, not all checklist elements are necessary for all security controls, and not all technical documents provided will be as neatly titled as the documents discussed here.[7]

7.2.1.2.1 Technical Security Reports Review

The security risk assessment team, or a member of the team, should review the available security reports to gain a perspective on the inputs to the current security risk assessment. The objective of this review is not to judge the completeness or correctness of past reviews, but to use information gathered during past efforts to double-check and improve the current effort. Table 7.5 provides a baseline checklist for reviewing security reports.

7.2.1.2.2 Technical Diagrams Review

The security risk assessment team, or a member of the team, should review the available technical diagrams to determine the security architecture of the information system. The objective of this review is to use information provided in the network diagrams to double-check information already gathered and to gain insight into the information system's security architecture. Table 7.6 provides a baseline checklist for reviewing network diagrams.

7.2.1.2.3 Technical Manuals Review

The security risk assessment team, or a member of the team, should review the available technical security manuals to gain a perspective on the inputs to the current security risk assessment. The objective of this review is to increase the security risk assessment team's understanding of the technology employed within the organization's information system. Table 7.7 provides a baseline checklist for reviewing technical security manuals.

7.2.1.3 Review Technical Security Designs

Security design review (also called architectural review) is an assessment of the system or architecture design to determine its ability to support the security

Table 7.2 RIIOT Method of Data Gathering for Technical Controls. The application of the RIIOT Method to technical controls indicates that the data gathering in this area will focus mainly on document review and testing controls.

Controls	Review Documents	Interview Key Personnel	Inspect Controls	Observe Behavior	Test Controls
Monitoring technology	X				X
Audit logs	X	X		X	X
Logical access controls	X				—*
Checksums	X				—
Encryption	X		X		—
Anti-virus system	X			X	X
Single sign on systems	X				—
Two-factor authentication	X				—
Identity management systems	X	X	X		
Automated password policies	X		X		X
Password crackers	X				
Password generators	X				
Data backup technologies	X	X			
RAID	X				
Forensic analysis tools	X				
Vulnerability scanning tools	X	X			
Patch management systems	X	X	X		
Screen savers	X			X	
Personal firewalls	X			X	
Anti-SPAM	X			X	
Spyware removal	X	X		X	
Penetration testing tools	X	X			
Digital signatures	X			X	
Configuration management systems	X	X		X	

Control				Test controls
Defense in depth	×			—
Network segmentation	×		×	
Security domains	×			
Redundancy	×		×	
Evaluated products	×		×	
Link encryption	×			—
Traffic flow security	×			—
Secure protocols	×			—
DMZ segmentation	×			—
NAT/PAT	×			—
Application-level FW	×	×	×	×
Session-level FW	×	×	×	×
Packet filter FW	×	×	×	×
Callback modems	×		×	—
Host IDS	×	×		×
Network IDS	×	×		×
System hardening	×	×	×	×
No default shared keys	×			
File encryption	×		×	
Network encryption	×			—
Virtual private network	×			×
E-mail encryption	×			—

*Almost all of the technical security safeguards *could* be tested. However, it is typically cost prohibitive to do so within the confines of a security risk assessment. For example, if an organization is using single DES to encrypt e-mail, the security risk assessment team could set up a system to attempt to decrypt the encrypted data through a brute-force attack. Such an attack may even yield a result which states that single DES encryption is too weak for the organization's application. But the resulting recommended safeguard would be to use a stronger key (e.g., Triple DES). Such a result can be gained without the expense of brute-force attacks and simply relies on the information security professional's judgment. The security risk assessment is exactly the place for such judgments and recommendations. The technical controls in this matrix with a "—" in the test controls column indicates a control that *could* be tested but which is not typically tested within the confines of a security risk assessment.

Table 7.3   Technical Documents to Request. The security risk assessment team should attempt to obtain and review as many relevant technical documents as possible within the data-gathering stage of the security risk assessment. This table provides a sample list of documents to request, but it is by no means exhaustive.

Document Type	Sample Titles
System information	• Network diagram/map • Addressing scheme
Previous security risk assessments	• Security risk assessment • Security audit report • Security test ng results • Certification package • System security authorization agreement (SSAA) • IT security review
Internal audit reports	• Audit results • Audit findings
Manuals	• Anti-virus system manual • Administrative guide for IDS • Functional specification for custom applications

Table 7.4   Technical Document Review Checklists. Checklists for reviewing various types of technical documents are provided in Tables 7.5 through 7.7.

Security Policy	Expected Elements Table
Security reports review checklist	Table 7.5
Technical diagrams review checklist	Table 7.6
Technical manuals review checklist	Table 7.7

requirements of the system. This is not a testing effort supported by the use of tools. Instead this is an engineering review of the system and the design of its security controls.

It is important to understand that this assessment is performed at the "design level," not the "implementation level." For example, a system design that places a critical database behind a packet-filtering firewall has a critical design error because the firewall cannot protect the critical database from direct communication with untrusted hosts outside the firewall. This is a design error, not an implementation error, because no packet-filtering firewall can protect the database in this design; this design requires a proxy filtering firewall (at the least). Design-level errors cannot be corrected through a change in the implementation (e.g., harden the firewall, change the firewall ruleset); they require a change in the design (e.g., implement both a packet-filtering firewall and an application proxy firewall to protect the database).

As with many of the tasks within a security risk assessment, it is difficult to completely assess the security design of critical systems. Exhaustive assessments are typically considered unachievable. Furthermore, many security risk assessments are bound by scope and budget that limit the ability to delve too deeply into the security of the system design. However, given that the security design of the system can certainly contain critical vulnerabilities, the security risk assessment team endeavor to review the security design of the critical system to the extent that time, budget, and expertise allow.

There are no known approaches to systematically review the security design of the system.[8] The ability to review a secure design is based on experience and analytical skill (but if I just left it at that, the readers would be disappointed). For the sake of extending the discussion of such approaches, the security risk assessment team should consider the following approaches:

1. Determine the security requirements of the critical systems.
2. Assess the security design against basic security engineering principles
3. Assess the security design against a set of common mistakes or investigation areas.

7.2.1.3.1 Determine Security Requirements

In government systems this process can typically be accomplished without too much effort, because the security requirements should be documented in the certification and accreditation package.[9] For those systems outside government agencies, determining the security requirements of the system may not be as easy, but the following approach can yield useful results quickly:

- Step 1: Recall System-Critical Assets — For each critical system, list the assets. This should have already been done during the preparation phase. It is best to identify categories of assets instead of specific ones. For example, it really does not matter that there are patient records, medical charts, admission forms, and medical test results on a system, but it does matter that there is protected healthcare information on the system.
- Step 2: Identify Security Requirements for Each Asset — For each asset identified above, determine the security requirement for its storage, processing, and transmission. Again, no need to get too involved here, we are assessing the system, not building it. Use categories of security requirements such as confidentiality, integrity, and availability. Some special-purpose systems may have additional or alternative security

Table 7.5 Security Reports Review Checklist. The security reports should be reviewed for previously identified and relevant information that may impact the current security risk assessment.

Objective	Subtopic	Review Tips
Gather information from past security review efforts to improve data gathering in the current security risk assessment	Mission statement	• Check mission statements recorded in other reports against the ones provided to you. If they are different, ask key personnel why this has changed.
	System components and boundaries	• Review named system components and indicated system boundaries and compare them to the current statement of work. If they are different, ask key personnel for an explanation. • Look for any components, subsystems, areas, or interfaces that have not been included in the last or present assessment. For example, some organizations never include physical security as a part of the assessment. Determine if the lack of review for organizational elements is a vulnerability.
	Roles and responsibilities	• Look for definitions of roles and responsibilities from previous reviews. Specifically, look for responsibilities such as running an internal vulnerability scan, account review, or other security activities.
	Threats	• Review the threats considered during the previous assessment efforts. Review the threats identified for this effort and consider adding previously identified threats.
	Assets and asset values	• Review the assets and the values assigned to those assets listed in previous assessment efforts. Consider listing additional assets previously identified. Reexamine asset values based on previous asset valuations.
	Current safeguards	• Review the list, description, and vulnerabilities of existing safeguards from previous assessments. Determine if those safeguards are still in place. Consider the previous vulnerabilities within those safeguards and ensure that they are either addressed or are listed in your current security risk assessment.
	Recommended safeguards and timelines	• Review the recommended safeguards and suggested timelines for implementation from previous assessments. If such timelines have passed, look for evidence that these safeguards were implemented, addressed in another manner, or ignored.

Table 7.6 Technical Diagrams Review Checklist. The technical diagrams should be reviewed for accuracy, currency, and the implementation of system security architecture safeguards.

Objective	Subtopic	Review Tips
Gather information from network diagrams to check accuracy of data gathered and security architecture safeguards employed	Accuracy	• Pick several connections shown in the drawings and inspect the actual equipment to verify the drawing (i.e., trace wires). • Use automated tools to develop a system diagram and compare against the drawings provided.
	Currency	• Inspect latest change management documents for changes that would affect the diagrams. Compare provided diagram against recent architectural changes. • Look at the date of the diagrams. The date should be relatively recent.
	Identification of external interfaces	• Review the network diagrams for external connections such as Internet connections, VPN connections, connections to other systems, modem pools, and any network component that may be reached by a modem.
	Identification of systems	• Check drawings against the system boundaries from the statement of work. Is there anything missing? Is there anything extra?
	System architecture	• Defense in depth: Use network diagrams to determine the extent of security components protecting the network. Specifically, look for networkwide authentication servers, placement of firewalls and IDSs, link encryptors, and NAT boxes. • DMZ: Review the network diagrams to identify the DMZ. Ensure that all components are identified and accounted for in the system identification from the statement of work. • Network segmentation: Review the network diagrams to identify any segmentation within the network. Note perimeter protection at each segment boundary and IDS sensors within each segment.

Table 7.7 Technical Manuals Review Checklist. The technical manuals should be reviewed for configuration options, warnings, and cautions.

Objective	Subtopic	Review Tips
Gather information from available technical manuals to understand security implications of the equipment deployed	Configuration options	• Review technical manuals for configuration options of the equipment, for example, high availability options for firewalls.
		• Review manuals for modes of operation for the equipment, for example, active mode for IDS.
	Warnings and cautions	• Administrator warnings: Many manuals provide warnings to administrators for the security settings, or security functions, for example, ordering of firewall rules, or the existence of default accounts.
		• User warnings: Many user manuals will provide warnings to users about the security features provided within the products, for example, digitally signed e-mail is not protected from disclosure.
		• Assumptions: Many manuals will state environmental assumptions that must be met to ensure security, for example, physical protection of the connection to the console.
	Encryption settings	• Symmetric keys: Symmetric keys less than 128 bits are generally considered weak.
		• Hash values: Hash values less than 160 bits are generally considered weak.
		• Asymmetric keys: Asymmetric keys less than 2048 bits are generally considered weak.

requirements. For example, trading systems have requirements for nonrepudiation and voting systems have requirements for anonymity.

- Step 3: Allocate Security Requirements to System Components — Systems can be deconstructed into subsystems to facilitate understanding. Subsystems could include network interface, storage, access control, administration, audit, and file management. Each of these systems will be responsible for a subset of the security requirements developed in step 2. For example, the confidentiality of protected health information should be allocated to the network interface, storage, access control, and file management.

- Step 4: Consider Additional Requirements for Components — Once you are able to view the security requirements allocated to system components, it may become obvious that some security requirements are absent. For example, each subsystem must be able to protect itself from tampering.

7.2.1.3.2 Basic Security Design Principles

One approach for reviewing a security design and determining if the security requirements are met is to assess the design against basic design principles. These principles are not always applicable to systems, instead they should be viewed as a set of tools that may be employed when the situation warrants. However, it is useful to review each of these principles when considering the design.

Defense in Depth — The principle of defense in depth states that the compromise of critical assets should require the compromise of more than a single security control. The use of multiple overlapping protection approaches means that the failure of any one mechanism will not result in the compromise of the protected asset. The jewelry in your home is likely protected by the following security controls: front-door locks, burglar alarm, barking dog, and a safe. Likewise, critical assets on a system are likely protected by multiple layers of security controls. Although this is not an exhaustive list, look for the following controls within a critical network:

- multiple levels and types of firewalls;
- network anti-virus protection;
- intrusion detection system and monitoring;
- access controls;
- network segmentation;
- encryption.

For each critical asset within the system, the security risk assessment team should determine the adequacy of the security controls that must be breached to compromise the asset.

Least Privilege — The principle of least privilege states that each person, role, or process is given no more privilege than required in order to perform the mission. The goal is to reduce the risk to the critical system by reducing the number of people and processes with access to critical system security controls. The application of this principle to the security design of the system means that user roles and privileged processes should only be given the privilege they need for the duties or functions they perform. For example, within an integrated system, a process that collects audit data from multiple network components needs the privilege of reading audit logs and creating a new one, but does not need other privileges such as reading password files and writing to sensitive databases.

There is not much the security risk assessment team can do about reviewing the internal processes of off-the-shelf software, but many critical systems in operation also contain custom-developed code for the specific environment in order to make different pieces of off-the-shelf software work together. This type of code (sometimes referred to as "glue" code) selcom receives the same scrutiny and development controls as the commercial code. Programmers have been known to take the "shortcut" of giving a process all privileges and not just the ones it needs to perform its functions. This practice of loading processes with privileges leads to catastrophic security vulnerabilities when the process can be manipulated or compromised.

The security risk assessment team should review the privileges of the processes within the system to determine if the principle of least privilege is enforced.

Enforce Reference Validation Mechanism Aspects — A reference validation mechanism is a conceptual model of how access control should be performed within a computer system. The model states that subjects may only obtain access to objects if they go through the reference monitor (see Figure 7.4). For the reference monitor to effectively enforce access control, it must possess the following attributes:

- Always Invoked — Every subject access to an object must go through the reference monitor. There must be no other communication path between a subject and an object.

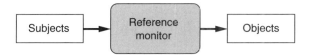

Figure 7.4   Reference monitor concept. The reference monitor is a conceptual model for access control that states that all subject accesses to objects must be approved by the reference monitor.

- Tamper-proof — The reference monitor must protect itself from tampering. No other process should be able to interfere with the reference monitor processes or security controls
- Simple — The implementation of the reference monitor (called the security kernel) must be small enough to be verified. A complex security kernel evades analysis and likely contains vulnerabilities.

To the extent that the security kernel is analyzable, the assessor should review the security kernel's ability to enforce each of the reference monitor aspects.

Enforce Domain of Execution — The principle of domain of execution states that a program in a privileged domain should be unaffected by programs in other domains. A domain of execution is enforced through the isolation of potentially shared resources including memory, processes, the CPU, the bus, and other shared objects. Trusted processes require protection through isolation of resources from other untrusted processes. For example, Java applets run within a virtual machine called a sandbox. Processes within this sandbox are protected from processes running outside the sandbox because specific resources are dedicated to the Java applets running within the sandbox. However, if multiple Java applets are running in the same sandbox, it is possible that they could affect the operation of each other through shared and unprotected resources.

The assessor should review the enforcement of domain of execution within critical systems to determine if trusted processes are isolated from untrusted processes.

Assume Those Untrusted Will Seek to Do Harm — When assessing security controls to determine vulnerabilities, it is always a good idea to assume that the worst will happen. With that in mind, assume that nonadministrative users will seek to gain unapproved access, and assume that those outside your control are untrusted. For example, during the security design review the assessor should assume that external domains are insecure. "Until an external domain has been deemed 'trusted' system engineers, architects, and IT specialists should presume the security measures of an external system are different than those of a trusted internal system and design the system security features accordingly."[10]

With this assumption in mind, consider what vulnerabilities may exist. For example, when you assume that nonadministrative users will seek to gain unapproved access, it becomes rather clear that a Trojan horse vulnerability, that seeks to modify access control lists on critical files, is a real possibility

The security risk assessment team should review the connections to external networks and the interfaces of untrusted users with a critical eye. Ask yourself, 'what is the worst they could do?"

Keep It Simple — Complex designs for security mechanisms are more likely to contain design flaws. When reviewing the security design of a critical system, the assessor should pay careful attention to security mechanisms that seem overly complex. These areas are typically a good place to find design flaws.

The security risk assessment team should critically review overly complex security mechanisms.

Accountability — The principle of accountability states that the additions, modifications, and deletions of critical assets need to be audited and associated with the user or process that performed the action. For each critical asset within a critical system, an audit record should be cut when the file is viewed, deleted, modified, or created.

The security risk assessment team should ensure that adequate audit records are generated for access to critical assets.

Avoid Single Points of Failure — A single point of failure is defined as a resource whose loss will in turn result in the loss of a critical service. If a single system component or resource fails, then the critical system also fails. Systems with secure designs and availability requirements should be designed to avoid single points of failure for critical system services.

The assessor should map critical systems to required resources and assess the extent of built-in redundancy for each of these required resources.

7.2.1.3.3 Common Areas for Investigation

Design analysis involves the review of the system design (not implementation) and its ability to enforce its security requirements. The best way to perform design analysis is to review the design of the system at a low level and create an argument for why it is able to enforce the security requirements. Unfortunately, such low-level design information is rarely available to anyone but the system developers. Moreover, such low-level analysis is not typically performed as a part of a security risk assessment. This discussion of security design analysis purposely takes a higher-level view.

The security design analysis approach described below concentrates on key areas in which system security design is typically flawed and areas in which the security risk assessment team is likely to be able to gain a view into the system design. These areas include transmission of sensitive data, storage of sensitive data, account setup and maintenance, perimeter controls, maintenance procedures, library routines, and backup procedures.[11]

Transmission of Sensitive Data — Anytime sensitive information is transferred from one system to another, the security assessor should take a careful look at the controls. Elements to review include transfer setup, transfer and transfer cleanup.

- Transfer Setup — Determine how the transfer is initiated. How does each party know that they are communicating with the other? How does each party know they are *only* communicating with each other and no one else? How are session keys exchanged? Is temporary storage utilized? What processes have access to the temporary storage?
- Transfer — How is the communication protected? What encryption algorithm is being used? How large is the key space? How often are keys changed?
- Transfer Cleanup — Is the temporary storage cleared? Is the communication channel properly closed? Does the sending party receive confirmation of the exchange?

Storage of Sensitive Data — Anytime sensitive information is stored on a system, the security assessor should take a careful look at the controls. Elements to review include storage area, labeling, and retrieval.

- Storage Area — Where is the data stored? How is the storage area protected from other processes? When the data is deleted? How do you ensure there is no data remaining?
- Labeling — Is the data labeled? How is the label used in access control?
- Retrieval — How is sensitive data retrieved from long-term storage? What other processes have control over the data? When should data be deleted? How is deletion enforced?

Use of Secure Protocols — There are many protocols for the transfer of information across a network that inherently does not provide confidentiality or integrity services. For example, the Password Authentication Protocol (PAP) uses a two-way handshake to establish communications and sends the password in the clear. The use of this protocol across a network that is assumed to be hostile is a design flaw. An authentication protocol that protects the confidentiality of the message should be used in this case, such as Challenge Handshake Authentication Protocol (CHAP) or Extensible Authentication Protocol (EAP).

- Use of Secure Protocols — Ensure that secure protocols are used as appropriate. What security requirements have been allocated to the protocol? Is the protocol designed to address those requirements?

Account Setup and Maintenance — When accounts are established, managed, or maintained, the security assessor should take a careful look at the controls. Elements to review include account privileges and rights, roles, resetting passwords, and administrative accounts.

- Account Privileges and Rights — What privileges and rights are available for accounts? How are these assignments determined? How often are the rights and privileges reviewed? Is it possible to gain additional rights through other mechanisms (e.g., su, superzap)? To what extent is the granting of privileges audited?
- Application to Application Access — How does one application gain access to another application? Is the application treated as "just another user?" If so, are passwords sent in the clear when accessing a password-protected application?
- Single Sign-On — Is single sign-on established within this design? What method of SSO is being used?
- Roles — What are the privileged roles within the system? Are there separation of duty concerns among any of these roles? How are these concerns addressed? How are individuals assigned to roles? Are such assignments reflected in the audit records?
- Password Recovery and Account Lockout — What does it take to lock up an account? Does it require administrator intervention to unlock the account? How are passwords recovered or reset? How does the administrator (or system) determine they are really talking to a user who forgot their password? How is the new password relayed to the legitimate user? Are they forced to change it?
- Administrative Accounts — Do all administrative accounts have the same privilege? How are individuals associated with administrative accounts? Who audits the actions of the administrators?

Perimeter Controls — The security controls that have been put in place to protect the perimeter of the system should be reviewed by the security assessor. Elements to review include perimeter coverage and protection strength.

- Perimeter Coverage — Using a system diagram, identify all interfaces to the system. Now identify the protection used on interface point (e.g., firewall, modem, VPN). Ensure that all interfaces have some type of protection.
- Protection Strength — Now assess the strength of each protection device. What type of firewall? Does the modem require a password? Is it a callback modem? What encryption is used to support the VPN?

Maintenance Procedures — Maintenance procedures associated with critical systems can sometimes represent an Achilles' heel to an otherwise secure system. Maintenance procedures are sometimes an afterthought and are performed when the system is outside its normal operating mode. It is for this reason that the maintenance process deserves some scrutiny.

- Maintenance Access — Many systems allow remote maintenance access. The access can be provided through rather insecure means such as open modems, group passwords, or unencrypted communications.
- Maintenance Updates — Some systems receive maintenance updates through a physical means such as tapes in the mail. How do you know who the tape really came from?

Proprietary Solutions — Be especially critical of proprietary solutions where open standards or well-known industry standards exist. A critical system that touts a proprietary encryption algorithm should be scrutinized.

- Encryption Algorithms — Who developed the algorithm? To what extent has this algorithm been reviewed, tested, and analyzed? By whom?

Group Identities — Although most users are likely to have unique identifiers for their accounts, many systems still have some group identities. The lack of unique identification for all accounts makes it impossible to enforce the following security principles: accountability, assignment of specific rights to individuals, non-repudiation services, access control decisions, and the prevention of masquerading.

- Group Accounts — Which accounts have group identities? Administration? Maintenance? Help desk? Guest?

Library Routines — Library routines are used by programmers to save the time it takes to rewrite subprograms that perform functions that are used by multiple programs. This practice is part of modular coding and is expected within well-designed systems. However, the system must carefully control access to the library routines. One easy way to compromise secure software is to replace a library routine with a Trojan horse. When this imposter routine is called it will likely run with privilege.

- Library Routines — Who has access to library routines? Are they protected through access controls? How would you know if one was changed inappropriately? Checksums? Do programs that call library routines use the full path name?

7.2.2 Interview Technical Personnel

Data gathering for technical security controls also involves interviewing key personnel. For the most part, data gathering in the technical area involves testing the system. However, it is important to interview the key technical personnel to understand the network, troubleshoot the testing effort, and understand the technical controls employed.

7.2.2.1 Technical Interview Topics

As mentioned before, the interviews with technical personnel are typically kept to a minimum. This is for several reasons. First, technical personnel are rarely available for formal interviews. You may find it easier to gain information by having several short and informal conversations. Second, the security risk assessment team istypically much more interested in how something really works instead of how someone says it works. Within the technical controls area, the security risk assessment team will find that interviews are useful as background information but will rely more on tests and inspections.

7.2.2.2 Technical Interview Subjects

The security risk assessment team should interview the technical personnel best able to provide information required to understand the network and assist in setting up the test effort. The selection of interview subjects will depend on who has the responsibility for the safeguards in question. All questions will be directed to security operations staff.

7.2.2.3 Technical Interview Questions

Prior to any interview, the security risk assessment team should review the available documents and prepare questions based on the information provided or concerns that surfaced during the document review. If several members of the security risk assessment team were responsible for reviewing the documents, these members should get together to create a list of questions that they have compiled on the technical documents.

7.2.2.3.1 Security Testing and Review Interview Questions

The security testing and review questions in Table 7.8 can be asked of anyone in the technical group who has the responsibility for the subjects discussed. The questions cover password cracking, vulnerability scanning, audit log review, and forensic analysis. If the organization has not implemented one or more of these controls, that section of the interview can be skipped as it is not applicable.

7.2.2.3.2 Security Components Interview Questions

The security components questions in Table 7.9 can be asked of anyone in the technical group who has the responsibility for the subjects discussed. The questions cover firewalls, intrusion detection, and anti-SPAM filtering.

If the organization has not implemented one cr more of these controls, that section of the interview can be skipped as it is not applicable.

7.2.2.3.3 Security Operations and Procedures Interview Questions

The security operations and procedures questions in Table 7.10 can be asked of anyone in the technical group who has the responsibility for the subjects discussed. The questions cover patch management, configuration management, hardening guidelines, and data backup. If the organization has not implemented one or more of these controls, that section of the interview can be skipped as it is not applicable.

7.2.3 Inspect Technical Security Controls

Data gathering for technical security controls also involves inspecting technical security controls. Recall that inspection differs from testing in that inspection is performed when testing is inappropriate or not feasible. Inspection involves the review of the security control and security control aspects such as configuration or arrangements. For the most part, the approach for performing a security control inspection includes the listing of the security controls under review, verifying information gathered, determining vulnerabilities, and documenting the results. Each of these phases is discussed within the context of technical data gathering.

7.2.3.1 Listing Technical Security Controls

The relevant security controls to be inspected include only those that lend themselves to inspection. In the case of technical controls this includes the following:

- audit logs;
- identity management system;
- data backup technologies;
- vulnerability scanning tools;
- penetration testing tools;
- patch management system;
- anti-SPAM tools;
- configuration management;
- firewalls;
- intrusion detection systems;
- system hardening guidance.

Of course, only those controls actually implemented by the organization can be inspected. The list of administrative security controls to be reviewed for a specific

Table 7.8 Security Testing and Review Interview Guideline. The interviewer should compile a list of questions to ask the responsible party to ensure that the security risk assessment team has a clear understanding of the technical safeguards.

Objective	Subtopic	Question
Increase knowledge of technical safeguards deployed within the organization	Password cracking	• What tools are used to test the strength of passwords? How often are these tools used?
		• What account do you log into to use those tools?
		• Where are the results kept? How are they disseminated within the organization?
		• How is access to the tool and the password file protected? Is such access logged?
	Vulnerability scanning	• What tools are used to test the vulnerabilities of the system?
		• What account do you log into to use those tools?
		• Where are the results kept? How are they disseminated within the organization?
		• How is access to the tool and the password file protected? Is such access logged?

Audit log review

- How many different audit logs are created?
- How often is each log reviewed?
- Do you have any tools or processes that assist in the review of these logs?
- What account do you log into to review these logs?
- How is access to these logs protected?
- Who else has access to these logs?
- How much information (in hours or days est.) can these logs store?
- What happens when is the log file gets full?
- Do you receive a warning when the file is nearly full?
- What information is available for each audit event? (i.e., log-on/log-off, policy changes, process tracking).
- How are events on the same system correlated?
- How are events that happen on different parts of the network correlated?
- How are audit files protected from deletion?
- How much audit log information do you retain and for how long?
- How are archived audit logs protected?

Forensic analysis

- What tools are used for forensic analysis?
- What training have you had on these tools?
- Do you hold any industry certifications in forensic analysis?
- What account do you log into to use those tools?
- How is access to the tool protected? Is such access logged?

Table 7.9 Security Component Interview Guideline. The interviewer should compile a list of questions to ask the responsible party to ensure that the security risk assessment team has a clear understanding of the technical safeguards.

Objective	Subtopic	Question

Increase knowledge of technical safeguards deployed within the organization	Firewalls	• What is the process for making changes to the firewall ruleset?
		• Who has authority/access to make these changes?
		  Are there unique IDs for each person authorized to make the change?
		• What events are tagged for alerts? Who gets these alerts?
		  How are the alerts delivered?
		• What events are tagged for audit? Who reviews the audit logs? How often?

	Intrusion detection systems	• Is the IDS in active or passive mode?
		• What has been your experience with false positives?
		  Did you make adjustments to the system?
		• How are IDS signatures updated?
		  Do these signatures work well within your environment?
		  Did you make adjustments to the rules to accommodate your environment?
		• What attacks are tagged for alerts? Who gets these alerts?
		  How are the alerts delivered?
		• What attacks are tagged for audit? Who reviews the audit logs? How often?

	Anti-SPAM filtering	• What has been your experience with false positives and false negatives? • Can users make their own adjustments to the system? • How are SPAM filters updated? • Is the blocked e-mail stored? Where? How long? Who has access?

Table 7.10 Security Operations and Procedures Interview Guideline. The interviewer should compile a list of questions to ask the responsible party to ensure that the security risk assessment team has a clear understanding of the technical safeguards.

Objective	Subtopic	Question
Increase knowledge of technical safeguards deployed within the organization	Patch management	• How do you verify the integrity of the patch? • How is the patch tested for correctness and effectiveness? • Is the system backed up prior to applying a new patch? • How do you ensure the patch worked? (A: Perform vulnerability scan.) • How are patches prioritized and scheduled for application? • How do you inform other administrators that the patch was applied? • Do you require external partners to apply critical patches?
	Configuration management	• Is there a configuration management plan in place? • What tools are used to implement configuration management? • Which of the following elements are under configuration control: network maps, firewall rulesets, IDS signatures, user accounts, operating system patches, application versions? • Who reviews and approves these configuration changes? • Does "security" have a review or approval "voice" in the configuration process?
	Hardening guidelines	• Do you have a hardening guideline or checklist? • Is there a specific checklist for each of your platforms and major COTS applications? • What is the source of information for the hardening guidance? • How often is your guideline updated? • How do you keep track of changes to the guidance and application of the guidance to your systems? • How do you test the effectiveness of your hardening guidance?
	Data backup	• How often do you test your data backups? • What is your backup schedule? What is your tape rotation schedule? • How often do you update your backup software? • Where are your backup tapes stored? • Where do you store your backup software? • Is there encryption or other logical controls on the backup data? • Are your backups automated? • Do you ensure that all critical files are closed prior to performing a backup?

organization comprises any of the controls that the organization stated are in place. Statements regarding technical controls in place could have come from interviews or provided as part of the document review process. The team should obtain a point of contact for each of these controls.

7.2.3.2 Verify Information Gathered

Information gathered regarding technical security controls should be confirmed through the inspection process. Team members should use various methods to confirm the existence of each of these security controls.

7.2.3.2.1 Audit Logs

The security risk assessment team should review a sample of available audit logs. Specifically, the team can ask to see the audit reports of specific events they suspect or know have happened:

- log files for security risk assessment team log-ins;
- log files associated with security risk assessment team testing;
- log files for last access to an excessive privileged application such as a password cracker;
- log files associated with the last documented incident.

7.2.3.2.2 Identity Management System

The security risk assessment team should identify a member of the technical team that "wears several hats," for example, a system operator who also reviews the audit log files. Then the team member should ask the operator to list *all* of the accounts he has at the organization and ask for a report on his identity. The team member can then compare the report against stated accounts for that user. This same process can be repeated for several different positions.

7.2.3.2.3 Data Backup Technologies

A member of the security risk assessment team should ask to see where the backup tapes are stored. The team member can then compare the condition of the actual tape backup site against what was discussed during the interview. For example, the team member can ask, "Where are the tapes really stored?" The team member should also inspect the tape label to ensure that it contains the date of the backup, the type of backup, the operating system version, and the retention period.

7.2.3.2.4 Vulnerability Scanning Tools

The security risk assessment team should compile a list of the vulnerability scanning testing tools that are used internally. Each of these tools should be checked for the latest updates. The team should ask the person responsible for running these tools a few questions to ascertain their experience and knowledge using these tools.

To ensure a complete coverage of vulnerability scanning testing tools within the organization, a member of the team should map each of the tools used against the following categories of internal checks that may be run:

- operating system vulnerability scanning;
- web application vulnerability scanning;
- database vulnerability scanning;
- wireless LAN vulnerability scanning;
- modem vulnerability scanning (e.g., wardialing).

7.2.3.2.5 Penetration Testing Tools

The security risk assessment team should compile a list of the penetration testing tools that are used internally. Each of these tools should be checked for the latest updates. The team should ask the person responsible for running these tools a few questions to ascertain their experience and knowledge using these tools.

To ensure a complete coverage of penetration testing tools within the organization, a member of the team should map each of the tools used against the following categories of internal checks that may be run:

- operating system penetration testing;
- web application penetration testing;
- database penetration testing;
- wireless LAN penetration testing;
- modem penetration testing.

7.2.3.2.6 Patch Management System

A member of the security risk assessment team should ask for a demonstration of the patch management system. During the demonstration the team member should determine the features of the patch management system (e.g., enterprisewide monitoring, report generation, delegation of duties, automatic deployment of patches).

7.2.3.2.7 Anti-SPAM Tools

A member of the security risk assessment team should check for false positives by asking to see the repository for filtered mail (i.e., mail identified as SPAM) and determining if filtered mail contains legitimate mail.[12] Alternatively, the team member could send an e-mail to several points of contact containing text that may be inappropriately flagged as SPAM. For example, send an e-mail with the word "Middlesex" in the subject line.

7.2.3.2.8 Configuration Management

A member of the security risk assessment team should ask for a demonstration of the configuration management system. The team member can then determine the features of the configuration management system (e.g., change identification, change tracking, integrated approval process). Also, the team member should ask to see the change management documentation for several recent changes that he may be aware of.

Also, the team should read available documentation to become familiar with the process. Then the team members should select several recent changes such as patch application, account creation, or firewall change, including at least one you know about through other data-gathering processes. Ask to see the documents that walk through the process of change control for those selected changes.

7.2.3.2.9 Firewalls

The inspection of firewalls comes down to the inspection of the firewall ruleset. Use Table 7.11 to guide your review of the firewall rulesets. Of course, firewalls are not one-size-fits-all, so treat this table as a guideline, not a rule.

7.2.3.2.10 Intrusion Detection Systems

The security risk assessment team should review the intrusion detection systems to ensure their effectiveness. Specifically, the team should examine the following elements of the IDSs for vulnerabilities:

- Definition Files — A member of the security risk assessment team should review the intrusion detection definition files. The team member can compare these definitions with vendor and CVE[13] latest known attacks.
- Adequate Coverage — The effectiveness of an intrusion detection system is based on the availability of the information it receives about network- or host-based activities. The assessor should ensure that IDS sensors are properly placed throughout the information system network to ensure proper coverage. The best approach to assessing adequate coverage is to indicate the presence of IDS sensors on a network diagram. The assessor should be cognizant of subnets, critical servers, and critical applications.

Table 7.11 Firewall Ruleset Inspection Guideline. The firewall ruleset is the collection of access control rules that govern the logical access control decision made by the firewall. Depending on the type of firewall, these rulesets can make access control decisions on IP address, protocol, and even recognized attacks.

Applicable Firewall Type	Ruleset Inspection Element

All	Look for the rules in these general classifications in the following order
	1. Anti-spoofing filters, including:
	  • Blocked private addresses
	  • Unroutable addresses
	  • Reserved addresses
	  • Illegal addresses
	  • Internal addresses over external ports
	2. Block UDP and ICMP echo requests.
	3. Block loose source routing and strict source routing.
	4. Block unused ports and services.
	5. Block unauthorized zone transfers (i.e., unauthorized packets for port 53).
	6. Apply egress filtering (i.e., outgoing traffic may only come from internal IP addresses).
	7. List user permitted behaviors (e.g., http to webserver).
	8. List management permitted behaviors (e.g., SNMP traps to the management server).
	9. Block "noise" packets (e.g., OSPF and HSRP chatter).
	10. Specify rules for traffic to be denied and administrator to be alerted.
	11. Specify rules for traffic to be denied and logged for later analysis.

Application-level	• Verify how often vulnerability updates are applied.
	• Determine process for verifying authenticity of vulnerability updates.
	• Ruleset should include rules for blocking the following commands:
	  • EXPN, VRFY, DEBUG, WIZARD
	  • PUT command for FTP servers

Stateful inspection	• Determine the adequacy of the session timeout values. • Ensure that the capability for striping scripts from traffic (e.g., ActiveX, Java) is activated.

- Capacity — An important element in ensuring that an IDS is effective is to ensure that it has the appropriate capacity for the network traffic (NIDS).

7.2.3.2.11 System Hardening Guidance

A member of the security risk assessment team should review the application of system hardening guidance to a sample of systems. Hardening guidance application can be reviewed by walking through the hardening guidance elements and checking the system being reviewed against each element. Also, the team member can check for documentation of who performed the hardening and when it was performed.

7.2.3.2.12 Operating Systems and Applications

Many operating systems and even some applications arrive from the manufacturer with a multitude of features and services that can result in security vulnerabilities (e.g., development tools, default settings). System hardening refers to the removal of those features, services, and default settings to establish a secure implementation of operating systems and applications. In addition, by ensuring that default settings are corrected, a configuration review also ensures that the services and features are properly used.

By far the most widely used approach for a configuration review is the use of a checklist. A checklist (also called lockdown procedures, hardening guidelines, or security technical implementation guide) is a document that contains instructions and procedures for the secure configuration of information technology products. A security configuration checklist can assist the security risk assessment team in efficiently reviewing the parameters of the secure implementation of a component of a security system. Using the checklists as a guide in the examination is a quick way to ensure that a reasonable review of the possible vulnerabilities has been performed.

Sources of Checklists — Security configuration checklists are developed by government, consortia, vendors, academia, and private industry. Below is a list of some of the sources for security configuration checklists:

- Government checklists:
  - The National Security Agency (www.nsa.gov/snac) — The NSA Systems and Network Attack Center (SNAC) provides security configuration guides for applications, database servers, operating systems, routers, switches, Web servers, and browsers.
  - Defense Information Systems Agency (DISA) Security Technical Implementation Guides (https://iase.disa.mil. techguid/stigs.html) — These guides are only available via .mil and .gov domains.

- National Institute of Standards and Technology (NIST) (http://csrc.nist.gov/pcig/cig.html) — The Cyber Security Research and Development Act requires NIST to develop security configuration checklists. This site contains checklists for VOIP, routers, biometrics, databases, applications, domain name servers, and many others. The NIST security configuration checklists will be stored at the following link as they become available: http://checklists.nist.gov.[16]
- Vendor checklists:
  - Microsoft TechNet: Standards, Regulations, and Government Issues (www.microsoft.com/technet/security/topics/issues) — This site provides links to security guides and configuration guides for Microsoft SQL Server, Windows 2000 Server, and Windows NT Server.
  - Oracle Technology Network (www.oracle.com/technology/deploy/security/oracle9i) — This site provides a white paper on Oracle9i security in operational environments.
- Academia checklists:
  - The CERT® Coordination Center (www.cert.org/tech_tips) — The CERT®/CC provides a set of hardening guidelines for Windows 95/98, NT, and UNIX.
- Consortia checklists:
  - Forum on Incident Response and Security Teams (FIRST) Best Practice Guide Library — (www.first.org/resources/guides). FIRST maintains a set of best practice guidelines that include hardening guidelines for a variety of products including Microsoft (IIS, NT, Windows 2003), Cisco (IOS), RedHat LINUX, Solaris, and others.
  - The SysAdmin, Audit, Network, Security (SANS) Institute SANS Security Consensus Operational Readiness Evaluation (SCORE) Effort (www.sans.org/score) — This site provides a set of security checklists, including ASP, firewalls, handheld computers, HP-UX, Web applications, Windows 2000 and XP, and others.
  - The Center for Internet Security (CIS) (http://www.cisecurity.org) — This site contains "benchmarks" for operating systems, network devices, and applications.

Use of Checklists — Checklists should never be considered as the only mechanism for performing a configuration review. A security configuration checklist can be used to assist or guide the security risk assessment team in reviewing the system components for possible vulnerabilities, but the assessors should use one or more of the following approaches:

- Approach 1: Review Components Against a Checklist — If the organization being assessed has no documented procedure for hardening system components, then this is the only approach you can take. This approach involves the following steps:

1. Select an appropriate checklist for the security components being reviewed. See the lists in the previous section for sources of such lists.

2. Customize the checklist to account for unique environmental and organizational concerns. Just as all customers do not use off-the-shelf software in the same manner, a security checklist will not apply equally to all environments. For example, almost all checklists include a section for disabling used services. The services used for each environment may differ. Therefore, you must know the services offered by the system components to customize a security checklist for appropriate use.

3. Walk through the customized security checklist indicating areas in which the actual implementation differs from the recommended implementation in the checklist.

4. Determine the possible vulnerabilities within the system component based on deviations from the recommended checklist. Note that some deviations may not result in an actual or material vulnerability. Most of the checklists will provide information as to the vulnerability that each step within the checklist prevents. If no such information is available, you must determine the vulnerability through research, analysis, or testing.

• Approach 2: Review Components Against Organization's Checklist — If the organization does have a documented procedure for hardening system components, then you can select a component to review and follow the documented guideline. This approach maps to the approach above with the sole exception where the checklist is one produced by the assessed organization and not an outside source.

• Approach 3: Review the Organization's Checklist Against a Checklist — Another approach to take if the organization has a documented procedure for hardening system components is to review their document against yours. This could be considered more of a procedure review in that it is a "desk check" exercise, in which you will note deficiencies in the organization's procedure wherein they fail to close a known vulnerability considered in the selected checklist. This approach is rather straightforward. Place the documents (their checklist and yours) side by side and indicate any vulnerability that is addressed in your document but not in theirs.

Next you determine the possible vulnerabilities within the system component based on the noted deviations. Again, some deviations may not result in an actual or material vulnerability. If your checklist provides information as to the vulnerability that each step within the checklist prevents, then record each vulnerability. If no such information is available, you must determine the vulnerability through research, analysis, or testing.

7.2.3.3 Determine Vulnerabilities

During inspection of the technical security controls, the security risk assessment team should look for vulnerabilities. The inspection process of these controls involves the recognition of ineffective mechanisms, configurations, or processes. The questions and tips within the previous section guide the security risk assessment team toward these vulnerabilities. For example, when inspecting the audit log features for adequate indication of potential security breaches, a vulnerability exists if the team determines that the audit logs are missing critical information (e.g., network time or access to critical files).

7.2.3.4 Document and Review Findings

As with all findings, the security risk assessment team must be sure to carefully record their findings in the area of technical controls through inspection. The team should include dates, evidence, team member names, and the vulnerabilities observed. These findings must be reviewed with the entire team and the point of contact for the control to give them a chance to clarify any misunderstandings.

7.2.4 Observe Technical Personnel Behavior

The process of gathering data through observation is a subtle one. With a few exceptions, this process is passive and depends on team members being aware of the organization's policies, procedures, and safeguards, while keeping an eye out for opportunities to confirm or disprove the organization's effective use of technology, although some observations can be active in nature, such as performing activities that should be audited and checking the audit logs. More experienced team members will find observation to be second nature and a side effect of being on site.

With a little guidance and teamwork, these observations can be recorded from most team members and add additional data points to the data-gathering process. Table 7.12 provides some guidance to the security risk assessment team for observing the behavior of the organization's staff in order to determine the strength of some of the technical controls. The security risk assessment team is encouraged to review Table 7.12 and add or modify table elements to suit its own needs and experiences.

7.2.5 Test Technical Security Controls

The last phase of data gathering for technical security controls in the RIIOT method is testing. Testing of technical security controls is the process of invoking conditions that test technical controls against their intended security functions. This type of data gathering provides excellent insight into the effectiveness of the controls.

Table 7.12 Technical Controls Observation Guideline. The security risk assessment team should be prepared to observe the behavior of the security staff, key personnel, and general employee population to check the effectiveness of technical controls.

Technical Control	Claim	Observation Test or Procedure Check
Audit Logs	• All security-relevant events are audited and reviewed	• Review audit logs for security-relevant events that transpired during the on-site inspection. • Wait a few days after an auditable event and check to see when the event was first reviewed.
Anti-virus systems	• System prevents virus infection	• Be aware of viruses that may be circulating during the time of the assessment. Determine from observation if the virus is having an effect on the information system.
	• Updates are performed regularly	• When given the chance to interview users or inspect a workstation, check to see if the latest updates have been applied. Also check to see if scans or updates can be blocked.
	• Users cannot block scans or updates	
Screen savers	• All workstations have active screen savers with passwords	• General observations of user behavior and workstations viewed while on site.
Personal firewalls	• Users cannot override settings	• Be aware of attacks that may be circulating during the time of the assessment. Determine from observation if the attacks have an effect on the information system.
	• Users understand how to use personal firewalls	
	• Updates are performed regularly	• When given the chance to interview users or inspect a workstation, check to see if the latest updates have been applied. Also check to see if scans or updates can be blocked.

Anti-SPAM filters	• SPAM is reduced or eliminated • False negatives are nonexistent or do not impact business	• When given the chance to interview users ask if they still receive any SPAM. • Ask if the SPAM filters have blocked any legitimate e-mail that they know of. Be careful of just taking the user's word for this. There can be many reasons for not receiving an important e-mail, including the possibility that it was never sent. Ask if they opened a trouble ticket or asked someone in IT about it. Follow up on the complaint to confirm that legitimate e-mail was actually blocked.
Spyware removal	• Spyware is removed • Updates are performed regularly • Users cannot override settings	• Determine from observation if spyware has infiltrated workstations and affects the mission. • When given the chance to interview users or inspect a workstation, check to see if the latest updates have been applied. Also check to see if scans or updates can be blocked.
Digital signatures	• Digital signatures are used for workflow processes	• Be aware of any security-relevant workflow process (e.g., account activation) that relies on e-mails. Confirm and document these processes, then ensure that each e-mail is only accepted if it has been digitally signed. Any instance where this is not the case should be documented as a finding because e-mail may be spoofed and the workflow process may be compromised.
Configuration management systems	• Security-relevant changes are documented, reviewed, and appropriately approved	• Be aware of security-relevant changes that happen while the team is on site. Follow up during the configuration management inspection if those changes have appropriately gone through the process.

The technical controls that lend themselves to testing include monitoring technology, audit logs, anti-virus systems, automated password policies, firewalls, IDSs, system hardening, and VPN. An approach for testing each of these controls is presented below. The security risk assessment team is encouraged to adopt, modify, or add to these test methods.

7.2.5.1 Monitoring Technology

The appropriate technologies to test include URL blocking. Testing procedures for URL blocking requires that the security risk assessment team perform activities that attempt to bypass the blocking controls in place. The following URL blocking tests should be attempted in order to gain a minimum level of confidence that the monitoring technology is effective:

- Attempt basic testing of various categories to be blocked:
  - Prohibited Content Sites — adult sites, hate groups.
  - Prohibited Use Sites — gambling sites, Web-based e-mail.
  - Waste of Resources — streaming media, shopping, real estate, dating, job search, games, financial, chats.
  - Security Violations — hacking, downloads, personal Web sites (hosted at GeoCities, AOL, etc.).
- Attempt to use remote proxies or Web anonymizers to bypass the URL blocking.
- Attempt to defeat mechanism if it is a client-side device.

7.2.5.2 Audit Logs

Testing procedures for audit logs require that the security risk assessment team perform activities that exercise security-relevant activities that should be audited. Additionally, the audit logs should be tested for protection from unauthorized modification. The following tests should be attempted in order to gain a minimum level of confidence that the audit log protections are effective:

- Audited Activities — The assessment team member should perform a sampling of security-relevant activities that should create audit records, for example, multiple authorization attempts, and attempted reading of protected files.
- Audit Log Information — The team member should review the created audit log files for the essential audit log event elements, for example, user identification, attempted access, success or failure, and network time stamp.
- Audit Log Protection — The team member should attempt to access audit log files from an unauthorized account.

7.2.5.3 Anti-Virus Systems

Testing procedures for anti-virus systems require that the security risk assessment team perform activities that attempt to bypass the anti-virus controls set for the system or workstations. The following tests should be attempted to gain a minimum level of confidence that the anti-virus technology is effective:

- Check Anti-Virus Settings — There are several settings essential to an anti-virus system that are important to its proper functioning. The assessment team member should review several deployed instances of the anti-virus software to check the following settings:
  - Automatic Updates — The anti-virus software should be configured to receive automatic updates at least daily.
  - Automatic Deletion — The anti-virus software should be set to automatically delete those viruses that it can
  - Automatic Scans — The anti-virus software should be configured to run automatic scans on all incoming e-mail and new files. The software should also be set to run a complete system scan at least once a week.
  - Locked Settings — The anti-virus software should be configured to block user attempts to bypass scanning, updates, or complete scans.
  - File Extension Settings — The anti-virus software should be configured to scan for the following file extensions: .exe, .com, .dll, .doc.
- Check Anti-Virus Currency — The assessment team member should check several deployed instances of the anti-virus software for the latest version and release.
- Check Anti-Virus Capabilities — The anti-virus software should be capable of scanning compressed (not encrypted) files.
- Run the Anti-Virus Test File (Optional) — To more completely test the anti-virus software, the security risk assessment team may elect to set up a test machine and run an anti-virus test file against it. The following Web site contains an updated anti-virus test file for just that purpose: www.eicar.org/anti_virus_test_file.htm

7.2.5.4 Automated Password Policies

Testing procedures for automated password policies require that the security risk assessment team perform activities that attempt to bypass the policies set and enforced. The following functional tests should be attempted to gain a minimum level of confidence that the automated password policy enforcement technology is effective:

- Password Length — The assessment team member should attempt to change the password on an issued account to a length less than the specified minimum. The team member should also attempt to change the password to an extraordinarily long length.

- Password Complexity — The team member should attempt to reset the password to a character string that does not meet the complexity requirements. Also the team member should attempt to set the password to a character string that includes illegal characters.
- Minimum Limit — The team member should attempt to change the password again within a short span of time (e.g. several minutes) to test any minimum password periods that may have been set.

7.2.5.5 Virtual Private Network

Testing procedures for virtual private networks (VPN) require that the security risk assessment team perform activities that attempt to bypass the authentication and authorization controls on virtual private networks. The following tests should be attempted to gain a minimum level of confidence that the VPN authentication technology is effective:

1. Username Enumeration — An assessment team member should test the VPN system for its susceptibility to user enumeration attacks. Some VPN systems respond differently to authentication attempts if the username is valid or invalid. Systems that exhibit such a behavior are more susceptible to dictionary and brute-force attacks on the authentication.
2. IKE Aggressive Mode Attack — This test is a little advanced, but tools exist that can largely automate the attack. The assessment team may consider testing the VPN through attempts to gain knowledge of the pre-shared key (PSK). If a VPN is set up to accept IKE Aggressive Mode connections, then the PSK transmitted prior to authentication is unencrypted. This unencrypted hashed key can be captured. A brute-force attack against the hash can be performed within minutes. If the assessment team does not need to demonstrate this vulnerability, it may suffice to ensure that the VPN is set to IKE Main Mode.

7.2.5.6 Firewalls, IDS, and System Hardening

The testing of firewalls, intrusion detection systems, and system hardening can be combined here because security professionals all use the same tools and techniques for testing these devices. In short, these tools include vulnerability scanners and automated penetration testing tools and these techniques include ad-hoc penetration testing. This section provides an overview of these tools and techniques to assist security risk assessment teams in ensuring completeness in their technical data-gathering effort.

Every security risk assessment team should have members who are expert in these tools and techniques. As any of these experts would tell you, these tools and techniques change all the time and they can get quite complex. This book does not attempt to provide the level of detail required to actually perform these tests, for several reasons. First, there are many other books in print and websites online that can provide that information. Second, the tools and techniques change too often to possibly print relevant and up-to-date information on these techniques. Instead, this section provides a description of the tools and techniques and a high-level review of how they should be employed in the technical data-gathering phase.

7.2.5.7 Vulnerability Scanning

Vulnerability scanning involves the testing of information system interfaces to identify obvious vulnerabilities.[15] A vulnerability scan is an important element of any security risk assessment because it provides a cost-effective way to identify vulnerabilities that exist within the system. All other data-gathering approaches result in indications of possible vulnerabilities and can be costly, but a vulnerability scan is both inexpensive (relatively) and effective.

The objective of the vulnerability scan is to identify the obvious configuration vulnerabilities that exist in the currently deployed systems. A configuration vulnerability means that the vulnerability can be safeguarded through improvements in the configuration of the servers or workstations (i.e., system hardening). This section provides a description of the vulnerability scanning process.

7.2.5.7.1 Stages of Vulnerability Scanning

A vulnerability scan is not simply the process of running the tool and printing out a report. A vulnerability scan actually incorporates a multistep process that includes the setup, mapping, scanning, and report generation. Most of these steps are described below:

- Setup — Setting up properly for a vulnerability scan is essential to the success of the scan itself. Several elements of the setup step need to be considered:
  - Administrator Presence — It is a good idea to have the administrator present during the setup process. This will give the assessor instant feedback if problems occur and the administrator can assist in problem resolution.
  - System Descriptions — The assessor should ask the organization to provide a list with each IP address to be scanned and the associated functions. Many vulnerability scanners can be set to scan only for relevant vulnerabilities given the function of the system or applications

on the system. This can significantly reduce false positives from the vulnerability scan.

- Subnets — The assessor must be aware of the network architecture and the subnets in order to properly place the vulnerability scanning device or software.
- Network Mapping — This step is described in the section below.
- Vulnerability Scanning — This step is described in the section below.
- Report Generation — When generating the vulnerability scanning report, several elements need to be considered:
  - More Than Raw Data — A vulnerability scan report should not simply be a dump of raw data generated by the vulnerability scanning tool. This should be a professional report that includes a description of the testing effort, the methodology, and the recommendations and timelines for correction.
  - Don't Point Fingers — The report should attempt to simply state facts and not overstep its bounds to guess at the cause. Keep it simple: state the vulnerability and the recommendation.
  - Various Views — The report should provide various views of the data. For example, include an executive summary that states the number of vulnerabilities and the overall risk level. Also include mid-level views of the data that categorize vulnerabilities by class. Lastly, make the raw data available on CD-ROM.

7.2.5.7.2 Vulnerability Scanning Tools

The availability and power of vulnerability scanning tools has increased tremendously over the past few years. These tools have both automated tasks previously performed manually and have increased the level of rigor and the depth of analysis commonly performed in security testing. In the past, security testing activities would include manual procedures or proprietary scripts to look for commonly known (called "obvious") vulnerabilities in many protocols, operating systems, and applications. Many vulnerability scanning tools have advanced and continue to advance by incorporating these procedures and scripts into available tools, some with intuitive graphical interfaces. This process has significantly reduced the effort and skill required to perform the task of vulnerability scanning.[16] Moreover, with the availability of such tools the depth of testing commonly performed on information security risk assessments has increased to a level that previously would have been prohibitively expensive to obtain.

As discussed previously, vulnerability scanning is a technique used to gather information about possible vulnerabilities within the target system. Vulnerability scanning tools support this task in one or more of the following areas:

- Network Mapping — Listing the available hosts and their open interfaces to be tested.
- Vulnerability Scanning — Provides an automated mapping of available hosts and ports to known vulnerabilities.

Network Mapping — The first phase of any vulnerability scanning activity involves the enumeration of the interfaces to be tested. This is generally referred to as network mapping. When the interfaces to be tested are unknown or when they need to be confirmed, network mapping is a useful technique.

- Definition — Network mapping tools run a port scan on the system to identify all reachable active hosts, network services operating on those hosts, and the name of the applications running those services.
- Result — The result is a list of IP addresses of the available hosts on the system and the associated ports, services, and applications run on those hosts.
- How They Work — Network mapping tools perform three tasks that together provide a listing of the hosts reachable on the system, their ports, and their services offered:
  - Finding Hosts — Network mapping tools generally determine available hosts through the use of ICMP_ECHO and ICMP_ REPLY packets. The TCP/IP protocol states that when a host receives a ICMP_ECHO packet, it responds with an ICMP_REPLY packet to the host that was the source of the packet. Network mapping tools generate ICMP_ECHO requests for every possible IP address within a specified range. Once the network mapping tool has completed sending and receiving these packets, it will know which hosts are available.
  - Determining Open Ports — Network mapping tools find open ports through TCP and UDP scanning:
    - TCP Scanning — TCP scanning is straightforward because the TCP protocol is a connection-oriented protocol and guarantees delivery of packets. By attempting to establish a connection with every port on an available host, a network mapping tool can determine the ports that are open because those that are "listening" will respond with a successful connection.
    - UDP Scanning — UDP scanning is more difficult and unpredictable because of the nature of the UDP protocol. The UDP protocol is a connectionless protocol that does not provide reliable delivery of data packets. This means that no connection is established between the sender and the receiver and that there is no guarantee that packets will be delivered either way.[17] Network mapping tools that implement UDP port scanning generally send

UDP packets, with no data, to a port. If the port does not provide an open service, then an "ICMP Port Unreachable" response is generated. If the port does provide an open service, then either the port will respond with an error or it will drop the packet altogether. So we can be sure of results that indicate ports are closed, but a result that indicates a port is open is only a guess because either the UDP packet or the ICMP response could have been dropped. Network mapping tools that implement UDP scanning generally will retransmit packets that appear to have been lost. Even with this improvement there are likely to be many false positives.

- Determine Services and Applications Associated with Open Ports — There are over 65,000 possible ports for each IP address. Ports are used to establish a specific communication between the source host and the destination host. Different types of communication are performed on different ports. Many specific communication types are performed on specific ports. For example, HTTP, the protocol used to communicate with Web servers, is performed on port 80, whereas the secure version of HTTP (HTTPS) is performed on port 443. Simply by reviewing the port numbers open and used, network mapping tools can determine the available services on the targeted machines.

- Limitations — Network mapping tools are considered rather low-level data-gathering devices. They can gather very useful information, but they can also be easily fooled or blocked. There are several important limitations of network mapping tools that security testers should be aware of:
  - No System Map — In general, network mapping tools do not provide a "map" of the system. All reachable hosts are simply listed without an indication of their arrangement within the internal system architecture.
  - Can Be Blocked and Fooled — Network mapping tools attempt to gain information through simple ICMP probing techniques. Many information systems that have been reasonably secured may have intrusion detection systems, honeypots, or even simple gateways that can block such inquiries or even send back erroneous data to confuse the suspected hacker.
  - Services May Be Different Than Expected — The assignment of services to port numbers is administered by the Internet Assigned Numbers Authority (IANA), which coordinates the use of the available port numbers to lessen confusion. The adherence to these assignments is not universal. Still, low-numbered ports (0–1024) are generally regarded as having specific services associated with them, and many well-known ports (1025–49151) follow the general registration of ports and services. Regardless, the mapping of an open port to an expected service is an educated guess and not a certainty.

- Overcoming Limitations — To overcome some of these limitations, many network mapping tools have developed additional functions and techniques to obtain the network, port, and application information on the target network:
  - Fingerprinting — This technique is used to identify the operating system at the other end of a connection. Information may have been blocked by configuring the system to not announce the operating system. However, the operating system can still be guessed with reasonable certainty, based on several fingerprinting techniques, including (a) response to invalid commands, (b) port pairs, and (c) banner grabbing.
    - (a) Response to Invalid Commands — Almost all operating systems would respond in a generic way to expected commands, but error messages sent for unexpected commands tend to be unique to operating systems. Using this information, some network mapping tools are able to "fingerprint" the operating system and report this information back to the tester.
    - (b) Port Pairs — Some operating systems can be spotted merely by the ports that remain open. For example, if a system has port 135 (DCE endpoint) and port 139 (NetBIOS), then the operating system is likely a Microsoft Windows 2000 or NT.
    - (c) Banner Grabbing — During the open connection the server sends configuration information to the requesting host. This information is not typically seen by the user, but a network mapping tool could intercept this "banner" and use the information in it to determine the application name and version.
  - Stealth Scanning — As you may expect, the process of scanning a system would be quite noticeable to anyone looking for such activity. If the target network has a firewall or an intrusion detection system with the ability to spot scanning or probing, the network mapping effort is likely to be cut short. Stealth scanning is a way to slow down the scan to such a level that it is not likely to be detected as a "port scan." For example, suppose you try to scan 65,535 ports with a scanner that can scan 300 ports per second. Then you will be able to scan one IP address every 3.64 minutes. That is pretty fast, but a stealth scan will slow the scan down to one port per second (for example) and would take over 18 hours to scan one host.
  - Strobing — This term refers to the scanning technique in which the system tester only looks for a specific set of open ports on the system. That set of open ports would include common ports where dangerous services are being offered but not secured, or where it is indicative of a Trojan horse already being installed. This technique is useful when

the testing effort is limited, fast scanning would likely be detected, and stealth scanning would take too long.

- Fragmented Packet Port Scans — Some networks will be protected by a packet-filtering firewall with rules designed to limit or block port scanning. By fragmenting a packet a port scan can still occur, even though the firewall is designed to block port scanning. This works by splitting (or fragmenting) the IP header into several different packets. The fragmented IP header may not be identified as part of a port scan because many packet-filtering firewalls do not reassemble the IP packet header before determining if the packets meet the ruleset for the firewall. Even packet-filtering firewalls with the ability to reassemble the header packet prior to determining the flow of the packet are typically configured to ignore this capability for performance reasons.

- SYN and FIN Scans — Another way around some firewalls discovering a port scan is to ensure that the TCP connect operation never completes and therefore the server process is not informed by the TCP layer that a connection was attempted. There are two approaches to port scanning while ensuring that a TCP connect never occurs:

  - SYN Scan — A SYN scan sends a SYN request to a port on the server. The SYN message is the first stage of the three-way handshake that occurs in opening a connection. If the server responds with a SYN-ACK message, then the port scanner assumes the port is listening. If the server responds with a RST, then the port scanner assumes there is no open service on that port. In either case a connection is never made and therefore the server process is not told of the messages by the TCP layer.

  - FIN Scan — A FIN scan sends a FIN request to a port on the server. If there is no open service on the port, then the server responds with a RST message. If there is an open service on the port, then the server ignores the message because it did not currently have a connection with the message sender. It is difficult to produce reliable results quickly with these scans because an open port is indicated by no response. There could be other reasons for no response, including accidentally dropped packets or packets blocked by the firewall.

- Network Mapping Tools — There are many network mapping tools available to information security professionals that can automate or significantly reduce the effort required to perform a listing of the network hosts and services. Below, one popular network mapping tools is discussed.

There are other tools such as SuperScan and Siphon, but the discussion below provides a general overview of such tools:

- Nmap — Nmap is a port scanning tool that can identify active hosts and open ports on those hosts (i.e., services). Nmap supports the following port scans:
  - TCP connect( ) — uses connect( ) system call to attempt to open a connection on user-selected ports on a remote host.
  - TCP SYN — uses root privileges of the host machine to initiate a connection (using a SYN packet). If a negative response is received (RST), then it is assumed the port is closed. If a positive response is received (SYN/ACK), then it is assumed the port is open and a cancel connection response is sent (RST).

Sidebar 7.1 Port Numbers and Ranges

There are a total of 65,536 (0–65535) possible port numbers. The port numbers are divided into ranges: well-known ports, registered ports, and (dynamic) private ports.

Well-known ports (0–1024)

These ports, also called low-numbered ports, are assigned by the IANA. They are unique because most operating systems restrict the association (called binding) of any service with these ports to trusted processes such as root. Table 7.13 shows a partial listing of the more common "well-known" port and service pairings.

Table 7.13   Well-Known Port Numbers. The following port numbers, below 1024, are important because they are associated with well-known services. Binding to well-known ports should be restricted to trusted processes.

Port Number	Service
7	ECHO
20	File Transfer Protocol — Data
21	File Transfer Protocol — Control
22	SSH Remote Login Protocol
23	Telnet
25	Simple Mail Transfer Protocol
42	Host Name Server
43	Who Is
53	Domain Name Server
69	Trivial File Transfer Protocol
110	Post Office Protocol v3
118	SQL Services

(Continued)

Table 7.13 (Continued)
Well-Known Port Numbers

Port Number	Service
137	NetBIOS Name Service
138	NetBIOS Datagram Service
139	NetBIOS Session Service
143	Interim Mail Access Protocol
156	SQL Server
161	SNMP
179	Border Gateway Protocol
194	Internet Relay Chat
389	Lightweight Directory Access Protocol
443	HTTPS
458	Apple Quick Time
546	DHCP Client
547	DHCP Server
666	DOOM

Registered ports (1025–49151)

These ports are not assigned by the IANA, but for convenience to the community the IANA lists the registered uses of these ports. This means that, although you may suspect a certain service to be performed on a given port, this may not be the case.

These port numbers are not considered "trusted" because in most operating systems ordinary users may establish an association with any of these port numbers. So, if a user beats another process to the establishment of a service on port number 1050, a client system opening a connection to that port may be looking for the Common Object Request Broker Architecture (CORBA) Management Agent but will be connected to the user process instead. Table 7.14 contains a partial listing of the more common port and service pairings in the registered port number range.

Table 7.14 Registered Ports. The following port numbers, 1025–49151, are not considered trusted since associations with these port numbers are not typically restricted.

Port Number	Service
1050	CORBA Management Agent
1243	SubSeven — Trojan horse
1352	Lotus Notes

(Continued)

Table 7.14   (Continued)
Registered Ports

Port Number	Service
1433	Microsoft SQL Server
1494	Citrix ICA Protocol
1521	Oracle SQL
1604	Citrix ICA/Microsoft Terminal Server
2049	Network File System
3306	MySQL
4000	ICQ
5010	Yahoo! Messenger
5190	AOL Instant Messenger
5632	PCAnywhere
5800	VNC
5900	VNC
6000	X Windowing System
6699	Napster
6776	SubSeven — Trojan horse
7070	RealServer/QuickTime
8080	HTTP
26000	Quake
27010	Half-Life
27960	Quake II
31337	BackOrifice — Trojan horse

Dynamic and Private Ports (49152–65535)
These ports are not assigned or registered There are no commonly known ports in this space.

Vulnerability Scanners — The second phase of the vulnerability scanning activity involves the identification of vulnerabilities of the hosts, operating systems, services, and applications identified during the network mapping phase. This is generally referred to as vulnerability scanning. When you need to confirm the existence of obvious vulnerabilities based on knowledge of available interfaces, a vulnerability scanner is a useful tool.[18]

- Definition — Vulnerability scanners attempt to identify vulnerabilities in identified hosts by looking for "obvious vulnerabilities." Vulnerability scanners are built by security engineers on the knowledge of how to identify vulnerabilities in specific systems. By coding this knowledge in an automated tool, these scanners can significantly reduce the work of the information security professional during this stage of security testing.
- Result — The result of running a vulnerability scan is a mapping between the results of the network mapping effort and known exploits for the systems it believes are present.

- How They Work — The vulnerability scanners are actually quite simple in that they look up known vulnerabilities for each port, service, operating system, or application that is known to be running on the system. Many vulnerability scanners also provide a risk index indicating the severity of the vulnerability as well as safeguard recommendations.
- Limitations — The limitation of the vulnerability scanners lies in the limited knowledge developed during the network mapping exercise. The network mapping efforts can produce incorrect data, such as misinterpreting information and reporting back that an operating system is running on the system when in fact it is not. Such incorrect information can lead to baseless assumptions about the target system and result in what is known as false positives. False positives are reported vulnerabilities that do not exist on the system.
- Overcoming Limitations — The tester may reduce false positive reading by using multiple network mapping programs and comparing the results. Another technique is to create a document of the systems being scanned and the known services on these systems. If these documents can be trusted, then the network mapping information can be corrected and therefore the vulnerability scanner will produce fewer false positives.

Virus and Pest Scanning — An optional phase of the vulnerability scanning activity within the security testing approach involves a search for executable code on the system that can lead to a breach in the protection requirements for the protected assets. This is generally referred to as virus or pest scanning. If the security risk assessment team needs to test for the presence of such software, virus and pest scanning tools are available.[19]

- Definition — Anti-virus software, spyware, and pest scanners can be used to search for installed malware such as viruses, worms, spybots, keyloggers, adware, and other uninvited code.
- Result — The running of these tools results in the identification and possibly the removal of malware.
- How They Work — These tools typically work on the basis of signature definitions. These definitions or fingerprints allow the tools to detect the signature of the virus or other malware. As mentioned previously, some of these tools also have the capability of removing the malware. Removal is possible if the tool is programmed with the knowledge of where all the pieces of the malware are stored.
- Limitations — These scanners are limited in their ability to detect malware based on limitations of the signature definitions. If the definitions stored with the tool are out of date or do not otherwise contain a matching signature, then the malware will go undetected. The scanners are limited in their ability to remove malware if they do not know where all the pieces

are stored or if the malware is integrated with another program that the user may not want deleted. Most of these programs are software that business users would not need, such as freeware games.

- Overcoming Limitations — The security assessment team member performing the malware scans should ensure that the signature definition files are up to date. Additionally, the team member may want to consider using at least two different malware scanners to increase coverage.

Application Scanners — Another optional phase of the vulnerability scanning activity within the security testing approach involves a search for vulnerabilities within deployed and custom applications. This is generally referred to as application vulnerability scanning. The security risk assessment team may elect to test for the presence of vulnerabilities within COTS and custom applications.[20]

- Definition — Application scanners, also known as Web application scanners, are tools that automate the testing of applications based on a set of known vulnerabilities. Many Web application scanners comply with the OWASP Top Ten. The Open Web Application Security Project (OWASP) Top Ten Most Critical Web Application Vulnerabilities are now considered an industry standard as the minimum set of vulnerabilities for which an application should be scanned.[21]
- Result — The running of these tools results in the identification of known vulnerabilities in the applications.
- How They Work — These tools typically work on the basis of signature definitions. These definitions or fingerprints allow the tools to detect the signature of the vulnerability.
- Limitations — These tools are limited in their ability to identify all application vulnerabilities based on limitations of the signature definitions and the inherent limitations in scanning. A more complete review of Web application security would include Web application code review.
- Overcoming Limitations — The security assessment team member performing the application scans should ensure that the signature definition files are up to date.

7.2.5.8 Penetration Testing

Penetration testing involves the exploitation of system vulnerabilities to gain system access or otherwise violate the organization's security policy. Penetration testing can take two forms.

The first form of penetration testing is simply an extension of vulnerability scanning. When vulnerability scanning is complete, the assessment team has a list of known vulnerabilities to the system. In this first form of penetration testing the team simply exploits the discovered vulnerabilities. Typically, this is not recommended because the vulnerability is already known and there is little or no benefit to the security risk assessment process in risking damage to the system or the organization's mission.

The second form of penetration testing is an ad-hoc testing method to look for less obvious vulnerabilities. This type of penetration testing requires a skilled team member. Based on the nature of this type of testing, which is ad hoc, it also eludes description, but the basic approach is as follows:

- Information Probing — The penetration tester will attempt to gain additional information on the systems to be tested. This information could simply be given to the tester or they could be gained through such efforts as reviewing newspapers and trade magazines, searching domain name registries, searching for information posted on Internet chat groups, and using network probing tools such as network sniffers.
- Vulnerability Scanning — This step was described above and was probably already performed at this stage in the testing effort. However, if the vulnerability scans were not performed, the penetration tester would perform them now.
- Penetration Techniques — There are various techniques that may be used to penetrate the system based on known systems and vulnerabilities. Some of the techniques that may be employed include: password cracking, privilege escalation, Web application hacking, social engineering, e-mail spoofing, and ad-hoc testing.

Sidebar 7.2 Zero-Knowledge Testing: Who Is Really Being Tested?

Many organizations assume that the external threats or hackers to their systems must truly be outsiders. As such, they expect that when hackers first begin to break into their systems these hackers start with no knowledge of the organization's systems, connections, partners, and employees.

The objective of an external penetration test is to test the adequacy of security controls in place and their resistance to attack from an external threat. Therefore, it is reasoned, such a test should emulate the external threat as realistically as possible. Using this reasoning, many organizations contract an independent security consultant to perform zero-knowledge testing. Zero-knowledge testing requires that the independent security consultants are given only the name of the company to be tested, a point of contact, a budget, and a few ground rules

This zero-knowledge restriction on the external testing service is unnecessary, misleading, costly, and will result in less useful results. The prevailing thought among organizations requesting this restriction on the service seems to be that the independent security consultants should "prove" themselves. The premise that a firm that is working for you should demonstrate their abilities to find information necessary to perform a thorough test is misguided. The qualifications of the firm you intend to hire should be carefully reviewed and assessed prior to the signing of the contract — not during the performance of the contract.

Another driver for placing the zero-knowledge restriction on external testing seems to be a misplaced belief that external threats come from those that will target the organization specifically. Although such targeted attacks are possible, the majority of the threat to organizations is manifested in the masses of script-kiddies and other deviants that exist in huge numbers. These pests are so ubiquitous that if your system exhibits a vulnerability for a small amount of time, chances are good that one of them will stumble upon it. For example, it is widely believed that an unprotected system exposed to the Internet will be compromised within three minutes. Therefore, a vulnerability in your system is more likely to be discovered by someone who stumbles upon it than it is by someone who targets your system. Restricting knowledge of your system to the security testers is not the best emulation of the real threats.

The work that must be performed to obtain knowledge of the organization's systems, connections, partners, and employees can be tedious but is not difficult. There is little doubt that any qualified security consultant could actually figure out the information typically given prior to testing anyway; it may take a bit of time though. Qualified security consultants know how to review public information (e.g., domain registries, press, bulletin boards, and annual reports) and perform social engineering to obtain the necessary information. Since it takes time to obtain this information, the security consultants will need to charge more for the service.

Lastly, the less information you give the security testers, the less complete the external testing can be. For example, your organization may have several areas that should be tested that may not be discovered in the initial search for information. These areas could include modem numbers on key equipment, systems registered under a different company name, and new interfaces. You can bet that these interfaces will be well exercised sooner or later by the masses of cyber-pests. If the security testers are not told about these interfaces and they go untested, the ultimate results of the test are questionable because of their incompleteness.

7.2.5.9 Testing Specific Technology

The sections below provide a description for how to perform testing on specific technology such as modems, wireless networks, and PBXs.

7.2.5.9.1 Modem Access Testing

Modem access testing, also known as wardialing, is a security-testing technique for identifying modems within the organization that may be attached to the information system and assessing the access controls of identified modems. The following tasks are performed during a wardialing effort:

- Footprint — The assessment team member scans a range of numbers belonging to the organization to identify phone numbers that give back a modem/carrier signal. Initially, this sweep of phone numbers within the range provided will be performed during the off hours so as to not alert suspicion. Additional sweeps of numbers can be performed during business hours as well. The advantages of such a sweep include the ability to find modems only available during working hours. The disadvantages of this additional sweep include disruption of phone lines and workers during business hours and increased risk of detection.
- Preparation — The assessment team member should now sort through the numbers identified in the footprint effort to prioritize candidate phone numbers for penetration. Candidate phone numbers should be sorted according to the following categories:
  - Default Passwords — Many systems may have default passwords still enabled. Based on response signatures or screens, wardialing tools may be able to identify the dial-up system.
  - Single Authentication/Unlimited Attempts — Systems at the other end of these phone numbers allow unlimited attempts at guessing log-in

credentials. The modems will not disconnect after a threshold of failed attempts. Moreover, these systems either only ask for a password (log-in ID is supplied or assumed), or worse only ask for log-in ID (which is typically easier to guess than a password).

- Dual Authentication/Unlimited Attempts — Systems at the other end of these phone numbers allow unlimited attempts at guessing log-in credentials. The modems will not disconnect after a threshold of failed attempts. These systems ask for both a log-in ID and a password.
- Limited Attempts — Systems at the other end of these phone numbers will disconnect after a threshold of failed attempts.
- Penetration — The assessment team member should attempt to gain access to the organization's systems through modem numbers identified and sorted during the previous steps. The assessor should use a dictionary of default and easy-to-guess passwords to attempt to log-in into these systems.
- Reporting — The assessment team member should log all wardialing efforts and report the results. This report should include the range of numbers scanned, identification of modem/carrier signals detected, and identification of systems penetrated.

7.2.5.9.2 Wireless Network Testing

Testing procedures for wireless networking systems require that the security risk assessment team perform activities that attempt to discover wireless networks within the network and determine the access controls placed on those networks. This testing can be performed rather simply using what is known as a wardriving technique:

- Wardriving — A member of the security risk assessment team should configure a laptop (or even a handheld PC) with a wireless scanning application such as AirMagnet or NetStumbler. The assessor should then walk or drive around the organization's complex in search of discovered wireless networks. These applications will discover all networks within range and report on the network name (if broadcast), signal strength, and its mode of protection. The mode of protection will either be open, WEP, WPA, or other stronger methods. Obviously open networks are insecure, but WEP-protected networks are also considered weak and insecure.

7.2.5.9.3 PBX Testing

Testing procedures for private branch exchange (PBX) systems require that the security risk assessment team perform activities that attempt to bypass the access controls for the PBX system. The following tests should be attempted to gain a minimum level of confidence that the PBX protections are effective:

- Attendant Terminals — The assessment team member should determine if attendant terminals are physically and logically protected. Attendant terminals provide access to the administration functions of a PBX and should be reserved for use by authorized individuals. Physical protection could mean locating the devices in a locked room. Logical protection could be accomplished through password or PIN codes.
- Remote Maintenance — The assessment team member should determine if remote maintenance is enabled on the PBX. If remote maintenance is enabled, the external access should be controlled, for example, turn off the modem when not in use, use a callback modem, change default passwords.
- Unassigned Numbers — The team member should attempt to find an unassigned number by guessing extension numbers that may not have been assigned yet. Then, by calling into the extension number, he may be asked for a password to set up the mailbox. The assessor should try default passwords such as 1111, 1234, and the extension number itself.[22]
- More Attacks — There are many more complex attacks that may be attempted as well. These attacks are well documented in the NIST Special Publication 800-24, *PBX Vulnerability Analysis.*

Notes

1. For those who are experts in this field or have a checklist they are comfortable with, you may skip this section without losing any context for the rest of the chapter.

2. Protecting access to a file via a password mechanism is considered inherently weak within information systems, because of the lack of accountability and the inability to revoke access. Password protection for files sent over an insecure network medium are more common but still considered insecure, because an unauthorized user may intercept the file and perform unlimited attempts at guessing the password.

3. Two-factor authentication has an additional requirement that the two authentication methods must be of different types (i.e., something you know, something you have, and something you are). For example, a password and a personal identification number (PIN) are not considered two-factor authentication because it simply reduces to a longer password.

4. This works well for threats such as eavesdropping, where network segmentation will limit the computers to which a would-be eavesdropper can listen to only those computers on the network segment they are listening on. However, network segmentation must be accounted for when deploying safeguards such as intrusion detection systems. The system designer must be careful to include IDS sensors on all segments of the network to ensure complete coverage. A network segment is

not bounded by hubs, since hubs are a layer 1 device that does not even recognize MAC addresess.

5. A more detailed understanding of encryption is important to any information security professional. However, such a discussion is beyond the scope of this book.

6. Many experienced security consultants will be tempted to simply review documents and provide comments on discovered security deficiencies, but fail to spot missing key elements. It is for this reason that a checklist is used to guide the review and ensure a more complete analysis.

7. For a more complete discussion of how to use the "review documents" approach, refer to section 5.2.2.1.

8. Some would argue that the Common Criteria Evaluation Methodology (CCEM) provides a systematic approach to design review. However, the Common Criteria requirements and evaluation methods only specify the form and content requirements for design documents and the approach for evaluating the sufficiency of the documents. Design analysis occurs, but there is no formal process for such an analysis in the CCEM.

9. Certification is the processes of examining technical and nontechnical security controls for the enforcement of the system's security policy. Accreditation is the decision by the appointed authority to accept the security risk of the system. The "C&A" process requires documentation of the security requirements, system boundaries, an examination of the controls, and a conclusion.

10. Note removed.

11. Each of these security design areas is treated at a rather high level. This is intended because a security risk assessment is not the same as a system evaluation. System evaluations can afford the time and effort it takes to review these controls in much more detail. Remember that security risk assessments are a periodic check based on changes in the threat environment; a security evaluation is performed prior to acceptance of the system in the first place.

12. Reviewing user's mail has legal implications. The Electronic Communications Privacy Act, and other laws, restricts the monitoring of electronic communications. At a minimum the team leader should have written permission to review communications in association with the assessment, ensure that such a policy exists within the organization, and ensure that users have been informed that communications may be monitored for performance or security reasons. Prior to inspecting any electronic communications, the security risk assessment team leader may want to get a legal opinion. Nothing in this book should be construed as legal advice.

13. The Common Vulnerabilities and Exposures (CVE) dictionary is a list of standardized names for known vulnerabilities and security exposures. The CVE dictionary is a project run by the MITRE Corporation and sponsored by the US-CERT at the U.S. Department of Homeland Security (www.cve. mitre.org).

14. The reader should also check out the ICAT Metabase (icat.nist.gov). This is not a checklist but a searchable index of information on computer vulnerabilities.

The user can enter the product and version into the database and get a list of applicable vulnerabilities. Most of these vulnerabilities are linked to additional vulnerability information and patches.

15.   Vulnerability scanning can be applied to any network device with an IP address. This includes firewalls, VPN servers, IDS, etc. This section deals with vulnerability scanning as it applies to any network-connected device. More specific testing of technology is covered in a later section.

16.   Vulnerability scanners have reduced the effort and skill required to perform the task of vulnerability scanning but not eliminated it. A good amount of skill is still required to set up the tests and review the results. Also, in larger systems the vulnerability scanning effort can easily be one of the largest tasks.

17.   At first glance this sounds like a useless protocol because it cannot guarantee anything. But this is not the case. The UDP protocol provides fast delivery of packets with low overhead in processing. This type of service is extremely useful in services such as voice and video streaming that do not care about an errant dropped packet from time to time, but do care about low overhead and fast performance.

18.   Many vulnerability scanners also perform network mapping (the first phase). In this section we are only concentrating on their ability to map vulnerabilities to known ports, services, operating systems, and applications.

19.   Many virus and pest scanners also have the ability to remove found malware or run resident and detect new attempts to place malware on the system. Although these are worthy features of these products, in this section we are only interested in their ability to discover malware.

20.   Note removed.

21.   For more information, or to download a copy of the OWASP Top Ten, see www.owasp.org.

22.   This same technique of password guessing could be used on assigned numbers as well. However, the security risk assessment team leader should be careful not to violate eavesdropping laws or the confines of the statement of work.

References

[1]   Hills, Roy, *VPN Security Flaws White Paper*, January 31, 2005. www.nta-monitor.com/news/vpn-flaws

[2]   Hills, Roy, "If you fail to prepare, be prepared to fail", *SC Magazine*, November 2004, p. 48.

[3]   *Generally Accepted Information Security Principles*, GAISP v3.0, Information Systems Security Association. http://www.issa.org/gaisp/_pdfs/v30.pdf

[4]   Common Criteria Evaluation Methodology, Version 1.0, CEM-99/045, August 1999.

[5]   *PBX Vulnerability Analysis: Finding Holes in Your PBX Before Someone Else Does*, NIST Special Publication 800-24, August 2000. http://csrc.nist.gov/publications/nistpubs/800-24/sp800-24pbx.pdf

[6] *Engineering Principles for Information Technology Security (A Baseline for Achieving Security)*, NIST Special Publication 800-27, June 2001. http://csrc.nist.gov/publications/nistpubs/800-27A/SP800-27-RevA.pdf

[7] *The NIST Security Configuration Checklists Program* NIST Special Publication 800-70, August 12, 2004. http://csrc.nist.gov/checklists/index.html

[8] Mateti, Prabhaker, Port Scanning Lecture. Wright State University, College of Engineering and Computer Science, Dayton, OH. www.cs.wright.edu/~pmateti/InternetSecurity/Lectures/Probing

[9] Fydor, "The Art of Port Scanning," 1997. www.nmap.org

[10] [NIST 800-42].

[11] [RFC 1700] Reynolds, J., Postel, J., Request for Comments: 1700, Assigned Numbers, October 1994.

[12] [VISA CISP] Visa International, Cardholder Information Security Program.

[13] [ISSAF] Rathore, Balwant, Information System Security Assessment Framework (ISSAF), Draft 0.1, Open Information Systems Security Group, December 25, 2004.

[14] [SANS] Naidu, Krishni, Firewall Checklist, SANS SCORE. www.sans.org/score/firewallchecklist.php

[15] [backup] Beaver, Kevin, Checklist: Performing data backups, November 23, 2004. SearchWinSystems.com

Chapter 8

Physical Data Gathering

Extending the security risk assessment to include the review of physical security mechanisms provides a more complete view of the overall security posture of the organization. Failure to consider physical vulnerabilities can lead to a false sense of security and increase the risk of a breach to capital or information assets. Attempts to breach the security of the organization can come from logical attacks or physical attacks. To ignore the physical side of the security risk equation is an invitation to disaster.

There are some organizations in which the physical security and the logical security are handled by distinctly separate groups (e.g., military bases). Even if the organization does have a distinct separation between the physical and logical security, the project sponsor should consider a joint (physical and logical) security risk assessment as an improvement to the assessment process.

Sidebar 8.1 Physical Security Assessments

As with any project, it is important to note the objective of the security risk assessment, especially when it comes to reviewing physical security controls. The objective of the assessment is to provide an accurate analysis of the current security controls and not to inspect the security controls for adherence to building codes, fire codes, or other legal regulations. In fact, certain licenses and credentials are required for the inspection of fire systems and installation of physical security controls.

Therefore, the material in this security risk assessment book is at an appropriate level to provide a security risk assessment team the information and approach needed to spot threats and vulnerabilities in the current security posture and to make recommendations for improvement. However, the design, installation, and inspection of physical security controls are beyond the scope of this book.

For more information on physical security controls and certifications, visit the following websites:

- *ASIS International:* www.asisonline.org
- *Underwriters Laboratories Fire Alarm System Certification — Listing Process:* www.ul.com/alarm systems/fire.html
- *DOE Physical Security Inspectors Guide:* www.oa.doe. gov/guidedocs/0009pssig/0009pssigpdf.html

8.1 Physical Threats and Safeguards

Threats, threat agents, and threat statements were covered earlier in section 4.5. Physical threats specifically are covered here as an approach to introducing physical data gathering. This section, on threats and safeguards, is intended as a primer or introduction to security threats in the physical area.[1]

A member of a security risk assessment team requires a basic understanding of the threats and safeguards within the physical security area to be an effective member of the team. There are numerous physical security threats; some of the more frequent physical threats are discussed in Table 8.1. This section describes the general physical security threats and safeguards as well as a process for gathering information regarding the adequacy of physical security mechanisms.

8.1.1 Utilities and Interior Climate

Protected assets, especially computer systems and components, need to be protected from adverse climate conditions to ensure continuous operation. Of primary concern in areas that house computer equipment (e.g., data centers) is monitoring and controlling of heat and humidity conditions.

Table 8.1 Physical Threats and Safeguards. Physical threats include utilities, fire, flood, other natural disasters, employment breaches, and perimeter breaches. Physical safeguards that may reduce these threats are numerous.

Area	Class	Threat	Safeguard
Utilities and interior climate	Power	• Inconsistent power • No power	• Surge suppressor • Line conditioner • Voltage regulator • Flywheel energy storage UPS • On-site power generation
	Heat	• Unavailable cooling • Insufficient cooling	• HVAC • Temperature alarm • Temperature log
	Humidity	• High humidity levels • Low humidity levels	• Humidifier/Dehumidifier • Humidity alarm • Humidity log
Fire	Fire exposure	• Asset damage • Death or injury to humans	• Building construction • Construction details • Storage of combustibles • Fire exits • Fire evacuation
	Fire detection	• Asset damage • Death or injury to humans	• Smoke detectors • Heat detectors • Flame detectors • Fire detector location

(Continued)

Table 8.1 (Continued)
Physical Threats and Safeguards

Area	Class	Threat	Safeguard
	Fire alarm	• Asset damage • Death or injury to humans	• Control panels • Local alarm • Municipal alarm • Auxiliary alarm • Proprietary system • Central station • Remote station
	Fire suppression	• Asset damage • Death or injury to humans	• Mobile • Water • Foam • Clean agent • Water damage safeguards
Flood	Water damage	• Asset damage • Death or injury to humans	• Water pipe safeguards • Raised floor safeguards
	Water exposure	• Asset damage • Death or injury to humans	
Other natural disasters	Elements exposure	• Asset damage • Death or injury to humans	• Lightning safeguards • Earthquake safeguards • Volcano safeguards • Landslide safeguards • Hurricane safeguards • Tornado safeguards
Employment protection	Personnel screening	• Misplaced trust • Legal troubles	• Proof of identity • Background check • Proof of citizenship • Military clearance

Category		Threats	Components
Perimeter protection	Barriers	• Unauthorized entry • Employee endangerment	• Fencing • Buildings • Doors • Locks • Vehicle barriers
	Lighting	• Unauthorized entry • Employee endangerment	• Continuous lighting • Standby lighting • Movable lighting • Emergency lighting
	Intrusion detection	• Unauthorized entry • Employee endangerment	• Exterior sensors • Interior sensors • Closed circuit television
	Physical access control	• Unauthorized entry • Employee endangerment • Unauthorized removal of property	• Badges • Card readers • Biometrics • Visitor control • Property pass • Package inspection

8.1.1.1 Power

All other critical systems depend on adequate, consistent, and "clean" power. Power delivery systems within the building and within the computer rooms must take adequate precautions against risks. The following risks to internal power should be considered:

- Power Loss — Many factors, including weather, sabotage, and equipment failure, can cause a loss of power to the building. A loss of power will obviously impact all critical systems.
- Degraded Power — Many factors, including weather, power load, and equipment failure, can cause a momentary or continuing voltage drop. Many pieces of equipment are unable to perform correctly when experiencing a voltage drop.
- Excessive Power — Another problem sometimes experienced in the power delivered to the building is excessive power. This can be caused by many factors, including lightning strikes and equipment failure.

8.1.1.1.1 Power Safeguards

The following safeguards should be exercised within the power distribution plant inside the building or on the ground of the organization's campus:

- Regulate Voltage — Power regulation devices to ensure consistent steady power. Devices include:
  - Surge Suppressor — These devices protect against temporary excessive voltages.
  - Line Conditioner — These devices regulate, filter, and suppress noise in AC power sources.
  - Voltage Regulators — Provides a constant DC output independent of input voltage, output load, or temperature.
  - Flywheel Energy Storage — These systems use the power provided by the grid to turn a rotor. The kinetic energy produced by the spinning rotor is in turn converted back to electricity. This configuration provides protection from power surges and from power losses for short durations.
  - Uninterruptible Power Supplies (UPS) — These devices sit between the AC power source and the electronic equipment. UPS devices provide power conditioning, distribute the power load, and provide backup power in case of a loss for longer durations.
  - On-Site Power Generation — Gasoline-or diesel-powered generators can be located on site to protect against power outages that last beyond the capacity of the UPS system. These systems must have a supply of fuel on site to ensure that they can continue operation in the event of an emergency.

8.1.1.2 Heat

Computer rooms are filled with equipment that produce heat. These rooms must be specially designed to handle the high-volume air conditioning (HVAC) needs of this equipment. Most manufacturers recommend that temperature levels stay between 70°F–74°F (21°C–23°C).

8.1.1.2.1 Heat Safeguards

Safeguards for ensuring that the computer room stays within established thresholds include:

- High-Volume Air Conditioners (HVAC) — These specialized systems should be rated to handle the anticipated load within the computer room. Redundant systems and redundant sources of air help to mitigate some of the risks of failure.
- Temperature Alarms — A temperature monitor can be set to alarm individuals responsible for the computer room climate when temperature thresholds are exceeded.
- Temperature Log — Special devices or computer peripherals can be installed to record the room temperature over time. These devices can alert those responsible when thresholds are exceeded but can also be used to track and identify cooling needs for planning purposes. If such a device exists in the organization being assessed, the security risk assessment team should review the logs for the last 90 days.

8.1.1.3 Humidity

The equipment in computer rooms is sensitive to both high and low humidity environments. High humidity environments can increase the risk of corrosion to sensitive equipment. Low humidity levels increase the chance of static buildup and discharge. Static discharge can reset or damage sensitive computer equipment.[2] Most manufacturers recommend that humidity levels stay between 40 and 60 percent relative humidity.

8.1.1.3.1 Humidity Safeguards

Safeguards for ensuring that the computer room stays within established thresholds include:

- Humidifiers/Dehumidifiers — A component can be added to the air handling system to add or remove humidity from the air. If these are used in areas that have hard water (i.e., high mineral content), then the water should be softened prior to being introduced into this expensive equipment.

- Humidity Alarms — A humidity monitor can be set to alarm individuals responsible for the computer room climate when humidity thresholds are exceeded.
- Humidity Log — Special devices or computer peripherals can be installed to record the room humidity levels over time. These devices can alert those responsible when thresholds are exceeded but can also be used to track and identify air conditioning needs for planning purposes. If such a device exists in the organization being assessed, the security risk assessment team should review the logs for the last 90 days.[3]

8.1.2 Fire

A fire is defined as the energy released in the form of light and heat when oxygen combines with a combustible material (fuel) at a suitable high temperature (heat). These three elements (oxygen, fuel, and heat) form what is known as the fire triangle (see Figure 8.1). The fire needs all three elements of the fire triangle to survive. Fire fighting is based on the removal of one or more of these elements. For example, heat is typically removed by spraying water on a fire; oxygen is removed by coating fuel with a chemical "blanket" such as foam, thus blocking the fuel from oxygen; and fuel is removed from the triangle by removing fuel sources in the proximity of the fire (i.e., digging a fire line).

There are three stages of a fire: the growth stage, the development stage, and the decay stage. The growth stage begins with the ignition of one or more of the materials. Flashover refers to the point in the growth stage when all materials are at their ignition temperatures. The development stage occurs when all materials are under combustion and the temperature of the fire increases at a much slower rate. The decay stage of the fire occurs when the fuel is burning out or the oxygen is becoming unavailable. At this stage the fire temperature slowly drops.

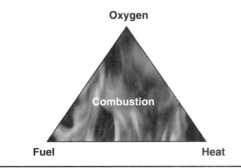

Figure 8.1 The fire triangle. A fire needs three things to survive: heat, oxygen, and fuel. A fire may be effectively suppressed by removing any of these elements.

To avoid fires or limit their damage to the organization there are many possible fire safety controls available. Fire safety controls range from controls that can detect possible fires to those that assist in the evacuation of the building.

Stage		Indication
1	Smoldering	Gas and submicron particles, initial heat
2	Open Burning	Invisible aerosol, visible smoke, increasing heat
3	Flashover	Extreme heat from combustible gases (1500° F or 815°C)

Figure 8.2A Fire Stages. A fire will go through well defined stages in which difference fire detection devices are well suited. Smoldering fires will not give off any appreciable heat or visible smoke, only invisible combustion particles. Open burning fires will give off significant heat and visible smoke. The Flashover stage, which can be reached in four (4) to ten (10) minutes perduces extreme heat from the collected combustible gases.

8.1.2.1 Fire Impact and Likelihood

Determining the likelihood of a fire is extremely difficult because there are many factors that go into such a calculation, such as the threat agent (natural or human), the building location, the building contents, and the service supported by the building. That said, there are some figures that will be useful to the security risk assessment team:

- Damage — Nonresidential fires have an average damage of $16,219.
- Deaths and Injuries — Nonresidential fires have an average of 5.7 deaths and 39.9 injuries per 1000 fires.
- Causes — The causes of nonresidential fires are summarized in Figure 8.2.

Some risk assessment tools have built-in estimation data. The following Web sites offer information and reports:

- National Fire Protection Association: www.nfpa.org
- Building and Fire Research Laboratory and NIST: www.bfrl.nist.gov
- U.S. Fire Administration — publications with fire statistics: www.usfa. fema.gov

8.1.2.2 Fire Safeguards

Organizations may protect their assets from the damaging effects of fire through limiting their exposure to fire, installing fire alarm systems, monitoring fire alarms, installing fire suppression equipment, and having fire evacuation plans.

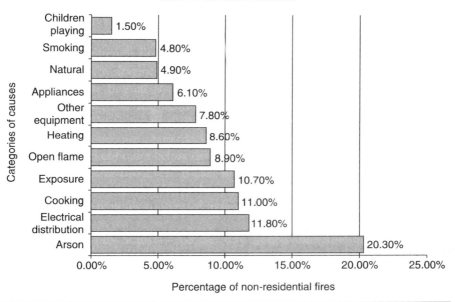

Figure 8.2B Causes of nonresidential fires. The most common cause of nonresidential fires, by far, is arson.

8.1.2.2.1 Fire Exposure Limitations

The best way to protect an organization's assets from fire is to avoid a fire altogether. A fire can be avoided (or damage reduced) by reducing the building's exposure to fire components. Below are key factors for consideration in fire exposure reduction through building design.

Building Construction — The materials used for construction of the building can greatly affect the combustibility of the building itself. Building construction types are classified according to the amount of time it takes a small fire to grow, consume the building, and lead to collapse. Fire safety standards and building codes for critical buildings call for a minimum fire resistance rating of 2 hours.[4] An indication of the fire classification of various construction types is detailed in Table 8.2.

Fire Exits — All buildings must comply with local and national fire codes, which require adequate fire exits, exit signs, and emergency and standby lighting.

8.1.2.3 Fire Alarm Systems

Fire alarm systems are composed of fire detectors, pull stations, a control panel, fire suppression equipment, speakers and bells, and possibly a link to the fire department (see Figure 8.3). Damage resulting from a fire can be limited or avoided

Table 8.2 Fire Classification for Various Types of Construction. Different types of construction provide vastly different protection from fire. A wood-frame construction provides little protection while heavy timber and fire-resistive construction can provide 1–3 hours of protection.

Type of Construction	Description	Fire Classification
Fire-resistive	Insulated noncombustible material*	2–3 hours
Heavy timber	Thick columns and beams	1+ hours
Noncombustible	No insulation	1 hour
Wood frame	2-inch framing	Minutes

Source: Federal Information Processing Standard (FIPS) 31. *The only difference between fire-resistive construction and noncombustible construction is the presence of insulation on the beams. This may seem like a minor improvement in fire construction, but it is the insulation that protects the beams from the intense heat of the fire and slows the beam failure and the building collapse.

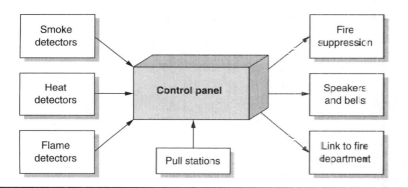

Figure 8.3 Fire alarm systems. A fire alarm system is an interconnected protection system consisting of fire detectors, pull stations, fire suppression equipment, speakers, a control panel, and optionally a link to the fire department.

if the building controls are capable of performing an early detection of a fire. Several types of fire detectors are described below, as well as considerations for their location and connection to a control panel.

8.1.2.3.1 Fire Detector

Fires can be detected through the proper selection and installation of fire detection equipment. There are three basic types of fire detectors: smoke, heat, and flame.[5]

Smoke Detectors — Smoke detectors deployed in nonresidential buildings should not be confused with those used in residential homes and apartment buildings. The devices used in homes are technically smoke alarms because they both detect smoke and signal with an audible alarm. Smoke detectors used in nonresidential buildings only detect smoke and signal the information back to a control panel, where data from the smoke detector can be assessed. If an alarm is to be sounded it can include the entire building. Smoke detectors can increase survivability chances in the event of a fire emergency by as much as 47 percent. All smoke detectors should be dual powered, interconnected, and have an indicator light.

- Dual Powered — Smoke detectors should be wired to a 120V AC circuit and also have a battery backup.
- Interconnected — Smoke detectors should be connected to one another so that smoke detection in one causes an alarm in all (within a specific zone).
- Indicator Light — Smoke detectors should have an indicator light to signal that they have sounded an alarm. This is especially useful when the alarm annunciator is centrally controlled and it may not be clear which detector has tripped.

There are three basic types of smoke detectors:

- Photoelectric Smoke Detectors — These detectors use a photoelectric eye that can detect visible byproducts of combustion (i.e., smoke).
- Ionization Smoke Detectors — These detectors contain a small amount of radioactive material in a dual detection chamber. The radioactive material ionizes the air, making it conductive and permitting a flow of current between the two chambers. Invisible byproducts of combustion (smoke particles) attach themselves to the air particles and reduce the conductance of the air. This interferes with the electrical conductivity between the chambers. Thus ionization smoke detectors can detect smoke that is not visible to the human eye. An ionization smoke detector can cover 200 to 300 square feet.
- Very Early Smoke Detection Alarm or Apparatus (VESDA) — A VESDA is a fire detection system based on the ability to sample air and to detect degrading materials during the precombustion stages of a fire (smoke). Depending on the levels of smoke in the air, a VESDA can provide the appropriate signal to the on-site response team or to a control panel. Signals can range from an early-stage alert to a late-stage declaration of fire.
  - VESDA systems have an advantage over smoke detectors in that they can detect smaller levels of invisible smoke (called obscuration) than ionization smoke detectors. The ability to draw the air in for sampling and the use of processors to interpret the data allows VESDA to detect levels of obscuration as low as 0.003 percent per foot, whereas ionization detectors can only detect levels of obscuration as low as 3 percent per foot.
  - A VESDA device can cover 5000 to 20,000 square feet.

- A VESDA system should not be considered in an area that allows smoking.
- A VESDA system should not be considered in an area that is "lights out" and is accessible within half an hour.

Heat Detectors — Properly functioning smoke detectors will almost always give an earlier warning than heat detectors because detectable levels of smoke almost always develop before detectable levels of heat. Heat detectors, however, have the lowest false alarm rate. Heat detectors can be installed in areas that may experience nonthreatening smoke, such as kitchens, or in other high-risk areas where smoke detectors cannot be placed, such as attics and mechanical rooms. There are two basic types of heat detectors:

- Heat Alarm — Heat alarms detect heat at a predefined level. Most heat alarms can be configured with a 117°F (47°C) 135°F (57°C) or 175°F (79°C) fuse.
- Rate of Rise — Rate of rise heat detectors are able to detect a rapid rise (e.g., 12°F–15°F (6°C–8°C) per minute) or extreme temperatures (e.g., 135°F (57°C) degrees). Rate of rise detectors can cover up to 2500 square feet. These detectors are typically deployed in areas where high heat may normally occur, such as kitchens or attics.

Flame Detectors — Flame detectors, or optical detectors, detect radiant energy (1800 to 7700 Angstroms). Flame detectors have a cone of vision outside of which they are unable to detect the presence of a flame. There are two basic types of flame detectors, UV and IR:

- Ultraviolet (UV) Flame Detectors — UV flame detectors are sensitive to both sunlight and artificial light. A UV flame, such as hydrogen, ammonia, or sulfur flame, radiates within the UV spectrum and is detected by the device. These devices can be used indoors or outdoors, but they must have a line of sight to the flame.
- Infrared (IR) Flame Detectors — An IR flame detector senses a flame by detecting energy on a cell that is sensitive to IR radiation. These devices can detect a flame based on its light component or flicker frequency. IR flame detectors are sensitive to most hydrocarbon fires, but not burning metal fires such as ammonia or sulfur. These devices may be used indoors or outdoors when shielded from the sun.

8.1.2.3.2 Control Panels

Fire alarm control panels are systems that receive inputs from a variety of fire detection equipment, process the data, and trigger a response (e.g., warnings or alarms).

Control panels should be located near the building entrance and the panel should be well labeled to identify which detector (or group of detectors) was alarmed.

Control panels also have an annunciator. An annuciator is a device that signals a change in the protection zones under the control of the monitoring system. Annunicators may log alarms or display a status of the alarm which identifies the zone of the origin of the alarm signal with an indicator light. There are several types of control panels:

- Simple — Simple control panels report on detectors that have tripped. Devices are typically grouped into zones through wiring circuits. The panels report on specific alarms in specific zones, such as a smoke alarm in a storage room.
- Addressable — These control panels are able to group individual devices into groups regardless of the wiring by use of a signaling technique. These signals allow the addressable (or intelligent) control unit to identify specific initiating devices or groups of devices. Some advanced control panels can report on the sensitivity setting of each sensor and even compensate for age, the accumulation of dust, or other factors.

8.1.2.4 Fire Alarm Installation Types

A fire alarm is the system that reacts to the detection of a fire. Fire alarms have a warning system and a response system. The warning system includes bells, speakers, and a visual alarm for the hearing impaired or in areas where there are high noise levels. The warning system signals to the building occupants to evacuate. The response system for nonresidential fire alarm systems can be installed to alarm and signal response teams in six different ways. Each approach has its own advantages and disadvantages.

8.1.2.4.1 Local Alarm Station

A local alarm station in an alarm that signals at the location of the alarm. These systems are unmanned and typically turn off automatically after a short duration. Local alarm systems are the oldest type of system and are typically found in schools and some hospitals. The basic system consists of manual fire pulls and bells. Local alarms may be linked to central or remote monitoring stations. Local stations must have a backup battery capable of 24 hours of standby power and able to sound an alarm for 5 minutes.

8.1.2.4.2 Municipal System

A municipal system is an alarm system run by a municipality and distinguished by "pull boxes" directly connected to the fire emergency response units. These systems, also called public alarm reporting systems, were popular decades ago because it would otherwise have been difficult to contact the fire department through lack of available phones and interconnected networks. Although such a system provides a direct connection to the emergency responders, these systems were susceptible to malicious false alarms. With the advent of ubiquitous networks and the availability of phones, very few municipalities maintain public alarm reporting systems.

8.1.2.4.3 Auxiliary System

An auxiliary system has an electrical circuit between the fire alarm control panel in the building and a municipal fire alarm box. When an alarm condition is detected, the municipal fire alarm box transmits an alarm signal to the dispatch center (just the same as if someone had manually pulled the municipal fire alarm box). This fire alarm system is the oldest remote alarm system.

8.1.2.4.4 Proprietary Systems

Proprietary systems are monitored on site by trained professionals. The on-site location must be isolated from other buildings and comply with national and local codes. It is rather costly to maintain a private proprietary system. Such systems are typically found in large industrial complexes, college campuses, and military installations.

8.1.2.4.5 Central Station

A central station is a business approved to monitor subscribers' alarm systems from a central location rather than on site. The central station notifies the police, fire, or emergency services upon receiving an alarm signal. Only approved central stations may maintain a direct connection with fire and police stations. Fire alarm systems monitored by central stations are required to have a 24-hour backup battery capable of sounding an alarm for 5 minutes.

8.1.2.4.6 Remote Station

A remote station is a secondary alarm station located on site but at a distance from the primary alarm site. Remote stations were designed to serve those areas that were not close enough to be monitored by central stations because of limitations in signaling. Digital communications advances removed limitations of central stations and remote stations are rarely used anymore. Most remote stations have been turned into central stations. Remote stations must have a backup battery capable of 60 hours of standby power and able to sound an alarm for 5 minutes.

8.1.2.5 Fire Suppression

A fire suppression system consists of the hardware (e.g., pipes and nozzles) and the suppression agent. The fire suppression hardware must be properly designed for the specific installation and use of the building. Fire suppression hardware can be classified as a mobile suppression system or a stationary suppression system.

8.1.2.5.1 Mobile Suppression Systems

These devices, also called handheld fire extinguishers, are an important element of an overall fire suppression system. Handheld fire extinguishers are essential to responders and their ability to extinguish small fires in early stages. This is the key to successful fire risk management; any fire that can be extinguished prior to a dump of suppression agent from the stationary systems can potentially save time, money, and information assets (see Figure 8.4).

8.1.2.5.2 Stationary Suppression Systems

Stationary suppression systems are in place throughout a building and connected to the fire alarm system. The pipe size, nozzle type, and pressure within the system are dependent upon the suppression agent within the pipes. Various suppression agents include water, foam, and clean agents.

Water Suppression — Water suppression systems, also called sprinkler systems, suppress fires through the application of water mist or spray, thus cooling the fire. These systems are required for heavy timber and wood-frame nonresidential

Figure 8.4 Mobile suppression systems. Commonly referred to as handheld fire extinguishers, these devices should be placed within 50 feet of equipment toward the door, inspected monthly, and tested annually.

buildings, whenever the maximum possible fire loss (MPFL) exceeds $1 million or there are other circumstances, such as adjacent buildings, highly sensitive areas. or central control centers within the building. The use of these systems is a good idea whenever an environment could be exposed to a fire composed of common combustibles such as wood, paper, cloth, rubber (i.e., class A fires). Water suppression systems are not recommended below raised floors. Some studies have found that the presence of water suppression systems increases the chance of survival in a fire by 97 percent.

There are two basic types of water suppression systems, wet pipe and dry pipe:

- Wet Pipe — The term "wet pipe" refers to the configuration of the water suppression system that leaves pressurized water in the pipes at all times These systems are simple and less costly than the dry pipe alternative but leave equipment or other assets beneath the pipes at risk in the event of a pipe leak or rupture.
- Dry Pipe — These systems store the water in tanks connected to the water suppression pipes, but those pipes are only filled with water when the fire detectors that are part of the system indicate a need. These systems are more expensive but introduce less risk to the assets being protected.

Foam Suppression — Foam suppression systems are normally used on, but not limited to, flammable liquid fires (class B). These systems require a method for mixing the foaming agent with water. Proportioning equipment ensures the proper concentration of foam and water, while balancing values (at the nozzle) regulate the foam concentrate pressure to match the water pressure. Foam suppression can be very effective because it fights the fire in three ways:

1. a foam blanket covers the fuel surface and smothers the fire;
2. the fire is cooled by the foam/water mix; and
3. the foam blanket restricts the release of flammable vapors that could further fuel the fire.

Clean Agent — Clean agent suppression systems, also called nonaqueous, are specifically designed to be used in areas where special equipment resides. These suppression agents not only have fire suppression capabilities but are nonconductive, noncorrosive, dry, and clean. The other advantage of clean agents over water mist systems is that these agents are deployed as a gas and will penetrate shielded enclosures. There are many alternative clean agents that can be used, and some of the most popular ones are described below:

- Carbon Dioxide (CO_2) — This suppression agent is an asphyxiant and is designed for nonoccupied areas and special industrial applications. CO_2 extinguishes fires by producing a heavy blanket of gas that reduces the oxygen level to the point where combustion cannot occur. CO_2 works on class A, B, and C fires, leaves no residual, and has a negligible effect on the environment. It has an ozone depleting potential (ODP) near zero and a global warming potential (GWP) of 1.0. CO_2 is inexpensive but it does require ten times more agent than halon-based systems.

- Halon — This suppression agent is a combination of hydrocarbons and halogen produced by the combination of the nonmetallic elements carbon, fluorine, chlorine, and bromine. For example, Halon 1301 is a combination of 1 parts carbon, 3 parts fluorine, and 1 part bromine. Halon is effective on class B (liquid) and C (electrical) fires. Halon suppresses the fire by cooling the fire, smothering the fire through the removal of oxygen, and disrupting the chemical reaction of combustion. Despite its fire-fighting capabilities, however, halon is not environmentally friendly. It has an ODP of 3–10 and a high GWP. Global treaties have mandated that halon not be used in new installations and production of halon ceased in 1993. Halon agents are being replaced by halon alternatives.
- Halon Alternatives — These suppression agents are commonly used as halon alternatives. These alternatives include Inergen, FE-13, and FM-200:
  - Inergen — Inergen[6] can be used for occupied and unoccupied areas, has an ODP near zero and a GWP near zero. Inergen requires ten times the amount of agent as halon and has a longer discharge time: 60 seconds vs. 10 seconds.
  - FE-13 — FE-13[7] can be used for occupied and unoccupied areas, has an ODP near zero but a high GWP. FE-13 may be subject to future environmental restrictions. This agent is good for areas with ceilings as high as 25 feet. FE-13 requires 2.5 times the amount of agent as halon.
  - FM-200 — FM-200[8] can be used for occupied and unoccupied areas, has an ODP near zero, and a low to medium GWP. FM-200 requires twice as much agent as halon. This agent cannot be used for areas in which the ceiling is higher than 12 feet unless two rows of nozzles are installed.

8.1.2.6 Fire Evacuation

The organization should have well-documented, approved, and tested fire evaluation procedures. These procedures are essential to ensure the effective use of fire safety equipment and the safety of the personnel within the building.

8.1.3 Flood and Water Damage

Next to fires, flooding is the most common and widespread natural disaster. A flood is defined by the National Flood Insurance Program as "a general and temporary condition of partial or complete inundation of two or more acres of normally dry land or of two or more properties from overflow of inland waters, unusual and rapid accumulation of runoff surface waters from any source, or a mudflow." Accidental water leakage is also covered here, since many of the safeguards to protect against natural flooding and accidental water leakage are similar.

The likelihood of a building being affected by a flood depends on its geographic location and the weather conditions in the general area. Data exists for determining this likelihood.

- U.S. Geological Survey — The map in Figure 3.5 outlines major watersheds that were affected by major floods during the years 1993–1997, including floods associated with hurricanes. The fact that a watershed was affected by a flood does not mean the entire area was under water. For a more precise measurement of likelihood of flooding, refer to flood insurance rate maps.

Flood insurance rate maps and data can be obtained from a variety of sources, including:

- The Multi-Hazard Mapping Initiative — This site generates an online map from a network of hazard and base map suppliers. Hazards that can be

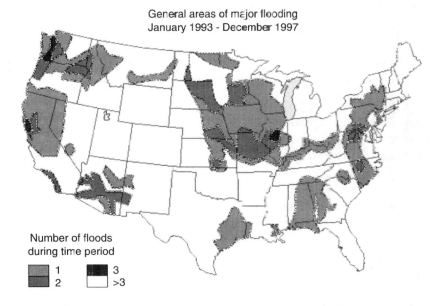

General areas of major flooding
January 1993 - December 1997

Number of floods
during time period

1   3
2   >3

Figure 8.5   U.S. flood hazard map. The map provides a visual representation of the relative incidence of major flooding and an indication of geographic areas that are likely to have a flood in the future. (Source: U.S. Geological Survey.)

plotted on the map include flood data, earthquakes, hurricanes, tornadoes, and many other hazards (www.HazardMaps.gov).

- ESRI Online Hazard Map — This site generates an online hazard map generated from existing flood insurance rate maps (FIRM). This data is approximate and should be fine for a risk assessment, but it is not a legal document sufficient for determining insurance rates (www.esri.com/hazards/makemap.html).
- National Atlas of the United States — This site generates maps of natural hazards such as floods, earthquakes, lightning, and hurricanes. You can also overlay other data maps regarding people, transportation, and biology (www.nationalatlas.gov).
- Paper FIRMs — These can typically be found in local or community flood plain management buildings or at the local tax assessor's office, or you can order one from the FEMA Flood Map store — Map Service Center at (800) 358-9616.

There are three hazardous flood areas noted on the flood plain maps, each caused by a unique natural occurrence:

- Riverine Flood Plains — Flooding in these plains is caused by heavy rainfall or snow-melt runoff or is due to an obstruction in a narrow channel.
- Coastal Flood Plains — These are areas near large bodies of water that are affected by floods resulting from high winds, tides, or wind-driven or underwater earthquake driven waves (tsunamis).
- Debris Cones — These are areas in which there can accumulate debris deposited at the base of a mountain by mountain streams that are subject to flash flooding.

Organizations may protect their assets from the damaging affects of flooding and water damage by limiting their exposure to water, protection from accidental leakage, and ensuring that raised floors are properly installed and monitored.

The best way to protect an organization's assets from floods and damaging waters is to avoid the water altogether. Floods can be somewhat avoided by choosing the proper geographic site for the organization's buildings. But for security risk assessments that are dealing with buildings already placed on the ground, and in order to deal with unpredictable and accidental water leakage, key considerations in water damage reduction through building design include drains, sump pumps, levees, and supplies such as sandbags and duct tape.

No matter where a building is geographically located, it may be susceptible to the risks of accidental water leakage. Considerations in limiting exposure to accidental water leakage through building design include water pipe safeguards and raised floor safeguards.

8.1.4 Lightning

Lightning from severe thunderstorms can cause electrical damage, interruption of electrical service, fires, and injury or death to people. The earth receives about 8 million lightning strikes a day. The likelihood of lightning in a general geographic area is directly related to the number of thunderstorm days that location experiences per year. Historical data has been compiled and put in map form, as shown in Figure 8.6. A map that shows geographic areas of thunderstorm days per year is called an isokeraunic map.

Based on the isokeraunic data, the likelihood of various lightning impacts can be estimated:

- Deaths — Given the frequency of thunderstorm days per year, the likelihood of a lightning death occurring depends on the location of employees. Lightning deaths occur most frequently in fields and ball parks (28 percent), but can also happen near bodies of water (17 percent), or heavy equipment (6 percent). If the organization has employees in these locations, then the likelihood of lightning-induced death is increased (see Figure 8.7).
- Electrical Outages — Lightning-induced transients (power surges) can cause equipment damage or loss of electrical service. The best source of data for likelihood of this occurring would be historical data from the power companies providing power to the building location.

Average number of thunderstorm days per year
(see key for explanation)

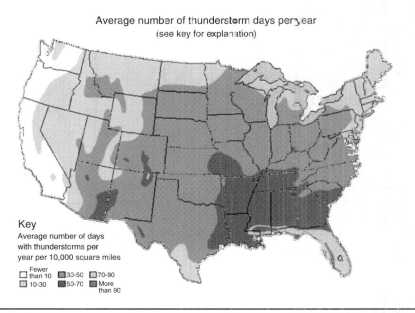

Key

Average number of days
with thunderstorms per
year per 10,000 square miles

- Fewer than 10
- 10-30
- 30-50
- 50-70
- 70-90
- More than 90

Figure 8.6   U.S. thunderstorm days hazard map. The map provides a visual representation of the relative incidence of thunderstorm activity. (Source: 1999 Oklahoma Climatological Survey.)

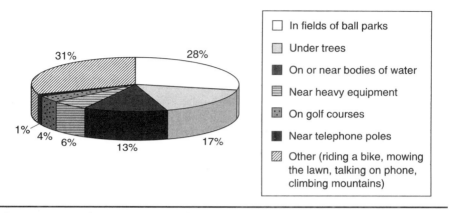

Figure 8.7 Lightning causes of death chart. Lightning deaths occur most frequently in ball fields or parks but are also quite frequent near bodies of water and heavy equipment. (Source: 1997 Oklahoma Climalotogical Survey.)

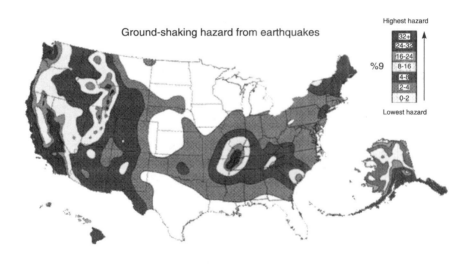

Figure 8.8 U.S. earthquakes hazard map. The map provides a visual representation of the frequency of earthquakes in the United States and an indication of geographic areas that are more likely to have earthquakes in the future. (Source: U.S. Geological Survey.)

8.1.5 Earthquakes

The U.S. Geological Survey produced the map in Figure 8.8 to show areas of the United States that have a 10 percent probability of having an earthquake of

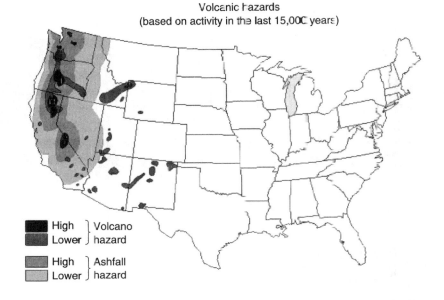

Volcanic Hazards
(based on activity in the last 15,000 years)

High ⎤ Volcano
Lower ⎦ hazard

High ⎤ Ashfall
Lower ⎦ hazard

Figure 8.9 U.S. volcanic hazard map. The map provides a visual representation of volcanic activity in the United States and an indication of geographic areas that are more likely to have volcanoes in the future. (Source: U.S. Geological Survey.)

appreciable damage in the next 50 years.[9] A more interactive map with even more data can be found at the following Web site:

- National Seismic Hazard Maps — This site generates an online map of earthquake predictions from a seismic data and predictions (http://eqmaps.cr.usgs.gov/website/nshmp).

8.1.6 Volcanoes

The hazard of volcanic activity includes local volcanic activity, lava flows, ash fall, and volcanic mud flows (called lahars). The map in Figure 8.9 shows the areas of greater and lower risk to local and fallout hazards from volcanic activity.

8.1.7 Landslides

The hazard of landslide incidents is greater in mountainous areas of the United States. The map in Figure 8.10 shows areas of high and moderate incidence and susceptibility to landslides.

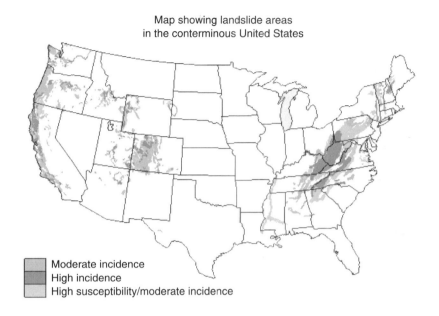

Figure 8.10   U.S. landslide hazard map. The map provides a visual representation
of landslide activity in the United States and an indication of geographic areas
that are more likely to have landslides in the future. (Source: U.S. Geological
Survey.)

8.1.8 Hurricanes

The incidence of hurricanes within the contiguous United States is concentrated on
the southeast coast. The map in Figure 8.11 shows areas of highest (60 hurricanes
in 100 years), high (40–60 hurricanes in 100 years), and moderate (20–40
hurricanes in 100 years) occurrence of hurricanes based on observations from
1888 to 1988.

8.1.9 Tornadoes

The incidence of tornadoes is concentrated along "tornado alley" but occurs
frequently in other areas in the eastern United States The map in Figure 8.12 shows
areas of highest (probability of a hurricane occurring in a single point is equal to
1 in 2000 years) and high (probability of a hurricane occurring in a single point
is equal to 1 in 5000 years) based on observations from 1954 to 1992.[10]

8.1.10 Natural Hazards Summary

Table 8.3 summarizes natural hazards, their impact, and possible safeguards.

Figure 8.11   U.S. hurricane hazard map. The map provides a visual representation of hurricane activity in the United States and an indication of geographic areas that are more likely to have hurricanes in the future. (Source: U.S. Geological Survey.)

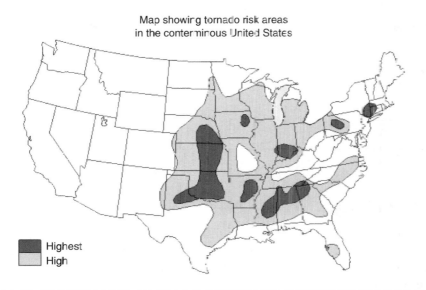

Figure 8.12   U.S. tornado hazard map. The tornado hazard map provides a visual representation of tornado activity in the United States and an indication of geographic areas that are more likely to have tornadoes in the future. (Source: U.S. Geological Survey.)

Table 8.3 Natural Hazards Summary. The natural hazards of flood, lightning, tornado, earthquake, hurricane, and fire can all lead to injury or death, disruption of utility service, or a physical breach in security. The table below provides a list of safeguards that may reduce the risk or impact of these natural hazards.

Natural Events	Injury/ Death	Disruption of Utility Service	Physical Breach	Safeguards
Flood	×	×	×	• Drains • Pumps • Levees • Sandbags • Duct tape
Lightning	×	×		• Lightning arrestors • Surge suppression
Tornado	×	×	×	• Building enhancements • Evacuation procedures • On-site tornado shelters • Stockpile plywood
Earthquake	×	×	×	• Building enhancements • Avoid tall structures • Evacuation procedures • Earthquake zones • On-site water supply
Hurricane	×	×	×	• Building enhancements • Evacuation procedures • Stockpile plywood
Fire	×	×	×	• Building enhancements • Fire alarm • Fire detector • Fire suppression • Evacuation procedures

8.1.11 Human Threats to Physical Security

The determination of physical security risks to an organization's building includes an analysis of natural and human hazards. The natural hazards were covered in the sections above. This section covers those hazards or risks that are initiated by humans.

Physical security controls should also be in place to deter, detect, and remove intruders. These controls cover employees, visitors, and outsiders. Controls include personnel screening, barriers, lighting, intrusion detection, access control, preventing unauthorized entry, and preventing unauthorized removal.

8.1.11.1 Personnel Screening

Organizations with security concerns (this should be all organizations) should perform some measure of screening on personnel prior to employment and possibly perform periodic updates. Personnel screening controls include proof of identity, background checks, citizenship checks, reference checks, and criminal checks.

- Proof of Identity — Prior to hiring an individual, employers are required to have a method by which they ensure the identity of the potential employee. Methods typically include checking a government-issued photographic identification card (e.g., driver's license, passport).
- Background Check — To confirm that information given on the employment application is accurate, employers should consider the performance of a background check. Such a review will require the permission of the applicant and will determine the accuracy of educational and professional qualifications, employment history, and personal references. The potential applicant should also be asked to sign a statement regarding criminal convictions.
- Verification of Citizenship and Right to Work — To be compliant with labor law, employers must determine the right of the potential employee to work and their citizenship. The employer should ask to see credentials that prove citizenship and right to work (e.g., birth certificate, passport, social security card, work permit, visa).
- Criminal and Credit Checks — In some positions it may be appropriate to request a criminal background investigation or a personal credit check.
- Military Clearances — For sensitive positions that expose the candidate to government-controlled sensitive information, much more rigorous personnel clearance processes are required. The procedures for such clearances are beyond the scope of this book.

8.1.11.2 Barriers

Barriers are used to control, limit, or exclude access to the physical premises. Control of access includes directing the flow of authorized pedestrian and vehicular traffic, providing entry points where identification can be checked, delaying forced entry, blocking visual inspection, and protecting individual assets. Physical access control is made easier by reducing the number of entry and exit paths for potential intruders and making more effective use of the protective force personnel.

- Fencing — Fences are used to indicate property boundaries and to enclose secure areas. To be effective, fences must be of the proper height and the fence line needs to be in good condition.

- Buildings — The building itself provides barriers such as walls, ceilings, floors, windows, and doors. Some of these barriers are rather weak, for example, drop ceilings and raised floors behind which walls do not extend to the hard deck.
- Doors — In addition to being a portion of the building barrier, some doors and windows are an extension of other systems such as the fire alarm system and the intrusion detection system. These doors have several control requirements and options to ensure that they work as an effective element of the overall system:
  - Fail Safe Lock — The lock on the door or window automatically opens during a power failure. This type of lock is essential to fire alarm systems to ensure the safe and speedy evacuation of personnel.
  - Fail Secure Lock — The lock on the door or window automatically closes during a power failure. This type of lock is essential to the protection of sensitive areas such as cash vaults.
  - Fail Soft Lock — The lock on the door or window can operate with a reduced capacity during a power failure. This type of lock may be used as part of a fire alarm system such as an automatically opening sliding door that will open, but not automatically, and must be pushed open.
- Locks — Locks are used to secure building entrances or security containers. The type and strength of the lock required depends on the information or area that it is safeguarding. Common vulnerabilities include weak locks and loose control over keys and combination changes.
- Vehicle Barriers — These are used to stop vehicles from entering the building. Barriers include bollards, pop-up barriers, cables, and natural terrain obstacles. Vehicle barriers, when employed, must be properly placed and monitored.

Sidebar 8.2 Natural and Architectural Barriers

Providing physical security to the perimeter of a protected building does not have to involve jersey walls, high fencing, and other "ugly" methods. An approach to providing external barriers to the building through environmental design can be used to provide esthetically pleasing and physically strong barriers. This approach is called Crime Prevention Through Environmental Design (CPTED—pronounced septed).

There are three basic elements to the CPTED approach: natural surveillance, natural access, and territorial reinforcement. Natural surveillance incorporates building and landscape elements to ensure that all external areas are under constant surveillance. This CPTED element includes placement of windows, landscaping, and lighting, to enable external and internal surveillance.

Natural access uses architectural and landscape elements to guide access to and within the building. Design elements that implement natural access include location of parking lots, sidewalks, doors, signage, and lighting. These elements conspire to control and direct traffic to those areas where would-be visitors are better scrutinized. Possible attack and escape routes are also significantly reduced through natural access designs.

The third design element of the CPTED approach is territorial reinforcement. This element reinforces the idea that the area is protected by ensuring that the grounds, seating areas, fence lines, and landscaping give the impression of a well-maintained and guarded area. This approach works two ways: (1) would-be intruders get the impression that exterior surveillance and barriers are well maintained and unlikely to have vulnerabilities, and (2) authorized personnel are more likely to challenge unauthorized visitors in a more defined and controlled area.

For more information see the following websites:

- International CPTED Association (ICA): www.cpted.net
- National Crime Prevention Council: www.ncpc.org
- Florida CPTED Network: www.flcpted.org

8.1.11.3 Lighting

Lighting is an essential physical security control that helps to prevent intrusions and endangerment to employees. In addition, lighting can increase the surveillance capabilities of the security force by correctly lighting property lines, entrances, and other critical areas. There are several types of lighting, including continuous lighting, standby lighting, movable lighting, and emergency lighting.

- Continuous Lighting — This is the most common type of lighting. Continuous lighting is a series of fixed lights that flood an area with continuous light. It is important to have a minimum safe light level and to avoid dark patches by implementing overlapping cones of light. There are two types of continuous lighting: glare lighting and controlled lighting. Glare lighting is used to direct light across a field of view to illuminate potential intruders and to hide internal guards. Controlled lighting is used to illuminate a patch of land such as a field or parking lot or a strip of land such as a pathway or fence line. Minimum and maximum lighting levels are determined by the governing laws and local ordinances. There is a lot of variation in these standards; however, the following figures can be used to provide a baseline understanding.

- Guard route .5 candle foot
- Building, fenceline, parking lot 1 candle foot
- Walkway, loading dock 3 candle feet
- Parking structure 5 candle feet

- Standby Lighting — Similar to continuous lighting in terms of arrangement of lights; however, standby lighting is configured to illuminate automatically when an intruder is detected or manually when guards become suspicious.
- Movable Lighting — This type of lighting refers to portable manually operated lighting devices such as spotlights and searchlights.
- Emergency Lighting — This type of lighting is used during a power failure and other emergencies to facilitate continued protection and safe evacuation. It depends on an alternative power source such as batteries or generators.

8.1.11.4 Intrusion Detection

Intrusion detection systems, also called electronic security systems (ESS), are designed to detect, delay, and respond to intruder activity. Unauthorized intrusion on the premises is a breach in physical security and is a risk to the organization's assets. Such intrusions should be detected by means of intrusion detection (alarm) sensors or visual surveillance. Regardless of the type of intrusion detection sensor there should be a guard force capable of responding within a reasonable amount of time (e.g. 5–10 minutes).

8.1.11.4.1 Intrusion Detection Sensors

The design and deployment of intrusion detection sensors depends on the site-specific characteristics of the building such as terrain, geography, climate, and type of protection required. Many sites require both interior and exterior sensors to completely protect the organization's assets.

Exterior sensors include fence sensors, line of sight sensors, and video motion sensors. These sensors are placed on the exterior of the building. As such they must be resistant to weather conditions (e.g., rain, snow, fog, extreme cold) and possible nuisance alarms from external disturbances (e.g., windblown objects, animals). Each of these exterior sensors is described briefly below:

- Fence Sensors — Fences are practical barriers that cover a large amount of terrain and cannot always be continually monitored through direct surveillance. A series of fence sensor technologies is available to extend the surveillance capabilities of the security protective force and detect breaches of attempted breaches to the fence line:

- Strain-Sensitive Cable — These fence sensors are cables that run the length of the fence and can detect fence movement (e.g., from an intruder climbing the fence) or fence penetration attempts (e.g., fence cutting).
- Taut Wire — A taut wire sensor is woven through a fence and protects the fence line by indicating when force is applied to the wire. Taut wires, when force is applied, signal intrusions through the closing of mechanical switches or a change in the monitored electrical output of strain gauges.
- Fiber Optic Cable — These sensors are established by stringing a fiber optic cable the length of a fence line and sending a modulated light signal through the cable. When force is exerted on the fiber optic cable, the modulated signal is modified and detected. This cause an alarm to be sent. Fiber optic cables are nonmetallic and are not susceptible to electrical interference and nuisance alarms such as lightning.
- Electric Field — Electric field sensors utilize alternating current to establish a constant electrostatic field (typically within a few feet of the fence line). Intruders entering the field will interrupt the constant field pattern and signal an alarm.
- Capacitance Proximity — These sensors consist of a capacitance sensor and several capacitance wires. Interference between the sensor and the wires is detected and set to signal an alarm condition. These sensors can be affectively installed on fence lines and roofs of buildings by placing horizontal strands of capacitance wires along the tops of fences or roofs of buildings.
- Buried Line — These sensors consist of a buried cable or a set of underground detection sensors. Because they are hidden they can be difficult to detect, but they are susceptible to environmental conditions such as a hard freeze or running water.
- Line of Sight (LOS) Sensors — Line of sight sensors detect intrusions when the field they protect is interrupted. LOS sensors work best on flat terrain with no obstructions.
  - Monostatic Microwave — This type of sensor incorporates a microwave transmitter and receiver at one end of the detection zone. Monostatic microwave sensors have a range of approximately 400 feet. Intruders are detected by a signal reflecting off their moving body. Monostatic microwave sensors provide volumetric protection for localized areas such as corners and around the base of a protected structure.
  - Bistatic Microwave — This type of sensor utilizes a separate microwave transmitter and receiver and has a range of up to 1500 feet. This type

of exterior sensor must incorporate overlapping zones because the area directly under and near the pole-mounted transmitter and receiver is not covered by the pair.

- Infrared (IR) — Infrared sensors provide alarms when IR beams are interrupted (active IR sensors) or when thermal IR radiation[11] is detected within the field of view (passive IP sensors).
- Video Motion Sensors — These intrusion detection systems work when an intruder enters a CCTV camera's field of view. The sensor is able to process the video image and trip an alarm in the event that the images match predefined criteria.

Interior sensors include boundary penetration sensors, volumetric motion sensors, point sensors, and duress alarms. These sensors are placed on the interior of the building. Interior sensors are categorized by the structure for which they are intended to provide protection, namely, barriers and interior spaces. Each of these interior sensors is described briefly below:

- Boundary Penetration Sensors — These sensors are designed to detect penetration of barriers such as walls, ceilings, duct openings, and windows.
  - Structural Vibration — These sensors are designed to detect for low-frequency vibrations that match those similar to the vibrations of attempted penetrations of a physical barrier (e.g., wall, ceilings). Structural vibration sensors detect attempts such as hammering, drilling, cutting, forcible entry, and explosive detonation.
  - Glass-Break — These sensors listen for the sound of breaking glass. The sound is picked up by microphone transducers that respond to specific frequencies that match the sound of breaking glass. These sensors typically cover a maximum of 100 square feet of glass surface.
  - Passive Ultrasonic — These sensors listen for sounds that could indicate the penetration of a barrier. Sounds detected by passive ultrasonic sensors include breaking glass, the snipping sound of bolt cutters, the hissing of an acetylene torch, the whining sound of a drill, and the shattering of brick or cinderblock. The effective range of passive ultrasonic sensors is between 3 feet (drilling) and 55 feet (bolt cutters).
  - Balance Magnetic Switches — These sensors have two parts: a switch mechanism mounted to a stationary object such as a door frame, and an actuating magnet mounted to a moving object such as a door. The switch is held open by a balanced magnetic force set up between the actuating magnet and a bias magnet mounted near the switch. This configuration is useful when an intruder may attempt to defeat the alarm with an external magnet. Either the door opening or the presence of an external magnet will cause the switch to become unbalanced and trigger the alarm.

- Grid Wire — These sensors are composed of a single electrical wire arranged in a grid pattern with an electric charge placed on it. The grid is either attached to the surface that it is designed to protect (e.g., a window or wall) or placed over an opening (e.g., a duct). When the grid wire is broken, an alarm is sounded.
- Volumetric Motion Sensors — These sensors are designed to detect the presence of an intruder in an interior space. All three of these technologies were previously described in the exterior sensor sections. They are included here for convenience.
  - Monostatic Microwave — This type of sensor incorporates a microwave transmitter and receiver at one end of the detection zone. Monostatic microwave sensors have a range of approximately 400 feet. Intruders are detected by a signal reflecting off their moving body. Monostatic microwave sensors provide volumetric protection for localized areas such as corners and around the base of a protected structure.
  - Infrared (IR) — Infrared sensors provide alarms when IR beams are interrupted (active IR sensors) or when thermal IR radiation is detected within the field of view (passive IP sensors).
  - Video Motion — These intrusion detection systems work when an intruder enters a CCTV camera's field of view. The sensor is able to process the video image and trip an alarm in the event that the images match predefined criteria.
- Point Sensors — These sensors are designed to protect a specific point or small area within the protected space. Intruders are detected when they come close to or touch a protected object.
  - Capacitance — These sensors set up a capacitance between the protected metal object and the ground. When an intruder touches or comes close to the protected metal object the capacitance is changed and an alarm sounds.
  - Pressure Mats — These sensors generate an alarm when weight is applied to the mat. An example of this type of sensor is two layers of copper separated by rubber with holes in it. These mats are typically placed at windows and doors to detect intruders before they get to a protected object.
  - Pressure Switches — Protected objects are placed on top of mechanically activated switches. When the object is removed, the weight of the object no longer holds the switch in the open position and an alarm sounds. Pressure switches are vulnerable to thin pieces of material slid underneath the protected object.
- Duress Alarms — These are fixed or portable alarms that signal the security protective force or an external alarm location to indicate an intrusion or other emergency. Duress alarms must not annunciate at the point of alarm because an audible alarm may endanger the person tripping the alarm.

8.1.11.4.2 Closed-Circuit Television (CCTV)

The surveillance and alarm response capabilities of the security protective force can be extended through the implementation of a closed-circuit television (CCTV) system. A CCTV system can have two distinct functions: alarm assessment and surveillance.

- Alarm Assessment — A CCTV alarm assessment system is design to enable the security protective force to respond rapidly to triggered alarms. The CCTV system can be used to perform preliminary investigations of the area and dispatch the security protective force to the appropriate areas.
- Surveillance — A CCTV surveillance system can effectively extend the surveillance capabilities of the security protective force. With a properly installed and maintained system, the standing security protective force can monitor more areas of the protective site and provide a greater frequency of physical and video monitoring.

8.1.11.5 Physical Access Control

Physical access control systems complement perimeter barriers, protective lighting, and other physical security safeguards by preventing unauthorized entry, the introduction of harmful devices, and the movement of information and materials from the protected location.

8.1.11.6 Preventing Unauthorized Entry

The protection of organizational assets relies on preventing unauthorized entry onto the premises and into sensitive areas. A variety of methods may be employed to prevent unauthorized entry. Identification methods are those mechanisms that use one or more methods of identification, together with authorization and access control, such as badge systems, card readers, or biometric controls. Visitor control procedures restrict the freedom by which a visitor can access the premises and place controls on their movement.

8.1.11.6.1 Identification Methods

For those people who are allowed to access the premises, identification methods provide a means to identify each individual, associate access authority with the identified person, and control access through integration with physical access devices. Examples of identification methods include badge systems, card readers, and biometric controls.

Badges — More sensitive facilities require additional protection to ensure that only authorized personnel enter, occupy, or leave a designated area. Security badging systems are used to implement and enforce controls to keep unauthorized visitors out. These controls include accountability procedures, badge storage, badge recovery, photo updating, and handling of lost badges and ensuring adherence to procedures.

- Accountability Procedures — The facility protective force must ensure that all badges are accounted for. Documentation specifying the disposition of badges should include date of issue, serial number, name of badge holder, organization, and date of destruction.
- Badge Storage — Facilities are especially susceptible if badges are stored in an insecure location. Badges should be stored in a locked drawer and protected at all times.
- Badge Recovery and Termination — When employees are terminated, facilities personnel must ensure that they retrieve and destroy the badge or otherwise terminate badge access immediately.
- Photo Update — Photo identification badges must be kept reasonably up to date such that the photo resembles the person to whom the badge was issued.
- Handling of Lost Badges — There must be complete and clear procedures for handling lost badges. These procedures should include rapid notification and termination of access on the lost badge. This can be accomplished automatically through a manual procedure of keeping up-to-date lost badge lists at all entrance points.
- Procedure Adherence — The safeguards listed above depend upon the establishment of and adherence to badge safeguarding procedures. The organization must ensure that the facility protective force and all employees and visitors understand and follow the established procedures.

Sidebar 8.3 Badges

The use of badges in many organizations provides little to no security. Unless the badging system has a logical control element, most implementations of these systems have significant vulnerabilities that severely reduce their effectiveness. Examples of logical control elements integrated into a badging system include badge readers and entry systems. For example, all entry points to the organization's campus and individual buildings have badge readers and turnstiles or mantraps activated by authorized badges.

Badging systems that only employ physical and pro-cedure controls typically offer little added security.

Consider the following vulnerabilities and possible observations:

- *Weak badge design and construction.* Replacement picture could be easily inserted without detectable damage to the badge.
- *Nonpicture badges.* Badges, even for permanent employees, have no identification picture. Lost badges can be used by anyone.
- *Sticker visitor badges.* These badges can be easily forged. Furthermore, these badges are rarely collected upon leaving the building and reusable badges can be found in the trash cans outside of visitor control.
- *Lack of inspection.* Badges are seldom reviewed close up by security personnel. Badges are viewed at a distance (i.e., badges are "flashed" as you drive by). In many cases, fake badges consisting of a white background and a colored blob in the middle would suffice.

Team members of the security risk assessment team should determine the effectiveness of the badging system through observation.

Card Readers — An improvement over picture-only badges is card readers. These authentication systems combine a badge (with or without a picture) with a mechanized system that further authenticates the badge holder or the badge itself. Simple card or badge readers encode information on the card through methods such as magnetic strips, smart cards, or proximity cards. The coded information on the card is compared with the information stored on the system and access determination is based on the results.

An additional control of a personal identification number (PIN) can be added to the automated-card reading system. The addition of this control makes the authentication mechanism stronger and is referred to as two-factor control. Care should be taken to ensure that PINs can be entered without others observing the secret PIN.

Card readers may be vulnerable to the extent that badges become lost and not reported or the ease with which the data stored in the card can be manipulated. Cards in which the data is stored in plaintext on a magnetic strip are the most vulnerable because devices to read and write to these cards are cheap and readily available.

Biometrics — Physical access control to an organization's buildings and protected areas can be improved through the implementation and deployment of biometric controls. Biometrics encompasses any technology that automates the authentication process through the use of physiological or behavioral characteristics. Physiological characteristics are measured by devices that implement retina, iris, finger, facial, or hand scanning technology. Behavioral characteristics are measured by devices that implement voice, signature, and keystroke scanning technologies.[12]

Biometric Authentication Vulnerabilities — The use of biometric systems to authenticate authorized individuals should be examined by the security risk assessment team to determine the level of risk incurred based on the biometric and implementation architecture of the authentication system. The following classes of biometric vulnerabilities should be considered:

- Authentication Device Protection — The authentication device itself must be protected from adverse weather conditions and possible destruction from potential adversaries. Both weather conditions and vandalism can degrade or destroy the capability of the authentication device from performing access control. In most cases, such a threat would have a denial of service impact on the authentication service. The team should observe the general location and accessibility of the device to unauthorized personnel and its exposure to the elements. Furthermore, the team should determine the effectiveness of the procedures in place to deal with the loss of function of one or more devices.

- Storage of Templates — A template is a distillation of the biometric characteristics measured and is unique to each catalogued individual. The storage of these templates must receive the same protection as the storage of system password files. The security risk assessment team should perform investigation and testing to ensure that the template files cannot be modified, replaced, or read through an unapproved process.

- Transmission of Templates — Centralized biometric authentication systems that store template files on a central server typically send the template file generated at the point of capture to the central server for comparison. The central server then sends back an approval code to the point of capture. The transmission of the template files and approval codes must be secured through physical protection of the transmission media, or encryption, or both.

- Crossover Error Rates — Each biometric device or technique has inherent errors within the system. Error rates, which can be false negative or false positive, are generally compared using the crossover error rate (CER), which is the error rate when false rejection and false acceptance rates are equal. Biometrics with a high CER should be considered somewhat vulnerable to the denial of access to authorized users and the allowed access of unauthorized users.[13] Furthermore, even higher CER values than may be reported by the manufacturer or industry sites may be present in a system deployed at the assessed site. Errors of implementation and configuration can introduce significant vulnerabilities for which tests should be conducted.

8.1.11.6.2 Visitor Control

The purpose of visitor control is to properly identify and control visitor access to the premises. The following elements of a visitor control program should be reviewed:

- Approval — All visitors should have prior approval to be on the premises from an authorized employee.
- Identification — The identification of a visitor should be established through the presentations and inspection of a government-issued identification card, such as a driver's license.
- Visitor Badges — All approved visitors should wear a conspicuous badge at all times. Visitor badges should be recovered when the visitor leaves.
- Escort — All visitors should be escorted in areas with a high sensitivity.
- Restrictions — For most installations, visitor access should be restricted to daytime work hours and non-sensitive buildings.

8.1.11.7 Preventing Unauthorized Removal

The security protective force should also provide controls for the prevention of unauthorized removal of equipment. Possible controls include:

- Property Pass — Authorized removal of equipment requires that a property pass be issued by an authorized individual. Property passes should protect against forgeries and reuse.
- Package Inspection — In order to ensure that all equipment removed from the premises is authorized, the security protective force should have the ability to inspect all packages (e.g., boxes, briefcases, purses).

8.2 The RIIOT Method: Physical Data Gathering

As introduced in Chapter 5, the RIIOT method of data gathering can be applied to any security risk assessment technique and helps to ensure a more complete and well-managed data-gathering process. The RIIOT method is applied to any area of security controls by reasoning about the most appropriate approach for gathering data on each security control under review. Applying the RIIOT method to the technical area shows that a majority of the data-gathering techniques to be applied to physical security controls will be document review, personnel interviews and control inspection of controls. Table 8.4 provides suggested reasonable approaches to gathering data for each of the security controls described in this chapter.

Table 8.4 RIIOT Method of Data Gathering for Physical Controls. The application of the RIIOT method to physical controls indicates that the data gathering in this area will focus mainly on document review and inspection of physical controls.

Controls	Review Documents	Interview Key Personnel	Inspect Controls	Observe Behavior	Test Controls
Surge suppressor		×	×		
Line conditioner		×	×		
Voltage regulator		×	×		
Flywheel energy storage	×	×	×		
UPS	×	×	×		
On-site power generation	×	×	×		
HVAC	×				
Temperature alarm/log			×		
Humidifier		×			
Humidity alarm/log			×		
Building construction	×		×		
Construction details	×		×		
Storage of combustibles			×		
Fire exits	×		×		
Fire evacuation	×				
Smoke detectors			×		
Heat detectors			×		
Alarm type		×			
Mobile fire suppression	×		×		
Stationary fire suppression	×	×			
Water damage safeguards		×	×		
Water pipe safeguards		×	×		
Raised floor safeguards		×	×		
Lightning safeguards		×			
Earthquake safeguards	×	×	×		
Landslide safeguards		×	×		
Tornado safeguards		×	×		
Proof of identity	×	×	×		
Background check	×	×	×		
Proof of citizenship	×	×	×		
Military clearance	×	×	×		
Fencing			×		

(Continued)

Table 8.4 (Continued)
RIIOT Method of Data Gathering for Physical Controls

Controls	Review Documents	Interview Key Personnel	Inspect Controls	Observe Behavior	Test Controls
Buildings			×		
Doors			×		×
Locks			×		×
Vehicle barriers			×		
Lighting	×		×		
Intrusion detection			×		×
Badges			×	×	×
Card readers			×	×	×
Biometrics			×	×	×
Visitor control	×	×		×	×
Property pass	×	×		×	×
Package inspection	×	×		×	×

8.2.1 Review Physical Documents

As demonstrated in Table 8.4, gathering data on physical security control involves the review of documents. The bulk of the document review will be a review of logs and processes. The remaining document reviews will include a review of architectural drawings and schematics.

8.2.1.1 Physical Documents to Request

Using the RIIOT document review technique, the security risk assessment team should determine the set of documents to be reviewed (see Table 8.5). In some cases the team will be able to review all documents obtained through information requests. In most cases, because of time or budget constraints, the team will need to narrow the evidence reviewed to determine the strength of physical security controls.

8.2.1.2 Review Physical Documents for Information

It is important to create a checklist to guide the review of each document.[14] A checklist is simply a listing of all the things a reasonable security engineer would expect to find in the reviewed document. In order to assist those performing security risk assessments, the checklists for document review are provided in Table 8.6.

Tables 8.7 through 8.10 are an illustration of how to construct and use checklists for the review of physical security documents. However, the team

Table 8.5   Physical Documents to Request. The security risk assessment team should attempt to obtain and review as many relevant physical documents as possible within the data-gathering stage of the security risk assessment. This table provides a sample list of documents to request. but it is by no means exhaustive.

Document Type	Sample Titles
Safeguard information	• Product manuals • System schematics • nspection reports
Previous physical assessments	• Inspection • Physical audit • Incustrial security auc t
Building and site architecture	• Physical site diagram • Building drawings • Blueprints
Security work products	• Guard logs • Visitor logs • Incident reports

Table 8.6   Physical Document Review Checklists. Checklists for reviewing various types of physical documents are provided in Tables 8.7 through 8.10.

Security Policy	Expected Element's Table
Physical safeguard information review checklist	Table 8.7
Previous physical assessment review checklist	Table 8.8
Building and site architecture review checkl st	Table 8.9
Security work products review checklist	Table 8.10

must understand that not all documents are required for all environments, not all checklist elements are necessary for al security contro s, and not all physical documents provided will be as neatly titled as the documents discussed here.[15]

8.2.1.2.1 Physical Safeguard Information Review

The security risk assessment team, or a member of the team, should review the available physical safeguard information (e.g., manuals, specifications) to gain a perspective on the inputs to the current security risk assessment. The objective of this review is to increase the security risk assessment team's understanding of the physical safeguards employed at the organization's site. Table 8.7 provides a baseline checklist for reviewing physical safeguard information manuals.

Table 8.7 Physical Safeguard Information Review Checklist. The physical safeguard information should be reviewed for configuration options, current settings, warnings, and cautions.

Objective	Subtopic	Review Tips
Gather information from available physical safeguard to understand security implications of the equipment deployed	Safeguard types	• Determine the type of exterior and interior sensors. Look for layers of different sensor types (i.e., defense in depth).

	Settings	• *Power.* Appropriate settings for these devices are dependent upon the business mission, environmental conditions, and threat of power loss. However, reasonable settings are typically as follows:
		  • Flywheel energy storage:
		  • UPS capacity: 20–45 minutes
		  • OPG: 8 hours to 3 days (be sure to inquire about on-site fuel capacity)
		• *Fire.* Appropriate setting for fire detection and suppression devices is conditional upon the placement and purpose of each device. Specifically, team members should look at the settings of the following devices:
		• *Heat alarms.* Typically set for 117°F (47°C), 135°F (57°C), 165°F (74°C), or 200°F (93°C)
		• *Rate of rise detectors.* Typically set for 12°F–15°F (6°C–8°C) per minute

	Capabilities	• *Alarms.* All alarms (e.g., fire, smoke, heat) should be reviewed for the following capabilities:
		  • *Battery backup.* 24–60 hours backup
		  • *Separate circuit*
		  • *Line supervision.* For alarms that dial out (e.g., remote systems)
		  • *Coverage.* Review coverage capabilities of various alarms (e.g., smoke, heat, intrusion). Compare coverage capabilities to the need of the environment.
		• *Fire suppression.* Ensure that clean agent suppression chemicals are appropriate for the application. For example, FM-200 cannot be used for areas where ceilings are higher than 12 feet.
		• *Cameras.* Determine the camera's ability to focus, zoom, pan, capture video, and distinguish characteristics in different lighting conditions.

(Continued)

Table 8.7 (Continued)
Physical Safeguard Information Review Checklist

Objective	Subtopic	Review Tips
	Procedures	• *Fire evacuation procedures.* At a minimum these procedures should have the following elements: 　• Fire and emergency drill training 　• Door closing instructions 　• Fire extinguisher use instructions 　• Building clearing instructions 　• Tarp use and storage instructions 　• Designated meeting areas 　• Free egress in emergency for all physical restrictions (e.g., metal detectors, mantraps, doors)

*Heat sensors integrated into the sprinkler heads of fire suppression systems are typically color-coded. Metal-colored plugs are typically set to 165 degrees. Colored glass vials have the following coding: green, 165 degrees; red, 200 degrees.

8.2.1.2.2 Previous Physical Assessment Review

The security risk assessment team, or a member of the team, should review the available physical security assessment reports to gain a perspective on the inputs to the current security risk assessment. The objective of this review is not to judge the completeness or correctness of past reviews, but to use information gathered during past efforts to double-check and improve the current effort. Table 8.8 provides a baseline checklist for reviewing physical security assessment reports.

8.2.1.2.3 Building and Site Architecture Review

The security risk assessment team, or a member of the team, should review the available building and site architecture documents (e.g., building layout, site survey, architectural drawings) to gain a perspective on the inputs to the current security risk assessment. The objective of this review is to increase the security risk assessment team's understanding of the physical safeguards employed at the organization's site. Table 8.9 provides a baseline checklist for reviewing building and site architecture.

8.2.1.2.4 Physical Security Work Products Review

The security risk assessment team, or a member of the team, should review the available physical security work products to determine possible vulnerabilities in

Table 8.8 Physical Security Assessment Reports Review Checklist. The physical security assessment reports should be reviewed for previously identified and relevant information that may impact the current security risk assessment.

Objective	Sub-topic	Review Tips
Gather information from past security review efforts to improve data gathering in the current security risk assessment	Safeguard components and physical boundaries	• Review named safeguard components and indicated physical boundaries and compare them to the current statement of work. If they are different, ask key personnel for an explanation. • Look for any safeguards that have not been included in the last or present assessment. Determine if the lack of review for organizational elements is a vulnerability.
	Roles and responsibilities	• Look for definitions of roles and responsibilities from previous reviews. Specifically, look for responsibilities such as incident response and reporting, compliance, and asset control.
	Threats	• Review the physical threats considered during the previous assessment efforts. Review the threats identified for this effort and consider adding previously identified threats.
	Assets and asset values	• Review the assets and the values assigned to those assets listed in previous assessment efforts. Consider listing additional assets previously identified. Reexamine asset values based on previous asset valuations.
	Current safeguards	• Review the list, description, and vulnerabilities of existing physical safeguards from previous assessments. Determine if those safeguards are still in place. Consider the previous vulnerabilities within those safeguards and ensure that they are either addressed or are listed in your current security risk assessment.
	Recommended safeguards and timelines	• Review the recommended physical safeguards and suggested timelines for implementation from previous assessments. If such timelines have passed, look for evidence that these physical safeguards were implemented, addressed in another manner, or ignored.

Table 8.9   Building and Site Architecture Review Checklist. The building and site architecture reports should be reviewed for design errors and areas of high risk.

Objective	Subtopic	Review Tips
Gather information from available drawing and schematics to improve data gathering in the current security risk assessment	• Safeguard components and physical boundaries	• Review indicated safeguard components and indicated physical boundaries and compare them to the current statement of work. If they are different, ask key personnel for an explanation. • Look at the placement of sensitive areas, parking areas, access points, and storage areas. Review for the adequacy of camera coverage, intrusion detection coverage, and guard coverage. • Consider response times of the security protective force, when sensor activates, and what additional controls are in place between the breached sensor and the protected asset. For example, a good design would be a motion sensor in the yard leading up to a window, a window glass-break sensor, and a locked file cabinet.*
	• Power supply diagrams • Data transmission systems • Lighting circuits • Site topography	• Look for opportunities for sabotage such as critical components in public areas or unprotected critical components (i.e., lack of bollards, low light levels, and weak locks). • Look for low or high ground which may give an intruder the advantage.
	• Site lighting diagrams • Camera coverage • Guard routes	• Look for inadequate coverage and blind spots.

(Continued)

Table 8.9 (Continued)
Building and Site Architecture Review Checklist

Objective	Subtopic	Review Tips
	• CCTV design	• *Camera placement.* Cameras should be placed along the site perimeter, at controlled access points, and within protected areas. Look for gaps in coverage. • *Video signal.* Depending on site characteristics, one of the following video signal media should be used: metallic cable (limited distance),RF transmission (up to 50 miles line of sight), or fiber optic cable (low loss,high resolution). Look for correct use of technology. • *Synchronization.* Test the synchronization of events between various sources.** • *Video processing and display.* The video camera and the video monitoring station should have the required features to properly protect the site. Look for the ability of the video monitoring station to quickly select CCTV cameras associated with tripped alarms, the presence of a video recorder and a video-loss detector, and proper lighting levels of all cameras.

*Protective controls that must be defeated prior to a sensor activating are called "pre-alarm" controls. Protective controls that must be defeated after the first sensor is activated are called "post-alarm" controls.

**CCTV cameras process timing signals within the image scan area. The timing signal can come from an external signal source or be derived from the CCTV camera's internal power source. The internal power source time is a good backup when the external power is unavailable; however, a synchronized timing signal allows for smooth transitions for monitors that switch from one video source to another.

the existing physical safeguards. Table 8.10 provides a baseline checklist for reviewing physical security work products.

8.2.2 Interview Physical Personnel

Members of the security risk assessment team should discuss the effectiveness of physical security mechanisms with key members of the physical security staff. Key members may include the head of facilities, members of the security force, and others involved in the selection, operation, or maintenance of physical security controls.

Table 8.10 Physical Security Work Products Review Checklist. The physical security work products such as visitor logs and incident reports should be reviewed to give the team an indication of the relative threat levels and compliance to established procedures.

Objective	Subtopic	Review Tips
Gather information from physical security work products to understand threat levels and adherence to established procedures.	• Proof of identity • Background check • Verification of citizenship • Criminal and credit checks • Military clearance • Incident reports	• Review a statistically relevant sample of employment records (e.g., background checks, citizenship verification). Look for inaccurate records, records beyond the periodic review requirements, or missing employment checks. • Review incident reports looking for frequency of incidents and possible weaknesses in security controls.
	• Alarm sensitivity	• Review logs of alarm reporting devices and alarm plots. Look for large nuisance rates.
	• Control testing schedule	• Review the control testing schedules and look for inadequate testing depth, rigor, or frequency.
	• Test results	• Review test results and look for remaining vulnerabilities.
	• Badge disposition records • Visitor log • HR records	• Look for inaccurate records and evidence of lax procedures, for example, missing badges, visitors who did not check out. • Look for badges and physical access controls to be inconsistent with HR records.
	• List of terminated employees • List of reissued badges • List of lost badges at each post • Temporary badge procedure • Visitor badge procedure • Badge recovery procedure • Escort procedure • Badge protection measures • Lost badge reporting procedures	• Look for active badges of terminated employees. • Look for out-of-date photographs on active badges. • Look for evidence of abundance of lost badges. • Look for inaccurate records of lost badges. • Look for missing or inadequate procedures.

8.2.2.1 Physical Security Interview Topics

Within the physical security controls area, the security risk assessment team will find that interviews provided a detailed understanding of the physical security safeguards employed at the site.

8.2.2.2 Physical Security Interview Subjects

The security risk assessment team should interview the facilities personnel best able to provide information required to understand the physical safeguards. The selection of interview subjects will depend on who has the responsibility for the safeguards in question. All questions will be directed to physical security staff.

8.2.2.3 Physical Security Interview Questions

Prior to any interview the security risk assessment team should review the available documents and prepare questions based on the information provided or concerns that surfaced during the document review. If several members of the security risk assessment team were responsible for reviewing the documents, these members should get together to create a list of questions they have on the physical security documents.

8.2.2.3.1 Utilities Interview Questions

The utilities questions in Table 8.11 should be asked of facilities personnel in charge of various physical security controls. The questions cover utilities and alarms. If the organization has not implemented one or more of these controls, that section of the interview can be skipped as it is not applicable.

8.2.2.3.2 Physical Security Procedures Interview Questions

The physical security procedures questions in Table 8.12 should be asked of facilities personnel in charge of various physical security controls. The questions cover utilities and alarms. If the organization has not implemented one or more of these controls, that section of the interview can be skipped as it is not applicable.

8.2.3 Inspect Physical Security Controls

Data gathering for physical security controls also involves inspecting physical security controls. Recall that inspection differs from testing in that inspection is

Table 8.11 Physical Security Controls Review Interview Guideline. The interviewer should compile a list of questions to ask the responsible party to ensure that the security risk assessment team has a clear understanding of the physical safeguards.

Objective	Subtopic	Question
Increase knowledge of physical safeguards deployed within the organization	Utilities	• *Testing.* How often are these tested? How well have they performed in the tests? • *Capacity.* Has capacity significantly increased since the equipment was procured? • *Fuel.* How much fuel do you have on site? How long can the generators run on that fuel? What is your process for obtaining more fuel?
	Alarms	• *Components.* Is there an alarm system? How many zones of protection? Where are the annunciating units? • *Coverage.* Are there any areas not covered by the alarm? • *Testing.* How often is the alarm system inspected and tested? • *Response.* Who responds to the alarm? What procedures do they follow? • *Protection.* Does the alarm have tamper-proof protection? Does the system have weather-proof protection? Does the system have its own circuit? Backup power? Line supervision? • *Maintenance.* Who maintains the equipment? • *Records.* Are records kept on all alarms (time, date, location, resolution)? Is there a specific part of the alarm system that has a high nuisance rate?

performed when testing is inappropriate or infeasible. For almost all physical safeguards, testing is inappropriate. Inspection involves the review of the security control and security control aspects such as configuration or arrangements.

For the most part, the approach for performing a physical security control inspection includes the listing of the security controls under review, verifying information gathered, determining vulnerabilities, and documenting the results. Each of these phases is discussed within the context of physical data gathering.

8.2.3.1 Listing Physical Security Controls

The relevant physical security controls to be inspected include only those that lend themselves to inspection. Many physical security controls are actively protecting critical assets and it would be difficult to test them without interrupting operations.

Table 8.12 Physical Security Procedures Interview Guideline. The interviewer should compile a list of questions to ask the responsible party to ensure that the security risk assessment team has a clear understanding of the physical safeguards.

Objective	Subtopic	Question
Increase knowledge of physical safeguards deployed within the organization	Asset tracking and control	• *Asset tracking.* Are hardware assets (e.g., servers, telephones, laptops, projectors) tracked in an asset database? Are they signed out when needed offsite? • *Portable assets.* Are portable assets (e.g., laptops, projectors) physically secure to protect from removal? • *Property control.* Is there a mechanism for property control (bringing and removing laptops from the site?)
	Visitor control	• *Visitor control procedures.* What are the procedures for visitor control? Are logs kept? • *Escort procedures.* What are the procedures for escorting?
	Security protective force	• *Duties.* What are the duties of the security force? Is there a job description? Is there a manual? Is there a daily/nightly checklist?

However, the security risk assessment team can still gain valuable information based on a carefully planned inspection of critical elements.

In addition to the review of physical security documents and the interview of key personnel, the security risk assessment team can survey the organization's premises to further determine the existing controls present. Basic steps in a physical security survey are as follows:

- Fence Line — Survey the site perimeter noting fence lines. Include details such as type of fence, condition, number of openings, manned and unmanned posts.
- Parking Area — Survey the outside parking area. Include details such as area enclosures, parking lot controls, manned and unmanned posts.
- Building Perimeter — Survey the building perimeter. Include details such as pedestrian and vehicular entrances, and access controls. Check all doors and note how they are secured. Check the ground floor and basement windows or ventilation grills, manholes, and fire escapes. How are each of these controlled?
- Building Interior — Start either at the top floor or the bottom floor. Note fire alarm systems and devices. Include details such as number and type.

Check the telephone and electrical closets. Are they locked? Note any alarms. Include details such as the type, number, and location. Determine the location of manned posts and times manned. Determine guards shifts and rotation procedures.

Physical controls within the building are numerous and can be complex. Inspection procedures for these interior controls are discussed in more detail in Table 8.13.

Table 8.13 Physical Safeguards Inspection Guideline (Power, Fire, and Lighting). The security risk assessment team should be prepared to inspect physical security devices to determine the effectiveness of physical safeguards.*

Physical Control	Safeguard Inspection
Power	• *Monitor power fluctuations.* A strip chart recorder should be in place to log internal transients. • *Isolate power to critical systems.* Ensure that the computer room distribution panels are directly connected to primary feeder panels and do not share stepdown transformers with other loads, especially high-horsepower motors. • *Clearly mark controls.* Both the distribution panel and the master control switch should be clearly marked. The master control switch (turns off all power) should be located near the room entrance, but should be protected against accidental engagement. • *Protect power distribution rooms.* Rooms that house power distribution equipment should be physically protected from unauthorized personnel. • *Protect outdoor utilities.* Any elements of the power system that are housed outside the building should be protected. Transformer pods should be within locked rooms. Transformer pods and utility poles should be protected by barriers to prevent accidental or deliberate destruction. • *Protect master control switch.* The switch that shuts off all power should be clearly visible but protected (e.g.,hinged cover).
Hand-held fire extinguisher	• *Monthly inspection.* Check that fire extinguishers have recent inspections and are full. Extinguishers should be inspected monthly and tested annually. • *Placement.* Fire extinguishers should be placed within 50 feet of each piece of equipment and located near the entrance to the room. • *Marked location.* The location of the fire extinguishers should be clearly marked (e.g., red paint on the wall or column).

(Continued)

Table 8.13 (Continued)
Physical Safeguards Inspection Guideline (Power, Fire, and Lighting)

Physical Control	Safeguard Inspection
	• *Size.* Fire extinguishers should be 2.5 gallon water extinguishers or 15 lb carbon dioxide extinguishers. Smaller handheld extinguishers should be available if there is a concern about the ability of some occupants to lift larger extinguishers. • *Fire blanket.* A fire blanket for small kitchen fires or humans should be available in appropriate areas.
Fire resistant building construction	• *Penetrations.* When the building walls are penetrated by pipes, ducts, or conduit, the penetration must be sealed with a material that provides equal or better fire resistance. • *Walls and partitions.* Interior firewalls and partitions should be erected to slow the spread of smoke and fire in the building. • *Stairwells.* Stairwells should be fire rated and designed to reduce the spread of fire and smoke. • *Ducts.* Air-handling ducts should be fitted with shutters or dampers that are activated by the smoke and fire detection equipment to reduce the spread of smoke throughout the building (e.g., switch to outside air only). • *Material.* Building material such as paint and carpet should be low flame spreading.
Storage of combustibles	• Separate storage plus inspection elements discussed in "Fire resistant building construction"
Fire detectors	• *Smoke detectors.* All smoke detectors should be in good working order, i.e., firmly attached to ceiling or wall near ceiling, and with good batteries. • *Detector range.* All detectors (smoke, heat, flame, etc.) should be deployed in a manner that conforms to their specifications. For example, VESDA devices typically operate within an effective range of 5000–20,000 square feet; Rate of rise, 5000 square feet; smoke detectors, only 200 square feet. • *Detector location.* Smoke and heat detectors' ability to detect fire is based on the flow of air to the detector. Improperly placed detectors (e.g., not within 8 inches of the ceiling or near exit doors) are less effective than fire detectors placed on the ceiling or in central locations. • *Detector types.* Different fires behave differently; some smolder, others ignite quickly. All types of fire detectors should be centrally located or near potential sources of fire.

(Continued)

Table 8.13 (Continued)
Physical Safeguards Inspection Guideline (Power, Fire and Lighting)

Physical Control	Safeguard Inspection
	• *Closed spaces.* Certain closed spaces such as telephone closets, raised floors, and hung ceilings could harbor a fire unnoticed in the early stages. These areas require dedicated fire detectors because electrical shorts are a major source of fire.
Water pipes	• *No water over computer room.* Water used for plumbing and drains should not be routed over the computer room or other sensitive areas.
	• *Shut-off valves.* All water pipes, including fire suppression pipes, should have shut off valves properly placed and marked. These valves are used to limit the damage of an accidental leak or pipe burst.
	• *Avoid "wet columns."* All buildings must route plumbing pipes up and down floors somehow. Some buildings route these pipes near support columns and enclose the whole column. These columns are also called risers or wet columns. If possible, the computer room or other rooms with sensitive equipment should not contain these risers. Risers can be identified because they are generally thicker than others to allow room for the pipes.
	• *Supply of plastic sheeting.* Keep a supply of plastic sheeting handy. It can be used to cover equipment in the case of a fire or accidental leakage or pipe burst. Many insurance policies require that a supply of plastic sheeting is kept nearby.
Raised floors	• *Raise electric boxes.* Electrical boxes below raised flooring should be raised a minimum of 8 inches off the floor.
	• *Unbroken conduit.* Conduit used beneath raised flooring should be a single piece or unbroken.
	• *Water detector.* Organizations should consider the use of water detectors underneath raised flooring to detect water in these closed areas.
	• *Drains.* The hard slab flooring beneath raised flooring should have drains about every 18 feet. These drains need to be plumbed correctly to ensure that drainage always flow away, i.e., positive drains.
Natural hazard protection**	• *Drains.* Low-lying areas that receive runoff, also called sumps, need to have adequate drainage to move excess water away fast enough so that the sump does not overflow. These drains should be fitted with check valves that ensure the water flows only one way — out.

(Continued)

Table 8.13 (Continued)
Physical Safeguards Inspection Guideline (Power, Fire, and Lighting)

Physical Control	Safeguard Inspection
	• *Sump pumps.* In times of excess runoff the drains within a sump may be inadequate to remove the excess water. A sump pump (or several sump pumps) is a good safeguard to keep the area clear of water and to prevent the excess water from overflowing the sump and damaging other parts of the building. The sump pump should have gasoline-driven motors and a supply of gasoline should be available nearby.
	• *Levees, curbs, walls.* These building structures can divert or even hold back flood waters to a limited degree. Organizations with buildings located within a flood plain should consider the construction of permanent flood protection systems.
	• *Sandbags.* In the event of an impending flood, sandbags can be used to create an emergency levee, raise an existing levee, or fill the gaps in permanent flood protection systems. Organizations should keep a supply of sandbags, sand, and filling devices (shovels) nearby in case of such an emergency.†
	• *Duct tape.* The handyman's best friend, duct tape, can come in handy in many situations. During a potential flood emergency, duct tape can be used to seal door frames. This is an extremely inexpensive and easy to implement safeguard.
Lighting	• *Building.* Buildings should be illuminated at a minimum of 1 foot candle. Lighting should be to a height of 8 feet above grade level or top of window or door, whichever is greater. The lighting should not extend to above the illuminated structure.
	• *Fence line.* The fence line should be illuminated at a minimum of 1 foot candle. Lighting should be controlled by motion sensors located 5 feet inside the fence line. Such a system should supply illumination only upon the detection of an intruder.
	• *Parking lot.* The parking lot should be illuminated at a minimum of 1 foot candle. Lights should be placed to avoid dark patches through overlapping cones of light.
	• *Pedestrian walkway.* The walkway should be illuminated at a minimum of 3 foot candles.
	• *Parking structure.* The parking structure should be illuminated at a minimum of 5 foot candles
	• *Loading docks.* Loading docks should be illuminated at a minimum of 3 foot candles and a maximum of 5 foot candles. Lighting should be out 25 feet from the building.

(Continued)

Table 8.13   (Continued)
Physical Safeguards Inspection Guideline (Power, Fire, and Lighting)

Physical Control	Safeguard Inspection
	• *Guard route.* The route should be illuminated at a maximum of 0.5 foot candles. It is important to avoid overillumination which can decrease the guard's ability to see clearly at night.

*Physical security safeguard inspection is unique in that many inspection elements are focused on determining the presence of a safeguard and not always on inspecting a specific safeguard for the correct configuration and working order. Of course, all safeguards should be visibly inspected and determined to be in good working order.

**This set of safeguards for natural hazard protection specifically addresses floods. For a list of relevant safeguards for other natural disasters, see Table 8.3.

†For more information on preparing for and using sandbags and other flood-fighting equipment, see the Louisiana Floods Web site (www.louisianafloods.org/emergency.asp).

Sidebar 8.4 Physical Security Walk-Through

A physical walk-through was once described as "walk around and look for stuff." Even though this description is rather informal and could be viewed as treating the technique lightly, this is not how it was intended. If you ever witness someone who is very good at the physical security walk-through, it will seem as if they simply "walk around and look for stuff" but they seem to notice everything. This is because they are going through a complex thought process in their head when analyzing the presence, condition, or absence of security mechanisms and the behavior of the organization through observation. This thought process is partly checklist and partly intuition based on experience.

In advising the reader on how to perform effective physical walk-throughs, checklists can be devised but intuition must be learned on your own. The approach used in this book to empower the reader to be a more effective security risk assessment engineer is to expose the reader to both a proposed checklist and examples of results derived from pure intuition. The checklist presented here provides a logical dissection of physical security measures and essential elements and required aspects of those measures. Also included in this section are several examples of "things that were noticed" by experienced security engineers through their ability of perception. It is believed the exposure of these "things" will assist readers in developing their own intuition, but nothing compares to experience.

A physical security walk-through is an inspection through observation of the physical security access controls. In most cases a physical security walk-through can be accomplished by one or two individuals in less than a single day. The walk-through itself is simply the gathering of information. This information must still be documented, assessed, and presented. However, a physical security walk-through adds a small amount of effort and cost to a security risk assessment and should be heavily considered for all security risk assessments.

8.2.3.2 Verify Information Gathered

Information gathered regarding physical security controls should be confirmed through the inspection process. Team members should use various methods to confirm the existence of each of these security controls.

8.2.3.2.1 Logs, Records, and Audit Files

The security risk assessment team should review a sample of documents and other evidence that indicates the effectiveness and operation of physical security controls. Specifically, the team can ask to see the logs, log tapes, records, reports, and audit files covering the area and time of specific events they suspect or know have happened. For example, ask to see records of the team's badges being issued.

The team should also review temperature and humidity logs (e.g., tapes). The assessors should look for periods outside the ideal range. The ideal ranges are typically as follows:

- Temperature (computer room): 70°F–74°F (21°C–23°C)
- Humidity (computer room): 40–60 percent relative humidity.

8.2.3.2.2 Perimeter Security

The goal of perimeter security is access control and employee safety. Access control is implemented through a series of security mechanisms to permit only authorized users to gain physical access to the building. Table 8.14 provides some guidance to the security risk assessment team for inspecting perimeter access control to determine the strength of the physical access controls. The security risk assessment team is encouraged to review Table 8.14 and add or modify table elements to suit its own needs and experiences.

Of course, only those controls actually implemented by the organization can be inspected. The list of physical security controls to be reviewed for a specific organization comprises any of the controls that the organization stated are in place or that are observed by the security risk assessment team. Statements regarding physical controls in place could have come from interviews or provided as part of the document review process. The team should obtain a point of contact for each of these controls and should be escorted for many of the inspections, because these controls safeguard critical business functions.

8.2.3.3 Determine Physical Vulnerabilities

During inspection of the physical security controls, the security risk assessment team should look for vulnerabilities. The inspection process of these controls involves the recognition of ineffective mechanisms, configurations, or processes. The questions and tips within the previous section guide the security risk assessment team toward these vulnerabilities. For example, when inspecting the badge-issuing process log features for adequate and accurate information being captured, stored, and retrieved when needed, a vulnerability exists if the team determines that the log process creates confusion or does not record critical information (e.g., driver's license number, point of contact, badge number, and type of access granted).

8.2.3.4 Document and Review Physical Findings

As with all findings, the security risk assessment team must be sure to carefully record their findings in the area of physical controls through inspection. The team should include dates, evidence, team member names, and the vulnerabilities observed. These findings must be reviewed with the entire team and the point of contact for the control to give them a chance to clarify any misunderstandings.

8.2.4 Observe Physical Personnel Behavior

The process of gathering data through observation is a subtle one. With a few exceptions, this process is passive and depends on team members being aware of

Table 8.14 Physical Safeguards Inspection Guideline (Barriers). The security risk assessment team should be prepared to inspect physical security devices to determine the effectiveness of physical safeguards.*

Physical Control	Claim	Inspection Elements

Property line	• The property line has the appropriate number and type of controls.
	• The controls are in good repair.
		• *Fences.* Look for jump points (anything that can be used to circumvent property fence lines), for example, depressions in the earth, tunnels, pipelines, erosion, missing fence panels, trees or trash receptacle near the fence line, insecure attachment to poles, vegetation providing cover, or bent tops of fence wire
		• *Fence heights.* Fences should be an appropriate height for the intended purpose. Use the following as a guide:
		  • *Property demarcation:* 3–4 feet
		  • *Barrier:* 6–7 feet
		  • *Serious barrier:* 8 feet with 3 strands of barbed wire.
		• *Gates.* Ensure that gates work and leave no gaps large enough for a person to fit through.
		• *Cameras.* Look for adequate coverage, especially for parking lots and all entrances. Adequate coverage includes camera existence, placement and quality and capture of image (lighting, focus, granularity, and frames per second (fps)).

Building perimeter	• The building perimeter has the appropriate number and type of controls. • The controls are in good repair.	• *Windows.* Look for broken or unlocked windows. • *Skylights.* Look for unsecured skylights. • *Doors.* Look for unlocked doors, specifically, loading docks and doors near smoking lounges. Look for telltale signs that controlled access doors are held open. • *Lighting.* Look for consistent and adequate lighting in parking lots, walkways, perimeter walls, fence lines, and perimeter doors.
Vehicle barriers	• Vehicle barriers are appropriately placed. • Barriers are in good repair.	• *Bollard placement.* Vehicle barriers (bollards) should be placed in areas requiring protection of unauthorized vehicles, for example, power transmission boxes, utility sheds, pedestrian entrances. • *Bollard condition.* Visually inspect bollards to ensure that they are in good repair.

*Physical security safeguard inspection is unique in that many inspection elements are focused on determining the presence of a safeguard and not always on inspecting a specific safeguard for the correct configuration and working order. Of course, all safeguards should be visibly inspected and determined to be in good working order.

the organization's policies, procedures, and safeguards, while keeping an eye out for opportunities to confirm or disprove the organization's effective use of physical safeguards, although some observations can be active in nature, for example, placing an access badge in your pocket instead of wearing it. More experienced team members will find observation to be second nature and a side effect of being on site.

The observation of physical security controls will include a review of internal security:

- Controlled Access — Controlling access to the building through well-defined, monitored, and defended entrances allows for effective protection of the organization's assets. The building entrances should have the appropriate number and type of controls.
- Shared Access — When a building is shared by multiple tenants, it is not always possible to provide access controls at the building entrance. Special consideration must be given to environments that share building access or that have public access to the building.
- Internal Access Controls — The goal of internal access controls is to provide additional access control among authorized personnel. Not all personnel authorized to be on the premises are authorized to be everywhere on the premises. For example, visitors to the building must be escorted and cannot enter designated sensitive areas. Access control is implemented through designation of controlled areas, internal access controls, internal monitoring controls and work area controls.
    - Controlled Areas — Controlled areas are any areas that are not open to the general employees. These areas are restricted to a limited set of personnel that perform a specific function. Examples of controlled areas include telephone closets, computer rooms, shipping and receiving, secure compartmented information facilities (SCIF), and equipment rooms. When reviewing the controls in a controlled area, the security risk assessment team member should use judgment as to the effectiveness of the controls. For example, a padlock on a SCIF is a weak control because it could be easily defeated with a single blow of a hammer.[16]
    - Internal Access Controls — Internal areas are areas that are not open to the general public. These areas are restricted to employees and guests. Examples of internal areas include offices, work space, and internal meeting rooms. When reviewing the access controls in an internal area, the security risk assessment team member should determine the effectiveness of the existing controls through test and observation.
    - Internal Monitoring Controls — Most governmental or corporate buildings have a variety of internal controls — for example, heat, humidity, intrusion — that are monitored. The effective monitoring of

these alarms can be an important element of an organization's security posture.

- Work Areas — The protection of sensitive information is susceptible to bad user habits. An observation of work areas can reveal the effectiveness of awareness training and the security culture within the organization.

With a little guidance and teamwork, these observations can be recorded from most team members and add additional data points to the data-gathering process. Table 8.15 provides some guidance to the security risk assessment team for observing the behavior of the organization's staff to determine the strength of some of the physical safeguards. The security risk assessment team is encouraged to review Table 8.15 and add or modify table elements to suit its own needs and experiences.

8.2.5 Test Physical Security Safeguards

The last phase of data gathering for physical security safeguards in the RIIOT method is testing. Testing of physical security safeguards is the process of invoking conditions that test physical safeguards against their intended security functions. This type of data gathering provides excellent insight into the effectiveness of the controls.

The physical safeguards that lend themselves to testing are limited to doors and locks, physical intrusion detection, and physical access controls. An approach for testing each of these controls is presented below. The security risk assessment team is encouraged to adopt, modify, or add to these test methods.

8.2.5.1 Doors and Locks

Testing procedures for doors and locks require that the security risk assessment team perform activities that attempt to bypass the blocking controls in place. The areas protected by these doors and locks are likely to be sensitive areas. It is for this reason that the security risk assessment team leader must be sure to gain permission from the organization to test such controls. The tests listed in Table 8.16 should be attempted to gain a minimum level of confidence that the doors and locks are effective.

8.2.5.2 Intrusion Detection

Testing procedures for physical intrusion detection controls require that the security risk assessment team perform activities that attempt to bypass or defeat intrusion detection controls. In an effort to provide a more complete knowledge base, Table 8.17 provides many possible tests for these controls.

Table 8.15 Physical Safeguards Observation Guideline. The security risk assessment team should be prepared to observe the behavior of the security staff, key personnel, and general employee population to check the effectiveness of physical safeguards.

Physical Control	Claim	Observation Test or Procedure Check
Controlled access	• The building entrances have the appropriate number and type of controls. • The controls are in good repair.	• *Entrances.* Are all entrances to the controlled area protected? • *Walls.* Are there other ways into the controlled area? For example, false ceilings, large vents, or false floors. • *Doors.* Look for unlocked doors. Are the doors properly and consistently locked? Specifically, closets and areas where it is difficult to control the temperature. Look for telltale signs that controlled access doors are held open. Is there an alarm for doors held open? Is there an access log? • *Door hardware.* Are the hinges for the doors on the inside of the controlled area? Are the door bolts shielded? • *Telephone closets.* Are modem numbers recorded? Are the modems always on?
Shared access	• There are no gaps in the security opened up by sharing access to the building.	• Are there any other people who can gain access to the controlled area, e.g., shared access with other tenants? • Do others with access follow the same procedures?
Internal access controls	• There is an appropriate number of building internal controls. • The controls are in good repair.	• *Visitor controls.* Did you sign a visitor form advising you of the procedures for visitors? Do employees enforce escort procedures? Are visitors challenged? • *Badge control.* Is there unlocked or unprotected badge storage?

(Continued)

Table 8.15 (Continued)
Physical Safeguards Observation Guideline

Physical Control	Claim	Observation Test or Procedure Check
		• *Manned posts.* Determine location of manned posts and times manned. • *Public areas.* Are there any places to tap into the network or use the phone unnoticed? Are there any office computers or workstations in the area? Are they locked?
Internal monitoring controls	• Physical location has the appropriate number and type of internal controls. • The physical location is adequately monitored.	• Start at the top or bottom floor. Note fire alarm systems and devices. Record the number and type of each device. • Note any other alarm type, location, and number of devices (e.g. heat, humidity, intrusion). • Determine location of monitoring facility. What alarms are being monitored and at what times?
Work areas	• Sensitive data is always secured.	• *Recorded passwords.* Casually look for passwords on "sticky notes," under phones and keyboards, in index files, and various papers posted in plain view in individual work areas. Many users will clearly post their passwords on sticky notes stuck to their monitor, while others will attempt to hide or encode them by placing them under "XYZ" in their index files or writing them backwards under their keyboard. Regardless of how they are hidden, they are typically within plain view or an arm's reach. • *Trash receptacles.* Look in several trash cans to see if sensitive information may have been improperly disposed. Focus on high-probability areas such as trash cans near fax machines, near meeting rooms, and in executive assistant areas. • *Desk tops.* Look for papers or recordable media that may contain sensitive information that may be unsecured.

Table 8.16 Doors and Locks Testing Guideline. The security risk assessment team should be prepared to test the functioning and strength of doors and locks to check the effectiveness of these physical safeguards.

Technical Control	Claim	Observation Test or Procedure Check
Door and locks	• Doors and locks are in good working order. • Doors and locks are adequately protected.	• *Timed closure test.* Open the door to a 90 degree angle and time how long it takes to close. A rule of thumb is that 6 to 8 seconds is reasonable. Doors that close more slowly are susceptible to tailgating. • *Closing latch test.* Open door just one inch. Let go and witness if the door closes shut or stays open owing to the friction or pressure of the latch. • *Protected latch test.* Inspect door to determine if the door latch is exposed to the outside. This basically means there is a lack of shielding between the door frame and the door near the door handle. If latch is exposed, attempt to defeat the mechanism through the use of a credit card, butter knife, or other tool. • *Motion sensor activated doors.* Attempt to circumvent door lock through unprotected gaps in the door. Methods include sliding a coat hanger with a piece of foil on the end through the door gap. The motion and heat of the foil could trip the motion sensor to open the door as if someone from the inside was approaching.
Badge access	• Doors controlled by badge access provide adequate protection.	• *Failed access.* Test for audit or alarm upon successive failed accesses. • *Tailgating.* Test for prevention of tailgating through supervision or mantraps. Will attempts be prevented or detected? • *Tampering.* Test (if appropriate) for detection of tampering through line supervision or monitoring. • *Power loss.* Test (if appropriate) documented settings for controlled access to determine disposition (i.e., fail secure, fail safe, fail soft) upon power loss. • *Shoulder surfing.* Test to determine if the PIN can be observed without being noticed.

Table 8.17 Physical Intrusion Detection Testing Guideline. Susceptible physical intrusion detection systems are those that may be bypassed easily through various means such as magnet substitution or removal for balance magnetic switches, wearing dark clothing to fool CCTVs, and walking slowly to fool motion sensors.*

Exterior Sensors	Nuisance Alarms	Vulnerable to:
Structural vibration	• Mounting on walls exposed to external vibration. • Vibrating machinery	• Bypass coverage area • Persistent random false alarms
Glass-break	• Sharp impact noises • Industrial background noise	• Bypass by cutting glass • Sound muffling
Passive ultrasonic	• HVAC air movement • Ringing telephone • Hissing pipes	• Sounds outside of range (e.g., drilling)
Balanced magnetic switches (BMS)	• Vibration • Improper installation • Poorly fitted doors and windows • Extreme hot and cold (expansion and contraction)	• Bypass protected opening • Line tampering • Cut door or window and hold actuating magnet
Grid Wire	• Wall abuse	• Bypass protected wall • Line tampering
Monostatic microwave	• Movement beyond detection area (microwaves penetrate standard walls and glass) • Fluorescent lights	• Bypass coverage area • Slow movement • Metal obstacles
Passive infrared (PIR)	• Sunlight-heated objects • Target masking • Overheated room	• Bypass coverage area • Obstacles
Video motion	• Internal lights	• Very slow motion • Intruders wearing clothes similar to background
Capacitance	• Rodents	• Control unit tampering • Low temperature • Surface water
Pressure mat	• Nearby vibrating machinery	• Bypass (step over) • Planking over
Pressure switch	• Accidental object movement	• Slide a thin metal strip under object
Duress alarm	• Accidental alarms	• Surprise and defeat
Strain-sensitive cable	• Lightning • Vegetation • Animals • Vibrations (railroad, highway)	• Tunneling • Trenching • Bridging
Taut wire	• Lightning • Vegetation • Animals • Vibrations (railroad, highway)	• Tunneling • Trenching • Bridging

(Continued)

Table 8.17 (Continued)
Physical Intrusion Detection Testing Guideline

Exterior Sensors	Nuisance Alarms	Vulnerable to:
Fiber optic cable	• Vegetation • Animals • Vibrations (railroad, highway)	• Tunneling • Trenching • Bridging
Electric field	• Vegetation • Animals	• Tunneling • Bridging
Capacitance proximity	• Birds • Vegetation	• Tunneling • Bridging
Buried line	• Lightning • Low levels of seismic activity	• Sidewalks and roads • Frozen ground • Bridging
Monostatic microwave	• Movement beyond detection area (microwaves penetrate standard walls and glass)	• Tunneling • Trenching • Bridging • Slow movement • Uneven terrain • Metal obstacles
Bistatic microwave	• Movement beyond detection area (microwaves penetrate standard walls and glass) • Fluorescent lights	• Tunneling • Trenching • Bridging • Slow movement • Uneven terrain • Metal obstacles
Infrared	• Windblown objects • Sunlight heated objects • Target masking	• Tunneling • Trenching • Bridging • Uneven terrain • Obstacles • Heavy snow, fog, rain • Warm weather
Video motion	• Headlights, sunlight, sunset • Birds and animals • Windblown objects • Large bushes and trees • Cloud movement and shadows • Severe weather	• Very slow motion • Intruders wearing clothes similar to background

*Many motion sensors are equipped with light-emitting diodes (LEDs) that light up when the motion sensor detects movement. If motion sensors are so equipped the assessors can use this signal as a method of testing for areas without coverage and the success of defeat tests. The typical motion sensor test is called the "four-step method." The tester takes four consecutive steps in single direction within one (1) second per step. This is called a "Trial" the sensor should trip in 3 out of 4 trials. Trials are to be taken with 3–5 second rests in between each and started in a new direction.

The security risk assessment team is expected to review these tests and select the appropriate test for the required coverage and rigor of their specific security risk assessment.

Notes

1. For those who are experts in this field or have a checklist they are comfortable with, you may skip this section without losing any context for the rest of the chapter.

2. For a human to even feel a static discharge the voltage level must be at least 3000 volts. Static discharges below this level can damage CMOS components, erase hard-drive data, and even cause system shutdowns. You do not have to feel it for it to do damage.

3. There are many devices on the market that combine these two functions (temperature and humidity).

4. NFPA Standard 221 and FM Data Sheet 1–22.

5. Although it is still an area of research, development has begun on some devices that can detect the noise of a fire. As fires of different fuel types put out different sounds, these devices can detect those sounds and signal the presence and type of fire. These devices are limited to solid fuel fires only.

6. Inergen is a registered trademark of the INSUL Corporation.

7. FE-13 is a trademark of DuPont.

8. FM-200 is a registered trademark of the Great Lakes Chemical Corporation.

9. The prediction of these events is inherently difficult to quantify. Several studies during the 1980s and 1990s came up with a 30-year probability for an earthquake in the San Francisco Bay area of between 50 and 90 percent. For a security risk assessment it is enough to note areas of high risk as compared to other areas of the country. For scientists it is a far more difficult task.

10. After hearing the statistics for hurricanes, floods, and earthquakes, these figures may seem exceedingly low. But remember that hurricanes, floods, and earthquakes affect a large area nearly completely, whereas a tornado typically has a narrow swath of destruction.

11. All objects with a temperature above absolute zero generate thermal energy. Humans generate between 7 and 14 microns. PIR motion sensors typically operate within the 4 to 20 micron IR wavelength.

12. These are only the most popular biometrics in use today. Other biometric technologies currently being researched include gait (or walk), vein patterns, DNA, and even odor.

13. CER values can range from near zero to 50 percent. These values are difficult to obtain because there seems to be no freely available test data on a variety of biometric devices. One group, the International Biometric Group, does provide industrywide testing, but the results are contained within a report that must be purchased.

14.   Many experienced security consultants will be tempted to simply review documents and provide comments on discovered security deficiencies but fail to spot missing key elements. It is for this reason that a checklist is used to guide the review and ensure a more complete analysis

15.   For a more complete discussion of how to use the "review documents" approach, refer to section 5.2.2.1.

16.   The security controls required for the proper protection of SCIFs are beyond the scope of this book. The proper place to find this information is in the National Industrial Security Program Operating Manual (NISPOM).

References

[1]   *Perimeter Security Sensor Technologies Handbook*, Defense Advanced Research Projects Agency (DARPA), 1996. www.justnet.org/perimetr/full3.htm

[2]   *Glossary of Security Terms*, ASIS International. www.asisonline.org/library/ glossary/index.xml

[3]   *Physical Security Inspectors Guide*. U.S. Department of Energy, September 2000.

[4]   Mathewson, Stuart B., U.S. earthquake frequency estimation — ratemaking for unusual events, 1999 Casualty Actuarial Society Forum Conference Proceedings.

[5]   *Shore Facilities Ozone-Depleting Substances (ODS) Conversion Guide for Heating, Ventilation, Air-Conditioning and Refrigeration (HVAC&R) and Fire Protection Systems*, January 2002. http://enviro.nfesc.navy.mil/ps/FacilityODSCOnv/ halon.htm

[6]   *National Fire Alarm Code*, NFPA 72(02), National Fire Protection Association, 2002.

[7]   McEwen, R.H.L., Fire alarm and detection systems, *Canadian Building Digest*, CBD-233, August 1984.

[8]   Early Detection, *Data Center Journal*, June 14, 2004.

[9]   U.S. Fire Administration/National Fire Data Center, Non-residential structure fires in 2000, *Topical Fire Research Series*, Vol. 3, issue 10, June 2004. www.usfa.fema.gov

[10] *Fire Protection Design Criteria*, DOE Standard, DoE-STD-1066-99, U.S. Department of Energy, Washington, DC 20585, July 1999.

[11] *National Industrial Security Program Operating Manual (NISPOM)*, DoD 5220.22-M, January 1995. http://www.dss.mil/isec/nispom_0195.htm

[12] Physical Security Standards For Sensitive Compartmented Information Facilities, Director of Central Intelligence Directive (DCID) 6/9-Manual, 18 November 2002.

Chapter 9

Security Risk Analysis

The fourth phase of a security risk assessment is security risk analysis. The security risk analysis depends on all the previous stages to supply the information required to analyze the security risk to the organization. The risk assessment phase consists of techniques and approaches for determining individual and overall risk levels. This process can take many different forms depending upon the security risk assessment method performed. The security risk assessment process will be discussed here by describing the process in the following three steps:

1. Determine risk.
2. Create risk statements.
3. Team review of risk statements.

Each of these steps is described in more detail in the sections that follow.

9.1 Determining Risk

The overall objective of the security risk assessment analysis process is to determine and convey the risk to the organization's assets. While a composite security risk will be determined at a later point in the process, the objective here is to determine the security risk to the organization's assets based on threat/vulnerability pairings. The security risk determination therefore is dependent upon the identified threats and vulnerabilities measured, based on the probability of the threat/vulnerability pair, the value of the asset affected, and the impact that the threat/vulnerability pair will have on the asset.

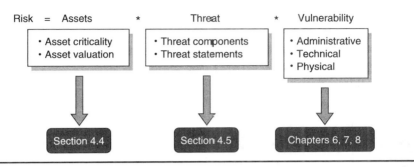

Figure 9.1   Basic risk equation. The basic risk equation computes the relationship between assets, threats, and vulnerabilities. Each of these areas has been covered in a previous section of this book.

This information was determined throughout the data-gathering phase of the security risk assessment. Once the team has all the data in order, the calculation of the security risk can be performed. The basic equation for risk calculation is:

$$\text{Risk} = \text{Assets} * \text{Threat} * \text{Vulnerability}.$$

For several reasons, this simple equation is merely an illustration of the principle that risk is calculated based on an understanding of the asset value, the extent of the threat, and the likelihood of the threat exploiting an existing vulnerability. Various security risk assessment approaches have different approaches for specifying the risk equation variables and for calculating their result.

The methods discussed in this book (e.g., data gathering, reporting, evidence collection) should apply equally well to any existing security risk assessment such as NIST 800-30, FRAP, OCTAVE, and proprietary methods. This book is not intended to create yet another security risk assessment method, but to prepare teams and individuals to participate effectively in any security risk assessment effort.

The basic risk equation simply computes the relationship between asset value, threat frequency, and vulnerability likelihood. This basic equation is illustrated in Figure 9.1. Since each of these areas has been previously covered in this book, it is tempting to think that determining risk is a simple calculation. However, the determination of the value of assets, the frequency of the threat, and the likelihood of a vulnerability existing is clouded by uncertainty.

9.1.1 Uncertainty and Reducing Uncertainty

When dealing with probabilities of threat and impact, we must recognize that the measurements we use (whether quantitative or qualitative) have an element of uncertainty. The agreement as to the probability that a threat will compromise

Sidebar 9.1 Interpreting Requirements

Many security risk assessment projects include a requirement to compare the current security posture against a set of requirements, a regulation, or a standard. These will collectively be referred to as requirements. *Despite the intentions of the requirement authors, security compliance requirements rarely have a straightforward interpretation. Because of the ambiguity of the language an interpretation process or professional judgment is required to resolve areas of confusion.

Some requirements, such as the Common Criteria for Information Technology Security Evaluations, have a formal interpretation process. Such a formal process requires procedures for requests for interpretation, draft and formal rulings, and a catalog of previous rulings.

Other requirements simply depend upon the professional judgment of the security risk assessment team and team leader. The judgment of adequate interpretations is based on the situation and an understanding of the intention of the requirement. Table 9.1 provides an example of the interpretation process.

> * The term "requirements" is used loosely
> here to mean any statement within the
> standard, regulation, or guidance that
> speaks to the security controls that
> should be in the information system being
> assessed.

Table 9.1 Interpretation Process Example. The interpretation process involves an interpretation of the requirement, a discussion of the environment and application a finding, and a recommendation to the organization based on the interpretation.

Step	Discussion/Example
Requirement	Automatic log-off: Implement electronic procedures that terminate an electronic session after a predetermined period of inactivity. HIPAA 164.312(a)(2)(iii)

(Continued)

Table 9.1 (Continued)
Interpretation Process Example

Step	Discussion/Example
Interpretation	The organization must ensure that any session on an organizational information system with PHI is terminated after a reasonable period of inactivity. A reasonable period can be anywhere between 5 and 15 minutes for most sessions. There could be reasonable explanations for why a session would need to be inactive longer (e.g., a batch session that runs long and the system does not recognize the processing as an activity). The termination of the session can take place on any of the following elements of the session: • *The user terminal.* This can be a workstation within the organization's buildings or a remote computer. • *The media.* This could be a modem pool or a LAN, etc. • *The end system.* This could be an organizational information system with PHI.
Discussion	After interviewing the organization's systems administrators it is found that workstations' default configuration currently locks after 15 minutes of inactivity but this is not documented in policy and is not enforced. Session controllers have the capability to automatically disconnect the session after a period of inactivity but are not configured to do so. For some session users this could produce a problem because the line looks inactive but a process could still be running. Use of the automatic log-out feature could impact the business mission for some users.
Findings	The organization *does not* currently meet this requirement because it does not automatically terminate idle and inactive remote sessions.
Recommendation	Use of the system automatic disconnect feature would likely interfere with operations if it is set to a reasonable limit such as 5–15 minutes. However, the organization should set this control to terminate access after 4 hours of recorded inactivity. Because this control does not adequately protect unattended workstations, the organization should document and implement a policy to lock workstations after 5–15 minutes of inactivity.

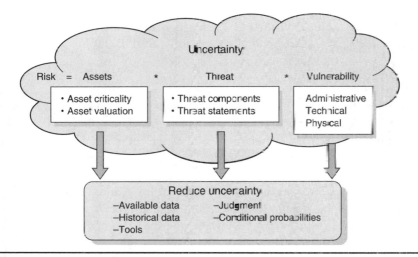

Figure 9.2 Introduction of uncertainty into determining risk. The basic components of the risk equation are clouded by uncertainty. Uncertainty may be reduced by gathering additional information or using consensus techniques.

an asset can be an oversimplification of a more complex measurement. The question may now become, "How sure are you about that probability?"

To continue with a security risk assessment, the assessment team must either reduce or accept uncertainty (see Figure 9.2). In this section we shall discuss various ways for reducing and controlling uncertainty.

9.1.1.1 Review Available Data

If any data is available on specific behavior — use it. Possible sources of data include crime statistics, analysis from previous risk assessments, or knowledge regarding related industries. Be sure to adjust the data up or down for the specific circumstances of the organization and environment. For example, when determining possible employee theft, the team should review records of past employee theft at the organization or at similar organizations.

In some cases the team may be able to find official statistics or actuarial information. Examples of this type of information are given extensively in Chapter 8. Information gathered may have to be extrapolated for the unique environment of the assessed organization. Examples of extrapolated information include reported frequency plus an estimated unreported frequency or official statistics modified by local conditions.

9.1.1.2 Examine Historical Data

Past events provide some indication as to the likelihood of similar events. For example, if employee theft occurred three times last year and no significant safeguards have been put in place since then, it may be reasonable to assume that employee theft has a annual rate of occurrence (ARO) of 3.0.

9.1.1.3 Use Judgment

Although other sources of information may provide some insight as to a number or rating that a specific threat should receive, it really comes down to the use of professional judgment. The security risk assessment team should document their reasons for each likelihood rating and be prepared to defend it to the security risk assessment sponsor.[1]

Various techniques exist for using judgment to reduce uncertainty. These include the Delphi technique, a decision-making process that polls experts individually and gradually works toward a group consensus, and bounding the problem:

- Bounding the Problem — When attempting to determine risk compoent factors through the use of judgment, it is useful to first bound the problem with best and worst case scenarios. The team developing the values should use reasonableness when considering the best and worst case.
- Develop a Probability Distribution — Once the problem has been bound, the team should develop a range of values with probabilities for each value. This is called a probability distribution.

Table 9.2 provides an example of reducing uncertainty through bounding the problem and developing a probability distribution. For example, it is reasonable to consider that a power outage would last a minimum of 5 minutes and a maximum of 2 days.[2] Most power outages are estimated to last less than 1 hour. Experts are polled to determine probable occurrences of various power outage times.

Table 9.2 Probability Distribution. The use of judgment can be improved through the use of a range of values and probability distributions.

Upper and Lower Bound	Range of Values	Probability Distribution
5 minutes	5–10 minutes	7%
	10–15 minutes	8%
	15–30 minutes	36%
	30–60 minutes	18%
	1–2 hours	14%
	2–4 hours	8%
	8–16 hours	6%
	16–24 hours	3%
2 days	1–2 days	2%

The use of probability distributions adds another level of accuracy in the estimation or measurement of security risk to an organization's assets. This additional information allows the use of statistics, probability functions, and mathematical modeling. However, the complexity of these calculations necessitates the use of tools.

9.1.1.4 Use Tools

There are many tools available that can assist in the process of reducing uncertainty. Several examples of these tools include Microsoft Excel,[3] @RISK,[4] RiskWatch,[5] and BDSS.[6] Each of these tools has multiple capabilities to assist in the process of performing a security risk assessment. Microsoft Excel has built-in statistical functions; many plug-ins, such as StatPro and others, allow for the extension of Excel functions to include higher-level statistical modeling such as regression analysis and forecasting. @RISK allows for the modeling of uncertainty in risk assessment decisions, by replacing uncertain values with probability distributions. RiskWatch is risk analysis software that can address complications such as unavailability of information over time, and has built-in values for many standard vulnerabilities and threats. BDSS (Bayesian Decision Support System) integrates the concept of uncertainty into the risk calculations. This is just a small sampling of the many risk assessment tools available. The security risk assessment team should decide if such a tool would be useful to their effort.

9.1.1.5 Use Conditional Probabilities

Some threat/vulnerability pairs should be considered with respect to the chain of events that must occur for the threat/vulnerability pair to ultimately impact the security of the organization's assets. In such a chain of events, each event must occur for the next event to be considered. These are referred to as "conditional probabilities." It is the probabilities of the final event taking place (considering all the other events in the chain), not the first event, that is used as the probabilities for the threat/vulnerability pair.

When determining the probabilities of a threat/vulnerability pair having an impact on the organization's assets, consider the chain of events that must take place for the threat to exploit the vulnerability. For example, consider the threat/vulnerability pair of an ex-employee gaining access to your routers and switches by dialing in and using the administrator password. The probabilities of such an event may seem difficult to determine because there are many factors involved, but, by considering the chain of events, determining the probabilities becomes more tractable.

First, determine the events that must occur for the threat/vulnerability pair to impact the system. In this case the employee would have to be terminated, have knowledge of the passwords, and attempt to access the system before the passwords are changed.

- Conditional Events for Example Threat:
    1. Employee is terminated.
    2. Employee has knowledge of passwords.
    3. Employee has desire to gain access.
    4. Passwords are not changed before employee attempts access.

Second, determine the probabilities of each event (see Table 9.3):

1. Terminated Employees — Continuing with this example, start with how many employees are likely to be terminated this year. In the absence of any other knowledge, like a planned layoff or merger, historical records will provide a fairly accurate measurement. In our example, the organization of 1000 employees has terminated an average of 30 employees per year over the last five years. Most terminations were friendly, such as the employee changing careers or moving away, but about 10 percent of the time the termination was for cause. At this stage we are considering 30 ex-employees per year.

2. Terminated System Administrators — Not all terminated employees would even have access to the router and switch passwords. Only system administrators have such knowledge. 11 percent of the terminated employees were system administrators. At this stage we are considering 3.3 system administrators: 3.0 system administrators terminated and 0.3 terminated for cause.

3. Terminated System Administrators with Desire to Gain Access — Not all terminated system administrators would even want to gain access to the routers and switches of their ex-employer. After all, if they get caught their career (and freedom) could be jeopardized. Here we must use some judgment. Based on experience and intuition, let us say the team comes up with the judgment that 25 percent of the system administrators would have the desire to attempt access. This may seem like a high number, but consider that (a) they might just be "checking" the system to see if the passwords were changed, (b) anyone who would catch them would likely be their friend and may not turn them in, and (c) the system administrator's knowledge of the system allows him or her to believe that they can get around without anyone detecting their presence. The percentage for system administrators terminated for cause increases to 50 percent because the same reasons (a)–(c), apply, but now we have reason (d), they are out to hurt the organization for hurting them. At this point in the chain we are now considering 0.75 terminated system administrators with desire to access the routers and switches and 0.15 system administrators terminated for cause with the same desire.[7]

Table 9.3 Conditional Probabilities. Determining the probability of an ex-employee gaining access to the organization's routers and switches by dialing in and using the administrative password can be a rather difficult figure to develop. The use of conditional probabilities together with some known data reduces the complexity and uncertainty of such an estimate.

Event Number	Event	Probabilities	Discussion
1	Employee is terminated	30 (30 times per year someone is terminated)	The organization (of roughly 1000 employees) has terminated an average of 30 employees a year over the last 5 years. 10% of those employees were terminated for cause.
2	Employee has knowledge of passwords	3 sys. admin. terminated per year 0.3 sys. admin. terminated for cause	Only system administrators have passwords to routers and switches. 11% of the terminated employees were system administrators (for cause termination was proportional).
3	Employee has desire to gain access	0.75 sys. admin. 0.15 sys. admin. for cause	15% of terminated employees desire to gain access, but 25% among sys. admin. 50% of those terminated for cause desire to gain access.
4	Passwords are not changed in time	0.075 sys. admin. 0.015 sys. admin. for cause	Passwords are typically changed prior to the terminated employee leaving the building, but occasionally (10% of the time) personnel performing this duty are busy on other tasks and cannot get to it until the end of the day.
Annual expected breach		0.09	9% chance of this happening per year.

4. Terminated System Administrators with Desire and Means to Gain Access — Fully realizing the dangerous situation of terminated employees with sensitive passwords, this organization has procedures in place to change all passwords on systems if the passwords were known by an employee being terminated. The procedure calls for the system administrators to change the passwords as a part of the termination procedures. However, because system administrators are understaffed and overworked, the procedure is not always completed prior to the employee leaving the

building. About 10 percent of the time the personnel performing this task cannot get to it until the end of the day. It is only in these circumstances that the terminated system administrator can access the system. At this final stage we are now considering 0.075 terminated system administrators with the desire and means to access the routers and switches and 0.015 system administrators terminated for cause with the same desire. This gives us an annual expected breach of the system through this chain of events of 0.09. Put another way, there is a 9 percent chance of this scenario happening.

9.2 Creating Risk Statements

Between asset valuation, threat frequency, vulnerability probability, and impact affect, there are many values or numbers of which to keep track. If the security risk assessment team is using a tool, the tool can be used to keep track of and report the values and numbers. If the team is using a process without an automated tool, then an approach is required to track these values.

One such approach is the creation of security risk statements. A security risk statement is a method of presenting related information in the expression of a security risk. Three examples of security risk statements are given in Table 9.4. In the first example, the security risk statements are informal language expressions combining the threat agent, vulnerability, policy violated, and the asset exposed. This simple set of security risk statements is useful in smaller-scale assessments where there are not numerous security risk statements to be made. Notice that these statements lack the ability to express the impact of the risk,

Table 9.4 Example Risk Statement 1. A security risk statement is a method of presenting related information in the expression of a security risk. This table provides several examples of security risk statements using sentence constructs for threat agents, vulnerabilities, policy violated, and asset exposed.

Threat Agent	Vulnerability	Vulnerability Target	Policy Violated	Asset Exposed
A competitor	may social engineer	the sales office	to reveal	key customer lists
A hacker	may exploit known vulnerabilities	in the remote authentication protocol	to disrupt	remote authentication services
An intruder	may gain access	to the telephone closet	to eavesdrop on	sensitive conversations

the likelihood of the scenario, existing security controls, overall risk, and recommended solutions.

The second approach to developing security risk statements incorporates all of these components into a single row within a spreadsheet. This more complex approach has the advantage of documenting all of the constituent components of a security risk statement, while still providing a reasonably understandable and compact format for what could be a complex set of information.

As with the other approaches presented in this book, these are just a few of the many approaches currently in use by information security professionals. Again, if the team is using a tool or other method, it is likely that the tool or method provides its own approach for consolidating and presenting this information (see Table 9.5).

9.3 Team Review of Security Risk Statements

Because of the large amount of data generally compiled during the data-gathering stage, it is a good idea for the security risk assessment team to divide up the task of creating security risk statements. Generally, the statements can be divided up along the areas of study, that is, administrative, physical, and technical. Further division can be accomplished by subdividing the technical areas according to systems or subgroups of the systems.

Team members should work alone or in small groups (e.g., two people) to create the security risk statements covering the data assigned to them. Once the draft statements are complete, the team leader should compile the complete list and distribute them to all team members. The next task is for the entire team to review the draft statements and arrive at a consensus for the statements and the data values contained in the statements.

9.3.1 Obtaining Consensus

Arriving at a consensus for the elements within the security risk statements is an important step in the security risk analysis process. This step ensures that all members of the team have a chance to express their findings. Furthermore, obtaining a team consensus on the security risk statements allows all team members to gain a perspective of the overall security risk of the organization through a better understanding of all of the elements.

While obtaining consensus on these statements, the team should be wary of too much overlap. The following advice on obtaining security risk statement consensus may prove useful during this exercise:

- Avoid Overlap — While reviewing draft security risk statements, the team may find that some security risk statements may completely overlap or duplicate others. In this case the statements should be reduced to a single

Table 9.5   Example Risk Statement 2. A security risk statement is a method of presenting related information in the expression of a security risk. Below are several example security risk statements using a security risk assessment approach modified from Department of Defense Methods.

Ref. No.	Area	Vulnerability	Threat Source	Impact (1–4)			Existing Controls	Likelihood		Risk	Recommendation
				Conf.	Integrity	Availability		Attempt (1–4)	Exploit (1–4)		
8	Physical security	Telephone demarcation: access to telephone closet by guests	Cleared customers, visitors, and maintenance	Access to internal networks; access to internal phone conversations		Disruption of telephone service	Area restricted to cleared customers	3: Remote	1: Easy	1	Add locking cabinets to telephone and network connections in shared area
					1: System Disruption						
32	Admin. security	Hackers may gain unauthorized access to information system through password guessing and social engineering	Hackers, social engineers, customers	Access to sensitive information	Threatens integrity of resources and sensitive information	Interruption of service, monetary losses, credibility losses	Employee awareness of sensitive information	2: Possible	2: Moderate	1	Create and enforce strong password policies, consider two-factor authentication
								C: Occasional			
					1: Serious Risk. Exposure of sensitive information			B: Probable			Create and apply a strong security awareness program
56	Technical security	Hackers may gain unauthorized access through RPC call services	Hackers or disgruntled employees	Access to sensitive information	Modify sensitive data	Interruption of service, monetary losses, credibility losses	Some logging with minimal review	1: Likely	1: Easy	1	Create firewall rulesets, apply latest patches, harden servers, and install IDS
								A: Frequent			
				1: Serious Risk. Exposure of sensitive information.							

statement. In fact, the team should institute some type of ordering of the statements (e.g., according to subject) so that all duplicates may be found.

- Group Like Findings — There are likely to be some components of the system with many findings. For example, it is typical to find many vulnerabilities within the external interfaces provided by the information system that can be addressed through the latest software patch. Although a security vulnerability tool will produce volumes of information on each of these findings, it is more useful to the customer to group these findings into relatively few findings with common recommendations, such as install latest patches.

9.3.2 Deriving Overall Security Risk

Lastly, the security risk assessment team should derive an overall security risk. The overall security risk measurement should be consistent with the statement of work and the ranges used to describe individual security risks. For organizations regulated by information security laws such as HIPAA, the overall security risk should indicate a level of compliance. For all other organizations, the overall security risk level should indicate a relative security risk, for example, Moderate Security Risk, and a comparison to others in the same industry. The details provided in such a measurement do not need to be listed. This only has to provide the decision makers an indication of their current security risk in comparison to their security risk tolerance.

Notes

1. This last approach for determining the likelihood of an event is one of the main reasons why many security professionals opt for the qualitative security risk assessment approach. This is a realization that even if you choose a number such as 3.0, it is still based on judgment and therefore is subjective.

2. An example where this would be a reasonable assumption is in an organization that has a UPS and 2 days of fuel for on-site generators. A power outage of less than 5 minutes can be handled by a UPS. A power outage of more than 2 days would, in all likelihood, be the result of a major natural disaster and require another level of support.

3. XL is a trademark of the Microsoft Corporation.

4. @RISK is a trademark of the Palisade Corporation.

5. RiskWatch is a trademark of Expert Systems Software, Inc.

6. BDSS (Bayesian Decision Support System) is a trademark of OPA, Inc.

7. Expressions such as "0.75 terminated system administrators" may seem strange because we typically discuss humans in whole numbers. However this expression is interpreted to mean "on average we would expect 0.75 terminated system administrators to attempt to gain access per year" or put another way there

is a 75% chance that at least 1 terminated system administration will attempt to gain access this year.

References

[1]   *CMS Information Security Risk Assessment Methodology,* Department of Health and Human Services, Centers for Medicare and Medicaid Services, Version 1.1, September 2002.

[2]   Krause, Micki, and Tipton, Harold F., *Handbook of Information Security Management,* ISBN: 0849399475.

[3]   *Approach to Risk: Position Paper on the Approach to Risk, Methodologies Dealing with This and the Technical and Community Information Required for Implementation,* Environmental Risk Management Authority, New Zealand, December 2002, ER-OP-03-02 12/02.

[4]   *Preparing Information on Risks, Costs and Benefits for Applications Under the Hazardous Substances and New Organisms Act 1996,* Environmental Risk Management Authority, New Zealand, July 2000, ISBN 0-478-21507-1, ER-TG-03-01 07/00.

[5]   Common Criteria for Information Technology Security Evaluation, Version 2.1, CCIMB-99-031, August 1999.

[6]   *Guidelines for Automatic Data Processing Physical Security and Risk Management,* Federal Information Processing Standards Publication 31 (FIPS Pub. 31), National Bureau of Standards, June 1974.

Chapter 10

Security Risk Mitigation

Once the security risk to an organization's assets is known, the security risk assessment team must develop recommendations for reducing this risk. These recommendations are referred to as safeguards. This chapter discusses the selection of safeguards, the compiling safeguard solution sets, justifying the implementation of safeguards, and an understanding of the security risk parameters regulating the acceptance of safeguard recommendations.

10.1 Selecting Safeguards

Safeguards are selected based on their effectiveness in addressing the indicated security risks. The pool of available safeguards to employ is infinite and is expanding all the time. The security risk assessment team can only suggest those safeguards with which it is familiar. The more experienced the team, the larger the pool of safeguards it has to draw from during this stage of the security risk assessment. The safeguards listed in Chapters 6, 7, and 8 are a good start, but the team should not limit itself to those listed in this book.

An approach for more systematically considering possible safeguards is to consider safeguards within the people, process, and technology categories. The people, process, and technology categories are used rather extensively within the information technology arena, and for good reason. These categories effectively describe three separate areas from which information technology is affected.

These categories are a good fit for framing the discussion of safeguard selection.[1]

- People Safeguards — The team should consider people-based safeguards such as qualified and trusted individuals.
- Process Safeguards — The team should consider process-based safeguards such as security awareness training, account review, or change management.
- Technology Safeguards — The team should consider technology-based safeguards such as two-factor authentication, intrusion detection systems, or SPAM filtering.

10.2 Safeguard Solution Sets

The discussion regarding safeguard selections above assumes a one-to-one relationship between vulnerabilities and safeguards. For example, systems are vulnerable to obvious holes — apply latest security patches. However, the relationship between safeguards and vulnerabilities is many-to-many (see Table 10.1). This means that some safeguards address more than a single vulnerability and some vulnerabilities are addressed by several safeguards. In fact, the application of several safeguards to address a single vulnerability is the implementation of the design principle of defense in depth.

Determining a recommended mix of safeguards to effectively address the identified vulnerabilities can be something of a trial-and-error exercise. Available tools typically supply scenario-based or "what if" calculations that can provide some measure of solution set analysis. Team members with a working knowledge of the application and effectiveness of current industry solutions will be of particularly good use at this stage. Although some safeguards have well-known properties that can be easily modeled and presented in tools and methodologies, many others are

Table 10.1 The Many-to-Many Relationship between Safeguards and Threats. Any given remedial measure can address more than one threat. Conversely, any threat can be addressed by multiple remedial measures.

Remedial Measures	Threats				
	Fire	*Internal Theft*	*External Theft*	*Hurricane*	*Sabotage*
Fire detection system	×				×
Loss control team	×			×	×
Roving guard patrol	×	×	×		×
Intrusion detectors		×	×		×
Personnel screening		×			×
On-site power generator				×	×
Backup plan	×			×	×

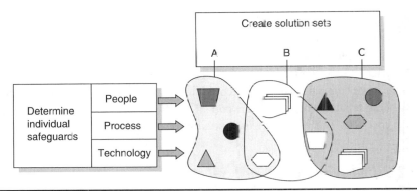

Figure 10.1 Individual safeguards and solution sets. The security risk assessment team should identify many individual safeguards for addressing the identified vulnerabilities, but to consider how those safeguards can work together the team should then consider candidate solution sets.

new or have unique application factors that are not accounted for in the tools and methods (see Figure 10.1).

A solution set is a composition of complementary and compensating safeguards that work well together to address the identified risks and provide cost-effective solutions to reduce the security risk to an acceptable level. The security risk assessment team should work together to produce a variety of safeguard solution sets prior to settling on a recommended set. The three factors that will determine the recommended set are cost, effectiveness, and accepted res dual risk.

10.2.1 Safeguard Cost Calculations

Many security risk assessments include (as specified in their statement of work) a rough calculation of the safeguard cost as well as the indication of the effectiveness of the safeguard. The cost of a safeguard includes several components, namely, purchase price, installation charges, training costs, operational costs, and maintenance costs. Each of these safeguard costs is described below:

- Purchase Price — Many technology-based safeguards are additional system components that must be purchased. The purchase price is simply the cost to purchase the safeguard component from the vendor.
- Installation Charges — Many safeguards have an associated cost for installing or implementing the safeguard. The installation cost is the cost of integrating the safeguard into the organization's information system.
- Training Costs — The implementation and operation of many safeguards will require that the organization's staff receive training on the safeguard. The training costs are the cost associated with properly training the affected staff on the security safeguard.

- Operational Costs — All safeguards have some operational cost associated with them. The operational cost is the day-to-day cost of ensuring that the safeguard is working as intended.
- Maintenance Costs — Many safeguards have an associated cost for maintaining the safeguard. This could be in the form of a software update/maintenance contract or the cost of yearly maintenance. The maintenance cost is the annual cost of maintaining the safeguard in good working order.

10.2.2 Justifying Safeguard Selections

Once the effectiveness of safeguards and safeguard solutions sets is known, the next task is to justify the recommended safeguards to the senior management of the organization.

10.2.2.1 Justification through Judgment

Safeguard justification typically comes down to a cost-benefit analysis, but there are many safeguards that should be implemented without the cost of justifying them through a cost-benefit analysis. These safeguards include those required by law, and low and moderate cost safeguards.

- Required by Law — For those organizations within regulated industries, many of the recommended safeguards are simply those required by the regulations. For example, all financial institutions with individual financial records must comply with the Gramm-Leach-Bliley Act, which requires, among other things, annual security awareness training. It would be a waste of effort to perform a cost-benefit analysis on security awareness training. Rather the organization should accept the safeguard because it is required by law.
- Low Cost with Material Benefit — Many safeguards have a very low cost and a clear benefit to the organization's security posture. Such safeguards should not undergo rigorous cost-benefit analysis calculations in order to justify their implementation. These safeguards should simply be accepted at face value and implemented to improve the protection of the organization's assets. For example, applying security patches to servers has a relatively low cost and certainly provides a clear benefit to the organization's security posture.
- Moderate Cost with Critical Reductions in Risk — Other safeguards have a moderate or reasonable cost with the potential to avoid a fatal loss. Again these safeguards should not be subject to cost-benefit analysis and instead should be accepted as an improvement to the organization's security program. For example, implementing an effective security awareness program has a moderate cost but provides a great potential for

avoiding fatal losses through social engineering, user error, and system misuse.

The use of safeguard justification through judgment should not be overlooked. Even though there exist formulas for determining safeguard cost and approaches for estimating safeguard effectiveness, it is not always in the best interest of the organization to spend valuable engineering time on the exercise of formally justifying all recommendations. Many business decisions are based on the judgment of experienced and trusted consultants. In many instances it makes sense to take the recommendations as presented without asking for extensive and costly additional analysis. For example, organizations in the early stage of developing a security program to protect their assets are likely to have predictable gaps in their security program such as security policies, awareness training, adequate staff and review of logs. If the conclusions of the security risk assessment recommend these improvements, most organizations would be well advised to get busy implementing, instead of calling for more data.

On the other hand, there are times when a more complete cost-benefit analysis is required.

10.2.2.2 Cost–Benefit Analysis

Cost–benefit analysis is a precise method for determining and comparing the value and cost of a proposed safeguard. Cost-benefit analysis, therefore, provides a quantitative method for justifying proposed safeguards. But this precision comes at a cost and has several required components:

- Common Unit of Measurement — A cost-benefit analysis is a mathematical comparison of costs and benefits and requires that all costs and benefits be expressed or converted into a common unit of measurement. The unit of measurement used could be risk or even societal benefit, but it is typically dollars. In the case of dollars as a common unit of measurement, all dollars must be expressed in terms of "today's dollars." Although this expression may sound like a complicated economic concept, it is actually quite simple and is based on the concept that being paid a dollar today is worth more than being paid a dollar next year. This concept is referred to as present value of money.
- Estimating the Costs — When performing the cost–benefit analysis for any recommended safeguard, the complete costs of the safeguard must be accounted for. These costs include all costs over the life-cycle or useful life of the safeguard and include acquisition costs, implementation costs, training costs, operational costs, and residual risk costs.
- Estimating the Benefits — When performing the cost–benefit analysis for any recommended safeguard, the complete benefits of the safeguard must

be accounted for as well. These benefits include all benefits over the life cycle or useful life of the safeguard and include not only reduction in threat frequency and threat impact, but also nonsecurity gains such as productivity gains, staffing reductions, and improved organizational effectiveness.[2]

- Discount Costs and Benefits — The costs and benefits of the recommended safeguard are not required or realized right away. Some costs or benefits are attributed to the start of the safeguard implementation project, while others are applied later in its life cycle. As discussed above, a dollar two years from now is worth less than a dollar today and its exact value depends upon the rate of inflation or return you could otherwise get for investing the dollar somewhere else. The technique of converting future dollar costs and revenues to today's dollars is called discounting. This next step requires that the costs and benefits be discounted.
- Compute Cost Benefit — Project have both negative cash flows (expenses) and positive cash flows (revenues). These cash flows can be realized at different times. In order to compare these values fairly all cash flows are normalized to 'today's dollars' (NPV). Even projects with positive NPV may not be selected by management. Management has a limited budget from which to fund projects only those with the best returns get funding. The hurdle rates for funding within the organization is called the internal rate of return (IRR).

Sidebar 10.1 Economic Terms

- *Present Value of Money (PV).* PV relates the value of future dollars to a present-day dollar. An investment that would pay $1000 five years from today and earns 10 percent per year interest has a present value of $620.
- *Net Present Value of Money (NPV).* NPV relates the combined negative and positive cash flows from the project in today's dollars. A positive net present value indicates a worthwhile project while a negative NPV indicates that the organization should forgo the project.
- *Internal Rate of Return (IRR).* IRR is the return an organization requires to invest in internal projects.

The example in Tables 10.2 and 10.3 shows the information and calculations necessary for a cost-benefit analysis. In the example below, the safeguard of implementing a secure coding effort is reviewed. The costs of a secure coding effort include the development of standards, training, additional coding steps, and additional review steps. The benefits of this effort include reduction in rework

Table 10.2 Estimating Costs. The costs of a secure coding project include the development of standards, training, additional coding steps, and additional review steps.

Estimate Costs	1st Year	2nd Year	3rd Year	4th Year	5th Year	Assumptions
Secure coding standards	$8,000	$1,000	$1,000	$1,000	$1,000	1st year 80 hours to develop (in-house); 10 hours to maintain in later years
Secure coding training	$14,000	$7,000	$3,500	$3,500	$3,500	1st year: 20 developers; 2 sessions; same course 1 session next year; self-taught from tapes in later years
Impact on coding	$200,000	$100,000	$50,000	$50,000	$50,000	1st year: 10% additional effort; 2 extra developers; savings over later years due to organizational maturity
Impact on review cycle	$200,000	$200,000	$200,000	$200,000	$200,000	$20,000 per app., 10 apps. per year
Total costs	$422,000	$308,000	$254,500	$254,500	$254,500	

Table 10.3 Estimating Benefits. The benefits of a secure coding project include reduction in rework and reduction of threat impact.

Estimate Benefits	1st Year	2nd Year	3rd Year	4th Year	5th Year	Assumptions
Reduction in rework	—	$120,000	$240,000	$360,000	$360,000	1st year no reduction (learning curve); 2nd year, 10% reduction; 3rd, 20% reduction; 4th and 5th, 30% reduction; rework is 30% of coders' time
Reduction of threat impact:						
Disclosure	$180,000	$180,000	$180,000	$180,000	$180,000	$10,000/disclosure; ALE = 1.5 disclosures per app.; reduction = 60%
Integrity	$75,000	$75,000	$75,000	$75,000	$75,000	$5,000/mistake; ALE −1 mistake/app.; reduction = 75%
Availability	$125,000	$125,000	$125,000	$125,000	$125,000	$25,000/hour; ALE = 1 hour/app.; Reduction in DOS attacks = 50%
Total benefits	$380,000	$500,000	$620,000	$740,000	$740,000	
Total costs	$422,000	$308,000	$254,500	$254,500	$254,500	
Net cost/benefit	**$(42,000)**	**$192,000**	**$365,500**	**$485,500**	**$485,500**	

and reduction of threat impact. The net present value of the effort is computed based on the expected incomes or costs over a number of years:

$$NPV = \sum_{i=1}^{n} \frac{incomes_i}{(1 + rate)^i}$$

The net present value for the incomes presented in Tables 10.2 and 10.3 and a rate of return of 8 percent = $1,103,146. This means that, all costs considered, the secure coding effort has a positive present-day value of over $1 million. Some organizations use the internal rate of return (IRR) as a gating factor for projects. The advantage of the IRR approach is that the organization is able to prioritize all possible projects for the available capital. The IRR s based on the return of a similar investment. The IRR for the secure coding effort is 529 percent.[3]

10.3 Establishing Risk Parameters

It is the duty of senior management to accept the security risk to the organization's assets. With this in mind, the security risk assessment team must have a good indication as to the security risk adversity of the organization's senior management. Recall earlier (see Table 4.2) that the business mission was discussed in terms of risk acceptance. A "tier 1" organization was deemed to have a low risk acceptance, meaning that the senior management would likely prefer to implement almost any reasonable safeguard to address vulnerabilities, whereas "tier 3" organizations were deemed to have a high risk acceptance, meaning that the senior management would likely prefer to implement only those safeguards absolutely necessary. The organization's level of risk acceptance should be considered when selecting recommended safeguards.

The security risk for each vulnerability found during the data-gathering phase can be addressed through one of four ways:

1. Reduce Risk — implement recommended safeguard to reduce specific risk.
2. Assign Risk — purchase insurance to assign or transfer the risk to another party.
3. Accept Risk — based on business mission and other factors, accept the identified risk.
4. Avoid Risk — avoid the risk by eliminating the risk cause, for example, shutting down a vulnerable system.

Notes

1. The categories are sometimes extended to include "environment" as well.
2. There is a significant level of difficulty associated with equating reductions in security risk to the common unit of measurement — money. Judgment will

need to be applied to make the conversions from qualitative to quantitative. In such a case, any assumptions used for the conversion should be well documented.
3. Microsoft Excel has functions for both net present value and internal rate of return, namely, NPV(rate, [value1], [value2],) and IRR(values).

References

[1] Krause, Micki, and Tipton, Harold F., *Handbook of Information Security Management*, ISBN: 0849399475
[2] "Cost-Benefit Analysis Guide for NIH IT Projects," May 1999. www.wwwoirm.nih.gov/itmra/cbaguide.html

Chapter 11

Security Risk Assessment Reporting

To the customer of the security risk assessment the project is not complete until it is documented. One of the most important elements of the security risk assessment effort is the reporting of the results. The security risk assessment team may have a clear understanding of the risks to the organization and the safeguards that should be employed, but that information must be conveyed to the organization in a clear and effective manner.

Recall that a security risk assessment is an objective analysis of the effectiveness of the current security controls that protect an organization's assets and a determination of the probability of losses to those assets. The objective of the security risk assessment is to provide information regarding risks to the organization's assets to senior management in support of their safeguard selection decisions or risk acceptance. Clear and effective security risk assessment reporting requires that the contents of the report be perceived as accurate, nonthreatening, relevant, and unambiguous. Each of these aspects of a quality report is discussed below.

11.1 Cautions in Reporting

A security risk assessment team can deliver a technically accurate report but still miss the objective of the security risk assessment effort by alienating those who receive the information or those who provide support to those senior managers. The security risk assessment team must be careful not only about what they say but also how they say it. The discussion below is meant to provide some advice on framing the assessment results in a manner that will be well received:

- Avoid Pointing Fingers — Again, the objective of the security risk assessment is to determine risk and recommend safeguards, not to assign blame. The security risk assessment team should avoid statements that may be interpreted as assigning blame (see Table 11.1).
- Avoid Delay in Reporting — Although security risk assessment reports include tactical and strategic analysis, many of the observations, findings, and recommendations are operational. This means that time is of the essence in delivering the security risk assessment report. On the other hand, the security risk assessment team needs to ensure that the report is accurate. Therefore, it is essential to create a draft report that can be delivered for initial customer review with the expectation that some components of the draft report may need to be revised to ensure accuracy and completion of the deliverable objectives. This first draft should be delivered without delay. Too much time elapsed between the last interaction with the organization and the first draft of the report leads to an impression of irrelevance of the report. The following quote, taken from Rochester

Table 11.1 Nonconfrontational, Nonjudgmental Risk Statements. The security risk assessment team must avoid confrontational or judgemental findings. Remember the objective of the assessment is to prioritize risks and not to assign blame.

Avoid Phrases Like	Instead Use Phrases Like
Finding. Administrators in group A failed to properly harden all servers in their area.	*Finding.* Procedures for hardening servers in group A were not completely effective. *Evidence.* Some servers in group A were not hardened in accordance with the stated policy.
Finding. Bad user habits leave passwords written in the clear around their workstations.	*Finding.* Security awareness training is not completely effective for all users. *Evidence.* Many user workstations areas had recorded passwords in plain sight (e.g., sticky notes on monitors, taped to pull-out drawer).

Institute of Technology's first experience with security risk assessment vendors, demonstrates the importance of timely delivery of the security risk assessment report:

"Some analysis was no longer relevant by the time the final report was delivered .... Our vendor estimated the delivery of the final report to take about three times the amount of time spent during the onsite interview and scanning phase."[1]

- Include Positive Findings — The security risk assessment report is an extremely important tool for the senior management of the organization. However, much like an audit report, it is filled with a list of many areas for improvement. The security risk assessment team must understand that a list of all these findings in a single report, delivered to the senior management of an organization, is understandably met with a mixed reaction from those who will eventually be asked to implement many of the recommendations.

11.2 Pointers in Reporting

Too many engineers believe that the important work is in the data gathering and analysis and forget that nothing matters unless it is communicated effectively. Security risk assessment reports are especially difficult to create because they are based on technical information that needs to reach both managerial and technical audiences. A few tips are provided below to assist the team in preparing a quality document:

- Use Tables and Figures — Many ideas are best presented in a table or a figure. Also understand that about half your audience will gain most of their information through visuals. Use them generously. Be sure to refer to every table or figure in the text. Label tables and figures correctly and consistently. Include a list of tables after the table of contents.
- Use Consistent Terminology — In any field there exist many ways to say the same thing. Within security risk assessments, the terms "safeguards", "countermeasures", and "compensating controls" are used interchangeably. This is fine between other professionals, but in a report to a diverse audience the switching from one term to another can completely lose your audience. It is a good idea for the team leader to produce a term sheet to be used throughout the report. The term sheet should cover technical terms to be used, as well as the long and short name to be used for the customer, the name of computer systems, and the name of locations.

11.3 Report Structure

The structure of the report can greatly enhance its readability and usability. Because the report is designed for different audiences, it should have different sections for each type of audience. These include executives and technical resources.

11.3.1 Executive-Level Report

The executive report is clearly designed for the senior management of the organization. As such, the executive section should cover the information the senior management requires to make an informed decision. The following recommendations should be followed when compiling the executive summary:

- Length — The executive management section is typically a 2–4-page summary of the entire report.
- Key Elements — Describe the purpose of the assessment, the assessment approach, major findings, recommendations, and next steps.
- Provide Clear Recommendations — The executives are quite comfortable making decisions based on recommendations and available information. They are typically not comfortable with analysis that provides no clear recommendation. You are the expert — state your opinion.
- Technical Detail — The executive summary should never contain detailed technical information. However, the report should be structured so that finding detail on high-level findings and recommendations is easy.

11.3.2 Base Report

The main body of the report should provide almost all of the information gathered during the assessment process. The structure of the report could be dictated by the statement of work. If so, follow the dictated structure. If not, the following recommended structure could be followed:

- Introduction — This section provides an introduction to the security risk assessment. It should contain all the information required for someone to come up to speed on the reason for the project and what the project entails. Those familiar with the project should be able to skip this section without missing any required information to make security risk decisions. This section should include the following subsections:
  - Background — Provide a background on why and how the security risk assessment is being performed. This may include regulatory requirements or other driving factors.
  - Security Risk Management Overview — Provide a primer on risk management to properly frame the role of the security risk assessment.

Section 1.4.1 provides a nice example of the security risk management overview.

- Scope — Provide a description of the scope of the assessment. This scope should be taken directly from the statement of work and logical and physical boundaries as well as coverage (e.g., administrative, physical, and technical) and rigor descriptions.
- Approach — Provide a description of the security risk assessment approach. If you are using a common approach or tool, use the standard description of the security risk assessment approach provided by the product literature. If you are using a proprietary method you may use the marketing literature or proposal response language.
- Site Characteristics — Describe the existing physical safeguards, environmental factors, and geographic location of the information systems to be assessed. This should include facility access controls, visitor procedures, restricted areas, power sources, safety features, and environmental systems.
- Information System Characteristics — Describe the existing technical safeguards. This should include data classification, virus protection, backup software, identification and authentication systems, and all other technical controls.
- Organizational Characteristics — Describe the existing administrative safeguards. This should include policies, procedures, and security activities currently performed by the organization's personnel or outsourced to trusted partners. A organizational chart highlighting the security organization should also be included and discussed.
- Asset and Threat Analysis — Include a report on the asset and threat analysis of the organization.
- Vulnerability Analysis — Include a report on the identified vulnerabilities.
- Security Risk Analysis — Include a discussion of the security risk analysis results. This could be recorded in tabular or other formats.
- Countermeasure Recommendations — Include a list of countermeasures recommended.

11.3.3 Appendices and Exhibits

A report can be made more clear by including details for those who want additional information to support the findings. Appendices can include anything that would assist in making the case for any recommendations in the main report body. Below are the typical appendices of a security risk assessment report:

- Resources and Evidence Information —Provide a list of the evidence used to determine asset values, threat statements, and identified vulnerabilities. Many of the findings within the report will be accepted at face value because of the credentials of the security risk assessment team and the recognition of the problem areas from the organization. However, some findings may be questioned. The evidence appendix can provide the required information to back up the findings of the team. Production of this appendix throughout the security risk assessment process is imperative to ensure its accuracy.

- Detailed Findings — Many findings are too detailed for the body of the report, but provide information that will be needed by the organization. For example, the output of a vulnerability scanner provides in-depth information that will be needed by the organization's administrator fixing the problems.
- Cost Estimate Worksheets — If considerable effort was put into calculations such as cost-benefit analysis or recommended countermeasure estimates, these calculations can be recorded in an appendix.
- References — It is common practice to provide a list of references used and cited throughout the report.

11.4 Document Review Methodology: Create the Report Using a Top-Down Approach

The first description of what the customer expects in the final security risk assessment report is in the statement of work (SOW). Although the SOW does not provide great detail as to the contents of the report, the project manager should ensure that the final report meets the minimum description contained in the SOW.

A good start for the report development is a description of what the report will look like: format, approximate length, key concerns of the customer, details contained within, and so on. This information is captured in a document specification. The document specification should be reviewed and approved by the customer. The customer may comment on certain elements of the document specification such as the key concerns or the extent to which recommendations will provide details. Comments such as these should be encouraged and even solicited from the customer. A careful review and wording of the document specification assists in a greater understanding of the intended contents of the final deliverable.

The security assessment team leader should negotiate requested changes to the document specification to address the comments of the customer and seek approval of the revised document specification. Once approval has been obtained, the document specification becomes the new deliverable description. This is advantageous to both the customer and the assessment team because it is a refinement of the SOW. Any differences between what is expected and what is planned to be delivered should be dealt with as early as possible.

The next level of document development is an annotated outline. These refinements of the deliverable will lay out the topics to be covered in the document and the order in which they are presented. Moreover, an annotated outline contains a one- or two-sentence description of the document sections to more clearly identify the topic to be covered. The document authors should not assume that a section title alone explains its contents. For example, a section of a risk assessment report called "security controls" could have a sub-section entitled "security policies." It is not immediately clear if this section is intended to discuss rules and regulations that govern the behavior of authorized individuals or if this section is referring to the rulesets for the firewalls. As "security policies" is an overloaded term, different individuals could infer quite different meanings. This inference regarding the contents of the final deliverable would lead to a miscommunication and perhaps ultimately to a dissatisfaction or rejection of the final report.

11.4.1 Document Specification

A document specification is a formal document describing the deliverables of the engagement. Even though the deliverable may have been listed in the statement of work, the document specification is a useful document that can lead to project efficiencies through increased communication and feedback. The document specification documents the following aspects and details of the security risk assessment report to be created and delivered:

- Project — The official name of the project. This should be consistent with the statement of work and be used on site as well. Use of a consistent name can eliminate confusion, especially if there are multiple assessment projects within the organization at any one time.
- Audience — Clearly state the primary and secondary audience of the document. In the case of a security risk assessment, the primary audience is the senior management of the organization being assessed and the secondary audience is the staff who will be asked to implement some of the controls described in the report. An understanding of the audience helps to ensure that the report is compiled and written in a manner that assists the audience in reading, understanding, and using the document, for example, inclusion of an executive summary and a technical appendix.
- Key Topics — List any specific considerations for this particular assessment that the team or the customer should be aware of, for example, "This assessment is being performed as a pre-audit for a Sarbanes-Oxley assessment." Such instructions give the project leader and the team members a heads-up for unique considerations within the environment.
- Production Issues — Identify any specific production or delivery issues regarding the final or intermediate deliverables. For example, identify the format, number of copies, and delivery method for the final report. Mention here if a formal presentation is expected and if other formats of the report, for example, slides or a summary are expected.

- References and Prototypes — List any references such as regulations or security risk assessment methods to be followed. Also list any previous work such as last year's security risk assessment that could be used to garner information.

The sample document specification in Table 11.2 illustrates the format and use of a document specification in structuring the document development methodology.

11.4.2 Draft

The development of a draft security risk assessment report is essential to the success of the project. A draft report provides two important functions:

- Immediate Feedback — The draft security risk assessment report provides an immediate feedback to the customer for security gaps of high risk. If the assessment team has uncovered and documented high-risk security gaps that should be addressed immediately, the draft report is a useful vehicle for delivering a documented record and recommendations for addressing these areas. For example, a draft report should contain the results of vulnerability scans and recommendations for patches.
- Opportunity for Correction — In the course of reviewing documents, performing interviews, inspecting controls, observing behavior, and testing controls, mistakes will be made by the security risk assessment team. Those mistakes may be as simple as a misspelling of the name of an interviewee to as complex as documenting the current system architecture. In either case it is important to get the facts right so that the findings may be considered without undue prejudice.

11.4.3 Final

The final security risk assessment report is the corrected version of the draft report. The team leader should be careful to ensure that the final report only contains those corrections from the draft that have been discussed with the customer. This point is important and deserves clarification. It is not necessary that the final report findings are accepted or approved by the customer, but it is necessary that they be discussed with the customer and that the customer has been given an opportunity to clarify any misunderstandings.

The objectivity of the security risk assessment is essential to its value. The team must ensure that the final security risk assessment documents the security risk assessment team's beliefs and findings.

Table 11.2   Document Specification Example

Project: 081503001 — ABC Corporation Security Risk Assessment
Title: ABC Corporation Security Risk Assessment
Type: Security Risk Assessment Report

Audience:
- **Primary:** ABC Corporation management will use the findings of this report to determine required changes in their security program. Specifically, they will look for existing vulnerabilities and how to patch them; missing elements of the security program and how to implement them; and residual risk and how to mitigate it.
- **Secondary:** This document will be used in subsequent efforts to assess and improve the security posture of the ABC Corporation. Secondary audience may include security engineers/auditors and managed security vendors.

Purpose/Problem Statement:
- Assess ABC Corporation's current security architecture. ABC Corporation wants to be certain that it has done due diligence in analyzing its current security architecture.
- Provide recommendations for solutions to security deficiencies. Provide options, recommendations, and proposed solutions necessary to provide a secure environment.
- ABC Corporation also wants to prepare itself for a mandatory SAS70 Type I audit that will be performed early next year.

Key Topics
- Executive summary highlighting the most pertinent issues, high-level findings, and an assessment of the overall security posture of the network.
- The body of the report will provide a description of the approach, findings sorted by area, recommendations for improvements, and appendices containing detailed findings.
- This report will give ABC Corporation a straightforward description of the actions needed to address areas of concern.
- Specifically, the report will summarize the customer's security needs, identify relevant threats and vulnerabilities given the customer's current architecture, operational procedures, and risk level, specify architectural improvements and considerations, and summarize findings and recommendations, providing a framework for moving forward. The report will be organized as follows
  - Introduction (background, security risk management overview, scope, approach)
  - Site characteristics
  - Information system characteristics
  - Organizational characteristics
  - Asset and threat analysis
  - Vulnerability analysis
  - Security risk analysis
  - Countermeasure recommendations

(Continued)

Table 11.2 (Continued)
Document Specification Example

Specific Considerations:
Project management, project contributors, and document reviewers need to be aware of cost and time constraints and the impact of overages on other tasks.

Document Specification History:
Date: V1.0 Initial draft document specification
Date: V1.1 Changed _ in response to _

Production Issues:
- **Review:** Delivery relies upon timely review of document specification and rough draft of the assessment report by ABC Corporation.
- **Up-to-date:** Assessment findings and solution recommendations are based on available information of existing products and services, and known vulnerabilities at the time of the review.
- **Coordination:** Various sections of the report will rely on input from several different security engineers. However, recommendations for overall solutions will overlap these areas. Coordination in findings and recommendations is necessary for overall recommended security plan.
- **Changing Environment:** Assessment requires a freeze on the scope of the assessment. This includes the infrastructure, policies, organization, and configurations. The assessment team lead must be notified of any changes that will take effect during the assessment. We would expect such changes to follow a change control process.

References/Prototypes:
1. *ABC Corporation/Veridyn Inc. Statement of Work for Security Assessment*, August 15, 2003.
2. *Site Security Handbook, RFC 2196*, Network Working Group, B. Fraser, September 1997. http://www.faqs.org/rfcs/rfc2196.html
3. *Risk Management Guide: Recommendations of the National Institute of Standards and Technology*, NIST Special Publication 800-30, 1st Public Exposure Draft — June 2001 http://csrc.nist.gov/publications/drafts/riskmgmtguide-draft.doc
4. *The 60 Minute Network Security Guide: First Steps Towards a Secure Network Environment*, Systems and Network Attack Center (SNAC), October 16, 2001.

Resources:
Project lead:	Michelle Lee
Document lead:	Thomas Benton
Principal writers:	Kasey Nicole
Secondary writers:	Rachel Rose
Technical support:	J. F. Duit
Reviewer(s):	Internal: Billy Gilmore
	Customer: ABC (TBD)

11.5 Assessment Brief

It is recommended that the final security risk assessment report be presented to the organization's senior management. The assessment briefing is outlined below:

- Attendees — The attendees for the security risk assessment briefing should include representatives from the organization's senior management and the security risk assessment team. At a minimum the attendance should include the project sponsor and the security risk assessment team leader.
- Meeting Agenda — The presentation of the final report should be rather straightforward and follow the outline of the report itself. The meeting should start with introductions and a brief explanation of the effort. The security risk assessment team leader should briefly describe the process of the security risk assessment and then provide a review of the high-level findings, starting with positive findings. Next the team leader should list the recommended safeguards and a suggested timetable for implementation.
- Briefing Tips — As mentioned in many other places throughout this book, the security risk assessment effort can be a controversial effort within the organization. The team leader should be aware that the final presentation could be a place where such controversy comes to the surface. The following tips are provided to help ensure that the final briefing is successful and runs smoothly:
  - Iron out wording problems in the draft.
  - Ensure that all draft reviews included appropriate parties.
  - Bring plenty of copies for everyone.
  - Be sure to highlight positive findings, including the security risk assessment project itself.
  - Invite all interested parties.
  - Keep findings nonjudgmental (solutions not blame).

11.6 Action Plan

The final phase of the security risk assessment is to ensure that the organization creates an action plan for addressing all security risks identified in the final report. Each individual item should be assigned to a named individual and a date for action identified and tracked. Each of these identified risks should be reduced, accepted, avoided, or assigned. A good practice is to record the disposition of the risk on a master copy of the final security risk assessment report with a date and a signature of the senior official who accepts the residual risk after the selected mediation approach.

Note

1. Lessons learned from RITs first security posture assessment, Rochester Institute of Technology, January 1, 2004.

References

[1] *Information Security Risk Assessment: Practices of Leading Organizations*, A Supplement to GAO's May 1998 Executive Guide on Information Security Management. United States General Accounting Office, Accounting and Information Management Division, November 1999. GAO/AMID-00-33. http://www.gao.gov/special.pubs/ai00033.pdf

[2] *An Introduction to Computer Security: A NIST Handbook*, NIST Special Publication 800-12, October 1995. http://csrc.nist.gov/publications/nistpubs/800-12/800-12-html

[3] "Generally Accepted Information Security Principles" GAISP v3.0, Information Systems Security Association. http://www.issa.org/gaisp/_pdfs/v30.pdf

[4] "Lessons Learned from RITs First Security Posture Assessment," Rochester Institute of Technology, January 1, 2004. http://www.educause.edu/ep/ep_item_detail.asp?ITEM_ID=197

[5] *How to Get Action on Audit Recommendations*, U.S. General Accounting Office, July 1991.

[6] Rugh, David E., and Manning, Robert E., *Proposal Management Using the Modular Technique*, Peninsula Publishing, 1973.

Chapter 12

Security Risk Assessment Project Management

A security risk assessment is a project — a rather unique project that requires a specific skill set and activities but a project nonetheless. For the risk assessment to result in a successful effort, the project must be well managed. In this section the fundamental elements of project management are discussed. These elements are planning, tracking and correction, reporting, and staffing.

12.1 Project Planning

A project manager has the ultimate responsibility for the successful completion of a project. Success is defined in terms of customer satisfaction, technical quality of the work, and completion within budget and time constraints. In order to ensure a successful project, the project manager must properly plan the project.

12.1.1 Project Definition

Project planning begins with the project definition. A project is defined within the statement of work (SOW). This is the portion of the contract that is the basis for defining the work and the time and resource constraints on the project. Ideally, a project manager will have been involved in the negotiation process and the creation of the statement of work, but this is not always the case.

The first thing a project manager needs to do is to read the statement of work and ensure that the project expectations are understood. The project manager must then confirm that the deadlines and resource constraints are able to be met. If the project manager sees any problem with the SOW, including the deliverables, resources, or deadlines, these problems must be dealt with early as possible in the process. The project manager must articulate what changes need to take place before accepting the project from the senior manager or whoever signed the SOW. The project manager and senior management need to come to an agreement as to the parameters of the SOW. Any required changes could be to the SOW or as an internal charge or expected overrun.

At this point the project manager accepts the project and its parameters. It is now up to the project manager to ensure that the project completes successfully.

12.1.2 Project Planning Details

In order to effectively allocate hours and still ensure that the project will finish on time, the project manager will typically divide the project up into phases and activities within each phase. Tools such as Microsoft Project provide a useful way to quickly create project plans.

12.1.2.1 Project Phases and Activities

The first step is to divide the project into phases. There is no hard-and-fast rule about phases. Project managers want to strike a balance between the ability to adequately track progress (thus siding for small phases) and the overhead of managing many phases (thus siding for larger phases). But a good rule of thumb is that each phase should be at least a few days and not more than a month. For example, an average risk assessment project may be divided into the phases shown in Table 12.1.

Each phase can be further broken down into activities. Again, there are no hard-and-fast rules here either, but a good rule of thumb is that each activity should be at least a day and not longer than a week or two. You will find that exceptions are more the rule, though. For example, reviewers are typically given 4–8 hours to review a document. Continuing the risk assessment example, each phase can be broken into tasks as shown in Table 12.2.

12.1.2.2 Phases and Activities Scheduling

Now that the project has been divided up into phases and activities, the project manager needs to schedule the phases and activities such that the project will

Table 12.1   Project Phases. Divide the project into "manageable" phases.

Phase	Name	Description
1	Pre-on-site	Complete project initiation tasks and prepare for on-site activities
2	On-site assessment	Perform on-site data gathering and testing
3	Results analysis	Review data gathered and compile results
4	Reporting	Document and present findings to the customer

Table 12.2   Project Tasks. Divide each phase into an "assignable" task.

Phase	Tasks
Phase 1: Pre-on-site	Project initiation (letter of introduction, kickoff meeting, obtaining proper signatures, permissions, and accesses, requests for documents)
	Document review (review of policies, procedures, training material, previous risk assessments, organization, charts, etc.)
	Interview preparation (preparing interviews with key personnel)
Phase 2: On-site assessment	Document follow-up
	Observation of security practices (walk-throughs, TRASHINT)
	Interviews
	Technical assessment (internal security scanning, wardialing, firewall ruleset review, architecture review)
Phase 3: Results analysis	Data analysis
	Create risk statements (including recommendations)
	Team review and consensus of risk statements
	Additional research for recommendations
Phase 4: Reporting	Document specification
	Annotated outline (with section assignments to team members)
	Draft
	Final
	Briefing (if required)

complete on time (see Figure 12.1). Experience is the best teacher for doing this correctly, but a few tips are offered below:

- Determine Start Times — Work backwards from the due date.
- Review Time — Be sure to leave adequate time for internal and customer review. Customer review time is typically 2–3 times as long as internal

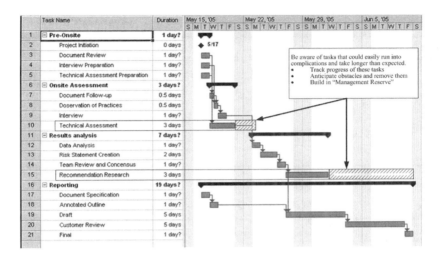

Figure 12.1 Using Microsoft Project™ to schedule tasks. The Gantt chart view in MS Project is a useful way to plan and visualize how the project tasks interrelate.

review time because we do not have control over how the customer spends their time.

- Critical Paths — Be aware of dependencies and critical paths. Some activities can be performed at any time, while others require the results of a previous activity being performed. If you are using a tool such as Microsoft Project™, the tool can take these inputs and assist with efficient planning.
- Efficiencies — When defining activities, consider time and travel efficiencies by grouping activities, using identical resources or requiring travel to the same location together. For example, both internal scanning and key personnel interviews will require the security risk assessment team to be on site. Consider scheduling these activities in the same timeframe (e.g., in the same week). On the other hand, consider the resources required to support these activities and ensure that enough slack time is allowed for slips in the schedule due to testing delays, organizational meetings, or key personnel who may be needed for both activities.

12.1.2.3 Allocating Hours to Activities

With resources allocated to activities, the project manager now assigns hours to activities. This is a careful balance. The project manager needs to assign enough hours to the activity so that the resource can complete the task. At the same time, the project manager needs to ensure that the project can be completed within budget. Again experience is the best teacher here, but below are a few tips:

- Management Reserve — Set aside a 10 percent "management reserve." As stated before, something always comes up or you will find that you underestimated at least one of the tasks. This reserve can be dipped into if you are going over budget.
- Project Management Hours — Be sure to assign hours to project management. This typically translates to 5–10 percent of the total hours on many projects.
- Engineering Estimates — Don't be afraid to ask the resource directly, "How many hours would you need to review a company's security policies?" or "Can you review their policies in 16 hours?"

Let us say that a security risk assessment project was bid at $35,000 and four weeks to complete the project. At the current rate of $200/hour, that gives you 175 hours of labor to complete the project in four weeks. Sketch out the hours and calendar time it may take to get the job done. Ideally, this was already done during the proposal stage. An example is provided in Table 12.3.

The team leader should share with the project members the MS Project Gantt chart and the hours allocation table. Now your project members know what you expect from them, when you need it, and with whom they will be working. Be sure to give them enough information, worked examples, and guidance so that they understand how to complete the task. One of the keys to successful project management is effective delegation.

12.1.3 Project Resources

The project manager needs to ensure that the project can be performed successfully with the resources assigned. The project manager should first consider any contractual requirements on resources. The contract may have specified a named individual or specific experience or credentials for some of the team. Given these constraints, the project manager must first address contractual issues.

Once contractual issues are handled, the project manager must then ensure that the project team has the necessary skill sets and availability to get the job done. A successful risk assessment project will depend largely on the skill of the project manager and the quality of the project team. The ability of the project team members is dependent on their objectivity, knowledge of the system, and risk assessment skills.

12.1.3.1 Objectivity vs. Independence

An objective team member is one whose view is not distorted or influenced by emotion or personal bias. Those who assess the relative strengths and weakness of

Table 12.3 Hours Allocation Example. The project manager should sketch out the allocation of the hours to the project's tasks in order to determine how the project can be completed within budget. Notice the "management reserve" under the heading "Management."

Phase/Task	Resource 1	Resource 2	Resource 3
Pre-on-site:			
Project planning	6		2
Document review		8	
Interview preparation		2	
On-site assessment:			
Document follow-up		3	
Interviews		3	
Inspection		2	
Observations		2	
Testing	16		
Results analysis:			
Data analysis	8	8	2
Create risk statements	6	6	
Team review	6	6	6
Additional research	8	8	
Reporting:			
Document specification		2	
Annotated outline		4	
Draft	8	20	
Final	2	6	2
Briefing	4	2	
Task total: 158 hours	64	82	12
Management: 17 hours			
Net: 175 hours			

the security controls must be able to do so without pride of ownership, undue influence from bosses, internal political pressures, or any other factor that may pollute neutral analysis. Even if a team member is able to professionally perform the tasks within a security risk assessment, there will remain the appearance of a conflict of interest. Furthermore, team members with the best intentions of remaining objective are typically unable to remain objective because they are too close to the "problem." A security architect who designed and assembled the current system architecture is unlikely to look at the problem with a fresh set of eyes. The architect will naturally be hesitant and perhaps unable to view the current architecture with the same detached emotion as an outsider.

Human nature practically dictates that independence is required to ensure objectivity. There are many reasons why a member of a security risk assessment team may not be able to provide an objective review. The customer and project leader should take reasonable precautions to ensure that team members are objective. The customer and the team leader should carefully consider removing any team member who fits one of the following categories as a voting member of the risk assessment team:

- Builder — A team member who was or is currently involved in the design, development, or operation of any of the security controls under scrutiny (e.g., members of the current security team).
- Interested Party — A team member who is in a position within the organization that will be affected by the results of the security risk assessment (e.g., candidates for a security team, project managers for projects that may require additional security measures).
- Stakeholder — A team member who is in a position to benefit or be harmed from the results of a security risk assessment (e.g., project managers, "competing organizations").

12.1.3.2 Internal vs. External Team Members

Many arguments have been made for the inclusion of internal resources on the risk assessment team. These arguments point out that complex systems and security controls can best be understood by those who are more familiar with these systems. There is no doubt that internal resources will have a better understanding of the systems and even the business objectives if these internal resources include members sufficiently high up in the organization. However, the inclusion of internal resources on a security risk assessment team can have many setbacks as well.

Internal resources added as members of the risk assessment team tend to be biased and inexperienced in risk assessment methods. Anyone who cannot provide an objective assessment of the security controls should not be a voting member of the security risk assessment team. Moreover, internal resources tend to have expertise in the organization's systems and not in the risk assessment method being employed on the project. Unfamiliarity with general risk assessment concepts can slow the team down or lead to inaccurate results. For these reasons, internal resources should not be part of a risk assessment team.

That being said, internal resources are incredibly valuable to the risk assessment process. The team will rely on these resources to explain the operation of systems and security controls employed. It is not unusual to have internal resources "drive" when reviewing configurations or performing some internal testing of the systems and their controls.

12.1.3.3 Skills Required

The project manager or customer will also want to ensure that an appropriate team is assembled for the security risk assessment. It is not always possible for the project manager to choose the team. However, if the project manager has a choice, a team composed of objective and experienced members would be best. When assembling the team, the project manager should consider both team expertise and team member expertise.

12.1.3.4 Team Skills

The team as a whole will require the skills necessary to test all security controls within the defined scope of the project. The team requires skills of leadership, writing, presentation and, depending on the scope of the project, various technical skills.

12.1.3.5 Team Member Skills

Each member of the team requires specific security risk assessment skills, general consulting skills, general team member skills, and general writing skills. Specific security risk assessment skills are largely discussed in this book. The other required team member skills mentioned here are discussed briefly below. Security professionals should refer to other texts or courses to develop the proper skills listed here.

Sidebar 12.1 How to Destroy Credibility in Five Letters or Less

Every interaction between a consultant and the customer results in the establishment or the modification of the credibility of the consultant. This is why it is just as important to dress and communicate appropriately as it is to perform quality work. I once gave a seminar on the Health Insurance Portability and Accountability Act to a group of state auditors, hospital administrators, and healthcare organizations. During this two-day seminar we discussed the history of the legislation, covered entities, dates, and penalties, and the privacy and security regulations and their implications on their administrative, physical, and technical controls.

The seminar was co-sponsored by a company who intended to resell HIPAA integration services. As a sponsor of the seminar they added several slides to the end of the presentation that described the services they offered. There was a small but noticeable mistake in these final slides. The final slide describing their credentials claimed that the company employed "HIPPA experts." It is rather difficult to establish credibility if you cannot ever spell the topic you claim to be an expert in.

12.1.3.5.1 Specific Security Risk Assessment Skills

This book is intended to assist in the teaching of specific security risk assessment skills. By reading this book and referring to its contents through the security risk assessment process, team members can increase their specific security risk assessment skills and become more productive team members. However, it is expected that the members of the security risk assessment team have a general knowledge of security.

A general knowledge of security can be gained from working within the information security profession on a variety of assignments and roles. The elements of the information security profession vary from the development of policies and procedures, to an understanding of the laws and regulations, to technical knowledge of the security controls. The best indication of a professional's experience is gained from observing their work. However, customers do not always have previous experience with the information security professionals and therefore an observation of their work is not possible until they are under contract and working for you. More and more organizations are relying on a review of the certifications held by information security professionals as a measurement and indication of their experience, trustworthiness, and knowledge.

Within the information security field, the amount of certifications can be overwhelming. Sorting of these certifications can be a monumental task. Although there are well over a dozen information security certifications available, they can be categorized as major certifications, advanced certifications, vendor certifications, and other certifications. The purpose of this section is to highlight the most recognized and therefore sought-after certifications in the information security field.

Major Information Security Certifications — The certifications discussed in this section are considered the major information security certifications. These certifications are among the most popular within the industry, recognized by other professionals, and most frequently found in job descriptions or listings. For example, in a recent (nonscientific) study of information security jobs posted on monster.com, 383 job postings requested or required the CISSP® certification, the CISA® certification yielded 186 such postings, the GSEC® yielded a total of 84. All other information security certifications rarely showed up at all.

- CISSP® — The International Information Systems Security Certification Consortium (ISC²) calls the Certified Information System Security Professional (CISSP®) the "Gold Standard in information system security certifications." It is hard to argue with this bold statement. The stringency of the requirements, the breadth of the tested knowledge, and the recognition of the CISSP® have made this the most sought-after information security certification in the industry. Candidates wishing to obtain a CISSP® certification must pass a 250-question, 6-hour exam covering ten areas of information security, called the Common Body of Knowledge (CBK). This certification also requires that candidates have a minimum of four years of experience, comply with a strict code of ethics, be endorsed by an information security professional, and attest to a clean criminal history.

- CISA® — The Information Systems Audit and Control Association (ISACA) has created the longest standing of any of these certifications. The Certified Information Security Auditor (CISA®) certification is *the* information security auditor credential. The exam is 200 questions, 4 hours long, and offered only twice per year at 136 locations worldwide. CISA® candidates must also adhere to a strict code of ethics, and have five years of experience to obtain this certification.

- GSEC® — The SANS® (SysAdmin, Audit, Network, Security) Institute developed the Global Information Assurance Certification (GIAC) Security Essentials Certification (GSEC®) to validate a security professional's skills. The GSEC® has established itself as the "technical" security certification, largely because it not only tests candidate knowledge of security areas but also the pragmatic application of security principles. GSEC® candidates must complete an 8-page research paper or case study, comply with a strict code of ethics, and pass two separate 100-question, 3-hour exams covering the CBK topics.

Sidebar 12.2 Should You Hire a Hacker?

Short answer: No, but first a quick disclaimer on the use of the term "hacker." Throughout this book the term is used to describe an unethical lawbreaker who targets an organization's assets through information security vulnerabilities. There has been considerable debate on the history and use of this word. Decades ago it was used as a compliment to describe someone who could construct elegant code in their sleep, or someone that could always find a way to make systems integrate even if they were not meant to. However, that is not how the word is used now. The term "hacker" here is only used to describe the criminals.

When shopping for a quality organization or individual to test an information system or to assist in securing an organization's information system, some people are confused as to whether or not they should hire an "ex" hacker. Some would argue that hackers are likely the best people suited to help organizations protect their assets. They often ask, "Who else would know better how to defend against hacker attacks than a hacker himself?" This is a naïve concept based on little more than misguided guesswork. The fact is that hackers may be skilled at breaking into systems, but that skill does not always translate into the same skills required when performing a security risk assessment. In fact there are three principal reasons not to hire a hacker to defend your system: trust, skill, and threats.

Trust. An information system security consultant must be a trusted individual with the highest integrity. These consultants, by the nature of their work, will have knowledge of your system vulnerabilities. These consultants will also likely have physical and logical access beyond that of an outsider. Trust in such an individual is paramount.

Hackers have already demonstrated that they cannot be trusted. Known or admitted hackers usually violated laws and certainly violated the ethics held by information security professionals.

Skill. An information security professional must also have the skill to determine all the possible vulnerabilities of your system and to provide recommendations for how to mitigate your overall risk. These consultants must be knowledgeable in all domains of information security, as security will often break at the weakest link.

Hackers are much like cat burglars, or any career criminal; they have a certain technique or approach to breaking into systems that they use again and again. This approach is often referred to as their *modus operandi* or "MO." A cat burglar who breaks into homes knows one or two tricks for breaking in. For example, he knows how to jump a sliding glass door off the tracks or how to pop a garage door off its tracks. If you hired this "reformed" thief to protect your home he would be great at showing you how to put a safety bar on your glass door and how to lock your garage door instead of just closing it. However, this thief would likely know nothing about quality alarm systems, lighting, camera placement, strength of door jambs, and teaching your kids not to answer the door or the phone when you are out for the evening.

Threats. The idea that hackers are the best suited to help protect an organization's assets is misguided because it also assumes that the only threats are from an external hacker. It should be clear to any reader of this book that threat sources can also be from internal employees or nature. It would be a severe error in risk management to disregard the other threats such as errors and omissions, loss of physical or infrastructure support, malicious code, and fraud.

Your best bet when selecting outside assistance for the testing or securing of your organization's assets is an information security professional and not a hobbyist or criminal.

Advanced Information Security Certifications — The certifications discussed above are only a part of a more complex structure of certifications in which more advanced credentials can be obtained by specializing in other areas. Professionals wishing to expand their knowledge on specific aspects of information security can obtain these advanced credentials.

- ISC2, the organization that administers the CISSP® certification, also offers additional advanced certifications for professionals who have already obtained the CISSP® and want to specialize in architecture (Information Systems Security Architectural Professional — ISSAP), management (Information Systems Security Management Professional) ISSMP, or government criteria and processes (Information Systems Security Engineering Professional — ISSEP).
- ISACA, the organization that administers the CISA certification, also offers a companion certification for professionals who want to specialize in management (Certified Information Security Manager — CISM). Both the CISM and ISC2's ISSMP target information security professionals in management. Because both of these certifications are so new it has yet to be determined which will be more in demand for senior security positions such as the Chief Security Officer (CSC) or the director of information security within an organization.

- SANS, the organization that administers the GIAC GSEC certification, has the most complex — or robust (depending on your point of view) — certification scheme for information security professionals. The scheme is based on a fundamental certification (GSEC) and can be built on from there. Specific areas of concentration include technology such as firewalls, intrusion detection, and forensics. The SANS tops off the information security certification mountain with the GSE. GSEs must complete all GIAC certifications.

Vendor Information Security Certifications — Nearly every security product has an accompanying certification associated with the product or product lines. These certifications are valuable for those who will be working extensively with the products, especially those who work with these products day to day. Among these certifications are the Cisco, ISS, RedHat, and other certifications.

Specialty Security Certifications — The major information security certifications recognize the need for information security professionals to have a working knowledge of associated fields such as computer forensics, physical security, and business continuity planning. But each of these areas has its own credentials as well. For those who will specialize in these fields, the following certifications should be investigated. There are undoubtedly other certifications covering these areas, but the ones listed below are the best known and most accepted by other professionals:

- CBCP — The Disaster Recovery Institute certifies professionals in the area of business continuity and disaster recovery planning. The Certified Business Continuity Professional (CBCP) is well recognized and accepted internationally. The exam covers ten subject areas in business continuity. CBCP candidates have two years of relevant experience to obtain this certification. There are currently over 2500 professionals certified as CBCPs worldwide.
- CPP — The American Society for Industrial Security (ASIS[1]) established the Certified Protection Professional (CPP) certification in 1977. A CPP is a well-recognized distinction within the field of industrial security (referred to by some as physical security). The exam is 200 questions and covers subject areas in security management, investigations, and legal aspects. CPP candidates must pass a criminal background investigation and have nine years of relevant experience to obtain this certification.

Other Information Security Certifications — There are still more information security certifications available for those who do not meet the experience requirements of the major certifications or who just want another approach. The most popular of these is the Computing Technology Industry Association

(CompTIA) Security+ certification. CompTIA is best known for its A+ certification for entry-level computer technicians. Although the Security+ certification does not carry the weight of any of the major security certifications, it is well known. Security+ candidates are required to have two year's experience in networking with an emphasis on security. The exam covers general security issues, cryptography, communications, infrastructure, and organizational security.

12.1.3.5.2 General Consulting Skills

Consulting is the process of assessing a business problem or challenge from an outside perspective and providing recommendations to resolve the problem or overcome the challenge. Consultants need to understand the many obstacles they may face in their endeavor to assist an organization.

12.1.3.5.3 Criticisms of Consultants

Consultants belong to a much maligned profession. Criticisms of the profession are a mixture of reality and perception. At worst, consultants are sometimes considered insensitive, inexperienced, and unable to produce real results:

- Insensitive — Whenever a consultant is on the job, they are also a visitor in someone else's workplace. Every workplace has a unique culture and set of normative values that have evolved within the group of people who work together daily. Any visitor to the workplace may be considered insensitive if they violate these normative behaviors. Furthermore, consultants are sometimes called in to assess a current situation or assist in a project that has been stalling. In either case, the consultant's advice or mere presence can be taken as criticism of the existing work.
- Inexperienced — Every project a consultant works on is unique. Even if they are an expert in a specific service and have led numerous efforts within the area, each project presents unique characteristics. These unique characteristics include the customer mission, custom systems and application, and specific technology. No consultant is going to know as much as the customer regarding these characteristics. Employees within the customer organization may sometimes criticize the consultants for not understanding their systems. Often this is a reaction to the real or perceived criticism mentioned above.
- No Real Results — As mentioned before, consulting is the process of assessing a business problem or challenge from an outside perspective and providing recommendations to resolve the problem or overcome the challenge. This type of engagement is complete once the recommendations are complete and the report is accepted. The process of implementing

the results would be a different contract and is often not part of the engagement. When the customer organization has determined that they will implement the recommendations without the assistance of the consultants (for cost or even independence reasons), the consultants are often viewed by others within the organization as a group that cannot produce real results.

12.1.3.5.4 Overcoming Critics

Not everyone is cut out to be a consultant. The business of consulting can be demanding and tricky. Just because you have technical skills does not mean you will be a good consultant. Consulting is not simply the application of technical know-how. The underlying technical skills required are a necessary but by no means a sufficient skill. Consulting is instead a mix between listening, observing, analyzing, researching, presenting, and teaching, with an emphasis on diplomacy. To be a productive consultant and overcome the criticisms mentioned above, the consultant should first understand the criticisms and then consider the following advice:

- Sensitivity — Consider that you are a guest in someone else's workplace. Do your best to understand and comply with the normative values of the organization. Also understand that you may have been called into a situation that has already accumulated baggage. Various members of the organization may have already drawn up sides on issues that you have yet to discover. Be aware that when you point out areas for improvement you may also be pointing out gaps in someone else's work. Carefully phrase your speech when conducting interviews, briefing findings, and creating the report.
- Experience — Seek to understand the unique elements of the specific job as early as possible. Research the organization's mission from Web site, annual reports, press releases and other sources. Ask for a brief description of the company mission and the systems and applications that are within the project scope. Attempt to talk less and listen more during interviews. This will not make you an expert on the organization and its systems, but it will lead you to a reasonable understanding of the project's unique characteristics and toward more targeted analysis. The result will be recognition by the customer that you understand that they are unique and will treat them with respect and not apply "cookie cutter" solutions.
- Results — Much of the problem with the criticism of "no real results" comes from a lack of understanding within the organization regarding the scope of the contract. Most contracts are limited to providing recommendations and stop short of having an assessment team implement recommendations within the same contract. When you are part of a team

that will not be providing the implementation of the recommendations, be clear in interviews, presentations, and the final report regarding the scope of the work.

Recommendations should provide as much detail as possible to the implementation team. Specific information regarding the implementation will be appreciated by those who inherit these recommendations.

12.1.3.5.5 Conflict of Interest

To avoid a conflict of interest, many contracted assessment efforts strictly cover the assessment and not any follow-on work. The concern is that the assessment team may have a conflict of interest between providing well-researched, targeted recommendations and "cookie cutter" solutions that lead the organization into purchasing more services or product from the assessment team. This concern is reasonable and should be carefully considered by both the customer and the security service consultant vendor.

12.1.3.5.6 General Writing Skills

All team members should have the ability to write effectively. They should be able to present their ideas in a clear and concise manner. In this section we offer some high-level advice for general technical writing skills that should be well understood and practiced by each member of the security risk assessment team.

- Understand and Write to Your Audience — The audience of the security risk assessment report can be rather mixed. You should expect senior-level managers, mid-level managers, and technical personnel within the organization to read the security risk assessment. Writing to such a diverse audience can be problematic. Therefore, you should create an executive summary designed specifically for the senior-level executive who wants the "bottom line" and technical appendices for the technical readers who want to know the results of the vulnerability scan, for example. The body of the report should be written to the security risk assessment sponsor or mid-level managers. The report should be thorough in terms of explaining the findings, their impacts, and the recommendations.
- Don't Lecture — The authors of the document should state facts and opinions but never emotion. Understand that you must carefully word your descriptions and findings within the report to ensure not only accuracy but also sensitivity. Leave emotion out of it. Simply state the facts as they present themselves and render an opinion as to the findings.
- Write Clearly — Contributing authors to the security risk assessment report must be able to clearly express their technical ideas and findings

to a wide audience that is not necessarily a security expert. Furthermore, the audience reading the report is likely to have very different expectations, expertise, and motivations for reading the report. It is for this reason that the report should be divided into distinct areas designed for these groups. An executive summary is designed for the executives and those who need a high-level understanding of the report's results and conclusions. The body of the report is designed for the majority of the audience that is interested in the approach, techniques, and findings of the report to a greater level of detail. Lastly, appendices may be developed to place more technical and detailed information such as scanning reports, lists of tools used, or other technical information.

The authors of the report must be able to determine their intended audience and use the appropriate terms and concepts to convey the information most appropriately. For example, someone reading the executive summary is not interested in the tools used to scan a workstation or in a listing of the ports that remain open. In fact, such information is likely to be confusing or, at the very least, distracting within the executive summary. Instead the author of the executive summary should state that some workstations remain vulnerable to Internet-based attacks. The body of the report could contain a description of the techniques used to determine susceptibility and the appendix should contain the results of a vulnerability scan on that system.

12.2 Project Tracking

An essential element of project management is tracking the progress of the project. Project tracking is required to correctly report on the project status and to detect and correct any deviations from the plan. A project manager may choose to track the progress of the project on several different levels, including tracking hours only, tracking time elapsed only, or tracking both hours and calendar time against the completion of tasks within the project. The level of tracking performed by the project manager should be determined based on the complexity and length of the project.

12.2.1 Hours Tracking

Security risk assessments that are less rigorous and involve a relatively small scope could be adequately managed simply by tracking the hours expended on the effort against the completion of the tasks within the project. For example, if the task of reviewing the existing security policies and procedures is expected to take 8 hours and the task of performing interviews with key personnel is expected to take 12 hours, then it may be adequate to simply record the number of hours actually expended for each of these tasks.

Table 12.4 Hours Tracking. Project managers can effectively track the progress of small and simple projects through tracking the hours planned and expended on each task. Here we see that the project is trending over budget going into the results analysis task.

Phase/Task	Resource 1 Plan	Resource 1 Actual	Resource 2 Plan	Resource 2 Actual	Resource 3 Plan	Resource 3 Actual	Hours Tracking
Pre-on-site:							
Project planning	6	4			2	3	−1
Document review			8	10			+1
Interview preparation			2	4			+3
On-site assessment:							
Document follow-up			3	6			+6
Interviews			3	4			+7
Inspection			2	4			+9
Observations			2	4			+11
Testing	16	12					+7
Results analysis:							
Data analysis	8		8		2		
Create risk statements	6		6				
Team review	6		6		6		
Additional research	8		8				
Reporting:							
Document specification			2				
Annotated outline			4				
Draft	8		20				
Final	2		6		2		
Briefing	4		2				
Task Total: 158 hours	64		82		12		
Management: 17 hours							
Net: 175 hours							

In this case, project tracking could be accomplished in a simple table (Table 12.4) that indicates the planned and actual hours for each task along with an indication of their completion. For simple security risk assessments, the information available from this type of tracking is adequate to record hours expended and to determine when it may be time to take corrective action.

12.2.2 Calendar Time Tracking

Another way to track the progress of security risk assessments that are less rigorous and involve a relatively small scope is to track planned and actual completion times for each task. For example, if the task of reviewing the existing security policies and procedures is expected to start on September 1 and take one day, while the task of performing interviews with key personnel is expected to start on September 3 and take two days, then it may be adequate to track planned and actual calendar time.

Project tracking using only calendar time could be accomplished in a simple table that indicated the planned and actual start and completion dates for each task. For simple security risk assessments bid at a firm-fixed price, the information available from this type of tracking is adequate to task completions and to indicate when it may be time to take corrective action.

12.2.3 Project Progress Tracking

While hours and calendar tracking may be adequate for relatively small security risk assessment projects, larger and more complex projects require more insight into indications of project progress. It is not enough to know how many hours over or under budget the project is or how many days behind it may be. Instead the project manager needs to be able to view both of these indicators and more to properly manage the project.

The project manager should continually track progress on the project to ensure that the technical, calendar, and budget constraints are met. The technical constraints (quality of the work) can be tracked through your technical lead or through involvement in the technical reviews of the work products. The calendar and budget constraints may be tracked through updating the project plan and comparing the planned calendar time and budget to the expended calendar time and budget. Again, Microsoft Project™ or other project management software can provide useful tools for tracking project progress (see Figure 12.2).[2]

12.3 Taking Corrective Measures

If the project manager notices that the project is no longer on track, the project manager must take corrective measures to get it back on track. These measures can range from getting more resources, working longer hours, or asking the customer for a larger budget.

12.3.1 Obtaining More Resources

When a project falls behind, the project manager must create a plan to bring it back "in line." If the project manager noticed this problem early, then they have more choices of how to correct the situation. These choices include putting more resources into the project or extending the hours of the current resources. This approach assumes that the project can be "saved" or, in other words, the project can still be performed on time and perhaps even within budget.

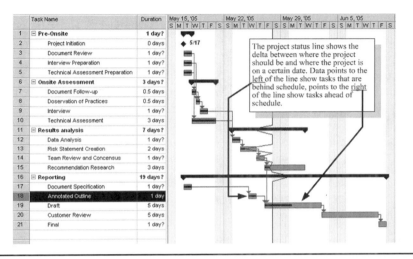

Figure 12.2   Using Microsoft Project™ to track your project. The tracking Gantt chart view in MS Project is a useful way to track progress on your project tasks to present to the customer or to provide you with an indication of when to take corrective action.

If the project manager determines that the project cannot be saved and the statement of work cannot be satisfied with the resources at the disposal of the project manager, then another path must be taken. In this case, the scope of the work is changed to meet the projected product and delivery date. This is commonly referred to as a change order. The cause for a change order could be from a customer demand or from a lack of proper planning for potential obstacles. If the change order is a cause of a customer demand and the project will require additional effort because of the change, then it is typically reasonable to also pursue an increase in the budget. This will allow the project manager to obtain the appropriate resources to complete the project. If the change order was caused by the team, then an increase in the budget may not be appropriate.

12.3.2 Using Management Reserve

A management reserve of hours and calendar time can come in handy in the situation when you find your project is running behind schedule. Management reserve should not be thought of as a "fudge factor," as if the project manager is not skilled at estimating the project. Instead, the reservation of a small amount of hours and time as a buffer is a technique used by project managers to give them the capability to actively manage the project and meet customer satisfaction goals.

Any good project manager will tell you that every project, no matter how well planned, will have obstacles and unforeseen delays. You know there will be some challenges during the project but you just don't know what they are going to be. Based on the complexity of the project and an experienced estimate of the magnitude and frequency of delays, a good project manager can provide reasonable estimates for management reserve. This ability to estimate adequate management reserve will come with experience. If you have such experience — use it. If not, for now, just use 10 percent for both hours and calendar time. If the deviations from the project are caught soon enough or are small enough, you can basically make an adjustment without affecting the final deliverable or the bottom line.

Sidebar 12.3 Keys to Ensuring Project Success

This book is filled with practical approaches for performing a security risk assessment. This viewpoint, however, is mostly from the perspective of the information security engineer performing the security risk assessment. It is the organization management and not the information security engineer who commissions or coordinates the security risk assessment project and in many ways is responsible for its success through the organizational treatment of this task.

In 1999 the Government Accounting Office performed a study of best practices in industry for performing security risk assessments. The GAO report concluded that the following success factors were crucial to the organization's success in performing security risk assessments.

- Obtain Senior Management Support and Involvement — This has been stated several times but it deserves reiteration here. The GAO study found that senior management support was important to ensure that lower-level organizations took the security risk assessment seriously, that adequate resources were made available for the project, and that the results of the assessment were implemented. Senior management involvement is not simply the provision of adequate budget. The study found that successful organizations involve senior management in the determination of the security risk assessment scope selecting participants in the process, and approving the final action plan resulting from the assessment.
- Designate Focal Points — Security risk assessment projects that had oversight by champions at a senior

level within the organization were more successful and coordinated than those security risk assessment projects that did not have designated focal points. Security risk assessment focal points assisted with the organizational planning, performance, and reporting associated with multiple security risk assessments within the organization.

- Define Procedures — All organizations within the GAO study had developed and documented security risk assessment procedures and even tools to facilitate and standardize the process. These procedures helped to ensure consistency between security risk assessment projects within the organization, but they also had an added benefit. Security risk assessment procedures limited the time and cost of security risk assessments because the security risk assessment teams did not have to perform the effort from scratch and could leverage techniques, processes, and templates developed previously in other security risk assessments.*

- Involve Business and Technical Experts — The GAO study found that the use of business managers and technical specialists was helpful to the security risk assessment process. Business managers were considered valuable for their deep understanding of business operations, criticality of systems, and sensitivity of data. Technical personnel were found to be experts in system architecture, system vulnerabilities, and the effect of changes on operational procedures. The involvement of other experts, such as internal auditors, contractors, and even federal agencies, proved to be useful to some organizations studied.

- Hold Business Units Responsible — When it comes to assigning responsibility for implementing the recommendations of a security risk assessment, the organizations studied concluded that individual business units were the best positioned for ensuring follow-through. Business units were also determined to be well suited for determining when the next security risk assessment should be performed.

- Limit the Scope of Individual Assessments — The organizations that were the subject of this study found that conducting individual assessments with a narrow and specific scope helped to keep each security risk assessment more manageable. These organizations conducted a series of individual security risk assessments and used the results to compare and rank business units.

- Document and Maintain Results — Documentation of a security risk assessment is essential. The final security risk assessment report must be maintained and made available to the appropriate individuals. Uses of the security risk assessment report include providing a record of the security posture of the system, providing valuable information to internal auditors and future security risk assessment teams, and as a method for holding management accountable.

*This is precisely why security risk assessments performed by information security professionals are so efficient. Information security professionals perform security risk assessments for multiple organizations and have well-developed processes and tools.

12.4 Project Status Reporting

One of the most important aspects of project management is project reporting and control. This is because project reporting serves two major functions:

1. *It provides the customer with the confidence that the project is going well and they are getting value.* Even though the technical team may be making great progress, the lack of clear project reporting to the customer may leave the customer thinking that nothing much is going on. Similarly, the lack of efficient and complete information exchange with the customer concerning the project reflects on the professionalism of the company.
2. *It provides team members and senior management with a view of the project's progress.* Team members and senior management tend to become frustrated when they are left in the dark as to the progress of the project.

12.4.1 Report Detail

The detail provided in the status report depends upon the customer's need for insight and oversight of the project. The report should provide enough detail to let all those concerned understand the project's progress and current action items. However, the team leader should be careful not to include so much detail in the report as to spend a disproportionate amount of effort on tracking and reporting progress and less on performing the other tasks within the effort.

12.4.2 Report Frequency

The optimal frequency of project reports is determined by the complexity of the project, the length of the engagement, the number of people involved, and the preference of the project sponsor. Although almost any frequency could be demanded, weekly, bi-weekly, or monthly are the most popular.

12.4.3 Status Report Content

The content of the project status report may be specific to a project, that is, specified in the statement of work (SOW). If the statement of work requires a specific format or specific content in the status report, then clearly a compliant status report should be developed. However, if no format or content is stated, the security risk assessment team should use their standard template. This standard template should include the following information:

- Project Name and Date of Report — The status report should be clearly labeled and named so that the reader can quickly ascertain the project and the timeframe for which this report was created.
- Progress Indication — To the customer this should be in terms of milestones reached and progress made on others. MS Project^{TM} creates a nice chart for this. To the team members and senior management, progress indication also includes hours expended and hours left.
- Plans for Next Period — that is what the team is doing next. The MS Project^{TM} chart mentioned above would cover this as well.
- Action Item Tracking — All projects have a series of action items for the team or for the customer. These are specific tasks that need to be completed to accomplish the project, for example, schedule interviews with key personnel, get access badges, and so on. It is best to record, assign, and track these for the project. It is not an action item until it is specified, assigned, and given a due date.
- Issues — Include any issues that cannot be resolved by the team.

12.5 Project Conclusion and Wrap-Up

Don't let down your guard just because the project is coming to a close. This is one of the most critical stages of the project. Dangers here include "scope creep," project run-on, and the inability to effectively go after follow-on work.

12.5.1 Eliminating "Scope Creep"

This refers to the phenomenon suffered by many projects where the customer keeps expecting more. As the customer asks for more, the inexperienced project manager gives more and it becomes increasingly difficult to ever end the engagement for which you were tasked.

For firm-fixed price (FFP) contracts, this results in cost overruns for which the contractor cannot charge, because the deliverable is the final report and individual hours are not charged. For time and materials (T&M) contracts this is not good either, because the customer will end up being charged more than was originally expected. Even though this will lead to more contracted hours and therefore more money for the contractor, this is not a good way to operate a consultancy because there is a big danger that the customer will be unhappy.

The best way to control these situations is to clearly define the scope of work and to manage the expectations of the customer throughout the project. If a customer wishes us to extend the scope of work, the project manager should write up a new task order, complete with an estimate of the hours it would take or the extra cost to complete the new task.

12.5.2 Eliminating Project Run-On

Whereas "scope creep" is the customer pushing for more work, project run-on is the project members not knowing when to quit. In almost all of security risk assessment engagements the team is limited by time or the customer's budget for the project. Many times this means that the completed work could always be better. The team can always find ways to spend more time writing up recommendations for a risk assessment. The team can always provide more references for why a security policy statement should be included in an acceptable use policy. The team can always continue to try to penetrate a system, but it is essential to clearly communicate to the customer the extent of the services, ensure that the team delivers and delights the customer, and complete the project within their budget.

The best way to eliminate project run-on is to be diligent about allocating hours to team members, tracking the project, and taking appropriate corrective action when the project gets behind.

Notes

1. Reflecting its international presence, this organization is now referred to as ASIS International.
2. Be careful of using the resource usage features of these software packages. They are typically far too complex to be useful for projects of this size and do not

translate well to projects in which your resource may be working on other projects at the same time. Stick with the pretty Gantt chart they make.

Reference

[1] Landoll, Douglas J. "Benefits of IT Certifications" Certification Magazine, March 2004.

Chapter 13

Security Risk Assessment Approaches

There are nearly as many security risk assessment approaches as there are organizations that perform them. It is not the intent of this book to define the best or only approach for performing security risk assessments. In fact it seems clear that different approaches to performing a security risk assessment are required for different situations. Various security risk assessment approaches are discussed here for two reasons.

First, it is important to understand the different approaches that have been developed and currently in use to perform a security risk assessment. Those performing these assessments should always be looking for ways to improve the process through the adoption of new techniques or the modification of current ones. To allow for the process of continuous improvement, those defining and performing security risk assessments must have an understanding of the other approaches currently being used.

Second, various security risk assessment approaches are discussed here to demonstrate the applicability of the advice in this book, regardless of the security risk assessment taken. Most activities described in this book (e.g., understanding business objectives, gathering data, conducting interviews) are required in all security risk assessment approaches. However, most other security risk assessment approaches lack a detailed description of the activity and offer little advice on actually performing the task. The reader can use the descriptions and advice in this book to gain a better understanding and more efficient approach to completing their own security risk assessment using nearly any security risk assessment approach.

The reader will also find specific activities described in detail in this book that are not discussed elsewhere and may not be a part of the current security risk assessment approach taken. For example, the document review methodology, physical security walk-throughs, or specific checklists, are not typically described or used in other security risk assessment approaches. The reader should carefully consider these activities as possible improvements to their current process.

The first step in performing a security risk assessment is to clearly define and understand the approach to be taken. There are many approaches for performing a security risk assessment. These approaches vary in terms of analysis, measurement, use of tools, and the definition of the project phases defined.

13.1 Quantitative vs. Qualitative Analysis

One of the most noted differences between various security risk assessment techniques is the way in which the risk decision variables are determined or computed. Risk decision variables include at least the following aspects:

- value of the asset;
- likelihood that a vulnerability will be exploited; and
- severity of the impact.

Sidebar 13.1 Likelihood and Probability

The terms "likelihood" and "probability" are both used to describe how likely an event is to occur. However, "likelihood" is used to qualitatively describe this occurrence and "probability" is used to quantitatively describe this occurrence.

Probability is a numerical measure of the chance of a specific event or outcome. The probability of an event is measured as the ratio of the sum of the events in question to the total number of possible events. Therefore, probability is always a numerical value between 0 and 1, 0 indicating no chance of the event happening and 1 indicating that the event is certain to happen.

Each of the risk decision variables may be determined through a complex computation or through subjective judgment. The computational approach to determining risk decision variables is called quantitative analysis. The subjective judgment approach is called qualitative analysis.

13.1.1 Quantitative Analysis

Quantitative analysis is an approach that relies on specific formulas and calculations to determine the value of the risk decision variables. There are several formulas that are commonly associated with quantitative security risk analysis. These formulas cover the expected loss for specific risks and the value of safeguards to reduce the risk. There are three classic quantitative risk analysis formulas: annual loss expectancy, single loss expectancy, and safeguard value:

1. Annual Loss Expectancy (ALE) = Single Loss Expectancy * Annual Rate of Occurrence.
2. Single Loss Expectancy = Asset Value * Exposure Factor.
3. Safeguard Value = ALE Before − ALE After − Annual Safeguard Cost.

Each of these formulas is explained in more detail below.

13.1.1.1 Expected Loss

Expected loss is a useful concept because, when dealing with risk, you are not dealing with certainty but instead with probabilities. Consider a situation in which a gambling friend proposes that he flip a coin to determine how much money you win. If the coin lands on heads you win $1.00; if the coin lands on tails you win $2.50. How much would you be willing to play such a game?

The value of this game (or your friend's expected loss) can be determined through the application of the concept of expected loss. First note that the probability of your friend losing $1.00 or $2.50 is equally likely. Using statistics we can compute the expected loss for a single event of $1.75. This means that if you play this game you may end up winning as much as $2.50 or as little as $1.00, but on average you will win $1.75:

$$Expected\_Loss = [probality(heads) * \$1.00 + probality(tails) * 2.50]$$

$$Expected\_Loss = [0.5 * \$1.00 + 0.5 * \$2.5]$$

$$Expected\_Loss = [\$0.50 + \$1.25]$$

$$Expected\_Loss = \$1.75$$

13.1.1.2 Single Loss Expectancy

In business we deal not with gambling friends but with hackers, disgruntled employees, viruses, and other events that are not certain but have an element of chance or prediction. Because these threats may have an impact on our organization's assets it is useful to predict and measure the expected loss. Single loss expectancy (SLE) is the expected loss as the result of a single incident. In the case of the gambling friend the single loss expectancy for the event is $1.75. Many risk assessment techniques use a specific formula for SLE which incorporates an exposure factor (EF) and the asset value. An exposure factor is the average amount of loss to the asset for a single incident. For example, a warehouse that catches on fire would on average only burn halfway or lose only half of its value. This would equate to an exposure factor of 0.50. Single loss expectancy is defined as asset value (AV) multiplied by the exposure factor (EF):

$$\text{Single Loss Expectancy} = \text{Asset Value} * \text{Exposure Factor}$$

13.1.1.3 Annualized Loss Expectancy

It is rare that a risk event happens exactly once a year. Some risk events like computer viruses happen several times a year, while others such as a fire in a warehouse only happen once every 20 years. Because budgets for avoiding or otherwise dealing with these incidents are on a yearly cycle, it is useful to compute the expected losses from these risks within a single year. This number is referred to as the annualized loss expectancy (ALE). The ALE is computed by multiplying the single loss expectancy by the annual rate of occurrence (ARO). An ARO is simply a prediction of how often a specific risk event is likely to happen each year. For example, the annual rate of occurrence for a virus may be six while the annual rate of occurrence for a fire in the warehouse could be 1/20 or 0.05:

$$\text{Annualized Loss Expectancy}$$
$$= \text{Single Loss Expectancy} * \text{Annual Rate of Occurrence}$$

13.1.1.4 Safeguard Value

Lastly, it is useful to determine how much you would be willing to spend on a countermeasure to reduce a specific risk. A countermeasure is any administrative, physical, or technical security mechanism that reduces the risk to the organization's assets. No countermeasure can completely eliminate the risk to an organization's assets. Instead a countermeasure may reduce the risk to an organization's asset by reducing the single loss expectancy, the annual loss expectancy, or both. A countermeasure can reduce the single loss expectancy by reducing the exposure factor or it may reduce the annualized loss expectancy by reducing the annual rate of occurrence. A countermeasure also costs money to implement. Sometimes a countermeasure may be worthwhile to implement because the expected losses to the organization's assets are severely reduced with a low-cost countermeasure. At other times a countermeasure may not be worth the cost because the organization only experiences a slight drop in the risk to their assets and a high cost of implementing the countermeasure.

This brings us to the last basic equation for risk assessment: countermeasure or safeguard value. Safeguard value is defined as the reduction experienced in the annualized loss expectancy minus the annual cost of implementing the countermeasure.

$$\text{Safeguard Value} = (\text{ALE Before} - \text{ALE After})$$
$$- \text{Annual Cost of Countermeasure}$$

13.1.1.5 Quantitative Analysis Advantages

By using well-documented formulas, the values of the risk decision variables have many benefits:

- Objective — A risk decision variable determined through quantitative analysis can be considered objective. Because the calculations that determine the value of the risk decision variables are based on predetermined formulas, the resultant value can be considered objective and not as likely to be influenced by subjective measures or judgment.
- Expressed in "Real" Number — Asset valuation and safeguard valuation can all be expressed in terms of specific costs (e.g., U.S. dollars). When considering the value of a single asset, consider all direct and indirect values of the asset. It also helps to consider the value of the asset in light of a specific threat.

Consider a warehouse that stores inventory and that is threatened by a fire. First, consider the direct costs of the building itself, and the inventory and equipment inside the building. These values are relatively easy to obtain because market value and replacement costs can usually be easily computed. Then consider the indirect costs. These costs may include, but are certainly not limited to, lost business due to the fire, lost business due to loss of reputation of the organization, and potential loss of life. The calculation of the indirect costs is typically more complicated than that of direct costs. This calculation becomes difficult as unknown elements and values that are difficult to obtain enter the equation.

In Table 13.1, three indirect costs are computed. The first indirect cost is that of lost business due to the fire in the warehouse. In the example it was determined that lost business would be equal to the profit that would have normally been made from orders during the time it takes to get the warehouse functions back to normal. The second indirect cost is the damage to the organization through the loss of

Table 13.1 Quantitative Measurements. **Quantitative analysis of asset valuation and safeguard valuation results in a specific cost.**

Asset Valuation Components	Value	Justification
Building	$100,000	Cost to rebuild
Inventory	$50,000	Cost to organization
Equipment	$48,000	Replacement cost
Lost business	$24,000	4 weeks to return to normal operations $6,000 profit from orders per week
Reputation	$31,099*	Expected loss of business — 10% of one year's business
Employee endangerment	$90,000	Risk of life is 3%; value of life = $3 million

*The reputation calculation is computed using a present value of money formula with an interest rate of 6% and a loss of 10% of the business profit or $600/week for a year.

reputation due to a fire in the warehouse. In this example, loss of reputation is considered to be a 10 percent drop in business for one year. When considering the loss of future monies, you must also consider the present value of the future revenues. A present value of money formula was used in the calculation in the example to account for the time value of money.[1] The third indirect cost considered here is potential loss of life. In the example of the warehouse, a single security guard was considered. The warehouse has no full- or part-time employees assigned to the building except for a single security guard. Because the guard is posted outside the building and charged with detecting and reporting a fire but not with building evacuation, the chances that the fire would injure or kill the security guard are considered low. Valuation of a human life is perhaps the toughest of all the quantitative risk decision variables. It is an absolutely political and moral nightmare to put a dollar value on a human life. If you plan to use quantitative analysis and you need a dollar figure, you should use a value produced by another source. In 2002 the United States Department of Transportation set the value of a human life at $3 million. Using this figure and backing it up with a reference is your best bet. In this example his life is considered to be worth $3 million, consistent with the U.S. DoT figure.[2]

- More Easily Understood — Third, the expected loss is better understood. Formulas are mathematical equations. The simplest of formulas, like those listed above, are very easy to understand. It is important to separate the concepts of understanding from those of agreement. I am not saying that you will not have heated debates about the value of a human life, for instance, but once the values of the variables in the formula are reached it is a simple and certain outcome. In assurance and validation circles, descriptions that are based on mathematical constructs are called "formal." This means that they have certain outcomes as mathematics is unambiguous.

- Meaningful Statistics — A quantitative analysis approach to determining risk decision variables can provide meaningful statistical analysis, because we have "real" numbers with which to work. For example, by comparing the annualized loss expectancy for an organization over a period of time, you could gain insight as to the extent of the value of the security improvements.
- Credible — Analysis based on a quantitative approach seems more credible because there are specific numbers attached to values, probabilities, and impacts. A risk assessment that results in the statement "The current annualized expected loss for this organization is 3.16 million dollars due to breaches in cyber-security" seems more credible than the statement "The current security posture of this organization is medium-high." Although both statements may be based on the same analysis and the same level of rigor in the assessment, the quantitative approach resulting in a dollar figure seems more credible.
- Provides a Basis for Cost-Benefit Analysis — Many corporate decisions requiring the expenditure of limited resources are made only after a careful cost–benefit analysis. This means that the perceived benefit of the project (e.g., develop a patch management system) must outweigh the cost involved in such a project. Quantitative analysis, namely safeguard value, can provide the information necessary to analyze the costs and benefits of proposed security controls.
- Supports Budget Decisions — Similarly, the dollar figures provided by the quantitative analysis can be used to support budget estimates for upcoming projects and budget cycles.

13.1.1.6 Quantitative Analysis Disadvantages

Although quantitative analysis has many benefits, the complexity of this approach results in some substantial disadvantages as well:

- Complex — The formulas used in quantitative analysis and the resulting volume of tables upon tables of numbers can be quite complex. This leads to several problems for the project, including the need for more experienced project members and overall increased costs.
- Calculations Not Understood — The calculations involved in the various formulas can appear daunting and confusing to the reader. This hinders the understanding of the analysis performed.

- Results Not Trusted — The complex formulas and lack of understanding of the calculations may lead to a general frustration and even mistrust of the results. It is difficult to accept the conclusion of a report if you do not understand the analysis. Understanding the analysis of some quantitative methods is a task on a par with understanding geometric proofs.
- A Lot of Work — A quantitative risk analysis can be labor-intensive because of the number of data elements required and calculations that need to be performed. Substantial information gathering is required to obtain the values needed for the quantitative formulas. The derivation of the value for each of the asset, threat, vulnerability, and safeguard variables for a single team member is difficult enough. Add to that the difficulty of arriving at a team consensus for each and every one of those values.
- False Sense of Accuracy — Perhaps the biggest disadvantage of a quantitative risk assessment method is the false sense of accuracy it portrays to most consumers of the information. When consumers of a security risk assessment report are presented with specific figures for expected loss or safeguard value, they tend to believe that the numbers are derived with a large degree of accuracy. The fact is that an accurate value for many variables that go into computing these figures is difficult if not impossible to obtain.

There are limited sources of data available to assist in determining values for probabilities of events such as the likelihood of a sophisticated attack by a hacker or a disgruntled employee sabotaging the system. The lack of such data makes any attempt to state such a probability educated guesswork at best. Values such as damage to corporate reputation or loss of competitive advantage are inherently difficult to determine.

Other values are extremely complex to determine even if data exists. For example, determining the magnitude of a loss caused by the loss of an e-mail server can be exceedingly difficult to estimate and must consider the following factors:

- Number of users served by the e-mail server.
- Value of communication capability offered by the e-mail server to each of the users.
- Value of the storage and retrieval capability offered by the e-mail server to each of the users.
- Alternative methods of communication available to each of the users.
- Length of time the e-mail server is down.
- Specific communication or storage and retrieval needs during the time of the outage for each user, for example, if a big proposal needs to go out.

Even areas in which it seems, at first glance, that it will be relatively easy to determine costs, other factors conspire to make this a difficult task. For example, it may seem like an easy task to determine the hardware, software, installation, and training costs of implementing a new firewall, such as the cost of implementing a safeguard. However, it is very difficult to accurately estimate other costs associated with this implementation, such as possible productivity loss during implementation or the cost of tuning the firewall policy to block potentially dangerous connections while still allowing custom applications and legacy systems to interact.

Lastly, even if this data was available it would be out of date within months or weeks because the threat environment in which most organizations operate changes so rapidly. New attacks are being developed daily and easy to use, downloadable tools quickly incorporate new attacks and make them available to many potential hackers.

13.1.2 Qualitative Analysis

Whereas quantitative analysis relies on complex formulas and monetary or frequency values for the variables, qualitative analysis relies on the subjective judgment of the security risk assessment members to determine the overall risk to the information systems. The same basic elements are required to determine risk, such as asset value, threat frequency, impact, and safeguard effectiveness, but these elements are now measured in subjective terms such as "high" or "not likely."

Even if the qualitative risk equation variables are not always expressed in terms of numbers, the values of these variables are often treated as if they do, in the following limited ways:

1. Qualitative values have order. These values are hierarchical. For example,

$$High > Medium > Low$$

2. Qualitative values compute. These values are used in equations to compute other values. For example,

$$Likelihood\ of\ Occurrence * Severity\ of\ Impact = Risk$$
$$Likelihood\ (Conceivable) * Severity\ (Major\ System\ Damage)$$
$$= Risk\ (Undesirable)$$

These qualitative risk equation variables are not treated as values in the same way that quantitative analysis variables are. Qualitative risk equation variables are not expressed in terms of monetary values but as a predicted frequency of occurrence. Therefore, unlike quantitative risk analysis, the results of qualitative risk analysis cannot be used to directly justify costs through a cost-benefit analysis.

Different qualitative security risk assessment methods have varying names, descriptions, and levels of qualitative values. An example of qualitative values is shown in Table 13.2

13.1.2.1 Qualitative Analysis Advantages

By using the subjective judgment of security risk assessment team members, qualitative methods have many benefits:

- Simple — Qualitative methods can be a welcome relief from the complexity of quantitative methods. The simplicity of these methods is their major feature and is the root of nearly all of the advantages of qualitative methods.
- Simple Measurement Values — Under quantitative methods it can be extremely difficult to derive exact numbers for each of the asset, threat,

Table 13.2 Qualitative Measurements. Qualitative analysis methods use levels, labels, and descriptions for qualitative values. The example shown here has qualitative values and descriptions for vulnerability measurements of attempt, exploitability, and potential impact.

Level	Attempt	Exploit	Impact
1	Likely	Easy	Exposure or loss of proprietary information Loss of integrity of critical information System disruption Major structural damage Loss of physical access control Exposure or loss of sensitive information Grave danger to building occupants
2	Conceivable	Moderate	Major system damage Significant structural damage Risks to access controls Potential exposure to sensitive information Serious danger to building occupants
3	Improbable	Difficult	Minor system damage or exposure Some structural damage Reduced access control effectiveness Moderate exposure to sensitive information Moderate danger to building occupants
4	Remote	Extremely difficult	Less than minor system damage or exposure Extremely limited structural damage Potential effect on access controls Control of sensitive information Safety of building occupants

impact, and safeguard variables. Under qualitative methods this task is still significant but can be performed with a lot less effort. Consider how difficult it would be to determine the impact of an e-mail server going down under the quantitative method. Now consider how easy it would be to get the team to agree that the impact of the e-mail server going down for a day would be a "major loss" as opposed to a "critical loss" or a "minor loss."

- Easy to Understand and Convey — The analysis and results of qualitative security risk assessment methods are easy to convey to others. Descriptive terms and relatively easy computations make it easy for others not involved in the analysis to review the results and comprehend the analysis contained in the security risk assessment report.
- Provides Adequate Identification of Problem Areas — In most situations a qualitative security risk assessment will provide enough information at an adequate level to influence the improvement of the organization's security posture. Although there is not a dollar value attached to recommended safeguards, qualitative security risk assessment methods still provide enough information to let the organization know what improvements are required to reduce the risk to their critical assets.

13.1.2.2 Qualitative Analysis Disadvantages

Although qualitative methods have many benefits, the simplicity of this approach results in some substantial disadvantages as well:

- Subjective Results — There is no getting around the fact that the value of the security risk assessment variables is subjective and based more on experience and judgment than cold hard facts. Therefore, the results are subjective as well and one could always argue that they may be inaccurate.[3]
- Subjective Asset Value — The same argument used above can be used for the valuation of assets. It is difficult to defend subjective values placed on assets other than to state that the judgment was based on experience. Although such estimates are typically accurate, the value can still be questioned and this can lead to difficulties in getting the results accepted.
- Subjective Recommendations — If the analysis is based on subjective asset values and results, then it follows that the resulting recommendations are subjective as well. Many will argue that this makes the results no less accurate, but the results may be more difficult to defend.
- Difficult to Track Improvements — For security programs that want to track their improvement from assessment to assessment, this becomes difficult when the assessment results in a "high-medium" or "medium-low" risk. Just how good an improvement would that be?

13.2 Tools

Performing an information security risk assessment is a complicated process. Even the most experienced of security risk assessment teams can find one or more of the tasks within a security risk assessment to be cumbersome, unwieldy, or complex. Some tasks within a security risk assessment are tedious, such as the listing of all vulnerabilities found and their mapping to recommended safeguards. Other tasks may be difficult because of the large number of items involved in the task, such as reviewing existing policies and procedures for relevant security gaps. Still other tasks can involve complex computations that may lead to mistakes, such as the computation of risk impact. To assist with these tasks there are a variety of checklists, templates, and software that may be incorporated into the security risk assessment process.

Checklists, templates, and software may be effectively employed in the security risk assessment process to increase its efficiency and accuracy. Consider the following security risk assessment tasks and how they may be improved through the use of checklists and tools:

- listing assets, threats, vulnerabilities;
- performing risk calculations;
- developing reports.

13.2.1 Lists

Checklists are useful when encountering a situation in which the risks are similar to those encountered in other situations. The extent to which the situations are similar dictates the usefulness of the checklist.

Other lists, such as a listing of all the threat agents and threats, can be useful as well. Creating this list for each security risk assessment can be a daunting task. There is literally no end to the number of ways an organization's system may be attacked by mankind or Mother Nature. When performing a security risk assessment, however, we must limit the threat agents and threats that we shall consider for the effort in some manner.

A checklist of possible threat agents and associated threats may be used to ensure that the security risk assessment team considers all relevant threat agents and threats. Much of the work here would be involved in compiling such a list, but that work can be reused for each security risk assessment performed. While the security risk assessment team will need to reconsider the threat agents and threats that are relevant for the specific security risk assessment, there is no need to reinvent the list.

13.2.2 Templates

Many templates are available to assist the security risk assessment team in performing the tasks of the security risk assessment. Many of the examples and approaches given in this book are in fact worked examples or templates that could be used or modified for use in a security risk assessment effort. Other templates are available on government Web sites and integrated within security risk assessment tools and methods.

13.3 Security Risk Assessment Methods

All security risk assessment processes have the same basic elements, namely, threat analysis, asset valuation, vulnerability analysis, and risk evaluation. Any process that results in an assessment of the current security controls and their ability to protect the organization's assets is a security risk assessment method. A security risk assessment method is a set of procedures and activities that structures the security risk assessment process.

Any given method for performing a security risk assessment may be ideal for one situation, budget, or industry but not for others. Security risk assessment methodologies are not a one-size-fits-all situation. Because of the various needs and various situations, a variety of security risk assessment methods have been developed. The list in Table 13.3 is by no means exhaustive but it does provide a good survey of many of the more popular security risk assessments available.

13.3.1 FAA Security Risk Management Process

The Security Risk Management Process was developed by the Federal Aviation Administration for achieving FAA's goals and objectives of applying risk management throughout the life-cycle management process. The FAA SRM was developed for FAA and is used there, but it is generally applicable to other organizations. The FAA SRM outlines a ten-step process. The FAA SRM is a qualitative method and provides levels, descriptions, and the formula for qualitative calculations; however, the FAA SRM does not provide much in the way of examples, templates, checklists, or tools.

13.3.2 OCTAVE

This risk assessment methodology was developed by the Software Engineering Institute of Carnegie Mellon University. The Operationally Critical Threat, Asset, and Vulnerability Evaluation (OCTAVE) method provides a process complete with guidelines, checklists, time estimates, and process descriptions for this three-phased security risk assessment process. The three phases include (1) asset-based threat profiles, (2) infrastructure vulnerability identification, and (3) security and strategy plan development. This method is designed to be run by a small team within a large organization (300 or more) with a multilayer hierarchy, an internally run computer infrastructure, and the ability to run their own vulnerability assessment

Table 13.3 Security Risk Assessment Methods. There are a variety of security risk assessment methods and tools. A few of the more popular security risk assessment methods are surveyed here.

Security Risk Assessment Approach	Type	Approach Phases	Resources Required	Application
FAA SRM	Open qualitative method	• Asset identification • Asset criticality determination • Criticality rating assignment • Threat identification • Existing countermeasure identification • Asset vulnerability rating assignment • Risk level determination • Decision making • Risk reduction determination • Cost-benefit analysis	• Program managers • Facility managers • Integrated product team leaders • Security representatives	FAA projects (required) General-purpose method
OCTAVE	Open qualitative method	• Profile threats and assets • Identify infrastructure vulnerabilities • Develop security strategy and plan	Internal, nonexperts	Large corporations with ability to run their own tools

FRAP	Open qualitative method	• Pre-FRAP meeting • FRAP session • Post-FRAP process	Facilitator and internal manager	Gap and initial assessment where time is of the essence
CRAMM	Commercial qualitative tool	• Asset identification • Threat and vulnerability assessment • Countermeasure recommendation	Qualified and experienced practitioners	Demonstrating BS 7799 compliance
NSA IAM	Open qualitative method	• Pre-assessment • On-site visit • Post-assessment	IAM-trained providers	Government agencies and Critical infrastructure required to meet PDD 63*

*Presidential Decision Directive 63, May 22, 1998, calls for frequent assessments on the critical infrastructure.

tools. The team may have had some training and exposure to performing security risk assessment, but they are not assumed to be experts.

13.3.3 FRAP

The Facilitated Risk Assessment Process (FRAP) was developed by Tom Peltier and was designed as a methodology that could be used by managers themselves with the assistance of a facilitator. The FRAP method consists of a three-step process that is designed to be completed with ten days. The FRAP method is a qualitative method and those who purchase the book are provided with templates and checklists.

13.3.4 CRAMM

The CCTA Risk Analysis and Management Method (CRAMM) was developed by the UK Government's Central Computer and Telecommunications Agency (CCTA) in 1985. The tool has evolved and has since been commercialized by Insight Consulting. CRAMM is a qualitative tool that provides the method, calculations, and report for a security risk assessment.

13.3.5 NSA IAM

The National Security Agency's (NSA) INFOSEC Assessment Methodology (IAM) was developed to train commercial entities how to perform assessments to NSA's standards. The NSA's IAM is based on the agency's approach for assessing information security inspections for government agencies. The IAM assessment consists of three phases: pre-assessment, on-site visit, and post-assessment phases. The IAM provides templates and guides for each step of the process, including a list of 18 baseline activities to review. The IAM process typically takes between five and fourteen weeks to complete. A team of 2–3 people is recommended.[4]

Notes

1. The present value of money is the total amount that the future payments would be worth now. Factors considered include the interest rate of the "loan" and the timing and amount of the payments. In this case we consider a loss of $600 of profits per week over a year.
2. "Revised Departmental Guidance: Treatment of Value of Life and Injuries in Preparing Economic Evaluations." United States Department of Transportation, January 29, 2002. http://os-pxweb.dot.gov/policy/EconStrat/treatmentoflife.htm

3. The astute reader will recognize that no matter what approach (qualitative or quantitative) is used, there are many security risk variables for which no cold hard facts are available. So, even though quantitative methods may result in a number, this does not mean that the number is any more accurate than the qualitative methods description.

4. The NSA has developed a program to assess IAM services providers for their ability to apply the IAM method. The assessment approach is a Capability Maturity Model (CMM) approach and is formalized in the Information Assurance Capability Maturity Model (IA-CMM).

References

[1] Passori, Al, "Selecting the Risk Assessment Method of Choice," META Group, July 21, 2004. http://searchcio.techtarget.com/originalContent/0,289142,sid19_gci994851,00.html

[2] Alberts, Christopher J., and Dorofee, Audrey J., "OCTAVE(SM) Method Implementation Guide Version 2.0," November 5, 2003. http://www.cert.org/octave/download/intro.html

[3] Alberts, Christopher J., and Dorofee, Audrey J., "OCTAVE Criteria, Version 2.0," December 2001.

[4] *Decision Making: A Technical Guide to Identifying, Assessing and Evaluating Risks, Costs and Benefits*. Environmental Risk Management Authority, New Zealand, ER-TG-05-1 03/04, March 2004, ISBN 0-473-21523-1.

[5] *Security Self-Assessment Guide for Information Technology Systems*, NIST Special Publication 800-26, November 2001. http://csrc.nist.gov/publications/nistpubs/800-26/sp800-26.pdf

[6] INFOSEC Assessment Methodology, "National Security Agency." http://www.iatrp.com/iam.cfm

[7] "Lessons Learned from RITs First Security Posture Assessment," Rochester Institute of Technology, January, 2004. http://www.educause.edu/ep/ep_item_detail.asp?ITEM_ID=197

[8] "FIRM: Fundamental Information Risk Management Implementation Guide," Information Security Forum, March 2001. http://www.securityforum.org/assests/pdf/firm.pdf

[9] *Guide for Selecting Automated Risk Analysis Tools*. NIST Special Publication 500-174, October 1989. http://csrc.nist.gov/publications/nistpubs/500-174/sp174.txt

[10] *Guidelines for Automatic Data Processing Physical Security and Risk Management*, Federal Information Processing Standards Publication 31 (FIPS Pub. 31), National Bureau of Standards, June 1974.

[11] Yazar, Zeki, "A Qualitative Risk Analysis and Management Tool — CRAMM," April 11, 2002. www.sans.org/rr/whitepapers/auditing/83.php

[12] "Acquisition Management Policy," Federal Aviation Administration, February 2005. http://fast.faa.gov

[13] Peltier, Thomas R., *Information Security Risk Analysis*, pp. 23–46. Auerbach Publications, 2001.

Appendix

Relevant Standards
and Regulations

This appendix contains a list and a brief description of most of the relevant information security standards and regulations that relate to the practice of security risk assessments.

GAISP

The Generally Accepted Information Security Practices (GAISP) is a project adopted and led by the Information System Security Association (ISSA). The objective of this project is to "create a common, international understanding of comprehensive, consistent, and coherent guidance on the protection of information assets." The GAISP is composed of "pervasive principles," "broad-functional principles," and "detailed properties."

Pervasive principles are described as general principles targeted at information security governance. As such they define and address information security policies such as confidentiality, integrity, and availability.

- Accountability, awareness, ethics, multidisciplinary, proportionality, integration, timeliness, assessment, equity.

Broad functional principles are described as being derived from the pervasive principles and provide guidance on how to operationally implement the pervasive principles.

- Information Security Policy — ensures that policy, procedures, standards, and guidelines are developed and maintained.
- Education and Awareness — deals with the communication of information security policy through education to all personnel given access to the organization's assets.
- Accountability — ensures that all personnel with access to the organization's assets are held accountable for their actions.
- Information Asset Management — deals with documentation and valuation of the organization's information assets.
- Environmental Management — ensures that risks that are inherent in the existing environment have been considered and addressed.
- Personnel Qualifications — ensures that sensitive positions have been identified, qualifications for these positions have been compiled, and a process is in place to ensure that sensitive positions are filled with qualified individuals.
- Incident Management — deals with the need to be able to detect and respond to information security incidents that could affect the enforcement of information security policies.
- Information Systems Life Cycle — ensures that information security needs are anticipated and considered at all stages of an information systems life cycle.
- Access Control — ensures that adequate access controls have been established to protect information assets.
- Operational Continuity and Contingency Planning — deals with the continuity of critical operations.
- Information Risk Management — ensures that appropriate information security measures are enacted, considering the likely threats, potential vulnerabilities, and the value of organizational assets.
- Network and Internet Security — ensures that the security implications of connecting to other networks or the Internet are considered when implementing security measures.
- Legal, Regulatory, and Contractual Requirements of Information Security — ensures that management is aware of all relevant legal, regulatory, and contractual information security requirements.
- Ethical Practices — deals with preserving individual rights while enforcing information security measures.

Detailed security principles are described as the specific methods of implementing the broad functional principles for a specific environment or technology.

The current version of the GAISP is not populated with detailed security principles.

CobiT

The Common Objectives for IT (CobiT) is issued by the IT Governance Institute of the Information Systems Audit and Control Foundation. The objective of CobiT is to provide a generally applicable and accepted standard for information technology security and control practices. CobiT comprises the CobiT Framework, Management Guidelines, Audit Guidelines, and an Implementation Tool Set.

The CobiT Framework is a set of 34 high-level control objectives for information security management grouped into the domains of planning and organization, acquisition and implementation, delivery and support, and monitoring. The Management Guidelines are a set of "action-oriented" guidelines that assist organizational management with controlling, monitoring progress, and measuring the organization's achievements. The Audit Guidelines are associated with each of the 34 high-level control objectives and provide guidance on how to review the organization's existing IT processes against CobiT's control objectives. The Implementation Tool Set provides organizations considering the use and adoption of CobiT with examples and lessons learned from organizations that have been there before.

Of the various elements of CobiT, the CobiT Framework provides us with a view into determining the IT Governance Institute's definition of information security best practices on the level of activities to be performed. The CobiT Framework comprises 34 high-level CobiT control objectives, but these are for IT, not just for IT security. A synopsis of the CobiT control objectives from an information security only standpoint is presented below.[1] Note that the CobiT Framework and the controls it comprises is designed for a more general IT audit and is not focused solely on information security. As such, almost all of the controls described here have many other important elements outside of the information security only treatment they receive here.

- PO2: Define Information Architecture — ensures that a business information model is created and maintained. This includes assigning data ownership and information classification.
- PO4: Define Information Technology Organization and Relationships — ensures that the information security group is defined and its reporting structure and staff are adequate to ensure that organizational information security objectives are met. This control also ensures that the information security roles and responsibilities are defined.
- PO6: Communicate Management Aims and Directions — ensures that information security policies are developed and communicated.

- PO7: Manage Human Resources — ensures that personnel management controls are in place. This control objective includes hiring and termination procedures and cross-training.
- PO8: Ensure Compliance with External Requirements — ensures that external requirements, including laws, regulations, and contractual agreements, are assessed and recognized as system requirements.
- PO9: Assess Risk — ensures that an information security risk assessment is performed.
- PO11: Manage Quality — ensures that quality controls are planned and implemented throughout the life-cycle stages.
- DS2: Manage Third-Party Services — ensures that the roles and responsibilities of third-party services are defined. This control also ensures that third-party services are audited to ensure their compliance with their roles and responsibilities.
- DS3: Manage Performance and Capacity — ensures that the performance and availability requirements for the information system are defined and met.
- DS4: Ensure Continuous Service — ensures that adequate controls are in place to ensure continuity of operations. This control includes disaster recovery planning, maintenance, and testing.
- DS5: Ensure Systems Security — ensures that controls are in place to protect information from unauthorized use, disclosure, modification, and loss.
- DS7: Educate and Train Users — ensures that users are aware of information security risks and their responsibilities in preserving the security posture of the organization.
- DS10: Manage Problems and Incidents — ensures that information security-related incidents are resolved.
- DS11: Manage Data — ensures that sensitive data is processed, stored, transmitted, and disposed of consistent with the security policy.
- DS12: Manage Facilities — ensures that physical and environmental controls are adequate.
- AI5: Install and Accredit Systems — ensures that systems are evaluated for their ability to meet information security requirements and accredited for use by the senior manager in charge of the system.
- AI6: Manage Change — ensures that information security risks introduced into the system are minimized through careful review, analysis, and approval of changes.

ISO 17799

The *Information Technology — Code of Practice for Information Security Management* (ISO 17799) was issued by the International Organization for

Standardization. The objective of the standard is to provide a common basis for organizations developing information security management programs. The ISO 17799 comprises a set of information security controls seen as best practices and applicable to most organizations. A quick review of these controls is presented below:

- Risk Assessment — ensures that security controls are selected from a risk-based approach to information security.
- Information Security Policy (3.1) — establishes and maintains an information security policy that defines information security, establishes roles and responsibilities, and defines additional information security standards and guidelines.
- Information Security Infrastructure (4.1) — establishes the information security organization.
- Security of Third-Party Access (4.2) — ensures that third-party access to information-processing facilities maintains the security of the organization's assets.
- Outsourcing (4.3) — ensures that the security of the organization's assets is maintained with respect to outsourcing of services.
- Accountability of Assets (5.1) — ensures that all assets are accounted for and assigned an owner.
- Information Classification (5.2) — ensures that an information classification system is developed and that all assets are classified.
- Security in Job Definition and Resourcing (6.1) — ensures that personnel in sensitive positions have been properly screened and have signed the appropriate documents.
- User Training (6.2) — ensures that all users are properly trained in their security responsibilities and use information system controls.
- Responding to Security Incidents and Malfunctions (6.3) — ensures that information security incidents are properly reported.
- Secure Areas (7.1) — ensures that critical systems are physically protected.
- Equipment Security (7.2) — ensures that critical equipment is physically protected.
- General Controls (7.3) — ensures that information and information systems are generally protected from theft and disclosure.
- Operational Procedures and Responsibilities (8.1) — ensures that proper procedures are developed for the operation of the information systems (including incident response procedures) and ensures that responsibilities are assigned while preserving adequate separation of duties.
- System Planning and Acceptance (8.2) — ensures that information systems are developed with respect to planned needs, including capacity, and that the developed system goes through a formal acceptance process.

- Protection Against Malicious Software (8.3) — ensures that proper precautions are taken to avoid and control the introduction of malicious software into the environment.
- Housekeeping (8.4) — ensures that backup, event logging, and equipment monitoring are performed.
- Network Management (8.5) — ensures that adequate network security controls are in place.
- Media Handling and Security (8.6) — ensures that media is properly labeled, handled, and disposed of.
- Exchanges of Information and Software (8.7) — ensures that security procedures are in place for the exchange of information and software between organizations.
- Business Requirement for Access Control (9.1) — ensures that decisions to grant or prevent access to information and information systems are based on business objectives.
- User Access Management (9.2) — ensures that user access to data is granted and controlled in a secure manner. This includes account registration, access control decisions, and account termination.
- User Responsibilities (9.3) — ensures that users are aware of the security responsibilities for keeping information and information systems secure.
- Network Access Control (9.4) — ensures that access to internal and external networks is done in a secure manner. This includes a review of the network interfaces, access controls, and authorization controls.
- Operating System Access Control (9.5) — ensures appropriate security controls at the operating system level. These controls include user identification, access audit, authentication, and access controls.
- Application Access Control (9.6) — ensures appropriate security controls at the operating system level. These controls include access controls, protection from operating system utilities, and isolation from other processes.
- Monitoring System Access and Use (9.7) — ensures that systems are monitored for possible access violations or inappropriate use.
- Mobile Computing and Teleworking (9.8) — ensures that security is preserved within mobile computing devices and personnel who work from other locations such as the home or on the road.
- Security Requirements of Systems (10.1) — ensures that adequate security controls are built into the system from the start of the project.
- Security in Application Systems (10.2) — ensures that appropriate security controls are built into application systems. This includes validation of input and output variables, and proper internal controls.
- Cryptographic Controls (10.3) — ensures that encryption is appropriately and properly employed to protect the security of the organization's assets. This includes proper encryption techniques, use of digital signatures and nonrepudiation services, and proper key management.

- Security of System Files (10.4) — ensures that system files such as audit logs, library routines, and configuration files are properly protected.
- Security in Development and Support Processes (10.5) — ensures that changes to operational systems and software are appropriately controlled, reviewed, and approved.
- Aspects of Business Continuity Management (11 1) — ensures that critical systems are protected from possible interruptions from disasters.
- Compliance with Legal Requirements (12.1) — ensures that legal, regulatory, and contractual requirements are considered in the development of security controls for the organization.
- Reviews of Security Policy and Technical Compliance (12.2) — ensures that information systems are reviewed periodically for compliance with existing security policies and procedures.
- System Audit Considerations (12.3) — ensures that the security auditing process is controlled and that information systems are protected from auditing tools and techniques.

NIST Handbook

The National Institute of Standards and Technology (NIST) Special Publication 800-12, also known as the *NIST Computer Security Handbook*, is an introduction to computer security controls. The handbook discusses the basic security controls that should be considered for securing information systems at the time of publication in 1995. The security controls discussed in the *NIST Computer Security Handbook* are categorized into management operational, and technical controls. Each of these security controls is briefly described below.[2]

Management Controls

The following set of security controls are referred to as management controls because they are usually handled by the management of the organization:

- Computer Security Policy (5) — These controls deal with computer security policies on all levels. The computer security program policy is the policy from organizational management that establishes the computer security program. Other policies, such as issue-specific policies and system-specific policies, are more focused policies that deal with specific topics or technology to preserve the security of the organization.
- Computer Security Program Management (6) — These controls establish a comprehensive management approach to the implementation of a computer security program. Specific controls include the organizational structure of the computer security program, and techniques to ensure its effectiveness.

- Computer Security Risk Management (7) — These controls ensure that the risk to the organization's assets are known and properly mitigated.
- Security and Planning in the Computer System Life Cycle (8) — These controls ensure that computer security considerations are adopted throughout the life cycle of systems and applications. Controls include security requirements analysis, security testing, installation, accreditation, change management, and secure disposal of sensitive information.
- Assurance (9) — These controls refer to any measure taken to gain confidence that the existing security controls operate effectively. Assurance measures may include proper planning, design, system review and approval, and other measures.

Operational Controls

The security controls listed below are called operational controls because they are implemented by the operational staff:

- Staffing (10.1) — These controls ensure that security was established and preserved through the selection, management, and even termination of staff. Controls include proper job definition, identification of sensitive positions, screening potential employees, and providing security awareness training and continuous education.
- User Administration (10.2) — These controls ensure that users' accounts are properly established and maintained. User administration controls include account creation and management, periodic account review, detection of misused and dormant accounts, the establishment of temporary accounts, and proper account termination.
- Contractor Access (10.3) — These controls ensure that access to computer systems granted to outside support is properly controlled.
- Public Access (10.4) — These controls ensure that access to computer systems granted to public users of the system is properly controlled.
- Preparing for Contingencies and Disasters (11) — These controls ensure that critical business systems continue to be available in the event of a disaster. These controls include the identification of critical business functions, listing of support resources required for critical systems, identification of potential disasters, development of contingency plan strategies, implementation of those strategies, and testing and revision of the contingency plan strategies.
- Computer Incident Handling (12)—These controls ensure that those computer incidents that may lead to a breach in security are identified, investigated, handled, and reported.
- Awareness, Training, and Education (13) — These controls ensure that all those with access to the computer systems understand their security

responsibly and are aware of the impact of their behavior on the security of the system.

- Secure Operations (14) — These controls ensure that the operations of the information systems and the security controls are performed in a manner that preserves the security of the information system. Security controls addressed here include support for user operations and software implementations, configuration management of key work products, backups of critical and operational data, secure controls on media, documentation of operational procedures, and maintenance of the information system.
- Physical and Environmental Security (15) — These controls ensure the security of the information system and organizational assets through physical and environmental controls. Security controls addressed here include physical access controls, fire safety, redundancy of supporting utilities, protection from structural collapse, avoidance of plumbing leaks, protection from interception of data, and controls for mobile and portable systems.

Technical Controls

The security controls described below are all referred to as technical controls in that they depend on technology (i.e., the information systems themselves) to enforce the security policy:

- Identification and Authentication (16) — These controls prevent unauthorized personnel from entering the computer system. Security controls include passwords, tokens, and biometrics.
- Logical Access Control (17) — These controls ensure that sensitive information assets and information systems are only accessed by authorized individuals. Security controls include access criteria, access policy, technical mechanisms (such as access control lists, encryption, and information labeling), and access control administration.
- Audit Trails (18) — These controls ensure that users are accountable for their actions and that indications of system instability or security problems are identified and tracked. Security controls include keystroke monitoring, audit events, and review of audit trails.
- Cryptography (19) — These controls provide for the protection of information and the implementation of confidentiality integrity, and availability (basic cryptography, integrity, digital signatures, key distribution, key management).

HIPAA: Security

On August 21, 1996, the Congress enacted the Health Insurance Portability and Accountability Act (HIPAA), Public Law 104-191. HIPAA was designed to improve the efficiency and effectiveness of the healthcare system by facilitating electronic interchange of healthcare information, including financial and administrative transactions transmitted electronically between healthcare organizations. Congress directed the Department of Health and Human Services to develop standards for transactions, unique health identifiers, transaction code sets, electronic signature, privacy, and security. The HIPAA Privacy rule documents the necessary protections for maintaining the privacy of "individually identifiable health information." Although the HIPAA privacy standard, issued on August 14, 2002, impacts the security requirements of an organization, only the HIPAA security standard impacts our discussion on core security practices.

The "Health Insurance Reform: Security Standards; Final Rule," commonly known as the HIPAA Security Rule, was issued by the Department of Health and Human Service on April 21, 2003. The HIPAA Security Rule was designed to assure patients, insured individuals, providers, and health plans that the security (i.e., integrity, confidentiality, and availability) of electronic protected health information (e-PHI) is protected through its collection, maintenance, use, and transmission. The purpose of this rule was to adopt national security standards for the healthcare industry for safeguards to protect the confidentiality, integrity, and availability of electronic protected health information.

The security controls within the HIPAA Security Rule are categorized into administrative, physical, and technical controls. Each of the administrative, physical, and technical controls is either required or "addressable." A status of "addressable" is interpreted to mean that the security control must be implemented if it is considered reasonable and appropriate for the intended environment. If the addressable security control is not considered reasonable and appropriate, then the reasons why must be documented and an equivalent measure must be adopted.

"Reasonable and appropriate" is a subjective measure and requires the use of judgment to determine and logic to explain. The use of these terms in the HIPAA Security Rule is by design and should be viewed as flexibility rather than ambiguity. Use of professional or managerial judgment is an integral part of business. Although this approach requires interpretation of the rule and explanation of your findings, this flexibility allows for a greater applicability of the regulation, adoption of new technology and methods, and the exercise of sound judgment.

All security controls mentioned in the HIPAA Security Rule are presented below regardless of their status as "required" or "addressable." Controls that are required have no special indication below. Controls that are addressable are indicated as such.

Administrative Safeguards

Administrative safeguards are administrative actions, policies, and procedures that manage the selection, development, implementation, and maintenance of security measures to protect sensitive information and to manage the conduct of the organization's workforce in relation to the protection of that information.[3]

- Security Management Process [164.308(a)(1)(i)] — This set of controls ensures that the security program of the organization is managed appropriately and that adequate processes are in place. The following elements of a security program are required:
  - Risk Analysis — The healthcare organization must conduct an accurate and thorough assessment of the potential risks and vulnerabilities to the confidentiality, integrity, and availability of electronic protected health information that it holds. This means that the organization must conduct or commission a security risk analysis of information systems that contain PHI and the policies, procedures, and other controls that affect these systems.
  - Risk Management — The healthcare organization is required to implement a set of security measures that reduce the security risk at the healthcare organization to a reasonable and appropriate level. This means that the organization must address all risks identified in the risk analysis but not necessarily implement every security measure suggested in the completed risk analysis document. The organization may decide to mitigate the risk through an alternative measure, reduce the risk through other measures, or accept the risk.
  - Sanction Policy — The healthcare organization is required to apply appropriate sanctions against members of the workforce who fail to comply with security policies and procedures. This means that the healthcare organization must ensure that security policies and procedures are followed and enforced. A policy must be in place to address the sanctions to be followed when an employee does not follow the established security policies.
  - Information System Activity Review — The healthcare organization is required to implement procedures to regularly review records of information system activity, such as audit logs, access reports, and security incident tracking reports. This means that the healthcare organization must collect and review information regarding possible, suspected, and known security incidents.
- Assigned Security Responsibility [164. 308(a)(2)] — This set of controls ensures that a security official with the responsibility for the development and implementation of the required security policies and procedures is identified.
- Workforce Security [164.308(a)(3)(i)] — This set of controls ensures that the organization implements policies and procedures to ensure that all employees have appropriate access to PHI and to prevent employees

who do not have access from obtaining access to PHI. Specifically, the covered entity must implement the following:

- Authorization and Supervision (Addressable) — The healthcare organization is required to implement procedures for the authorization and supervision of employees who work with PHI or in locations where it might be accessed. Procedures for authorization and supervision of employees working with PHI would be addressed in typical account authorization procedures. Procedures that recognize the "data owner" and require the data owner's approval prior to giving an employee access to PHI, would meet this requirement.

- Workforce Clearance Procedures (Addressable) — The healthcare organization is required to implement procedures to determine that the access of an employee to PHI is appropriate. Procedures such as criminal background checks and conflict of interest reviews could be required prior to the organization's employees being authorized access to PHI. A formal decision as to the appropriateness of this safeguard would be addressed as a result of a risk analysis.

- Termination Procedures (Addressable) — The healthcare organization is required to implement procedures for terminating access to PHI when employment is terminated. Procedures for the termination of access to PHI would be addressed in typical termination procedures. However, there are several areas and checks, including ensuring complete removal of PHI access, that are affected. These include partner notification, voicemail, cell phone, e-mail account termination, key and lock combination changes, reminder of continuing obligations, and group account and e-mail forwarding reviews.

- Information Access Management [164.308(a)(4)(i)] — This set of controls ensures that the organization implements policies and procedures for authorizing access to electronic protected health information. Specifically, the covered entity must implement the following:

  - Isolating Healthcare Clearinghouse Functions — If a healthcare clearinghouse is part of a larger organization, the clearinghouse must implement policies and procedures that protect the electronic protected health information of the clearinghouse from unauthorized access by the larger organization. If the healthcare organization is not a clearinghouse, then this requirement is not applicable.

  - Access Authorization (Addressable) — The healthcare organization is required to implement policies and procedures for granting access to PHI. Examples of appropriate policies and procedures include restrictions on access to workstations, transactions, programs, or processes.

  - Access Establishment and Modification (Addressable) — The healthcare organization is required to implement policies and procedures that, based upon the organization's access authorization policies, establish, document, review, and modify a user's right of access to a workstation, transaction, program, or process. If the access authorization requirement is appropriate, then the healthcare organization needs to implement the policies and procedures to enforce, modify, and update access authorizations.

- Security Awareness Training [164.308(a)(5)(i)] — This set of controls requires that the healthcare organization implement a security awareness and training program for all employees including management. Specifically, the covered entity must implement the following:
  - Security Reminders (Addressable) — The healthcare organization is required to implement a security awareness program that includes periodic security reminders to all employees. Security reminders are a way to keep the healthcare organization employees informed of their security responsibilities. These reminders can take many forms, including message of the day at log-in, security posters, and memos addressing specific security issues.
  - Protection from Malicious Software (Addressable) — The healthcare organization is required to implement a program that provides protection from malicious software. This shall include procedures for guarding against, detecting, and reporting malicious software.
  - Log-in Monitoring (Addressable) — The healthcare organization is required to implement a security awareness program that includes procedures for monitoring log-in attempts and reporting discrepancies.
  - Password Management (Addressable) — The healthcare organization is required to implement a security awareness program that includes procedures for creating, changing, and safeguarding passwords. When passwords are used as an element of the authentication process to the information systems, it is of paramount importance that users understand the role these passwords play in the healthcare organization's security and the users' role in ensuring that they are used effectively. Good password management includes strong password selection, frequent password changes, and safeguarding the secrecy of passwords. The healthcare organization's users should be trained in how to create or select strong passwords, why they should not "cycle" their passwords, why the healthcare organization enforces password changes frequently, how to recognize a "social engineering" attack, and how to safeguard their password.
- Security Incident Procedures [164.308(a)(6)(i)] — This set of controls ensures that the covered entity implement policies and procedures to address security incidents. Specifically, the covered entity must implement the following:
  - Response and Reporting (Addressable) — The healthcare organization is required to identify and respond to suspected or known security

incidents; mitigate, to the extent practicable, the harmful effect of security incidents that are known to the organization; and document security incidents and their outcomes. The healthcare organization must put into place a security incident and response capability. This includes technology and procedures to recognize a security incident; technology and procedures to mitigate the damage caused by the incident; and procedures for documenting the security incident. Many appropriate approaches are available to the healthcare organization.

- Contingency Plan [164.308(a)(7)(i)] — This set of controls requires that the covered entity establish (and implement as needed) policies and procedures for responding to an emergency or other occurrence (for example, fire, vandalism, system failure, and natural disaster) that damages systems that contain PHI. Specifically, the covered entity must implement the following:
  - Data Backup Plan — The healthcare organization is required to establish and implement procedures to create and maintain retrievable exact copies of PHI. This requirement applies to all systems upon which the organization relies to store master copies of PHI data.
  - Disaster Recovery Plan — The healthcare organization is required to establish procedures to restore any loss of data. The healthcare organization must create procedures for the restoration of all data if lost for systems that store data. This includes data on all organizational information systems that are relied upon to store master copies of PHI data.
  - Emergency Mode Operation Plan — The healthcare organization is required to establish procedures to enable continuation of critical business processes for protection of the security of PHI while operating in emergency mode. The healthcare organization must implement a business continuity and disaster recovery plan, which includes a plan for operations during and immediately after a disaster. This plan should cover customer interface procedures, work-around procedures, emergency management, public relations, emergency notification process, activation/deactivation procedures, voice communication procedures, identification of the crisis management team, crisis management procedures, and maintenance procedures for the plan.
  - Testing and Revision Procedures (Addressable) — The healthcare organization is required to implement procedures for periodic testing and revision of contingency plans. These plans and procedures should be tested annually.
  - Application and Data Criticality Analysis (Addressable) — The healthcare organization is required to assess the relative criticality of specific applications and data in support of other contingency plan

components. The healthcare organization should perform a data criticality analysis as part of the overall BCP DRP effort.

- Evaluation [164.308(a)(8)] — This set of controls requires that the healthcare organization perform a periodic technical and nontechnical evaluation, based initially upon the standards implemented under this rule and subsequently in response to environmental or operational changes affecting the security of PHI, that establishes the extent to which the healthcare organization's security policies and procedures meet the requirements of this subpart. This means that the healthcare organization needs to periodically perform a review of their technical and nontechnical (administrative and physical) controls to ensure that they meet the HIPAA rules. Healthcare organizations will be required to perform such analyses again when there have been significant changes to the architecture or when a selected period of time has expired. A reasonable interpretation of this time would be two years for many organizations, but this is a judgment call.

- Business Associate Contracts — The final HIPAA Security Rule [section 164.308(b)(1)] allows the healthcare organization to permit a business associate to create, receive, maintain, or transmit PHI on the healthcare organization's behalf, provided that the healthcare organization obtains satisfactory assurances that the business associate will appropriately safeguard the information. Specifically, the healthcare organization must implement the following:

  - Written Contract — The healthcare organization is required to document the satisfactory assurances through a written contract or other arrangement with the business associate. The contract must meet the requirements below. If the healthcare organization has knowledge of a pattern of activity or practice of the business associate that constitutes a material breach or violation of the business associate's obligation under the contract, unless the covered entity took reasonable steps to cure the breach or end the violation, then the healthcare organization must either
    1. Terminate the contract, if feasible; or
    2. Report the problem to the Secretary of Health and Human Services.

  - Implement Safeguards — The business associate contract must provide that the business associate will implement administrative, physical, and technical safeguards that reasonably and appropriately protect the confidentiality, integrity, and availability of PHI that it creates, receives, maintains, or transmits on behalf of the healthcare organization.

  - Agents and Subcontractors — The business associate contract must provide that the business associate will ensure that any agent, including a subcontractor, to whom it provides such information, agrees to implement reasonable and appropriate safeguards to protect it.

- Report Security Incidents — The business associate contract must provide that the business associate will report to the healthcare organization any security incident of which it becomes aware.
- Contract Termination — The business associate contract must provide that the business associate will authorize the termination of the contract by the healthcare organization, if the healthcare organization determines that the business associate has violated a material term of the contract.

Physical Safeguards

Physical safeguards are physical measures, policies, and procedures designed to protect an organization's sensitive information, information systems, and related buildings and equipment from natural and environmental hazards and unauthorized intrusion.

- Facility Access Control — The healthcare organization is required to implement policies and procedures to limit physical access to its electronic information systems and the facility in which they are housed, while ensuring that properly authorized access is allowed. Specifically, the organization must implement the following:
  - Contingency Operations (Addressable) — The healthcare organization is required to establish procedures that allow facility access in support of restoration of lost data under the disaster recovery plan and emergency mode operations plan in the event of an emergency. This means that the healthcare organization must establish procedures that allow access to the facility, which will be used to restore lost data in the event of an emergency.
  - Facility Security Plan (Addressable) — The healthcare organization is required to implement policies and procedures to safeguard the facility and the equipment therein from unauthorized physical access, tampering, and theft.
  - Access Control and Validation Procedures (Addressable) — The health care organization is required to implement procedures to control and validate a person's access to facilities based on their role or function, including visitor control, and control of access to software programs for testing and revision.
  - Maintenance Records (Addressable) — The healthcare organization is required to implement policies and procedures to document repairs and modifications to the physical components of a facility that are related to security (for example, hardware, walls, doors, and locks).
- Workstation Use — The healthcare organization is required to implement policies and procedures that specify the proper functions to be performed, the manner in which those functions are to be performed, and the physical

attributes of the surroundings of a specific workstation or class of workstation that can access PHI. This means that the healthcare organization must establish policies and procedures that dictate the use and placement of workstations.

- Workstation Security — The healthcare organization is required to implement physical safeguards for all workstations that access PHI to restrict access to authorized users. The covered entity must ensure that all workstations with access to PHI are physically secured. Of particular interest will be off-site workstations (and laptops) for telecommuters, executives, and others who access the healthcare organization's systems remotely.
- Device and Media Control — The healthcare organization is required to implement policies and procedures that govern the receipt and removal of hardware and electronic media that contain PHI into and out of the facility, and the movement of these items within the facility. Specifically, the healthcare organization must implement the following:
  - Disposal — The healthcare organization is required to implement policies and procedures to address the final disposition of PHI, and the hardware or electronic media on which it is stored. This means that the healthcare organization is required to have a policy and procedure for the secure disposal of hardware or electronic media that currently or ever did house PHI. These policies and procedures should include instructions for the proper sanitization of computer equipment, tapes, disks, and other electronic media prior to discarding it.
  - Media Reuse — The healthcare organization is required to implement procedures for removal of PHI from electronic media before media are made available for reuse. This means that the healthcare organization must have a documented procedure to ensure that no residual PHI is contained on electronic media that is exposed to those outside of the healthcare organization.
  - Accountability (Addressable) — The healthcare organization is required to maintain records of the movements of hardware and electronic media and any person responsible therefor. This means that the healthcare organization is required to have documented records for destruction and removal (e.g., gifts of computer equipment) of electronic media and hardware.
  - Data Backup and Storage (Addressable) — The healthcare organization is required to create a retrievable, exact copy of PHI, when needed, before movement of equipment. This means that the healthcare organization must ensure that a backup exists for the PHI data stored on hardware or electronic media prior to removal or destruction.

Technical Safeguards

Technical safeguards include specific technology and the policies and procedures for its use that protect sensitive information and provide logical access control.

- Access Control — The healthcare organization is required to have access controls in place. Access control is implemented through a series of controls, including unique user identification, emergency access procedures, automatic log-off, and encryption and decryption methods. The healthcare organization must review their current logical access controls and develop a logical protection architecture to control access to sensitive information on their information systems. Specifically, the healthcare organization must implement the following to obtain compliance:

    - Unique User Identification — The healthcare organization is required to implement policies and procedures that assign a unique name or user number to identify and track user identity. Each user ID on healthcare organization information systems must map back to a single and unique individual. The healthcare organization must identify all user accounts and ensure that the account identifier is associated with a single, unique user. No accounts may be shared. The practice of generic accounts, accounts without passwords, and accounts with passwords that are shared violate this principle and requirement.

    - Emergency Access Procedure — The healthcare organization must establish and implement the necessary procedures to obtain necessary sensitive information in an emergency. This means that the healthcare organization must ensure a method of gaining access to a system in case of an emergency, with the ability of upgrading privileges and levels of appropriate users in case of an emergency when other privileged users are unavailable. These procedures must be accomplished while still ensuring the security of the system and the sensitive information it contains.

    - Automatic Log-off (Addressable) — The healthcare organization must implement electronic procedures that terminate an electronic session after a predetermined period of inactivity. This means that the healthcare organization must ensure that any session on an information system with sensitive information is terminated after a reasonable period of inactivity.

    - Encryption and Decryption (Addressable) — The healthcare organization must implement a mechanism to encrypt and decrypt sensitive information. Encryption and decryption is an "addressable" requirement. Access control could be accomplished through a variety of other means. However, if encryption and decryption are performed, it must be done in accordance with best practices.

- Audit: Record and Examine Activity — Healthcare organizations are required to have audit controls in place. This means that the healthcare organization must have mechanisms that record and examine activity on the information systems that contain sensitive information. These controls may be implemented in hardware, software, or through procedural mechanisms.
- Integrity: Mechanism to Authenticate (Addressable) — Healthcare organizations must have integrity controls in place. This means that the healthcare organization must implement electronic mechanisms to corroborate that sensitive information has not been altered or destroyed in an unauthorized manner. Examples of electronic mechanisms that ensure integrity include error-correcting memory and magnetic disk storage.
- Authentication: Verify User Identification — Healthcare organizations must have authentication mechanisms in place. This means that these organizations must implement procedures to verify that a person or entity seeking to access sensitive information is the person or entity claimed.
- Transmission Security [164.312(e)(1)] — The healthcare organization is required to have transmission controls in place. Transmission controls may be implemented through a series of controls including integrity controls or encryption. Specifically, the healthcare organization must implement the following to obtain compliance:
  - Integrity Controls (Addressable) — The healthcare organization must implement security measures to ensure that electronically transmitted sensitive information is not improperly modified without detection until the sensitive information is disposed of. Examples of adequate controls may include cyclical redundancy checks (CRCs) or checksums.
  - Encryption (Addressable) — The healthcare organization must implement a mechanism to encrypt sensitive information whenever it is deemed appropriate. This means that the healthcare organization should address specific instances where sensitive information is vulnerable to interception or unauthorized access and ensure that sensitive information is protected.

Gramm-Leach-Bliley Act (GLB Act)

The Financial Modernization Act of 1999, known as the Gramm-Leach-Bliley Act, was passed by Congress to protect the personal information of banking consumers. The Gramm-Leach-Bliley (GLB) Act comprises the Financial Privacy Rule, the Safeguards Rule, and the pretexting provisions. The GLB Act applies to all financial institutions. These include traditional financial institutions (such as banks, securities firms, and insurance companies) but also any company that provides financial products and services, such as mortgage brokering, tax preparation, financial counseling, real estate settlement, real estate appraisal, check cashing, and consumer debt collection.

The Financial Privacy Rule regulates the practice of collection and disclosure of personal financial information by financial institutions. This regulation applies to any organization that receives consumer financial information in the course of their business.

The Safeguards Rule specifies information security requirements for financial institutions for the design, implementation, and maintenance of safeguards that protect consumer financial information.

"Pretexting" is a term used to describe the unlawful practice of individuals or organizations obtaining personal financial information from consumers under false pretenses. The pretexting provisions protect consumers from this behavior.

Although all three of these provisions of the GLB Act impact the security requirements of an organization, only the GLB Safeguards Rule impacts our discussion on core security practices. The GLB Act Safeguards Rule is outlined in the paragraphs below:

- Information Security Program Coordinator — The financial institution must designate an employee to coordinate the information security program.
- Security Risk Assessment — The financial institution is required to perform a security risk assessment that will identify "reasonably foreseeable" information security risks to confidentiality, integrity, or availability of consumer information. The security risk assessment must review the adequacy of current safeguards and cover, at a minimum, the areas of employee training, information systems (network and software design, information processing, storage, transmission, disposal), intrusion detection, prevention, and response.
- Appropriate Safeguards — The financial institution is required to implement information safeguards necessary to control the risks identified in the security risk assessment. These safeguards must be monitored or regularly tested to ensure the effectiveness of the safeguard's controls, systems, and procedures.
- Third-Party Oversight — The financial institution must ensure that the security of consumer information is not endangered by providing access to third parties. The financial institution must have measures in place to ensure that the service providers they select and retain are capable of maintaining appropriate safeguards to protect the consumer information. This means that the financial institution must require service providers to implement and maintain these safeguards contractually.
- Maintain Security Program — The financial institution must adjust its information security program to ensure that consumer financial information is protected. Adjustments to the program could be necessary after a

change in business arrangements, operations, or even a change in the threat environment in which the financial institution operates.[4]

Notes

1. The CobiT Framework indicates the extent to which each of the 34 CobiT control objectives meets business requirements. An indication of "primary" means that the business objective is directly impacted by the control measure. An indication of "secondary" means that the business objective is somewhat impacted by the control measure. The business requirements of confidentiality, integrity, and availability are commonly associated with information security. The analysis presented above regarding the use of the CobiT Framework control objectives being discussed from an information security standpoint is not simply a listing of the CobiT control objectives with primary or secondary satisfaction of the confidentiality, integrity, and availability business requirements.

2. The chapter number of the NIST Handbook chapter for each security control is included in parentheses as a reference.

3. For many information security professionals, and other technical professionals, the term "administrative" is commonly interpreted as "paperwork," "tedious," and even "nontechnical." This belief is not consistent with the current practice and use of the term "administrative controls." As can be seen in the HIPAA Security Rule, administrative controls actually include some quite "technical" activities such as risk assessment and security incident response.

4. Notice that, between the "appropriate security controls" and "maintain security program," the GLB Act Safeguards Rule requirements implicitly cover all reasonable safeguards. Many regulations are written purposely vague in order to be flexible. For these regulations it is important to state the "what" but not the "how."

Index